The Crown and the Courts

The Crown *and* the Courts

SEPARATION *of* POWERS

in the EARLY JEWISH IMAGINATION

David C. Flatto

Harvard University Press

CAMBRIDGE, MASSACHUSETTS

LONDON, ENGLAND

2020

Publication of this book has been supported through the generous
provisions of the Maurice and Lula Bradley Smith Memorial Fund

Second printing

Cataloging-in-Publication Data is available from the Library of Congress

ISBN: 978-0-674-73710-5 (alk. paper)

To the beloved memory of my mother, Dr. Zehava Flatto z'l
And in honor of my father, Dr. Leopold Flatto

Contents

The Crown and the Courts

Introduction

Law and Power in Biblical and Western Jurisprudence

"It is not in Heaven," announces the biblical verse (Deut 30:12) that, according to rabbinic exegesis, describes an everlasting transfer of the Torah to human hands.[1] Yet Scripture provides little guidance about who will serve over time as the Torah's earthly custodian following its revelation at Sinai: The ruler or king? The priests? The elders? A leading sage? The entire nation? A celebrated Midrash depicts the angels' immediate envy of Moses when he received the Torah.[2] Who is the object of their enduring jealousy across the generations?

The capsule chain of transmission recorded in rabbinic literature ("Moses received the Torah at Sinai, and passed it to Joshua, etc.,") offers only the faintest of hints.[3] A comprehensive response must focus instead upon the fundamental calling of revelation, and canvass relevant sources that distinguish a principal official(s) or type of figure(s), who can best fulfill this mandate in perpetuity.[4] Only by examining who becomes entrusted with the august duty of implementing the ideals of God's revelation on a systemic level, can one identify its leading executor(s).

Sinaitic revelation, as represented in Scripture, inaugurated a covenantal relationship between God and Israel, in which Israel pledged its absolute commitment to observe the divine commandments. Subsequent generations therefore proceeded to interpret the Torah as a legal charter, meticulously translating its ideals into an elaborate system of rules. Accordingly, the Torah's primary heirs are responsible for overseeing its normative order.[5] The above inquiry can then be reformulated in a more nuanced manner: Who is charged with interpreting, instructing, and administering the sacred laws and traditions of the Torah?

This book addresses this question by focusing upon the commission of judicial power. Analyzing programmatic writings depicting how justice should ideally be administered (rather than empirical descriptions, which reflect the substantial limits on jurisdiction that were imposed on Jews during various historical periods), it evaluates who is delegated a supreme role, and explores the underlying axiological values advanced by this assignment.[6] This book thereby offers an in-depth study of paradigmatic biblical accounts of the administration of justice as expounded by its foremost early interpreters, ranging from the fourth century BCE through the third century CE. Throughout the formative centuries of the Second Temple and early rabbinic periods, leading commentators presented crucial amplifications of the relatively inchoate depictions of legal authority found in the Bible. In the course of elaborating upon the biblical foundation, they also incorporated new and substantial juristic ideas of their own. Emerging out of the classical phase of biblical hermeneutics, these rich expositions delineate, or perhaps even constitute, its core legacy. A foundational study of early Jewish conceptions of legal authority must pore over this seminal corpus.

Surveying representations of legal authority illuminates an essential aspect of Judaism. Tracing back to Sinaitic discourses,[7] the fundamental role of law continued to define Judaism throughout the Second Temple and rabbinic periods. Due to the centrality of law, eminent Jewish thinkers focused upon this sphere (far more than on philosophy, or even theology), and developed some of their most profound and lasting insights as a result. Whereas much secondary literature examines the substance and doctrines of Jewish law, the jurisprudential theories or ideo-logical values implicit in its notions of legal authority have hardly been explored.[8]

Contemplating the structure of legal authority in early Jewish writings also has enduring significance from a wider perspective. Despite their important variances, the early Jewish texts analyzed below largely coalesce around what was at the time an extraordinary conception of the relationship between the legal domain and sovereign power, which had far-reaching implications concerning the role of law in society. Certain similar notions surfaced in the classical world, and reverberate even more loudly in contemporary Western jurisprudence, informing the construction of modern constitutional regimes. Approached from a comparative vantage point, the story of early Jewish jurisprudence represents a pivotal chapter in the general history of legal and political thought.

A clear theme runs through the primary early Jewish depictions of legal authority examined in this book and reveals the stakes of this study. More than reflecting upon the nature of law,[9] these texts revolve around the fundamental issue of hegemony over its jurisdiction. Repeatedly situating the administration of justice within the context of leadership and governance, these writings project the exercise of jurisdiction as a formidable authority, which corresponds to, or competes with, other forms of "political" power (more on terminology below).[10] In grappling with the vital relationship between law and power, early Jewish writings confront a core tension familiar to modern jurisprudence—especially manifest in the bedrock constitutional concepts of separation of powers, an independent judiciary, and the rule of law. Here is where a distinctive strand of early Jewish jurisprudence proves most fascinating from a comparative perspective.[11]

In many societies, controlling law is a way of wielding substantial power.[12] For this reason, the most powerful have historically sought to preside over the legal enterprise.[13] Especially in antiquity, laws emanated from the sovereign body, and justice was administered by the politically powerful. Absolute kings, emperors, and rulers left little room for a discrete sphere of justice.

This book will argue that an important strand in early Jewish jurisprudential writings sharply diverges from ancient legal traditions in this respect. The texts surveyed here share certain affinities with classical and Western legal traditions that create some space between sovereign power and law. Yet the Jewish tradition breaks new ground by envisioning the construction of independent institutions for administering justice, and articulating different versions of an ideal of separation. In order to provide further context for these claims, the survey below will briefly outline the relationship between law and sovereign power in antiquity (i.e., the contemporary world of the Bible) and the Greco-Roman world (i.e., the contemporary world of Second Temple and early rabbinic literature), and look beyond to pivotal phases of subsequent Western history until the early modern period. While this account follows a broad arc, the contrast to other legal traditions is nevertheless useful as a heuristic tool that helps isolate salient features of early Jewish legal jurisprudence, which will be introduced in the pages that follow.

Law and Power in Historical Perspective

Throughout much of legal history,[14] the judiciary, in its various guises, revolved around the axis of political power. In the Ancient Near East, a quasi-divine king commanded ultimate legal authority. Beyond adjudicating and enforcing legal rules, ancient regimes empowered the king with full legislative powers.[15] Hammurabi's Code—a collection of legal rules attributed to the eighteenth-century-BCE Babylonian king[16]— offers a vivid illustration of law's subordination to political power.[17] The prologue states that King Hammurabi was blessed with divine gifts and a special ability to perceive the principles of "justice and righteousness" that inform his laws, which he then proceeds to delineate. Implicit in his royal prerogative to pronounce legal rules is also his ultimate power to resolve all legal disputes. A matching epilogue states that an aggrieved party should stand before Hammurabi's image (engraved on top of the stele recording the laws) to find out his or her legal recourse, and then proclaim, "Hammurabi is a ruler ... who has bestowed benefits for ever and ever on his subjects, and has established order in the land."

Frequently, of course, the king would delegate judicial authority to inferior judges and magistrates. He nevertheless retained the ultimate power to overrule any legal verdict, and when he did not, his tacit approval was understood.[18] In the memorable words of Ernst Kantorowicz (describing a general typology, which helpfully characterizes ancient legal systems), "His majesty in the eyes of the law is always present in all his courts, though he cannot personally distribute justice."[19] Similar notions of the just king (*sar mesarim*) pervade the Laws of Lipit-Ishtar, Eshnunna, Ur Nammu, and other Ancient Near Eastern writings.

Just as ancient legal systems, from Mesopotamia to Egypt, were led by powerful, quasi-divine rulers,[20] certain classical legal systems were headed by rulers, although often of a more "secular" variety.[21] Other juridical schemes in the classical world were configured differently. Most famously: Athenian trials were conducted by a large group of jurors, a civic body that mirrored the constitutional form of a radical democracy. In Sparta, a couple of kings, several ephors, and a council of elders controlled the highest forms of judicial power.[22] Republican Rome relied on magistrates, the senate, and the popular assembly for various aspects of legal authority.[23] Still, even in these polities, jurisdiction was controlled by the sovereign entity.

Significantly, from among the Roman administration, one magisterial office emerged as a distinct focus of power, that of the praetor. By formulating annual edicts of remedies, the praetor essentially controlled the administration of justice.[24] Parallel to this development, an impressive class of jurists mushroomed in the latter half of the Roman Republic; these jurists were gradually recognized as the primary source of legal expertise. Through their prodigious oral and written responses, commentaries, and treatises, the jurists routinely advised judges on decisions and magistrates on remedies. Crossing over into the Principate, the praetor and jurists stood out as the dominant figures in Rome's flourishing jurisprudence.[25]

Building blocks of legal autonomy were thus laid in Rome, but formally and functionally such autonomy had its limits. The praetor, an annual appointee, officiated under the consul, and in any event the promulgated praetorian edicts ossified over time. Meanwhile, the jurists, whose star continued to rise, lacked binding authority and had to channel their abundant influence through administering officials.[26] Moreover, the entire legal enterprise operated under the shadow of the emperor.[27] And sure enough, the emperor found ways to co-opt or contain these alternate sources of juridical power. Hadrian commissioned a finalized version of the praetorian edict. Meanwhile, from Augustus onward jurists received selective sanction from the emperor, and by the third century CE some of the most prominent jurists were folded into the imperial bureaucracy.[28]

Admittedly, classical legal theory presented a broader set of ideas that severed law from the grip of political power. Greek cities took seriously notions of fundamental and customary law, and Roman law operated with conceptions of *ius* alongside the substantial accrual of statutes, edicts, and constitutions. But they did not, ultimately, implement these ideas by constructing institutional mechanisms for law's autonomous administration. In a similar vein, the great classical philosophers and thinkers articulated a stunning constellation of ideas about justice, the rule of law, natural law, nomos, universal law, unwritten law, divine law, and onward. Yet they hardly theorized about the institutional foundations of an independent judiciary. This absence looms even larger given their intellectual boldness in reexamining the most fundamental questions of political and constitutional life.[29]

Although the medieval period is largely beyond the scope of this book, it is important to briefly note the emergence of the two great Western legal traditions that further freed the domain of law from sovereign power, as well as the outer limits of this process. The early phase of medieval law in Continental Europe was marked by pluralism and fragmentation, as an amalgam of Roman, Germanic, canon, and local laws functioned unevenly among many territories and locales that were geo-graphically confined.[30] But over the course of the twelfth and thirteenth centuries, the revival and transformative study of Roman law in leading scholastic centers like Bologna, coupled with the expansion of canonist jurisprudence across monastic quarters throughout a powerful Chris-tendom, led to the formation of a *ius commune,* "a law potentially common to all."[31] Spreading across a wide swath of the continent, the *ius commune* surged for several centuries.[32]

In broad terms, the *ius commune* can be loosely characterized as a legal tradition that transcended political boundaries, even though its relation-ship to sovereign authorities was obviously more intricate.[33] Rulers har-nessed and exploited it to consolidate their powers (as did ecclesiastic authorities with the canon law), while others tried, albeit less success-fully, to limit and contain it.[34] In any event, this substantial evolution toward a fuller form of legal autonomy transpired through complex his-torical processes of interpenetration of a common legal tradition, not by institutional design. There was scant theorizing about an independent network of courts, and certainly no open efforts to repudiate sovereign control (with the singular exception of an emboldened papacy, begin-ning with the Investiture Controversy).[35]

By contrast, in the other main branch of Western law, the English common law, the formative role of institutionalization of the courts was paramount from early on—but as a way of anchoring royal authority. In order to assert central jurisdiction throughout the realm, and miti-gate the influence of county and seignorial courts, English kings (from Henry II onward) established the institutions of the medieval English common law, including the courts of the King's Bench, Common Pleas, and Exchequer.[36] But due to the mounting complexity of an idiosyn-cratic system of writs and remedies and abstruse doctrines, the common law increasingly became the province of a specialized judiciary.[37] More-over, throughout the sixteenth and seventeenth centuries a more frontal struggle ensued wherein the judiciary staked their claim to a relative in-dependence from the crown,[38] culminating in the legendary confronta-tions between Lord Coke and King James.[39]

It would take another century or more for the West to fully articulate and structure this institutional independence. Only with the rising emphasis in Enlightenment and democratic thought on delimiting the normative rights of all citizens, did autonomous legal institutions, with independent jurisdiction, materialize in the West. Concurrently, formal constitutional schemes were crafted to structure such arrangements, and conceptual doctrines (such as the separation of powers, an independent judiciary, and the rule of law) were developed to support their establishment.[40]

This brief survey of aspects of Western legal history provides a comparative framework for evaluating the nature of legal authority in early Jewish jurisprudence. Although the Bible conceives of the origin and nature of law in a unique manner that traces back to Sinai (see below), its general embrace of an absolutist form of judicial authority following the formation of a monarchy in Israel conforms with the surrounding political culture. Yet the Bible also introduces an anomalous secondary scheme dividing between royalty and justice, which subsequently flourished in postbiblical jurisprudence. This latter arrangement departs not only from regnant assumptions that characterized ancient legal systems, but also from those that continued to inform Western legal systems for centuries to come. The heart of this book will describe its remarkable content and contours.

Biblical Administration of Justice

Whereas the essence of law in much Ancient Near Eastern literature revolved around the king,[41] in the Hebrew Bible it does not.[42] In lieu of Hammurabi's prologue, the preamble to the Sinaitic laws announces, "I am the Lord your God, who brought you out of the land of Egypt, out of the house of slavery" (Exod 20:2).[43] In an influential article contrasting aspects of criminal law in the Bible and the rest of Ancient Near Eastern literature, Moshe Greenberg relates several substantive and procedural differences to their disparate underlying conceptions of legal authority.[44] In the Bible, God is "the fountainhead of the law," and the law is an embodiment of God's will. Accordingly, instead of a royal lawgiver, the Bible presents the law as deriving from divine revelation at Sinai.[45] Greenberg proceeds to demonstrate how certain features of biblical criminal law reflect this fundamentally different discourse on the origin of the law, including the stringency of capital offenses, absence of ransom, and the highly restricted possibility of waiver and pardon. In a similar vein, scholars have long noted the ways in which the Sinaitic covenant employs, but transforms, the Ancient Near Eastern model of suzerainty treaties.[46] Rather than a powerful suzerain contracting with a vassal king, the Bible represents God as entering into a pact directly with the people of Israel.[47] In the words leading up to revelation, God promises all of Israel that in return for their fulfillment of the laws, "you shall be for me a priestly kingdom and a holy nation" (Exod 19:6). By adapting the template of Ancient Near Eastern treaties, the Bible marginalizes the constitutive role of an absolutist king.[48] Instead, the Bible anchors the covenantal scheme in God's consecration of the entire people of Israel as a priestly-royal nation that receives an immediate revelation of sacred laws.[49]

Although the Bible's distinct perspective on the source and ontology of law may affect the optimal mode of judicial administration (a thread pursued in Chapter 8),[50] the explicit biblical treatment of this topic is more varied. Ultimate responsibility for the adjudication and enforcement of divine legal principles resides in the hands of human agents, according to the Bible, and the precise role of the monarch in this process—while clearly different from that of other Ancient Near Eastern legal regimes—requires further examination.[51] A survey of the Bible reveals a list of persons who possess legal authority to varying degrees: the paterfamilias, local townsmen, elders, priests, the high priest, (lay or professional) judges, military leaders, and the king.[52] Biblical scholars assume that in the primitive stages, before a centralized state developed, legal matters in ancient Israel were handled locally.[53] In the patriarchal and tribal world of biblical Israel, an informal network linked individuals, families, and tribes. Over time this system evolved into a hierarchical and organized social structure resembling the model of a kinship group.[54] As a centralized nation began to take shape, the extent of monarchic powers, including judicial authority, became a vital issue.[55]

Kingship and Justice

In the developed biblical scheme, according to most scholars, the king is pivotal to the legal system, and is possibly even the highest judicial authority.[56] Indeed, the initial request by the elders for a king in 1 Sam 8:6 emphasizes the judicial responsibilities of this new kind of leader: "Give us a king to govern / judge us [*le-shoftenu*]."[57] Similarly, 2 Sam 8:15 hails David as a king who executes justice (*mishpat*) throughout his realm.

Moreover, specific biblical episodes suggest that the king is the final body to whom one could appeal in legal disputes, whether as a supreme judge or based on a royal prerogative to repeal legal rulings. A classic illustration of this authority appears in 2 Sam 14. Appealing directly to King David, a woman requests royal intervention in a clan dispute that had erupted after an accidental homicide in her family. As the matter of an accidental murder plainly qualifies as a case of biblical law,[58] this text assumes a unique monarchic capacity to resolve legal controversies.[59]

In a nearby passage, Absalom contests his father's monarchic powers by luring people with the promise of his superior judicial verdicts:[60]

> Absalom used to rise early and stand beside the road into the gate; and when anyone brought a suit before the king for judgment, Absalom would call out and say, "From what city are you?" When the person said, "Your servant is of such and such a tribe in Israel," Absalom would say, "See, your claims are good and right; but there is no one designated by the king to hear you." Absalom said moreover, "If only I were judge in the land! Then all who had a suit or cause might come to me, and I would give them justice." Whenever people came near to do obeisance to him, he would put out his hand and take hold of them, and kiss them. Thus Absalom did to every Israelite who came to the

king for judgment; so Absalom stole the hearts of the people of Israel. (2 Sam 15:2–6)

Wresting away judicial power is the surest path for Absalom to achieve royal stature. Evidently, the person who controls the judiciary commands the monarchy.

Beyond such descriptive passages, other biblical sections project the notion of a "just king" administering justice as an ideal. A biblical maxim declares, "The king by justice establishes the land, but he that loves gifts overthrows it" (Prov. 29:4). When Solomon ascends the royal throne, he famously requests, in a dream, the wisdom to dispense justice from God (1 Kgs 3:5–14). Afterward, the narrative illustrates his sagacity in the trial of the harlots (1 Kgs 3:16–27). The chapter concludes, "When all Israel heard the decision that the king had rendered, they stood in awe of the king, for they saw that he possessed divine wisdom to execute justice" (1 Kgs 3:28).[61] Inscribed in these verses is a glorification of royal justice.[62] A later liturgical psalm expands on this typology of Solomon, the just king:[63] "Of Solomon. O God, endow the king with Your judgments, the king's son with Your righteousness. That he may judge Your people rightly, Your lowly ones, justly. Let the mountains produce well-being for the people, the hills the reward of justice. Let him vindicate the lowly among the people, deliver the needy folk, and crush those who wrong them" (Psalms 72:1–4).

Likewise, various prophetic writings laud an ideal of royal justice. Jeremiah 21:12 records a divine instruction to Davidic kings, "O House of David, thus said the Lord: Render just verdicts morning by morning, rescue him who is robbed from him who defrauded him." Several Isaiah passages extend this motif to an eschatological context, such as this depiction of a Davidic scion who will harness his preternatural skills in administering judgment:[64] "He shall sense the truth by his reverence for the Lord, he shall not judge by what his eyes behold, nor decide by what his ears perceive. Thus he shall judge the poor with equity and decide with justice for the lowly of the land. He shall strike down a land with the rod of his mouth and slay the wicked with the breath of his lips. Justice shall be the gird of his loins, and faithfulness the girdle of his waist" (Isaiah 11:3–5). Dispensing justice will be a defining task of messianic kingship.[65] A number of other passages relate to royal justice, whether the king is conceived of as an absolutist leader, a paragon of wisdom, or someone endowed with superior qualities.[66] Given the royalist form of surrounding political regimes, this fact is far from remarkable.

Deuteronomy 17: Separating Justice from Royal Power

In contrast with the above, Deuteronomy 17[67] advances a fundamentally different model that separates royal and judicial powers.[68] It juxtaposes two sets of verses, which will be referred to throughout this book. Deuteronomy 17:8–13 depicts the supreme administration of law:[69]

> If a legal matter is baffling for you between one kind of bloodshed and another, one kind of legal right and another, or one kind of assault and another—any such matters of dispute in your towns—then you shall immediately go up to the place that the LORD your God will choose, where you shall consult with the Levitical priests and the judge who is in office in those days; they shall announce to you the decision in the case. Carry out exactly the decision that they announce to you from the place that the LORD will choose, diligently observing everything they instruct you. You must carry out fully the law [*ha-torah*] that they interpret for you or the ruling that they announce to you; do not stray from the word that they proclaim to you either to the right or to the left. As for anyone who presumes to disobey the priest appointed to minister there to the LORD your God, or the judge, that person shall die. So you shall purge the evil from Israel. All the people will hear and be afraid, and will not act presumptuously again.

Afterward, Deuteronomy 17:14–20 describes the monarchy:[70]

> When you have come into the land that the LORD your God is giving you, and have taken possession of it and settled in it, and

you say, "I will set a king over me, like all the nations that are around me," you may indeed set over you a king whom the LORD your God will choose. One of your own community you may set as king over you; you are not permitted to put a foreigner over you, who is not of your own community. Even so, he must not acquire many horses for himself, or return the people to Egypt in order to acquire more horses, since the LORD has said to you, "You must never return that way again." And he must not acquire many wives for himself, or else his heart will turn away; also silver and gold he must not acquire in great quantity for himself. When he has taken the throne of his kingdom, he shall transcribe a summary of the law [*mishneh ha-torah*] on a scroll in the presence of the Levitical priests. It shall remain with him and he shall read in it all the days of his life, so that he may learn to fear the LORD his God, diligently observing all the words of this law and these statutes, in order that he not exalt himself above other members of the community and in order that he not turn aside from the commandment either to the right or to the left, so that he and his descendants may reign long over his kingdom in Israel.

According to Deuteronomy 17, difficult legal matters that cannot be resolved locally are referred to a centralized assembly of jurists, composed of Levitical priests and a judge.[71] Issuing supreme instructions, arguably based on divine inspiration, traditions, or reasoning,[72] their rulings are binding upon the entire people. As for the king's role, Deuteronomy's arrangement presents, in the words of Bernard Levinson, a "double anomaly."[73] The judicial section (Deut 17:8–13) never suggests that the king administers justice. The subsequent royal section (Deut 17:14–20) likewise omits any judicial function for the king. A pair of verses employs a deliberate rhetorical technique to further accent this point. A verse in the first section describes the final jurisdiction of the supreme judicial officials by stating, "Do not stray from the word that they proclaim to you *either to the right or to the left*" (Deut 17:11; emphasis added). In contrast, a verse in the second section explains the purpose of the king repeatedly reading the summary of the law that he transcribed: "In order that he not turn aside from the commandment *either to the right or to the left*" (Deut 17:20; emphasis added). So the central judicial officials supply the authoritative interpretation of the Torah's laws, while the king is relegated to a passive role of reading, not interpreting, the Torah. Further, the king is enjoined not to stray from the Torah's laws—which are interpreted by the judicial officials. The leading jurists have mastery over the Torah's laws, whereas the king is subservient to the Torah, and, accordingly, to them as well.[74] This hierarchy is symbolically reinforced and ritualized in the act of the king transcribing the summary of the Torah, "in the presence of the Levitical Priests" (Deut 17:18).[75]

Deuteronomy's jurisprudence, which separates legal authority from the king, hardly surfaces elsewhere in the Bible, at least not explicitly.[76] One passage that does resonate with it to a certain extent involves King Ahab and the vineyard of Naboth.[77] Reviewing this story from the angle of jurisdiction, the ruthless king astoundingly has no recourse for confiscating Naboth's property without initiating a legal procedure. Not only does this seem to undermine the king's right of eminent domain,[78] but it also belies the notion that the king monopolizes legal authority.[79] According to the Naboth story, the king is at least formally subservient to the rule of law.[80] Overall the Deuteronomy scheme is far less pronounced in the Bible than is the model of a royal judiciary.

To summarize the biblical corpus, then, this diverse and chronologically diffuse material relating to royalty and the administration of justice can be largely segregated into two strands. The dominant strand depicts the king as the ultimate force behind the legal apparatus. Whether as the final arbiter or an ideal embodiment of wisdom, the king has supreme authority. An alternate strand recognizes distinct judicial officials who operate independently of the monarch. Moreover, the rhetoric and content of the primary verses that formulate this latter position subordinate the king to the laws of the Torah, as interpreted by these officials.[81]

The Postbiblical Legacy of Deuteronomy's Jurisprudence

Both strands of biblical jurisprudence reverberate throughout later writings that are the subject of this book (these writings were formulated against the backdrop of a gradually emerging sense of a canon of sacred Scripture).[82] The dominant model finds distinct expression in certain Second Temple texts such as the Psalms of Solomon, and a more complex articulation, where a core tension between the strands is manifest, in several sections of Philo, Qumran, and rabbinic literature. Most of this book focuses on postbiblical writings that surprisingly expound on the second strand in various ways. Despite its anomalous position within biblical literature, the second strand assumes prominence among leading Second Temple and rabbinic writings—including various influential passages in Philo,[83] Josephus, Qumran, and rabbinic literature—which were among the many works from these centuries to deem the norms of Deuteronomy (and rest of the Pentateuch) to be binding.[84] Through their commentaries and discourses, these works not only preserve the Deuteronomic strand, but regard it as a foundational text.

Moreover, in enlarging upon the Deuteronomic strand, these writings develop its jurisprudence in substantial ways—muting, echoing, amplifying, or transforming its principal teaching in the process of transmission. In all, one can discern three different conceptual iterations that are manifest in these postbiblical elaborations, which will be discussed at length throughout this book. The first closely tracks the cleavage between sacral law and royal authority that surfaces in Deuteronomy, but erects institutional barriers to further circumscribe each one of these spheres. In this moderate version, the independence of law is adequately preserved by segregating the juridical and political domains (the "basic version—separation of powers"). The second maintains this divide but further secures justice from the corrosive influence of power in an additional respect. Rather than focusing outwardly on the potential intervention of the political organ, this conception turns inward and (re)constructs the internal makeup of the judiciary. Vertical hierarchies within the court are flattened, and judicial authority is widely diffused (the "internal version—dissemination of powers"). A third, bolder jurisprudence undertakes an audacious rethinking of the essence of the political enterprise in its totality. Animated by a profound distrust of political authority that perpetually threatens to undermine justice, this stronger version declares the autonomy and sufficiency of law, and aims to reconstitute the entire polity upon the foundation of law alone (the "stronger version—elimination of powers"). Abandoning the regnant notion of imperial law, all three iterations—each in their own way[85]—advance robust visions of law's empire.[86]

Observing the afterlife of Deuteronomy in important jurisprudential texts of the Second Temple and rabbinic periods, including the ways its various iterations are constructed and articulated, the chapters below expose the startling answer that these formative texts provide to the question posed at the outset: Who controls the revealed Torah by way of exercising legal authority? Jettisoning widespread assumptions, these writings principally present a negative answer, collectively announcing that legal authority should *not* be controlled by the politically powerful. Conceiving of the Torah's laws as supernal—deriving from heaven and entrusted to humans—leading Jewish jurists and thinkers instead cultivate an autonomous sphere of law and design juridical schemes (this is the positive aspect of their responses) that aim to secure norms from the damaging intervention of powerful leaders.[87]

This remarkable jurisprudential turn must, of course, be evaluated in context. This book will therefore repeatedly situate this Jewish discourse within the world of Jewish antiquity and late antiquity. Facing the colossal forces of Greece and Rome, Jewish thinkers and exegetes responded by developing their own juristic concepts and normative structures. Proclaiming the supremacy of law and the striking capacity of legal authority to expand in the absence of power, Jewish jurists and thinkers formulated ideas that revitalized Jewish life, and along the way contributed an extraordinary—and thus far, untold—chapter to the history of law and civilization. At the same time, it is a principal thesis of this book that Jewish legalism is not a reluctant response to disempowerment or merely functional in its aims, but instead a deeply rooted ideology, anchored in the themes of revelation[88] and revolving around the centrality of law and its profound potential to structure a society and polity.

In an overview of the history of jurisprudence from antiquity until the present titled *About Law*, the legal historian Tony Honoré offers the following synopsis, which contains the standard description of the emergence of the concept of judicial autonomy:

> It may seem strange that in the Roman world, which valued law highly, legal experts were advisers rather than judges. But so long as a society thinks that the ruler should do justice personally, the legal input has to come from elsewhere. . . . The role of lawyers is then to advise the ruler about the law rather than to sit in judgment themselves. The idea that the ruler should not himself be a judge, and should not interfere with judges, comes much later. It was not until 1607 that James I of England was told by Chief Justice Coke that he was not learned in the law and so could not judge a lawsuit himself. . . . In the next century (1748) the French writer Montesquieu argued that, for citizens to be truly free, the main powers of government must be in the hands of different people.[89]

This book offers a revision of this summary account. It argues that well before the seventeenth and eighteenth centuries, leading Jewish thinkers, among others, insisted that legal authority should reside in the hands of learned jurists, and not rulers. Confronting a prevailing political order with certain contrary assumptions, postbiblical writers built upon an anomalous strand of biblical jurisprudence, and formulated profound ideologies that promote the rule of law, and insist that a judiciary must operate independently of powerful, political rulers. Renowned as a religion of law from an early phase, Judaism inspired rich articulations of a novel, and in certain senses unparalleled, jurisprudence.

Methodology and Terminology

The body of this book will examine portraits of judicial administration that are recorded in influential writings from the Second Temple and rabbinic periods. Certain texts surveyed below narrowly address this theme, while others extend to related aspects of the legal system at large. Several sections will also evaluate texts depicting royal powers in order to gauge what, if any, are the judicial prerogatives of the king, and how the king interacts with other legal officials. Further, even writings that demote the king's legal authority largely define their jurisprudence in response to the royal archetype. Likewise, certain sections will discuss the jurisdiction of priests and charismatic sages in the judicial process. After reviewing the key texts for a given writer or period, I will then broaden the inquiry in order to examine the role of law within the wider socioreligious and political-theological vision of a given writer, text, or period.

Over the past couple of decades, the study of Jewish political and legal thought has burgeoned in the academy.[90] This books aims to complement several recent works that have focused on other dimensions of early Jewish law, including studies by Christine Hayes (on the divine nature of law),[91] Aharon Shemesh (the sources of law), and Beth Berkowitz and Devora Steinmetz (penology), as well as works on political theory and ideology by Michael Walzer (political philosophy in the Bible), Steven Fraade (political motifs in early Judaism), and Gerald Blidstein and Yair Lorberbaum (rabbinic conceptions of kingship).[92]

The principal question that animates this study—How do early Jewish writings configure the relationship between law and power?—almost inevitably evokes its modern analog of how contemporary societies delegate authority. While perpetually debating and revising the proper distribution of powers, Western constitutional discourse generally concurs on certain indispensable elements of any satisfactory scheme, including separation of powers, an independent judiciary, and upholding the rule of law. In the case of American political culture, there are also entrenched ideas that are more indigenous, such as an antimonarchic tradition tracing back to the origins of the republic.[93] Although modern sensibilities can potentially color any study related to law and power, the outsized impact of these doctrines makes these topics worth interrogating,[94] and makes the possibility of gaining a new critical perspective on them tantalizing.

In order to illuminate the historically and socially contingent dynamics of law and power as represented in early Jewish writings, I have aspired to resist a presentist perspective as much as possible throughout Parts One and Two. In meticulously examining troves of ancient texts, I have sought to evaluate the varied materials on their own terms and in their respective contexts. Accordingly, these chapters chart a plurality of voices and perspectives,[95] and identify tensions among and within bodies of work.[96] When necessary, I have discarded standard taxonomies and adopted subtler formulations to more accurately express jurisprudential ideas that are embedded in these corpora.[97]

Many early texts cluster together into schemes that mediate the relationship between law and power by adopting modes of separation. Here is where (re)introducing (or forthrightly acknowledging) the presentist perspective becomes productive. One cannot help but see the ancient schemes as precursors of modern constitutional structures; my aim is to also highlight their distinctiveness. In the early materials one finds different forms of separation (e.g., stronger or internal iterations) arising from different circumstances (e.g., conditions of limited jurisdiction, within a socioreligious order) and addressing a different set of concerns (e.g., protecting an unadulterated legal sphere). Viewed in their own particularity, the early materials also refract aspects of contemporary structures and commitments. Following the spade work of the prior parts, Part Three is dedicated to engaging in a comparative analysis.

Ultimately, then, this book aims to reap the benefits of both the need to resist presentism in attempting to authentically understand the past and also the inescapable limits of one's ability to do so.[98] A critical distance enables one to discern some of the most distinctive ideas of the past, even if it means losing some access to the nuances of time and place.[99] Conversely, these early paradigms can help enlighten and unmask latent assumptions that animate one's present outlook and offer different permutations to consider for what lies ahead. Recovering a perspective from the past affords us what Christine Hayes has recently described as "a measure of control over the next chapter of the story," and "opens up the possibility that we might better negotiate" the vital question of how to best configure the relationship of law and power.[100]

A note on certain terminology employed throughout this book is in order. I use the term "political authority" generally to refer to the legitimate exercise of power to govern and administer public affairs.[101] I use the term "legal authority" to cover various dimensions of responsibility for the legal system. Although the focus of this book is on judicial authority, early Jewish writings frequently envision the judiciary exercising other legal powers, including legislating, issuing instructions, and teaching laws.[102] I use the term "law" broadly to refer to a body of norms that are understood to be binding,[103] rather than in a more culturally specific way, since the programmatic writings below tend to speak almost platonically about this sphere when envisioning its administration.[104]

Terms familiar from contemporary discourse, such as "constitutionalism," "the rule of law," "judicial independence," and "separation of powers," are used advisedly along the lines described above. Thus, "constitutional" questions pertain to issues of arranging governance; "judicial independence" connotes a construction of an independent sphere of legal authority; and so on. The larger point that informs this latter choice of vocabulary is conceptual. Early Jewish writings contain meaningful reflections on the administration of justice, the structure of courts, the nature of authority, the role of law, and law's relationship to power. Some of them contain fragmentary thoughts; others convey more coherent visions. One of my primary ambitions in this book is to recover these legal-political concepts, and to likewise also register when these ideas are partial, ambiguous, or inconsistent.[105] In order to draw out these ideas, modern terminology is a necessary tool, because it is the most developed conceptual language available.[106] Nevertheless, the reader should be fully aware of the approximate nature of this vocabulary.

Exploring these ideas will sometimes necessitate examining relatively obscure texts, but will also entail revisiting well-known passages from a different perspective. For example, when analyzing Josephus, instead of rehearsing standard scholarly inquiries addressing his relationship to Pharisaism or the priesthood, or his apologetic or historical motivations, or the identity of his intended audience, I have set out to answer a new set of questions: What is the ideal role of law within religion and society, according to Josephus? Who should serve as the leading legal and political authorities? What qualifies them for this role? How does legal authority compare to political power? Similarly, when confronting historical issues that inform the background to various texts, I will adopt a distinct approach. For instance, while much scholarship has examined the loss of Jewish sovereignty during antiquity and late antiquity, I shift the focus to uncharted terrain by asking: How did Jews think about authority when they lacked political power? How did their political condition inform the administrative models and the socioreligious ideologies they constructed during this period? What conceptions of legal authority were formulated in this setting? By exploring the early *Jewish legal and political imagination* in this manner, I aim not only to contribute to the study of Second Temple and rabbinic literature, but also to illuminate all-too-neglected aspects of the ideologies, philosophies, and values reflected in these corpora.[107]

Describing this work as a study of the imagination helps capture something about its scope. This book charts a history of early ideas about law and power, within their historical context.[108] My primary aim is to enter into the rich internal discourse of a selection of texts, and analyze the conceptual frameworks that they offer.[109] Distilled as texts, these ideas prove rich cultural artifacts, with their own resonances, especially in light of the textual investedness of Jewish culture.[110] This book also offers a foundation for other critical approaches,[111] to which it gestures at times, though they remain beyond its main focus.[112] As for the nature of the texts, while they vary in form—including exegesis, idyllic renditions of the past, eschatological visions, and apologetic statements—the legal-political paradigms they describe share a kind of utopian quality.

Indeed, when one considers the substantial practical constraints on the jurisdiction of Jews throughout most of the Second Temple and rabbinic periods, these elaborate designs could hardly be understood as prescribing a holistic arrangement to be implemented in the near future. Rather, by laying down these constructs Jewish jurists were aiming to achieve something more aspirational, ranging from initiating a modest project of reform to offering a radical critique of absolutist notions of justice[113] (an analogy to the aims of Plato and other utopian writers on justice comes to mind).[114] This latter interpretation particularly resonates with the anomalous nature of the jurisprudential vision advanced in many of these texts.

At a more basic level, these writings enabled Jewish thinkers to convey ideas about justice, the nature of law, the role of politics, and even the essence of revelation. Through their reflections, they underscored central values, including advancing the rule of law, checking political power, promoting deliberation in the pursuit of justice, and requiring collective action to administer legal affairs. Further, their notions no doubt oriented their paths in the world of antiquity and late antiquity.[115] Or, to invoke Clifford Geertz's formulation, they offered them ways of "imagining the real," as their various accounts of legal authority helped represent and shape the world they inhabited.[116]

Chapter Plan

This work is divided into three parts. Part One (Chapters 1–4) examines Second Temple literature; Part Two (Chapters 5–7) analyzes rabbinic literature; and Part Three (chapters 8–9 and the Conclusion) reflects on the roots, theoretical implications, and afterlife of the prior findings. Chapter 1 contrasts a pair of Second Temple works, and then surveys four interpretations of Deuteronomy 17: those of Philo, Qumran, Josephus, and the rabbis. These diverse interpretations will serve as a springboard for a wide-ranging exploration of jurisprudential themes throughout this book. Chapter 2 analyzes a discrete section in Philo's writings that reflects his conception of the ruler as an embodiment of justice, but still maintains a parallel role for the priests in the legal process. Chapter 3, devoted to Qumran, surveys numerous texts that depict elaborate juridical schemes linked to the king, priests, councils, and the sectarian community. Chapter 4 concludes this part by addressing the distinctive jurisprudence of Josephus, which intersects with his attitudes toward monarchy, aristocracy, and especially theocracy, as manifest in his exegetical, historical, and apologetic writings.

Part Two is devoted to rabbinic writings involving the administration of justice, and, more generally, the interplay of law, power, and politics. Chapter 5 begins with a comprehensive analysis of the relationship between the king and the legal regime according to early rabbinic literature, especially focusing on the Mishnah's separation between these spheres. Chapter 6 presents an overview of the various modes of administering justice that are recorded in early rabbinic literature, and charts the different kinds of juridical schemes that are evident in this corpus. Chapter 7 complicates the schematic configurations of the prior chapters by exploring unresolved tensions between law and power that nevertheless persist in later rabbinic literature, as reflected in the legal authority of the *Nasi* (a term discussed in this chapter). Collectively, these seven chapters highlight different amplifications of the Deuteronomic strand in Second Temple and rabbinic writings.

Part Three proceeds to evaluate these jurisprudential ideas from three significant angles related to the prisms of history and theory. Chapter 8 considers various factors that may have made the Deuteronomic strand appealing to postbiblical writers, including historical conditions of disempowerment and axiological commitments deriving from the source and ontology of divine law. Chapter 9 compares and contrasts early Jewish notions of separation with parallel themes in modern jurisprudence, as described above. Even without advancing any genealogical claim, there is a phenomenological analogy that must be explored in order to better understand the nature of each and gain important insights into the theoretical underpinnings of constitutional doctrines. Finally, the Conclusion briefly explores later incarnations of this line of early Jewish jurisprudence as it extends from medieval to early modern times.

Even though the wide array of material surveyed in this work reveals alternate perspectives on the nature of legal authority, an important trajectory of postbiblical Jewish writings through late antiquity evinces a distinctive orientation. Proclaiming the supremacy of law, certain foundational early Jewish texts also insist on its independence. Transcending the circumstances of disempowerment, the appeal of their jurisprudence lies in a particular conception of law tracing back to the idea of revelation. Its enduring significance continues to characterize Jewish religion, society, and law to this very day. The chapters below portray the emergence of this extraordinary jurisprudence as it unfolds in assorted writings from the Second Temple and rabbinic periods.

Part One

Second Temple Literature

I

Postbiblical Jurisprudence

The two strands of biblical jurisprudence examined in the Introduction resurface throughout late biblical and postbiblical literature.[1] Given the centrality of the royalist strand in the Bible, its recurrence in subsequent strata is to be anticipated. By contrast, the strong resonance of the Deuteronomic tradition in postbiblical literature eclipses all expectations. What constitutes a marginal strand in the Bible becomes the dominant form of jurisprudence in these later corpora.

This chapter opens with a pair of contrasting Second Temple texts,[2] which respectively accentuate the two strands of jurisprudence that recur in postbiblical literature. Whereas the Psalms of Solomon (PS) extol the ideal reign of an absolutist king who promotes justice, Hecataeus proclaims the Jewish rejection of kingship[3] and the adoption of the leadership of priestly judges. So while PS follow the regnant scheme, Hecataeus presents a stark opposition between two modes of administration, and situates Jewish tradition on the nonroyalist side of the divide. Often considered a perplexing account, Hecataeus in fact portends the direction of much of postbiblical jurisprudence.

Propelling this surprising jurisprudential turn in subsequent phases is the decisive exegetical choice to build upon Deuteronomy 17 (the Hecataeus passage itself has no clear biblical antecedents). The next section in this chapter surveys the afterlife of this biblical source in the writings of Philo, Qumran, Josephus, and the rabbis, and serves as a portal into their broader jurisprudential ideas that will be analyzed throughout this book. Unlike the categorical formulations of PS and Hecataeus, these latter writings revise and transform Deuteronomy's teaching, and span a hermeneutic spectrum. Yet they each amplify essential aspects of Deuteronomy's unique juridical vision, and significantly advance its broader conception of law's autonomy.

Two Strands in Second Temple Literature

Psalms of Solomon

Among a collection of psalms composed in the wake of the Roman invasion of Judea in the first century BCE,[4] PS 17 offers an extended supplication for a Davidic messiah. The particulars of this psalm express a sweeping and spectacular royal ideology.[5] What should be underlined in this context is how the psalmist associates the future scion's flourishing rule with (a unique mode of) legal supremacy. In the psalmist's vision, the exalted sovereign will embody righteousness and accordingly execute justice throughout the land.[6]

After decrying the sinfulness of the people of Jerusalem who usurped the Davidic throne and installed a prideful imposter (17:5–6), and attesting to the latter's ouster by an alien empire led by a rogue king and disobedient judge (17:19–20),[7] the psalmist petitions for a different kind of leader: "See, Lord, and raise up for them their kin, the son of David, to rule over your servant Israel" (17:21). The next verses beseech God to endow the messianic king with ideal spiritual qualities in order to lead the righteous and vanquish the wicked. "Undergird him . . . in wisdom and in righteousness to drive out the sinners from the inheritance; to smash the arrogance of sinners like a potter's jar; to shatter all their substance with an iron rod; to destroy the unlawful nations with the word of his mouth . . . and he will condemn the sinners by the thoughts of their hearts. He will gather a holy people whom he will lead in righteousness" (17:22–26). After purging society of its sinners and vices, the king will assume the supreme role of a judge-ruler, "and he will judge the tribes of the people that have been made holy by the Lord their God. He will not tolerate unrighteousness (even) to pause among them, and any person who knows wickedness shall not live with them.... He will judge peoples and nations in the wisdom of his righteousness" (17:22–29).

In the continuation, the psalm lauds the future king's singular virtuosity, to the point of depicting him as flawless[8]—"he himself (will be) free from sin, (in order) to rule a great people" (17:36). The king's pure character will drive him to perpetually eradicate evil from his kingdom. "He will expose officials and drive out sinners by the strength of his word. And he will not weaken in his days" (17:36–37). The eschatological king will henceforth reign in glory, instructing and judging the people. "This is the beauty of the king of Israel which God knew, to raise him over the house of Israel. His words will be purer than the finest gold, the best. He will judge the peoples in the assemblies, the tribes of the sanctified. His words will be the words of the holy ones, among sanctified peoples" (17:42–43). Pristine and peerless, the messianic sovereign will dispense wisdom and justice to the world.

The biblical roots of the extraordinary theological-political vision of PS 17 are pronounced. Drawing on passages such as Isaiah 11, Psalms 2 and 72,[9] PS 17 concentrates some of the most avowedly royalist materials in Scripture. Building upon this scriptural foundation, PS 17 formulates a distinctive response to political realities of the second and first centuries BCE. Deeply critical of the Hasmonean dynasty,[10] the psalmist calls for a restoration of the Davidic dynasty.[11] In this respect, PS 17 differs from the principal Qumran opposition to the Hasmoneans, which focuses on transforming the priesthood rather than on reconstituting the monarchy (see Chapter 3). A second factor that informs the political conception of PS 17 is the confrontation of Judeans with Roman expansion and power. Traces of both of these influences can already be detected at the outset of PS 17 in the vehement denunciation of non-Davidic leaders (17:5–10), followed by the protest against the foreign powers who replaced them (17:11–14, 19–20).

The longing for a messianic ruler from the House of David, thus, encapsulates an intense yearning for an alternate religious and political landscape. Tellingly, the psalmist's redemptive vision encompasses a transformation of the social and legal order. Elaborating upon the primary strand of the Bible's jurisprudence, the psalmist petitions for a superior king to achieve this dramatic overhaul by reigning through sheer justice.

Hecataeus

A model of Jewish leadership and a jurisprudence that is the polar opposite from the royalism of PS 17 can be found in an excursus on the Jews that appears in the late fourth-century-BCE work "On the Egyptians" by the Greek author Hecataeus.[12] While there is considerable debate about the authenticity and dating of this passage, Bezalel Bar Kochva has recently defended the attribution to Hecataeus,[13] which would make this the oldest known account of Jewish origins in Greek literature (dating from the beginning of the Hellenistic period). For present purposes, what is of special interest is the passage's unique description of the political and juridical system of the Jews.[14] Employing standard Greek tropes about colonization and the establishment of institutions to govern the lives of settlers,[15] Hecataeus portrays Moses's leadership of the Jews who migrated from Egypt to settle Judea in the following terms: "The colony was headed by a man called Moses, outstanding both for his wisdom and for his courage. On taking possession of the land, he founded . . . Jerusalem. In addition, he established the temple that they hold in chief veneration, instituted their forms of worship and ritual, drew up the laws, and ordered their political institutions."

Mistakenly attributing a range of actions to the single figure of Moses,[16] Hecataeus describes him as the founder of the polity and giver of the law. Even more curious are his subsequent remarks about the nature of the Jewish polity.

> He picked out the men of most refinement and with the greatest ability to head the entire nation, and appointed them priests; and he ordained that they should occupy themselves with the temple and the honors and sacrifices offered to their God. These same men he appointed to be judges in all major

disputes, and entrusted to them the guardianship of the laws and customs. For this reason *the Jews never have a king*, and authority over the people is regularly vested in whichever priest is regarded as superior to his colleagues in wisdom and virtue. (emphasis added)

Notice how Hecataeus depicts the priestly leaders as masters of the law. The excerpt then concludes by describing the high priest, who heads the priestly caste and leads the Jews by way of his supreme legal authority.

They call this man the high priest, and believe that he acts as a messenger to them of God's commandments. It is he, we are told, who in their assemblies and other gatherings announces what is ordained, and the Jews are so docile in such matters that straightaway they fall to the ground and do reverence to the high priest when he expounds the commandments to them. And at the end of their laws there is even appended the statement: "These are the words that Moses heard from God and declares unto the Jews."[17]

Among several puzzling details in this account, perhaps the most bizarre and intriguing is Hecataeus's claim that the Jews never have a king, and that instead priestly jurists assume authority over the Jews.[18] The blatant inaccuracy of this remark has disturbed scholars, and several have concluded (for numerous reasons) that this entire passage is a later interpolation.[19] Others have even proposed that a Jewish informant deliberately misinformed Hecataeus for programmatic purposes.[20] Hecataeus's description of Jewish leadership must have also surprised his broader audience. Living during the late fourth century BCE, Hecataeus writes from within a Hellenistic world led by kings.[21] The importance of Hecataeus's description, though, lies not in its factual accuracy or wider currency, but instead in his perceptive intuition that Jewish ideology supports a unique form of governance.[22] Characterizing Jewish sovereignty as being led by priestly judges in lieu of a king, Hecataeus essentially articulates a version of the stronger thesis described in the Introduction, and thereby anticipates a future strand of Jewish thought that elevates sacral law over and against absolute power.

In this vein, the afterlife of Hecataeus's account is also noteworthy, as Bar Kochva has pointed out.[23] Preserved in Diodorus's *Bibliotheca Historica*, a first-century-BCE panoramic history of the ancient world culminating in the Roman conquest of the East, Hecataeus's description resonates with contemporary Judean political affairs reported by Diodorus. In the final volume (XL, 2), Diodorus intentionally records Hecataeus's account immediately after relaying the tale of the meeting between Judean leaders and Pompey in 63 BCE.[24] An examination of his description of this episode, especially the argument of the more than two hundred leading men of Judea (emphasized below), suggests that Diodorus saw it as intimately linked to Hecataeus's report:

> During Pompey's stay in Damascus of Syria, Aristobulus, the king of the Jews, and Hyrcanus his brother came to him with their dispute over kingship. Likewise the leading men, more than two hundred in number, gathered to address the general and explain that their forefathers, having revolted from Demetrius, had sent an embassy to the senate, and *received from them the leadership of the Jews, who were, moreover, to be free and autonomous, their ruler being called High Priest, not king.* Now, however, these men were lording it over them, having overthrown the ancient laws and enslaved the citizens in defiance of justice; for it was by means of a horde of mercenaries, and by outrages and countless impious murders that they had established themselves as kings.

Opposing both of the fraternal claimants to the throne, the more than two hundred men assert their inherited right to be led by a high priest rather than a king. Against this backdrop, Hecataeus's account documents that such an administrative structure dates all the way back to the original legislator, Moses. A hoary ancestral tradition mandates that Jews are led by the high priest and the ancient laws, and not by a royal regime.[25]

To summarize, Hecataeus presents a fascinating portrait of Jewish administration that is at variance with the royalism of much of the

Bible, certain postbiblical works of the Second Temple period, and contemporary modes of governance. Further, he not only suggests that Jews prefer priestly jurists to kings, but even intimates that they see the selection of the former as mutually exclusive to the coronation of the latter. Although the origins of Hecataeus's account are uncertain, this passage offers penetrating insight into certain Jewish conceptions of power as linked to the rule of sacral law. These conceptions reverberate in the argument of the Judean leaders recorded by Diodorus, and resonate with the subsequent shift toward legalism in postbiblical jurisprudence, and especially its stronger iteration.

In a more elementary sense, Hecataeus rightly discerns a deep tension in Jewish thought between royal power and sacral justice. For a conflict between these spheres often exists, and at times even percolates, in the jurisprudence of Jewish antiquity and late antiquity. By delineating opposite models of authority, Hecataeus exposes a critical fault line that runs through much of postbiblical jurisprudence. Its traces are already evident in a series of early interpretations of a single biblical passage.

Deuteronomy 17 and Its Interpreters

A broad array of models of jurisdiction are represented in four postbiblical works from the late Second Temple and rabbinic periods. While these works reflect different cultures and theologies, what makes their comparative analysis particularly instructive is a common point of origin: Deuteronomy 17 (cited in the Introduction). Despite the anomalous jurisprudence of this chapter relative to most of the Bible, it assumed a prominent position among early interpreters.[26] Using this biblical base influenced their orientation, even as its legacy was understood by them in markedly different ways. Below I will review selections from Philo's *Special Laws,* Qumran's Temple Scroll, Josephus's *Jewish Antiquities,* and Mishnah Sanhedrin that focus upon Deuteronomy 17 (subsequent chapters will evaluate a much broader selection of texts), considering how they conceive of judicial responsibility, and the role of the king, if any, in the judiciary.[27] Even an initial survey reveals a range of interpretations that reverse, revise, expand, or recalibrate the Deuteronomic subordination of the king to an independent judiciary.

Philo on the King and the Judiciary: Reversing the Separation

Philo promotes the king and depicts him as a supreme judicial figure, and thereby closes the gap between the king and the judiciary that surfaces in Deuteronomy 17.[28] In a lengthy excursus in *Special Laws* 4, titled "The Appointment of Rulers,"[29] Philo calls for the use of elections, as ratified by God, for selecting the ruler (4.151–157), and then elaborates on the powers and regulations of the monarch (4.158–188).[30] From the tone and substance of these passages it becomes clear that Philo considers the king to be the leading figurehead, a preference that Erwin Goodenough argued long ago appears throughout Philo's writings.[31] Thus, Philo states that the king possesses an "ensign of sovereignty which none can impeach, formed in the image of its archetype, the kingship of God" (4.160), and describes the king as "the person who has been judged worthy to fill the highest and most important office" (4.170). In contrast with the more equivocal orientation toward monarchy implied by the plain sense of Deuteronomy 17, Philo openly endorses a sovereign ruler.[32]

In detailing the responsibilities of the ruler, Philo specifies judging and appointing judges as leading duties. Strikingly, Philo relies principally on Deuteronomy 17 in his exposition, notwithstanding the plain sense of Scripture that judicial power does not reside with the king. In a loaded homiletic interpretation that will be unpacked in Chapter 2, Philo construes the biblical prescript in Deut 17:18–19—that the ruler must transcribe a summary of the law and repeatedly read it—to mean that he must immerse himself in the law (4.160–163). Eventually the ruler's "scepter will be this very law," ensuring his spirit of equality and ability to strike a proper balance between excess and deficiency (4.164–168). By observing the law, the ruler will overcome his arrogant impulses and remain allied with his people, an idea that Philo bases upon Deuteronomy 17:20a. The ruler will thereby achieve a virtuous balance, a theme Philo derives from the admonition in Deuteronomy 17:20b that the king not stray to the right or left. A ruler who adheres to the law will "honor equality, be impervious to bribes and give just judgments" (4.169)—all biblical prescripts for an upright judge.[33] His reward will be "that the days of his government shall be long" (4.169), echoing Deuteronomy 17:20c, which Philo interprets allegorically as a prediction of an enduring royal legacy.

Responsible for heading the government, including administering justice, the king should adjudicate only greater matters, Philo emphasizes, and he should delegate the rest of his docket to lower-level officials (4.170–172).[34] As a paradigm, Philo appeals to Moses, the ideal king (see Philo's *Life of Moses*),[35] who delegated judicial responsibilities in this manner at Jethro's recommendation (4.173–175).[36]

Within the range of positions charted in this section, Philo's jurisprudence stands out as the only work with a substantial royalist bent. Yet the fact that the royalism reflected in Philo's excursus is structured around Deut 17 already hints at a more complex scheme, relative to the absolutist template of royal justice encountered in the previous section in PS 17. Among other things, the judicial section of Deut 17 designates other officials, such as priests, as leading authorities. Sure enough, Philo explicitly registers this seemingly inconsistent fact at the end of his excursus. Therefore, Chapter 2 will further interrogate the degree of Philo's royalism, and the nature of a jurisprudence that is evidently linked to more than one official.

The Qumran Scrolls on the King and the Judiciary: Revising the Separation

Unlike Philo—who restores the king as a central figure in the administration of justice—the Qumran Temple Scroll (TS) affirms the basic hierarchy of Deuteronomy. According to TS, the king's position remains subordinate to the priestly judges. Yet TS revises the Deuteronomic tradition by linking the king to the judiciary, albeit in a secondary role that overall reinforces his inferior position.[37]

After restating the verses from Deuteronomy 17:8–13 regarding the judiciary's authority to resolve legal matters, TS reiterates the next sequence of verses from Deuteronomy 17:14–20 about the royal office (11 Q19 56). The scroll then segues into the "Law of the King" (LK), a discrete literary unit which the redactor of TS incorporates into the larger composition (11Q19 57–59).[38] This section specifies the duties and prerogatives of the monarch, supported by a pastiche of verses from Scripture. Among the prominent responsibilities of the king enumerated in LK is the duty to judge and instruct. He is duly enjoined to "not distort justice, nor take bribes in order to distort true justice" (11Q19 57, 19–20).

Nevertheless, LK also constricts the king's judicial autonomy. It requires the king to preside over legal matters with a council of thirty-six members, composed of twelve princes, twelve priests, and twelve Levites (11Q19 57, 12–13). Interpreting the verse, "that his heart should not become haughty over his brothers,"[39] as a binding protocol, LK stipulates,[40] "he [the king] shall not rise his heart above them [the council of thirty-six], nor shall he do anything in all his counsels outside of them" (11Q19 57, 14–15). The king must confer with the council in ruling on legal (and other) matters.[41] The narrow scope of the king's judicial powers is also implied by other parts of TS (56 and 61), which enumerate only the priests, Levites, and judges as leading judicial officials. The cumulative impression from this evidence is that according to TS, the judiciary is primarily composed of priests, Levites, and judges, and the king's judicial and political role is supplementary and limited.

In fact, LK, which constitutes the king's charter, is written by the priests on behalf of the king.[42] As the king derives his authority from this charter, his empowerment derives in some sense from the priests.[43] In a parallel arrangement, TS requires the king to consult with the high priest's *Urim* and *Thummim* (a special priestly vestment) before embarking on war (11Q19 58, 18–21), constraining the king's prerogatives in this domain as well. This, of course, raises the largely unexplored questions that will be taken up in Chapter 3 of how, on balance, to evaluate the standing and authority of the king in the TS, and whether the TS perspective on kingship and the king's role in administering justice represents an ideology found elsewhere in Qumran literature.

Josephus on the King and the Judiciary: Expanding the Separation

Differing from Philo and the TS, Josephus expands the Deuteronomic gulf separating the legal and royal spheres. Whereas Deuteronomy 17 depicts leading priestly judges, and then portrays a king who is subordinate to the (priestly) law, Josephus underscores the prominence of law, judicial officials, and priests, and altogether marginalizes the monarch.[44] Restating Deuteronomy (*Ant.* 4.214–218), Josephus refers to an autonomous network of municipal tribunals (each consisting of seven judges and a couple of Levites). The local tribunal refers hard cases to Jerusalem, where the high priest, prophet, and council of elders (*gerousia*) serve as higher judicial authorities (Deut 17:9 mentions only "the levitical priests and the judge"). Notice how the king is omitted from this expanded list of supreme judicial officials, as judicial administration according to Josephus operates independently from sovereign rule.

In a nearby section on kingship (4.223–224), Josephus expresses fundamental reservations about the monarchic institution that go well beyond the equivocation of Deuteronomy. In an emphatic statement, the precise implications of which have been debated by scholars since Wellhausen, Josephus proclaims the superiority of an aristocratic form of government.[45] Only if the people imprudently resist an aristocracy is a king appointed instead. The king must, then, be concerned with justice and remain subservient to the laws. Moreover, judicial officials will serve to check the authority of the king, as the king must solicit the counsel of the high priest and the advice of the elders (*gerousia*) before he acts. The king is thereby structurally subordinated to these latter two bodies. Read together, these two *Antiquities* sections complement one another. In the most basic sense, judicial authority is invested in officials aside from the king, because monarchy is a problematic institution.

An important elaboration on these themes is found in Josephus's later work, *Against Apion*, authored to defend Judaism against its detractors. Josephus frames his defense of the Torah as an analysis of its unique constitution, a "theocracy" (the implications of this new category that Josephus introduces in *Apion* will be explored in Chapter 4).[46] Here, too,

Josephus elides a political and legal discourse. In proximate passages, Josephus hails the historic, just, and immutable laws of the Torah as indicative of the singular achievements of Jewish civilization.[47] Given the emphasis on legal supremacy, the allocation of legal authority within this system is significant: the high priest and the priestly class are responsible for mediating the laws; not the king.

In sum, in his restatements of Deuteronomy 17, Josephus portrays the high priest and priests, perhaps with the assistance of the elders and the prophet, as the judicial leaders. In the optimal scheme, the monarchy is abolished altogether; less optimally, the king is relegated to a secondary role and must defer to some of these other officials. The substantial nexus between the legal and political order evident in these and other excerpts will be fleshed out in Chapter 4.

The late Second Temple texts examined thus far sharply diverge in their interpretation of Deuteronomy 17 and the degree to which the administrative structure aims for a separation of powers. In Philo, a monarchic ruler, who masters the law, is uniquely qualified to serve as a superior judge. According to the TS, the king participates in the judicial order, but administers alongside, or even beneath, the priests, Levites, and judges. Finally, according to Josephus, judicial officials operate autonomously, and monarchy is to be rejected or at least subordinated to other authorities. Beginning with the foundation of Deuteronomy 17, Philo restores the king to the administration of justice, the TS preserves its layered distribution of powers, while Josephus widens the hierarchy among these institutions by elevating the judiciary and demoting the king.

The Mishnah on the King and the Judiciary: Recalibrating the Separation

A full analysis of early rabbinic attitudes toward royal and judicial powers will be provided in Chapter 5, but a brief summary of a key mishnaic passage relating to Deuteronomy 17 is essential for rounding out this synopsis of the early hermeneutics of this biblical chapter.[48] The passage is recorded in Mishnah Sanhedrin chapter 2, which builds upon this biblical source (explicitly citing Deut 17:15, 16, 17, 19). Its conception of the king's relationship to the judiciary, which is formulated in a succinct manner, likely derives from the Deuteronomic tradition as well (this link is made explicit in a later rabbinic midrash):[49] "The king may neither judge nor be judged, testify nor be testified against" (*m. Sanh.* 2:2).

Following the lead of Deuteronomy 17, the Mishnah proclaims that justice is not the domain of the king, but instead is entrusted to a network of courts. Composed of the supreme court of the Sanhedrin and two tiers of lower tribunals, an expansive judiciary thus anchors the normative order.[50] In enhancing the autonomy of the courts, however, the Mishnah does not downgrade the king, as opposed to Deuteronomy, Josephus, and the Temple Scroll.[51] Rather, the Mishnah advances an original, recalibrated scheme where the king enjoys a prominent leadership position, but his role is separate from the judiciary and the broader normative system. The resonances and wider ramifications of this division, as well as the contrary voices it evokes, will be explored in Chapters 5–7.

Both biblical strands of jurisprudence resurface in late biblical and postbiblical literature. But whereas the royalist model is more dominant in the biblical corpus, an extraordinary reversal transpires in subsequent writings. Hecataeus first identifies a profound tension between competing models of political and legal authority, and privileges the independent leadership of priestly jurists (in contrast with the Psalms of Solomon). Over time, various formative works of late Second Temple and rabbinic literature turn to Deuteronomy 17 and expound on its teaching in manifold ways. While their respective interpretations of this chapter cover an entire gamut—reversing, revising, expanding, and recalibrating the Deuteronomic subordination of the king to an independent judiciary—the unmistakable influence of Deuteronomy's distinctive jurisprudence is evident throughout these varied works. Each writer grafts his own juridical conception—which includes a vision of legal supremacy,[52] and for some, legal autonomy—onto this biblical foundation.

The above survey also signals the importance of the underlying juridical and political issues for each one of these authors. Indeed, each one of these writers devotes much ink and energy to exploring related themes in numerous other contexts in their writings. Reviewing various interpretations of Deuteronomy 17 therefore constitutes only the first phase in a broader inquiry into aspects of postbiblical jurisprudence. The coming chapters will continue to unpack the above hermeneutic texts (and will fine-tune or even modify this initial summary) alongside a much wider selection of writings in order to analyze their political and juridical perspectives on the nature of legal authority, beginning with Philo in Chapter 2.

Overall the project of articulating notions of governance and power in Jewish antiquity and late antiquity precipitates a turn toward legalism, which affords the ultimate alternative to a royalist scheme for a religion whose identity revolves around the rule of law. While Hecataeus hints at this movement, more profound and far-reaching thrusts in this direction can be discerned in other writers who expand upon Deuteronomy, and also address related themes in various other contexts. This orientation is especially manifest in the vast, if complex, library from Qumran, the serial works of Josephus, and a cross section of normative teachings of the rabbis, whose works I will evaluate in subsequent chapters.

2

Philo's Jurisprudence

Chapter 1 introduced "The Appointment of Rulers" excursus in Philo's *Special Laws*, a philosophical-exegetical exposition of Pentateuchal norms written in the early first century CE. Elevating the monarchic ruler and situating him at the head of the legal order,[1] the excursus seems to echo the dominant strand of biblical jurisprudence. To wit, Philo inflates the sovereign's legal authority, even while recounting verses from Deuteronomy 17 that have a contrary connotation.

The analysis in the first section below will indeed highlight the royalist dimensions of Philo's excursus. The next section, however, will argue—on the basis of three interrelated motifs enumerated below—that the above characterization can be misleading, and is certainly incomplete. Far from being an absolutist figure who commandeers by way of legal edicts, Philo's ruler ideally upholds, and even personifies, universal laws that are indispensable for achieving justice within the polity. Moreover, the pursuit of justice relies on figures aside from the ruler. If from one perspective Philo's reconfiguration of legal authority reflects a royalist override of the plain sense of Deuteronomy 17, from another perspective his notion of rulership is more constrained, while his jurisprudence—informed to a certain extent by its underlying verses—is more capacious.[2] Simply situating Philo within the Bible's royalist tradition obscures important subtleties in his political vision and mischaracterizes the essence of his jurisprudence.[3]

Philo's Royalism

Philo's excursus comprises part of an appendix to the *Special Laws* on the virtue of justice.[4] Expounding upon the great science and art of governance ("a task which we might call an art of arts and a science of sciences" [4.156]), Philo identifies sovereign rule as the optimal mode of governance. Tracking Deuteronomy's monarchy section (17:14–20) systematically,[5] the excursus replaces the tentative and skeptical tone of these discrete verses with a grand and expansive portrait of sovereign rule. Proclaiming that the king is "formed in the image of its archetype the kingship of God" (4.164), Philo refracts the biblical image of God's majestic rule onto the sovereign.[6] Following in God's path, the monarch successfully governs the polity and achieves lasting gains. Elsewhere Philo offers a vivid depiction of Moses as the inaugural and ideal king of Israel.[7] Justice is evidently sustained for Philo by a political theology rooted in royalism.

The body of the excursus expounds upon the sovereign's political role. As the Deuteronomy 17 verses do not enumerate any powers or privileges of the ruler,[8] Philo fills this void on the basis of his novel exposition and exegesis. Eschewing the more obvious royal powers enumerated in the book of Samuel, such as waging wars,[9] Philo centers precisely upon what appears to be (intentionally) absent from Deuteronomy: the king's legal authority.[10]

In galvanizing support for his portrayal from the Pentateuch (with no obvious sources to draw on), Philo's royalist ideology is transparent. He appeals to several eclectic sources that only serve as prooftexts of royal justice for an exegete with prior conceptual commitments to this paradigm. Viewing Moses as an archetypal king, Philo invokes the Mosaic judiciary recorded in Exod 18:13–27 as a blueprint for the ruler's jurisdiction and delegation of authority (4.170–175).[11] Just as Moses sets up a judiciary, where he addresses "great [*megalos*]" matters and subordinate judges adjudicate inferior matters, so the royal judiciary adopts this same structure according to Philo, as the king presides over a network of lower judges.

Other sources that Philo uses to thicken his account of royal justice are even less explicit. In 4.169, Philo describes the tenets that guide the ruler's administration of justice by citing the standard rules of judicial conduct of Deut 16:19–20. He thus delineates the ways in which a law-abiding *ruler* honors equality, avoids bribery, and "gives just judgments justly"[12] (these same verses contain guidelines for all judges, as Philo emphasizes in an earlier section of the appendix).[13] In 4.177, Philo presents a fascinating reading of Deut 10:17–18,[14] which amplifies its notable judicial terminology: God is described as acting beyond favoritism, being immune to bribery, and executing justice for the downtrodden. According to Philo, these verses allude to God's *royal* administration of justice. Toward the end of the excursus (4.183), Philo invokes the broadly formulated prohibition of Lev 19:16 to "not deal basely [*lo telekh rakhil*] with your countrymen" as a specific warning to a *ruler* to not act corruptly, which may also relate to how he exercises legal authority.[15]

But none of these scriptural sources reference a ruler. Their explicit subject matter is a judge, God, and an unnamed subject,[16] respectively. Nevertheless, Philo identifies all three as monarchic figures, just as he does with Moses. Accordingly, the king must adjudicate justly, while protecting the vulnerable and standing upright in his exercise of authority. Philo invents a royal jurisprudence through his novel hermeneutics.

The climactic manifestation of Philo's royalist exegesis is the most immediate source he adduces, which is arguably the most problematic one, Deuteronomy 17. Beyond its skepticism toward monarchy and conspicuous omission of royal powers, this chapter plainly allocates legal authority to the Levitical priests and the judge in the Temple and subordinates the king to the Levitical priests (including the requirement that the king must record the law in their presence). Yet Philo remarkably bypasses these difficulties: Deliberately inverting the order of Deuteronomy 17 in his otherwise sequential exegesis, Philo presents the monarchy section before restating the judiciary section (see below). Further, when Philo expands on Deut 17:18's mandate that the ruler transcribe the summary of the law, he carefully omits the qualification recorded in its closing words: "in the presence of the Levitical priests."[17]

The advantages of these editorial decisions are readily apparent. Philo represents monarchy as the primary political institution. The king is in no way inferior to the Levitical priests, who have yet to be introduced or even referenced. Philo likewise mutes the equivocal language of 17:14 introducing the kingship section. Following these modifications that alter the tone of the section, Philo elaborates over several paragraphs on the king's juridical role.

Here, Philo appeals to Deut 17:18–20 as a pivotal source. Interpreting the king's commandment to write a summary of the law (Torah, i.e., *nomos*) as a literal charge with a foundational purpose, Philo construes these verses contrary to their plain sense as establishing the king's substantial legal authority and enhancing his sovereign powers. As Philo expounds in 4.160–169, the iterative act of recording and rehearsing the summary of the law forms an inextricable bond—a "cementing" and a "companionship"—between the king and the law. The king who fully immerses himself in this transformative process thereby achieves the Pythagorean ideal of becoming a *nomos empsychos* (a living law).[18] Figuring prominently in Philo's philosophy, this ideal characterizes the personality of Moses, the archetypal king and legislator in the *Life of Moses*, and is the aspiration of the Philonic king across the generations.[19] By invoking this powerful trope of classical kingship (see below), Philo caps off his magisterial reworking of Deuteronomy 17's political ideal and jurisprudence.

A More Complex Political and Jurisprudential Vision

Highlighting the extensive royalist dimensions of Philo's excursus, notwithstanding the plain sense of Deut 17 around which it is structured—in contradistinction with the other postbiblical works surveyed in Chapter 1—should not lead to the conclusion that his jurisprudence is monolithic. Rather than fitting squarely within the dominant strand (in its absolutist bent), there are significant nuances in his legal-political thought. In particular, three salient features can be discerned.

A Ruler without Muscle

Philo employs a revealing designation for the royal leader in the excursus, mostly labeling him an *archon* (ruler)—following the Septuagint translation of Deut 17²⁰—rather than a *basileos* (king).[21] For Philo, this shift in nomenclature evidently signals an alternate form of sovereign rule.[22] Thus, Philo stresses in the opening of the excursus (4.157) that the ruler is selected by the people on the basis of his merits, not by means of an arbitrary system of lots like the classical method of ancient Athens (4.151).[23] Implicitly, Philo also marginalizes Scripture's method of divine election of the ruler (Deut 17:15)[24] by declaring that God affirms the selection of the people. He likewise rejects the institution of dynastic succession prevalent in the Bible.[25] When restating the ample reward that is designated for a faithful king (Deut 17:20), in lieu of Scripture's promise of dynastic success ("so that he and his descendants may reign long over his kingdom in Israel"), Philo proclaims that the accomplishments of such a king will achieve a lasting legacy.[26] Reconstituting monarchy, Philo envisions a rule of an *archon* that better conforms to the democratic form, which Philo concludes is the best regime (see the peroration of the appendix, 4.237).

A further indication of the importance of these structural adjustments (absent the change of nomenclature) can be gleaned from Philo's depiction of Moses's royal appointment in the *Life of Moses*.[27] In his youth, Moses renounces the Egyptian dynasty that he was destined to inherit (*Moses* 1.149). At a later phase, Moses's coronation as the Israelite monarch follows the "democratic" template: "[by] having received the authority which they [the Israelites] willingly gave him [Moses], with the sanction and assent of God" (*Moses* 1.162–163). Chosen on the basis of his virtuous character, Moses ultimately refuses to bequeath his sovereignty to his progeny (*Moses* 1.150).

In this context, Philo notably contrasts the legitimacy of a meritocratic selection with a final alternative method of becoming a ruler—a brute power grab (*Moses* 1.148). Philonic sovereignty does not derive from an illegitimate monopoly of violence. Nor does the rule of a legitimate sovereign revolve around a show of strength. As stated, Philo glaringly omits any military role of the ruler.[28] In a similar vein, the ruler's administration of justice does not rely on force (indeed, a leitmotif in Philo's works is that the Mosaic laws are meant to be fulfilled in a voluntary manner).[29] If Philo is a royalist, he is no absolutist. His political vision calls for an *archon* who administers without coercion.

Embodying the Law

Rather than a muscular king who issues commands, Philo envisions a ruler with a different kind of nexus to the law. As we have seen, Philo invokes the Hellenistic Pythagorean ideal of *nomos empsychos* in a decisive passage (4.160–164) that builds upon the ruler's duty to transcribe the law (Deut 17:18). Far from clumsily imposing an alien, pro-monarchic trope onto this verse, Philo ingeniously weave this ideal into his hermeneutics. Along the way, he also substantially modifies this trope, further exposing the limits of simply labeling his approach as royalist.

The classical designation of the king as a living law classifies the king as an autonomous source of law, superior to any written law.[30] Philo's ruler, however, intensively studies the Torah's *nomos* or Mosaic law, and is bound by it.[31] A kind of dialectic then emerges, which Philo vividly encapsulates elsewhere when he describes Moses as the king and the lawgiver: "the king is a living law, and the law a just king."[32] In other words, the king (or ruler) simultaneously embodies and enacts the law by animating a law with defined content—the law of Moses. Moreover, as John Martens has argued in an important study, Philo uniquely conflates the *nomos empsychos* ideal with two other Greco-Roman conceptions of higher law—natural law and an unwritten law—and paradoxically equates them with the written Mosaic law.[33] He thereby unfastens this ideal from its exclusive attachment to the royal office.[34] In Philo's rendition, the just lives of the Patriarchs and Moses instinctively embodied the unwritten, universal law of nature, and prefigured the norms of the Torah.[35] Philo also sets this out as a prospective ideal for all future rulers.[36] The eternal law that they embody is beyond the control or scope of any one of them.

In the specific context here (paragraphs 4.160–164), Philo derives another layer of this ideal from the underlying verse, which sheds light on its ongoing political role in his thought: The embodiment of the law by the ruler grows out of an iterative and transformative process of consciously transcribing and studying the written law. In other words, the ultimate objective of writing the law is its *un-writing*. This striking process constitutes a deliberate reversal of the overarching trajectory charted by Philo elsewhere in his oeuvre, but ultimately serves as its complement.

In his exposition of the norms of the Torah, Philo repeatedly underscores that the opening books of the Pentateuch are essential prequels to the Mosaic law.[37] Beginning with creation and followed by the lives of the Patriarchs and Moses,[38] the Pentateuch exalts the universal, unwritten law of nature and its ultimate embodiment in the just lives of these protagonists. The written law of Moses, in turn, is a copy (*eikonon*) of the universal, unwritten law. Formulated "in agreement with the principles of eternal nature" (*Moses* 2.52)[39] and enacted as "memorials of the life of the ancients" (*Abraham* 3–6), Mosaic law is transcribed for posterity.

The primacy of the animate mode is thus readily apparent in Philo's scheme.[40] Inhering in the natural order, the perfected law is manifest through the visceral actions of the righteous. But in order to enable its widespread fulfillment, the law is necessarily reduced to writing. The masses, who are far from such a rarefied state, are henceforth guided by recorded precepts. The ideal ruler, however, must transcend the limits of this alternate, impersonal medium.[41]

Whereas the storied "ancients" organically achieved the state of *nomos empsychos*, the contemporary ruler is enjoined to pursue its attainment.[42] The ruler must therefore engage in a form of reverse engineering wherein he internalizes the written law so as to restore it to an unwritten, embodied state (i.e., by displaying virtue and exercising reason).[43] Instead of studying under the tutelage of the Levitical priests,[44] the ruler emulates the biblical paragons and cultivates his inner voice.[45] Replacing external mandates with an internal compass, the ruler finds a higher motive in fulfilling the law (akin to the "happy obedience to law" of the ancients).[46] Accordingly, Philo replaces the scriptural goal of the king's study as aiming to cultivate a sense of trepidation before God (Deut 17:19), with a description of the deep affection for the law that he will develop through this transformative process.[47]

The ruler's immersion in the Mosaic law also endows him with the capability to lead.[48] Serving as a living paradigm for others,[49] he likewise acquires an indispensable sovereign tool (a "scepter").[50] The laws of the Torah orient his political decisions in governing, judging, and managing all other matters that concern the public welfare—as he is "ever exercis[ing] himself in the laws" (4.169).[51] By executing the law, the ruler constructs a society that follows the universal, eternal, natural order. By heeding the spirit of the law, he leads justly and impartially adjudicates even "great matters" (discussed further below).[52]

So what distinguishes the ruler is not royal justice in an absolutist sense—the king is not the source of the law or above the law, nor can he commandeer it—but instead the perpetual charge (and capacity) to emulate Moses (and the Patriarchs) by embodying the law, which enables the king to serve as a model, leader, and judge. The ontology of law precedes the king and the polity,[53] and permeates the cosmos. The king ideally embodies the law and, in turn, enables its functioning in the political and judicial spheres.[54]

Divided Justice

A closer examination of Philo's selective use of Scripture in establishing the ruler's jurisdiction reveals another crucial dimension of his jurisprudence beyond its royalist slant. As we have seen, in his methodic exegesis of Deuteronomy 17 in the excursus, Philo initially bypasses the explicit verses of the judiciary section (Deut 17:8–13) that revolve around the Levitical priests and judge, not the king.[55] As the plain sense of this biblical pericope sharply distinguishes between royal and judicial powers, Philo of course has good reason to circumvent it. But presumably he cannot simply ignore several verses from the biblical chapter that he is systematically expounding, which speak explicitly about judicial power. Philo's affirmation of the ruler's legal authority necessarily raises the hermeneutic question of how he explains the contrary implication of these verses, which identify other supreme judges.[56]

When Philo finally restates Deut 17:8–13 at the tail end of his excursus (4.188–192), he shifts abruptly from the paradigm of royal justice. Directing a judge who is uncertain about a resolution to refer the matter to supreme judicial authorities on the basis of Deut 17:9 ("then you shall immediately go up to the place that the Lord your God will choose, where you shall consult with the Levitical priests and the judge who is in office in those days"), Philo identifies the "Levitical priests" as the priests, and the "judge" as the high priest: "he [a judge] should decline to judge the cases and send them up to more discerning judges. And who should these be but the priests, and the head and leader of the priests?" Likewise, elsewhere (3.31) Philo describes the high priest as the supreme judicial authority.[57]

The discordant juxtaposition of this concluding passage to the rest of the excursus is perplexing.[58] Failing to incorporate the ruler into this latter section, Philo never indicates how priestly supreme justice (4.188–192, anchored in Deut 17:8–13) coheres with the jurisdiction of the sovereign ruler (4.151–188, anchored in Deut 17:14–20, and other sources listed above). How do these two neighboring sections of the excursus fit together?

The key to understanding Philo's treatment of monarchy, priesthood, and the judiciary is to recognize that his jurisprudence distinguishes between the two different sections of Deuteronomy 17.[59] While the ruler has a leading judicial rank according to Philo, royal justice operates separately from the jurisdiction of the high priest and priests. Based upon a highly original exegesis, Philo advances a novel jurisprudence where the judiciary is comprised of two principal legal authorities, each with distinct posts.[60]

Parsing the respective passages in the excursus helps clarify the different nature of each of these supreme judicial roles, and the rationale behind their respective assignments to the high priest (and priests) and king. The latter paragraphs (4.188–192), which focus exclusively on priestly justice, openly address why priests should resolve the most factually obscure and difficult (or baffling) matters that confound local judges. As Philo explicates, the priests, who are especially alert and punctilious in observing God's laws (not brooking even slight errors), and additionally enjoy unique clairvoyance due to their prophetic capacities (i.e., an understanding that transcends hearing and reading),[61] are best equipped to resolve the most vexing matters.

In the earlier section (4.151–188, at 169–174), Philo addresses the ruler's jurisdiction. Here he notably describes a different set of challenging issues that are referred to the ruler for adjudication involving "great" questions, a term that appears in Exod 18:22.[62] Defining this term explicitly, Philo states, "And great [*megalos*] questions must not be understood, as some think, to mean cases where both the disputants are distinguished or rich or men in high office but rather where the commoner or the poor or the obscure are disputing with other more powerful, and where their one hope of escaping a fatal disaster lies in the judge." In other words, "great" matters arise when there is a gap in the social standing of the parties, which can lead to an abuse of justice. They require the oversight of the ruler[63] (in an extraordinary homiletical flourish, Philo describes how God the King judges the "great" matters of the people of Israel, who are routinely in a lowly position).[64]

By homing in on the class of "great" matters that fall under the ruler's (or Moses's) supreme jurisdiction, Philo invites a contrast to the "difficult" matters referred to in other relevant verses (Exod 18:26, Deut 1:17, and perhaps the "baffling"[65] matters described in Deut 17:8).[66] Apparently Philo distinguishes between "great" matters and "difficult" matters, identifying two discrete kinds of supreme legal matters that are to be adjudicated at the highest ranks.[67] "Difficult" matters (which cannot be resolved by common judges) are directed to the high priest and priests, who are punctilious and prophetic, and are therefore qualified to be the leading jurists. "Great" matters, which do not pose a substantive challenge but have high social stakes,[68] by contrast, are to be handled (perhaps as a matter of original jurisdiction) by the ruler, whose imposing presence brings stability to a vulnerable situation and who has the standing to declare a definitive resolution. Moreover, as the king comes to embody the law, he cultivates the balanced character and refined judgment necessary to resolve these disputes justly.[69] The adjudication of these two kinds of supreme legal matters requires distinct judicial venues.

What is crucial to note for the present inquiry is how Philo, following the allusions of Deuteronomy 17, incorporates royal justice into a more complex scheme. If the king is one arbiter of justice, the high priest and priests are another. Neither controls the law of Moses, but both are crucial intermediaries. More generally, Mosaic law reflects natural law and is universal in scope, beyond the province of any political institution. Still, achieving justice within a particular social order requires its optimal implementation within a polity. Here the institutional actors play a critical role, including the king and priests, as well as others.

Recall that most of the biblical sources adduced by Philo to support royal justice in the excursus are not expressly about the king (or ruler), and some are clearly not limited to him. Thus, the overt subject of Deut 16:18–20 are judges. Indeed, Philo construes these verses according to their plain meaning in a section that precedes the excursus labeled "Instructions to the Judges" (4.55–78, at 62, 66, 70).[70] It seems evident that ordinary judges also play an indispensable role in administering justice.

This point is crystallized when one recalls that the excursus is part of an appendix on justice. It opens with the statement that the institution of judges is a cornerstone of the pursuit of justice (4.136), which cross-references the earlier "Instructions to the Judges" section.[71] So multiple institutional actors are involved in administering justice, including a ruler, the priests, as well as judges.[72] Moreover, as referenced above, the appendix concludes by proclaiming democracy as the optimal constitutional framework for achieving justice. Ultimately, then, individual as well as institutional actors are necessary for attaining this virtue.

It is in this vein that immediately after the opening paragraph, the appendix (4.136–137) records a remarkable restatement of core verses from the "Shema" pericope ("These *words* shall be placed on your heart. . . . Bind them as a sign on your hand and let them serve as a frontlet between your eyes" [Deut 6:6, 8; emphasis added])—rendering the decisive term "words" as the "rules of justice [*prodidaskéto dí tá díkaia*]."[73] In other words, responsibility for executing justice—i.e., implementing the laws of Moses[74]—devolves upon each individual. Ideally, each person will even become a soul that is "charged through and through with justice" (4.141–142)[75]—a kind of living law—and thereby help construct a just society.[76]

Formulated in first-century-CE Alexandria, Philo's jurisprudence is well suited for a dispersed Judaism embedded within a host empire.[77] The universal law at its core transcends any intermediary, or even polity. Explaining elsewhere why the biblical legislator rejects the standard convention of first establishing a polity and then tailoring laws accordingly,[78] Philo writes that the law of Moses is "too good and godlike to be confined within any earthly walls."[79] Mosaic law matches the blueprint of the cosmic order, and is not derivative of sovereign institutions. It is this same perspective that informs Philo's jurisprudence in the excursus. Mosaic law thus crosses territorial and political boundaries, and is equally applicable in the Diaspora.[80] Forging a just community relies on the collective action of individuals dedicated to the teaching of the Shema pericope: upholding the law of Moses. The disempowered Jews of Alexandria are not compelled to abide by the law, but encouraged and instructed to embrace it—a softer approach, which also poses little threat to the imperial sovereign. In fact, rather than competing with the imperial host, the unenforced law of Moses merges into the values of the larger society.[81] Mosaic law mirrors natural law, and promoting justice is an enterprise prized by all.

It is a testament to the depth of Philo's political-philosophical thought that he supplements this universalistic account, notwithstanding its sufficiency for the contemporary conditions of diasporic Jewry. Blending revised classical tropes with original scriptural hermeneutics, Philo engages in the project of articulating an ideal political-juridical vision ("an art of arts and a science of sciences"), which he recognizes as the foundation of justice, even if this will remain a utopian quest in his lifetime. Several salient features of his political thought are reflected in the excursus examined above. First, Philo envisions a rulership molded in a democratic configuration, not an archetypal king. Second, the ruler's governance is to be driven by the embodiment and guidance of (natural-Mosaic) law. Finally, the law should ideally be administered by multiple institutional actors, who divide jurisdiction based on the kind of legal matter that arises.

Philo's distinctive vision is likely informed by, but also responsive to, the world he inhabits. A portrait of a limited, nonmuscular, sovereign who follows the dictates of universal reason does not have the subversive implications of an outright call for autonomous kingship.[82] Nevertheless, Philo also seems to be agitating against the contemporary realities of Roman imperial powers. Leading the embassy to Caligula, Philo witnessed firsthand the dangers of unbridled imperial rule.[83] Likewise, having lived through a transitional period when Ptolemaic Egypt came under the direct control of the early Principate,[84] Philo, like many of his peers, may have been disillusioned by the thinly veiled reality[85] of an absolutist emperor with consolidated powers.[86] His works boldly challenge the legitimacy of the centripetal force that characterizes imperial rule.

More generally, Philo's jurisprudence is not top-heavy. If the king (or ruler) is law, this is only because in a more sweeping sense the law is king. Universal law permeates nature, and is the pursuit of all. Legal authority thus does not reside in any one address, but straddles among several institutions.[87]

This captures the limits of conceptualizing Philo's jurisprudence under the model of royal justice. In the standard royalist model, sovereignty is vested in the body of the king, and legal authority is subsumed under the general powers of the ruler. By contrast, Philo's account in the excursus revolves around the role of law in the ideal polity. Trumpeting the supremacy of law, Philo associates its administration with the monarchy, priesthood, judges, and individuals. It is not the sole political prerogative or tool of the ruler.

Philo's jurisprudence thus reflects a far more interesting intersection between the two biblical strands than appears at first blush. To be sure, it bears obvious traces of the dominant royalist strand, which even leads Philo to read Deuteronomy 17 against its grain and identify the king at the head of the judiciary.[88] At the same time, Philo enlists the Deuteronomy verses in reconfiguring monarchy and projecting the ruler as an embodiment of law; and stretching jurisdiction beyond the grasp of any one office.[89] Other prominent postbiblical works that build upon Deuteronomy's jurisprudence likewise advance the supremacy of law but, unlike Philo, insist that the administration of justice be separated from the ruler's domain. These formative accounts of judicial independence will be examined in the coming chapters.

3

Qumran Literature on Kingship, Councils, and Law

Deuteronomy's prominence in early postbiblical jurisprudence, evident in Philo's writings, can also be discerned in Qumran literature. As we saw in Chapter 1, the Temple Scroll (TS) embeds the original composition of the "Law of the King" (LK) in a citation of verses from Deuteronomy 17.[1] The precise legacy of Deuteronomy's themes of kingship, priesthood, and legal authority reflected in this scroll, however, needs to be unpacked and evaluated.[2]

On one level, the LK revises Deuteronomy by elevating the king's significance and transforming its jurisprudence. Substantially supplementing Deuteronomy's monarchic verses, the LK mandates the formation of a royal guard, delineates the king's military role, establishes his priority in amassing spoils of war, and imposes more exclusive standards of eligibility for his spouse. Most germane to the present inquiry, the LK overrides Deut 17's separation of the king and the judiciary, and counts judging and offering legal instruction, alongside a council, among the king's leading responsibilities.[3] Yoav Barzilay has even argued that in an earlier recension, the LK advanced an absolutist jurisprudence controlled solely by the king.[4] The LK concludes by converting Deuteronomy's promise of longevity for a righteous king (17:20) into a covenantal pledge of eternal rule (11Q19 59:16–21). Overall, the LK underscores the principal role of the monarchy, which cannot be ascribed merely to exegesis or historical polemics, as some scholars have claimed.

At the same time, the inflated royalist interpretation of Moshe Weinfeld,[5] who argues that the broader aim of the entire TS (not just an early recension of the LK) is to enshrine the king at the helm of the ideal society, must also be rejected. The nucleus of this scroll is the Temple, and its overall theology revolves around this institution. Conferring the highest stature on the priestly caste, this scroll situates its ideology within a cultic framework. Evaluating monarchy through this lens, the TS's king has no role in the Temple nor any cultic responsibilities.[6] Moreover, he reveals weaknesses beneath his veneer of power. Vulnerable to sinning or being captured (57:10–11), or perverting justice (57:19–20), the king is sternly warned that his power will be revoked if he strays from God's commandments (59:13–15). In other words, the royal covenant of the TS is conditional.

In fact, even the LK affirms the supreme position of priestly officials,[7] especially in juridical matters, and in this sense upholds Deuteronomy's original hierarchy and jurisprudence.[8] They serve on an advisory council with Levites and chieftains (there are twelve representatives from each sector)[9]—a council of thirty-six to which the king must defer[10] (indeed, elsewhere in the TS, priests, judges, and Levites exercise legal authority, without the king).[11] In fact, the LK's royal charter is issued by the priests. Incorporated within a priestly scroll, the royalist LK also evinces a priestly orientation to leadership and legal authority.

Notably, elsewhere in Qumran writings, Deut 17 arguably serves as a backdrop for an exclusively priestly scheme, albeit in a highly specialized form of adjudication.[12] Conflating Deuteronomy's judiciary section with subsequent verses about prophecy (Deut 18:9–22; cf. Deut 13:1–6), 4Q375 describes a scenario where there is controversy surrounding a prophet's credibility (apparently involving a legal matter). In order to ascertain whether the prophet is a "true prophet" whose words must be heeded, or a "false prophet" who has committed a capital offense, the scroll mandates an extraordinary cultic-judicial proceeding (paraphrasing Deut 17:8–9):

> You (prophet) shall come with that tribe and your elders and your judges [t]o the place which your God will choose in one of your tribes before [the] anointed priest ...

> and he (i.e., the anointed priest) shall take [a young bullock] ... and shall study [all the precepts of] YKWK concerning all [... which have been hid]den from you. And he shall [g]o out before a[ll the chiefs] of the assembly ...

Evidently, the high priest (i.e., the anointed priest) "adjudicates" this prophetic controversy by offering a sacrifice, entering the Temple's inner sanctum, and studying and revealing the hidden law.[13] 4Q376 may imply that he relies on his priestly vestments to reach a decision.

Both the TS (including the LK) and 4Q375–376 build upon Deuteronomy's jurisprudence, highlighting the importance of administering law, and affirming the adjudicatory role of priests. But they diverge in a crucial respect, as only the TS accents a royalist motif (alongside the priestly one), projecting the king as a principal ruler and leading judge. This variance raises the questions of how to assess the monarchic dimension of the TS, and whether its perspective on kingship and the king's vital role in administering justice represents an ideology found elsewhere in Qumran literature.[14]

Beyond the Temple Scroll

While scholars debate how to evaluate the exact attitude of the TS toward monarchy,[15] the TS certainly recognizes the king's sovereign powers within the ideal regime. A few other texts discussed below likewise sanction majestic rule. In contrast, numerous scrolls distinguish other kinds of leaders. In a similar vein, the king is unquestionably involved in the judicial process, according to the TS. Elsewhere in the Qumran corpus, however, the judicial structure is differently constituted.

The limited role of kingship in Qumran literature corresponds to a larger point: Scholars largely concur that the TS and other early scrolls should be read against the backdrop of some phase of Hasmonean rule, and certain passages are intended as a polemic against failures of this dynasty (e.g., "the Wicked Priest" of Pesher Habaquq is commonly understood as a disparagement of Jonathan or Simon).[16] In theory, two distinct aspects of Hasmonean rule could have provided grist for the mill of anti-Hasmonean criticism: the assumption of royal authority by the sons of Mattathias, and their usurpation of the priesthood.[17] Although the former finds certain expressions in the (arguably early) scrolls (see this chapter's conclusion), significantly, the brunt of the Qumran opposition to the Hasmoneans relates to their pollution of the priesthood. Likewise, the alternative constructions of leadership promoted by the scrolls focus on elevating the priesthood (contra PS; see Chapter 1). Indeed, a fundamental objective of the scrolls is to reconceptualize and reconstitute the priesthood,[18] not monarchy.[19]

Accordingly, highlighting the TS as emblematic of Qumran's political and juridical vision is problematic. It is often trotted out for these purposes, but its multifaceted orientation described above is rarely noted, nor is the distinctiveness of its royalism adequately underscored.[20] A survey of additional Qumran writings on kingship and the nature of the king's legal authority will help to further contextualize the findings from the TS and bring its royalist ideology into sharper relief.

Further, a positive account of Qumran's jurisprudence requires moving beyond the royalist template in order to investigate the prevalent structures of political and judicial authority (in its various forms)[21] that are recorded in this oeuvre.[22] Although a comprehensive study of all relevant materials is beyond the scope of this work, and also raises notoriously knotty problems about the interrelationship among various Qumran texts,[23] a study of key passages is nevertheless illuminating in this regard. Transcending the particulars of Deuteronomy 17, these materials continue to echo its larger themes of a restricted monarchy, an exalted priesthood, and the paramount and autonomous nature of law.[24]

The first section of this chapter evaluates the standing of the king in other Qumran passages, and particularly the extent of his legal authority. In this section, I argue that the royalism of the TS reflects a minority voice in this corpus. Further, even texts that promote kingship strip the king of jurisdiction, while others with majestic themes have greater ambivalence upon closer inspection. Nevertheless, this secondary strand of Qumran writings has conceptual importance and its nuanced contours will be carefully adumbrated. The next section surveys the impressive, and in many respects original, list of officials and councils that are pervasive in Qumran writings. These nonroyal entities—priestly figures and other sectors of the community—are in fact the mainstay of Qumran jurisprudence. Finally, I will return to the TS and attempt to situate it—conceptually and chronologically—relative to numerous other Qumran writings that contract temporal power and expand the role of sacral law.

Kingship at Qumran

Despite the biblical foundation of kingship, its Hasmonean restoration, and eschatological future predicted by the Prophets,[25] monarchy receives scant attention in Qumran.[26] A suggestive line in the Cairo Damascus Document (CD)—a foundational scroll depicting the etiology of the sect—may expose the deeper roots of the king's marginalization. In the course of describing the "northern" flight of the faithful sectarians, CD records a revealing exegesis of a verse from Amos:[27]

> But those who held firmly [to the covenant] escaped to the land of the north *vacat* as he said, "And I will expel your king's booth[28] and the foundation of your images from my tent (to) Damascus" (Amos 5:26–27). *vacat The books of the Torah are the "king's booth,"* as he said, "I will raise up the fallen booth of David" (Amos 9:11).[29] *The "king" is the assembly.* (CD 7.13–17, MS A; emphasis added)

Defining "king" metaphorically, CD ascribes royal authority to the community.[30] It similarly interprets the royal encampment of the "king's booth" figuratively, as referring to the Torah, the legal foundation of the community. In other words, the popular assembly adhering to the rules of the Torah constitutes the political power base,[31] a theme that resonates throughout much of Qumran literature.[32] Withdrawing from the political center of Judea for the spiritual oasis near Qumran, the author of this passage locates sovereign power within the sectarian community.

If this citation epitomizes a larger political shift in Qumran ideology, however, it does not tell the full story. The continuation of this very passage refers to two leaders of the assembly, the "Interpreter of the Torah" (*Doresh ha-Torah*) and the "Prince of the Congregation" (*Nasi ha-Edah*),[33] where the latter apparently enjoys quasi-royal authority. Evidently there is a position of a political head(s), at least according to certain texts. Indeed, several royal figures are mentioned in Qumran writings under different titles, albeit mostly in eschatological contexts.[34]

Moreover, a few exegetical, polemical, or eschatological passages feature the sovereign ruler in various guises.[35] For instance, the epilogue of 4QMMT, the famous letter delineating contrasts between sectarian and nonsectarian laws, exhorts the opposition leader to reform his praxis by invoking the spiritual model of biblical kings. "Remember the kings of Israe[l] and reflect on their deeds, how whoever of them was respecting [the . . . La]w was freed from afflictions; and those so[u]ght the Law. . . . Remember David, one of the 'pious' [and] he, too, was freed from many afflictions and was forgiven" (4Q399 11–17).[36] Highlighting the successes and failures of historic kings, the epilogue may even be addressing the opposition leader as a misguided monarchic figure who can reform his ways and still serve as a beacon for his subjects.[37] Another text, the controversial Aramaic Apocalypse (4Q246), describes the kingdom of the "son of God," who will achieve a lasting (and perhaps fractious) rule after triumphing in apocalyptic battles: "His kingdom will be an eternal kingdom, and all his paths in truth" (4Q246 II:5–6).[38] The War Rule predicts that a royal messiah will battle in an apocalyptic campaign

(4Q285 Frag. 5 / 11Q14).[39] In the War Scroll, a princely ruler is armed with a shield that inscribes the names of the priestly and tribal heads of all of Israel (1QM V:1–2).[40] One much discussed fragment, the Prayer for the Welfare of King Jonathan (4Q448), formulates a rousing petition on behalf of the ruling sovereign (perhaps Alexander Jannaeus). Admittedly, this text is an outlier among the scrolls, which has made its tone and implications difficult to parse.[41]

Three Sets of Royalist Texts

Several other texts advance more elaborate royal ideologies; but, as fleshed out below, they also qualify their accounts in significant ways. 4Q161, a Pesher Isaiah fragment, depicts the commanding role of the "Prince of the Congregation" heading an apocalyptic battle against the *Kittim*.[42] The final section famously looks forward to the rule of the Davidic scion.[43] Heralding his future advent, the scroll's hermeneutic builds on some of the most memorable messianic verses in the Bible (Isaiah 11:1–5):

> [The interpretation of the word concerns the shoot] of David
> which will sprout in the fi[nal days, since] [with the breath of
> his lips he will execute] his [ene]my and God will support him
> with [the spirit of c]ourage ... [thro]ne of glory, h[oly] crown
> and multi-colour[ed] vestments [...] in his hand. He will rule
> over all the pe[ople]s and Magog [...] his sword will judge [al]l
> the peoples.

A towering messianic figure, as conjured by the scroll's vivid imagery, will reign supreme.

4Q174, the Florilegium of Eschatological Midrashim, likewise sets forth a brilliant eschatological vision with a dominant royal motif. Composing a florilegium from an assortment of royalist verses and interpretive additions (in the pesher style),[44] the scroll depicts an eschatological era when God will erect a purified, eternal temple and establish a lasting Davidic dynasty. Citing 2 Sam 7:11, the scroll reads: "'From the day on which [I appointed judges] over my people, Israel.' This (refers to) the house which [he will establish] for [him] in the last days."[45] In the following lines, the scroll adduces 2 Sam 7:12–14 and Amos 9:11 to describe the renewal of the Temple and the reestablishment of the Davidic dynasty.[46] By citing and interspersing these biblical verses, 4Q174 links the restored Temple—a centerpiece of Qumran theology—with the royal dynasty. Jacob Milgrom has further argued that this scroll deliberately conflates two different interpretations for the same biblical word, *bayit* (derived from 2 Sam 7:11): Temple and dynasty.[47] The cult and crown will both serve as cornerstones of an eternal edifice.

Finally, 1QSa, the Rule of the Congregation, and 1QSb, the Rule of Benedictions, arguably form a pair of texts with a pronounced pro-monarchic orientation. Possibly written as appendices to 1QS, the Rule of the Community, these two texts evidently announce protocols for the "final days."[48] 1QSa portrays the royal Messiah of Israel seated at the head of the eschatological banquet, and perhaps even describes him as God's direct progeny.[49]

A lengthier reference to a royal figure appears in 1QSb, which is composed of a series of elaborate blessings for various leaders and divisions, apparently intended to be recited at the dawn of the eschaton as part of a communal covenantal ceremony. Scholars have discerned five or six distinct blessings in this text (surviving in highly fragmentary form), the final one being for the "Prince of the Congregation."[50] Drawing on the opening of Isaiah 11—the same passage cited in Pesher Isaiah—alongside other verses,[51] this blessing delineates the supreme covenantal mission of the messianic prince:[52]

> Of the Instructor. To bless the Prince of the Congregation ...
> And he will renew the covenant of the [Com]munity for him,
> to establish the kingdom of his people foreve[r, to judge[53] the
> poor with justice,] to reproach the [hu]mble of the earth with
> upri[ghtness,] to walk in perfection before him on all the paths
> of [...] to establish his covenant as holy [during] the anguish
> of those seeking [it].

It concludes by appealing to God to endow the prince with extraordinary capacities:[54]

> May] the Lord rai[se y]ou to an everlasting height, like a forti[fied] tower upon a raised rampart. May you be [...] with the power of your [mouth.] With your scepter may you lay waste the earth. With the breath of your lips may you kill the wicked. May he give [you a spirit of coun]sel and of everlasting fortitude, a spirit of knowledge and of fear of God. May justice be the belt of [your loins, and loyalt]y the belt of your hips.... For God has raised you to a scepter for the rulers be[fore you ... all the na]tions will serve you, and he will make you strong by his holy Name.

Taken together, these two scrolls exalt a royal figure in their apocalyptic visions.

Trumpeting a messianic king, all of the above texts (4Q161, 4Q174, and 1QSa–1QSb) share similarities with the royalism of the TS. Yet just as the TS circumscribes the scope of royal power by ratifying the concurrent authority of priests, so too these eschatological texts also subtly, but unmistakably, reduce the royal figure's leadership role by dividing his jurisdiction with others. For instance, the last section of Pesher Isaiah, which magnifies the royalist eschatology of Isaiah 11, concludes in a markedly different tone. Citing Isaiah's description of the shoot of Jesse's supernatural mode of dispensing justice: "He (= the shoot of Jesse) will not [judge by what his eyes behold] or by what his ears perceive" (Is 11:3), Pesher Isaiah glosses: "which [...] and according to what they (the priests) teach him, he will judge, and upon their authority [...] with him will go out one of the priests of renown, holding in his hands clothes (of)" (4Q161, Frags. 8–10).[55] While the underlying verse extols the extraordinary innate resources of the Davidic scion, the scroll audaciously subordinates the royal messiah to priestly instruction,[56] and further stipulates that a leading priest join the king in judgment.[57]

In 4Q174 a similar phenomenon occurs. After citing a paraphrase of the resounding monarchic verses from 2 Sam 7:12–14 that culminate in the description of Davidic kings as children of God ("[And] YKWK [de]clares to you that he will build you a house. I will raise up your seed after you and establish the throne of his kingdom [for ev]er ... 'I will be a father to him and he will be a son to me'"), 4Q174 continues to interpret the verses: "This (refers to the) branch of David, *who will arise with the Interpreter of the Torah who [will rise up] in Zi[on in] the [l]ast days*" (emphasis added). Despite the blinding exclusivity of the relationship between God and the king announced by Scripture, the scroll implants another official alongside the king:[58] The (perhaps priestly)[59] "Interpreter of the Torah" (see below). Moreover, the latter is notably a legal authority (see below).

These passages thus daringly subvert the underlying biblical source texts. Whereas both Isaiah 11 and 2 Sam 7:12–14 categorically proclaim the sole rule of the Davidic scion, these Qumran passages insert priests into the eschatological regime. Moreover, they disseminate royal powers—particularly judicial powers—to these auxiliary officials. Even the most pro-monarchic Qumran passages recognize dual sovereignty.

The third set of texts arguably follows a loosely analogous pattern. Culling from Isaiah 11 in formulating its royal benediction, 1QSb situates the biblical verses in a wider context that colors their meaning. Prior to blessing the "Prince of the Congregation," the scroll records a blessing for the priestly sons of Zadok, and apparently another blessing for the high priest as well. The opening paragraph of the blessing of the sons of Zadok reads as follows:[60]

> Words of Blessing. Of the Inst[ructor (*Maskil*). To bless] the sons of Zadok, the priests whom God has chosen to strengthen his covenant, for [ever, to dis]tribute all his judgments[61] in the midst of his people, to teach them in accordance with his commandments. They have established [his covenant] in truth and have examined all his precepts in justice, and they have walked in accordance with wha[t] he chooses.

Scholars have characterized the blessings of the priests as being even more lavish in praise than the blessing of the prince.[62] Indeed, one can argue that the entire scheme of benedictions—arguably recited by a priest,[63] following the biblical template of the priestly blessings[64]—likewise confirms the preeminent status of the priests. The crux of the priestly calling, according to the above excerpt, involves dedicated stewardship over the covenantal law, including administering justice.[65] According to 1QSb, then, priestly authority equals or exceeds royal authority, and priests are recognized as supreme legal authorities (perhaps alongside the Prince of the Congregation).

Similarly, in the likely related 1QSa, the honor bestowed upon the priests at the session of the "men of renown" and the eschatological banquet exceeds that of the messiah. The high priest, bearing the eminent title "Chief of All the Congregation of Israel,"[66] and the other priests are seated first, and lead the ceremonial meal in blessing and tasting the new bread and wine. Moreover, an earlier section of 1QSa explicitly references the priests along with the chiefs of thousands, hundreds, fifties, and tens in the context of administering justice (see below).

Ambiguities in Royalist Texts

Several other passages, commonly branded as pro-monarchic, are in fact more ambiguous or nuanced than this label suggests. 4Q491 11 I,[67] the Self-Glorification Hymn, articulates a stunning self-description of an exalted figure who is given "a throne of power in the congregation of the divine beings."[68] His singular stature eclipses the "kings of old,"[69] including the unparalleled nature of his instruction and judgment.[70] Scholars are sharply divided on whether this figure is an angel or a human, an individual or the community, and whether, if a terrestrial figure, a king or a priest.[71] From among various theories, Morton Smith's identification of the speaker as a priestly figure who ascends to the celestial temple has garnered recent support.[72]

In 4Q521, the Messianic Apocalypse, a fragmentary text about the eschaton, the messiah is elevated to the apex of the universe, "[for the heav]ens and earth will listen to his anointed one" (4Q521 II:1). The identity of the messiah is uncertain, though, and some have seen him as more of a prophetic figure than a king.[73] Notably, a later clause in this passage that explicitly invokes a royal trope does not refer to the messiah, but instead diffuses the royal glory: "For He (God) will honor the pious upon the throne of an eternal kingdom" (4Q521 II:7). Humble multitudes will sit on the regal throne and preside in majesty.

An overtly royalist passage, 4Q252 V:1–6, 4Q, Patriarchal Blessings, expands upon Jacob's biblical blessing to Judah. Referring to a royal figure by several titles,[74] the passage predicts the perpetual rule of Davidic kings throughout the periods of Israel's sovereignty,[75] culminating in a lasting messianic reign:[76] "'A ruler[77] shall [no]t depart from the tribe of Judah (Gen. 49:10).' While Israel has the dominion, there [will not] be cut off someone who sits on the throne of David." When the scroll interprets the remainder of the verse, however, it widens its focus beyond the king. Whereas Scripture only mentions a ruler from Judah, 4Q252 refers in its final lines to a corresponding Davidic king as well as to various other sectors of the population—the "[thou]sands of Israel," "men of the Community," and "assembly of the men"—who evidently participate in leadership: "For 'the staff (ha-mehokek)' is the covenant of royalty, *and the [thou]sands of Israel are the standards (degalav)*[78] vacat Until the messiah of righteousness comes, the branch of David. For to him and to his descendants has been given the covenant of the kingship of his people for everlastings generations, which he observed [. . .] the Law (Torah) with the *men of the Community,* for [. . .] it is *the assembly of the men*" (emphasis added). Although the precise meaning of this fragmentary text is difficult to decipher,[79] it appears to subtly disseminate royal power to communal members.[80]

A CD passage that is conventionally portrayed as pro-Davidic[81] also highlights the king's inferiority to the priests and sectarians. Underscoring that the prohibition of polygamy also applies to the royal leader—labeled here "*Nasi*"—the scroll still exculpates King David for his multiple marriages.[82] It then lauds his general conduct, citing 1 Kings 15:5, "David's deeds were all excellent, except for the murder of Uriah," and adding, "but God forgave him for that" (CD 5:5). In short, the scroll exonerates David on one count, and records his pardon on another.

Yet even as the scroll expunges David's negative record, it accentuates that his multiple marriages violated biblical law. Further, consider the striking explanation advanced by this passage to excuse David's multiple marriages:[83] "And about the Prince (*Nasi*) it is written: 'He should not multiply wives to himself (Deut 17:17).' However, David had not read the sealed book of the law which was in the ark, for it had not been opened in Israel since the day of the death of Eleazar and of Jehoshua.... (And) one had hidden the public (copy) until Zadok's entry into office" (CD 5:1–4). Among the benighted of his generation, David is religiously ignorant, and therefore breaches the law inadvertently.[84] In contrast, the faithful custodians of revelation are past priests such as Eleazar and Zadok and contemporary sectarians.

Parenthetically, when citing Deut 17:17, this passage replaces the original term "*Melekh* [king]" with "*Nasi* [prince/patriarch]."[85] In fact, alternate terminology for kingship appears in numerous scrolls ("Prince of the Congregation," the "shoot of Jesse," etc.). Alexander Rofe has advanced the suggestive thesis that such substitutions signal a demotion of the status of the king in these writings.[86] Their widespread usage in Qumran may conform with a broader devaluation of royalty in this oeuvre.

The remaining passages that showcase a royal figure are mainly messianic ones, but in certain respects they, too, curb his role relative to other leaders. Adopting a diarchic or threefold scheme, the power structure they envision is distinctly hierarchical. As John Collins has emphasized, in the dual messiah texts the priest occupies the primary position, while the Judean quasi-monarchic leader supplements his authority.[87] Moreover, the eschatological references to the latter must be weighed against other texts that are more ambiguous or silent about a royal messiah. The uneven overall evidence has triggered a scholarly dispute about whether Qumran messianism anticipates one (priestly messiah), two (along with a Davidic figure)[88] or three (along with a prophet)[89] messianic leaders, or has conflicting visions.[90] Even texts that envision a royal messiah likely only represent a subset of Qumran eschatology.

In sum, whereas the TS is the most explicit text depicting a royal leader, there are several scrolls that refer to a monarchic figure, although in the aggregate they constitute only a minority among Qumran writings.[91] A few of these passages may project the ideal king in glowing terms, but the remainder present the royal leader as a secondary figure, or in other ways diffuse or undercut his sovereignty. Moreover, these latter passages confer legal authority on the priest(s) instead of treating it as the exclusive province of the king. These works often employ alternative labels for the ruler, which may signify his secondary status. Certain texts portray a messianic period where the ruler will follow the priest in leading the community.

Legal Authority in Qumran: Priestly Figures, Councils, and the Community

The above analysis evaluated the stature of the monarchy and the thin traces of royal justice in Qumran. The present section focuses directly on juridical writings, examining a selection of texts that depict how legal administration is structured in this corpus. Given the utopian nature of the scrolls, such materials not only afford insight into contemporary practices in Qumran, but also shed light on how its writings ideally configure legal authority.

As Joseph Baumgarten has remarked, "For what is generally considered to have been a small, self-enclosed community, the multiple references in the Qumran texts to juridical bodies are noteworthy."[92] Despite the diversity of viewpoints described below, the texts share certain common assumptions about the constitution of legal authority. They do not enumerate a royal figure among the supreme legal officials. Instead, legal authority is exercised by assorted figures, priests, and especially councils of different sizes and the community at large, as well as various combinations of the above entities. Indeed, a distinguishing feature of

Qumran jurisprudence is the ways it vests legal authority in the collective hands of the community.[93]

A couple of preliminary caveats are in order. The texts examined below are filled with inconclusive, or contradictory, evidence about the possible interrelationship among these various officials or arrangements.[94] Further, these passages blur various dimensions of the legal process, including legislating, interpreting, teaching, instructing, warning, testifying, punishing, and judging.[95] For present purposes, however, sorting through these complexities is less vital than reviewing the roster of personnel or entities who figure prominently, in order to discern the locus of legal authority in this corpus.[96]

A scholarly survey of leadership figures in Qumran literature enumerates the following personnel:[97] *Paqqid, Maskil, Mebaqqer,* priests, sons of Zadok, sons of Aaron, Levites, and judges (certain of these titles may overlap). The list should be prefaced with the names of two more officials: the Teacher of Righteousness (or a corresponding figure), and the Interpreter of the Torah. Most of these officers have priestly or Levitical ties; none are royal figures. This sizable roster, which includes various positions that seem to be original to this corpus,[98] signals the importance of administration in the sectarian community. Significantly, all of these personnel lead (in the present, or a utopian future) through the exercise of some form of legal authority. The most prominent ones will be considered in turn.

Leadership Figures

TEACHER OF RIGHTEOUSNESS: CD describes the covenantal commitment of communal members[99] to follow the supreme instruction of the Teacher of Righteousness:[100]

> But all those who remain steadfast in these regulations, [co]ming and going in accordance with the Torah, and listen to the Teacher's voice ... and they are instructed in the first ordinances in conformity with which the men of the community were

judged; and they lend their ear to the voice of the Teacher of Righteousness; and do not reject the just regulations when they hear them. (CD 20:27–31)

A historical figure, the Teacher likely personified the idyllic ruler whose memory long lingered,[101] and whose counterpart will lead the community, and act as the principal legal authority, at the end of days.[102] There are up to seventeen other references to this same figure in Qumran, including several important citations in Pesher Habakuk that describe him as being privy to ongoing revelation and delineating norms that are binding on the community.[103]

INTERPRETER OF THE TORAH: Possibly affiliated with the Teacher of Righteousness,[104] this figure was encountered above in citations from CD 7 and 4QFloriligeum. In both of these contexts, the Interpreter of the Torah (*Doresh ha-Torah*) leads along with another ruling official—the Prince of the Congregation (CD 7) or the messianic scion (4QFloriligeum).[105] Presumably, his standing in these contexts relates to his stature as a principal legal authority. In an earlier passage in CD 6:7–8 his role in this regard is more clearly articulated. Presenting an elaborate exegesis of the "Song of the Well" (Numbers 21:17–20), the scroll identifies the Interpreter as the "staff" (*mehoqeq*)[106] who guides the penitent sectarians through legal instruction (until the advent of the Teacher).[107] Based on such passages,[108] Paul Mandel has recently formulated the Interpreter's authoritative position within the community as follows: "The hierarchical structure of the community . . . supports the view of its leadership as functioning in the role of instructors to the people. . . . The *Doresh ha-Torah* was revered specifically because he *taught* laws—the revealed and the (previously) hidden."[109]

MEBAQQER: A primary administrator according to CD, the *Mebaqqer*'s responsibilities are sweeping and varied.[110] Examining the religious eligibility of initiates who wish to join the community and monitoring members' adherence to normative standards, this figure (possibly a Levite) also has additional juridical responsibilities.[111] Members of the assembly confer with the *Mebaqqer* concerning any dispute or judgment

(CD 14:8–11), and he officiates alongside judges (14:13). According to CD 9:16–23, he receives and records testimony, and presumably serves as a judge as well.[112] In CD 13:5–7, he functions as a legal expert who assists the officiating priest in ruling on questions of ritual purity. His position as a principal instructor and custodian of the community is elaborated upon in the continuation of CD 13 in effusive detail.[113]

MASKIL: A passage in CD introduces a supreme official who guides the normative life of the community: "And these are the ordinances for the *Maskil,* so that he walks in them with every living thing, according to the regulation of every time. And in accordance with this regulation shall the seed of Israel walk and it will not be cursed *vacat* (CD 12:20–22)."[114] After this introductory formula, however, the passage trails off (indicated by the *vacat*), never filling in the content of the instructor's ordinances. Scholars have puzzled over what exactly to make of this abbreviated formulation, and whether this signals a deliberate curtailment or transfer of the *Maskil's* authority.[115] In any event, the *Maskil* figures prominently in the Rule of the Community.[116] In an earlier passage, he is described as leading the righteous by teaching the doctrine of the two spirits (1QS 3:13–21). Later on, an extended section is dedicated to delineating rules for the *Maskil* as a principal guide and instructor (precisely what is missing from CD), who masters "all understanding" of the laws (1QS 9:12–26).[117] Other references include 4Q298, where he instructs those who join the community to heed his teachings; and a reconstruction of 4Q259 (parallel to 1QS8), where he evaluates the sons of righteousness (3:10) and promotes "just judgments" (3:15–16).[118]

PAQQID: A CD passage describes the priest as the head of the "Many" (i.e., an assembly, or representatives, of the community), who is a legal expert. Invoking a verbal form of the term *Paqqid,* the scroll legislates, "And the priest who is appointed (*ypkd*) (head) of the Many will be between thirty and sixty years old, learned in the book of H[A]GY and in all the regulations of the Torah, to formulate them in accordance with their regulation" (CD 14:6–8).[119] Likewise, 4Q289 1.4 and 1QS 6:14 refer to the *Paqqid* as head of the Many, and in the latter he serves in a kind of supervisory role over the communal council. Scholars nevertheless note the limited and somewhat ambiguous references to this official, and also debate whether he overlaps with the *Mebaqqer*.[120]

PRIEST: A couple of the references to the *Paqqid* identify him as a priest, and presumably other officials enumerated above are also priests or Levites. Additional texts explicitly refer to individual priests as leading legal authorities. Thus, CD 13:2–3 states, "And in the place of ten, a priest learned in the book of HAGY should not be lacking; by his authority all shall be governed."[121] Likewise, 1QS 6:3–4 designates a priest as an outstanding figure among a group of ten. The role of the priestly sector of society will be addressed below.

Councils

Alongside these vertical arrangements that rely on individual leaders, certain Qumran writings describe the legal authority of collective bodies, such as judicial councils.[122] These original schemes assume a variety of forms. All councils are composed of priests and non-priests. While some incorporate one of the leading officials enumerated above into the council[123]—thereby encompassing a hierarchical template within a wider circle—none (other than the LK section of the TS)[124] include a royal head. In the most horizontal structures, these councils share authority with a sector of the community or the whole community, and at times these larger populations are even depicted as being involved directly in the exercise of legal authority.

Consider CD's "Rule of the Judges," the most explicit Qumran passage relating to judicial authority:

> And [this is the Rule of the Judges of] the community: [A quorum of ten m]en chosen from the commun[ity] according to the time, fou[r from the tribe of Levi and] Aaron and [six from Isra]el, versed *vacat* in the Book of HAGY and the foun[dations of the covenant, between] twenty-five to sixty years old. And no one [sixty years and upwa]rd shall stand to judge [the congregation; for] through the failing of man [his days] have become few. (CD 10:4–10, 4Q266 8 iii 4–5, 4Q270 iv 15–17)

Specifying precise regulations for the size of the judicial quorum, the identity of the judges, their qualifications, and age requirements, this passage establishes a set protocol for the administration of justice, thereby underscoring the importance of this process. Evidently the ten-member judicial panel is intended to represent a cross section of the population, and therefore includes priests, Levites, and Israelites, a threefold division echoed elsewhere in Qumran literature (including the LK's tripartite division of the council of thirty-six).[125] Thus, supreme jurisdiction belongs to an autonomous body, rather than an empowered ruler or any official enumerated above.[126]

Another text refers to ten judges, supplemented by two priests,[127] collectively constituting a duodecimal council (the same size as each subdivision of the LK's council):[128] "Ten men and two priests, and there shall be judged before these twelve [and every] case concerning anyone in Israel, according to them shall they ask and anyone who rebels *vacat* He will be put to death one who transgresses intentionally" (4Q159 [Ordinances], Frags. 2–4).[129] The passage concludes with a warning that those who defy the council's rulings will be subject to capital punishment— arguably transposing a biblical rule that underwrites the paramount legal authority of the "Levitical priests and the judge" (see Deut 17:8–13) to the council.

An exegetical passage from a (reconstructed) Pesher Isaiah fragment (4Q164 Frag. 1:1–7) that depicts a utopian juridical arrangement similarly refers to a duodecimal council of priests, which perhaps adjudicates alongside a second duodecimal council of tribal leaders:[130]

"And I will found you in Sapphi[res (Is. 54:11)," Its interpretation:] they will found the council of the community, [the] priests and the peo[ple . . .] the assembly of their elect, like a sapphire in the midst of stones. "[I will make] all your battlements [of rubies] (Is. 54:12)," *Its interpretation concerns the twelve [chiefs of the priests who] illuminate with the judgment of the Urim and Thummim* . . . Its interpretation concerns the chiefs of the tribes of Israel in the l[ast days . . .]. (4Q164) (emphasis added)

Even as the passage invokes the priestly role of consulting with the *Urim* and *Thummim,* it envisions the priests adjudicating collectively in a quorum. Likewise, the passage may elevate the legal authority of tribal leaders, presumably administering justice in concert.

Councils and Community

Two other 1QS passages that concern conciliar arrangements notably combine, coordinate, and even suggestively elide their depictions with those of the broader community. While the responsibility of these councils extends to broader communal representation or leadership, they clearly have a leading normative role. Some scholars have inferred an implicit adjudicative function as well.

One passage refers to a fifteen-person community council (*atzat ha-yahad*).[131] They are charged to embody the highest normative principles:[132] "In the community council (there shall be) twelve men and three priests, perfect in everything that has been revealed from all the law to implement truth, justice, judgment" (1QS 8:1–4).[133] Representing the holy house of Israel and the sacred chambers of Aaron (1QS 8:8–9),[134] the council also serves as true witnesses and delivers retribution to the wicked (1QS 8:5–7). The council thereby fulfills the covenant of justice (1QS 8:9–10).[135]

An earlier passage—inserted between regulations pertaining to dwellings of the community and the session of the Many[136]—depicts a council of ten.[137] According to this passage, when a quorum of ten members of the community council convenes, it must be led by a priest, followed by additional members who preside in sequence (1QS 6:3–4, referenced above). Other people from the community will consult with them on all matters (1QS 6:4). The next line continues by mandating that the ten[138] should include a person who constantly instructs or interprets the Torah (*Doresh ha-Torah*), day and night (1QS 6:6–7). A possibly related CD passage (sharing similar sources and literary constructions, referenced above),[139] likewise mandates that a gathering of ten include a priest (otherwise, a Levite) who has mastery of the law (13:2–3).

The larger context of the 1QS prescripts about the juridical role of the ten (1QS 6:3–7) are disparate teachings filling column 5–7 about the community and the Many, which repeatedly emphasize their normative commitments and juridical responsibilities. Before the prescripts, 1QS introduces the exacting normative standards of the community (1QS 5:1–7); describes admission procedures for members who are fully dedicated to "the Law of Moses, according to all that he commanded, with whole heart and whole soul, in compliance with all that has been revealed" (1QS 5:7–25); stipulates that the Many convene in order to process legal accusations (1QS 5:25–6:1);[140] and mandates that members live in their dwellings in a hierarchical manner, and gather for counsel (1QS6:1–3). After the prescripts, 1QS orders the session of the Many to devote a third of each night to reading and instruction of the law (1QS 6:7–8);[141] regulates the session, composed of a hierarchy of sectors of the community, which confers on judgment with the council of the community (1QS 6:8–10);[142] prescribes a protocol for inquiry on behalf of the Many, and the *Mebaqqer*,[143] to the council (1QS 6:10–13); delineates the procedure by which a *Paqqid* admits new members, with the assent of the Many, into the council to administer justice (1QS 6:13–23); and records a fragmentary penal code that perhaps is enforced during the session (1QS 6:24–7:25).[144]

These passages, then, establish the legal authority of councils, but also emphasize the participatory role of the whole community in the legal sphere.[145] In fact, the composite literary record is sufficiently interwoven (or ambiguous) that some scholars essentially equate the council with the community (arguing that the council is an embryonic form of the community, or some variation of this thesis).[146] But even for those scholars who maintain that the council is a distinct band of elite members, what stands out is how 1QS quickly shifts from the council to the community and back. Moreover, 1QS regulates modes of inquiry, advisement, and sanction of the Many before the council. Whereas the entire Rule of the Community is structured to forge a normative, covenantal community, the middle section (1QS 5–7) indicates that the communal members are themselves agents of the juridical process.

Priests and Others

Numerous Qumran writings distinguish the role of the priestly sector of the community in administering legal matters. Various sources cited above amplify the jurisdiction of the priests (and Levites),[147] whether by sharing responsibility with a royal figurehead, serving in prominent positions of legal authority, or spearheading judicial councils. Further, the elevated position of the priests even casts a shadow over the collective nature of Qumran jurisprudence. Thus, the middle section of 1QS 5–7 that underlines the centrality of the normative community begins with the formulation: "This is the rule of the men of the Community who freely volunteer . . . to keep themselves steadfast in all He commanded in compliance with His will . . . to constitute a Community in law . . . *and acquiesce to the authority of the sons of Zadok, the priests who safeguard the covenant,* and to the authority of the men of the Community" (1QS 5:1–3; emphasis added). Similarly, the continuation that describes admission procedures of members demands complete "compliance with all that has been revealed of it to the sons of Zadok, the priests who keep the covenant and interpret the will and to the multitude of men of their covenant" (1QS 5:7–9). A later passage in 1QS exceeds these formulations by exclusively allocating legal authority to the (Aaronite)[148] priests. "Only the sons of Aaron shall have control over the law and property and according to them shall the decision go forth for every norm of the men of the community" (1QS 9:7).[149] Elsewhere in the scrolls, the priests and other officials are regarded as the legal experts on both revealed and concealed matters.[150]

At the same time, while the dominant role of priests in Qumran jurisprudence cannot be gainsaid, the wider dissemination of priestly authority is also apparent. Supreme priestly figures such as the *Mebaqqer* and the *Paqqid* help administer the legal authority of the council and the Many.[151] Likewise, even as all of the exemplars of the conciliar model stipulate that the council must be led by, or include (one, two, three, four, or twelve)[152] priests, they adjudicate alongside a larger pool of non-priests. In various texts, the priests adjudicate as a sector or division of the population, often alongside other sectors. Even as stirring an expression of priestly dominance as the opening lines of 1QS 5 cited above registers a perhaps secondary role of the council and community. Moreover, in parallel recensions of the Rule of the Community from the fourth cave (4QSb [4Q256] and 4QSd [4Q258]), these powers are vested in the council and Many alone.

By revolving entirely around the council and community, these parallels from cave four exhibit a coherence that is less apparent in 1QS, a likely later expansion,[153] which simultaneously focuses on priestly and communal authority. The ultimate result is that 1QS reflects an uncertain balance between these two foci of power, or at least one that is difficult to parse.[154] A similar ambiguity can be discerned in 1QSa.[155] Portraying the congregation at the end of days, 1QSa anticipates an epoch of Zadokite priestly supervision (1QSa 1:1–5), when all members will shoulder responsibility for the legal process. Abiding by the regulations and covenant of the Zadokites, communal members will undertake escalating legal responsibilities within the community at successive stages of maturity,[156] culminating with a remarkable mandate (or notice of potential eligibility) that devolves upon each member to join the judiciary:[157] "And at thirty years he shall approach to arbitrate in disputes and ju[dg]-ments, and to take his place among the chiefs of the thousands of Israel, the commanders of a hundred, commanders of fi[f]ty, [commanders of] ten, the judges and officials of their tribes in all their families, [according to the dec]ision of the sons of [Aar]on, the priests" (1QSa 1:13–16). As a result, mature members of the community fill the ranks of judicial officers and implement the supreme instruction of the priests.

Coupling the elite stature of the priestly class with the authority of the entire community, this last set of Qumran texts reflects a complex jurisprudence.[158] An elitist priestly pull as well as a more popular impulse coincide to shape its idiosyncratic form.[159] The convergence of these forces captures two of the main vectors of Qumran jurisprudence; as opposed to a royalist model, which only surfaces at its margins.

Revisiting the Temple Scroll and the "Law of the King"

This survey confirms the limited political role of the monarch in Qumran writings outside of the TS (specifically the LK section), and his near complete absence from judicial affairs. Instead, Qumran jurisprudence relies upon (priestly) officials, priests, councils, and the community. While the TS parts ways with other Qumran materials in assigning judicial authority to the king, it still betrays traces of the prevailing models by dispersing vertical power, relying upon a council of thirty-six (a cross section of three sectors of the population), and elevating the role of the priests.[160] It is as if the TS fuses a royalist ideology with juridical templates that are prevalent in Qumran.[161]

Given the TS's distinctive orientation,[162] and its stature as a fundamental text in the Qumran corpus,[163] it is important to tentatively situate this scroll in a general chronological framework alongside other significant texts, which will enable further reflections on how certain Qumran conceptions of kingship and justice may have developed diachronically.[164] Although scholars debate about the origins of the TS, many concur that it is a relatively early Qumran text, predating, or dating to the initial phases of, the sect.[165] Another foundational text with a royalist dimension, 4QMMT, is similarly understood by many scholars to be early,[166] or roughly contemporaneous to the TS,[167] and bears certain additional resemblances to the TS.[168] Most importantly, both of these texts lack the language of sectarian antagonism thought to be characteristic of later writings in Qumran.[169]

Turning to CD—a Qumran text that many scholars associate with (the beginning of) the next phase in the formation of the sect[170]—the role of the king assumes a decidedly different form. CD 7:13–20 records a metaphoric reading of the term "king" that implies a vesting of royal power in the community. This shift is largely emblematic of later Qumran writings, with their paucity of meaningful references to a monarchic leader. What emerges, then, is that whereas the early stratum of Qumran writings, which likely precedes the formation of the sect, affirms the centrality of the king's position, later sectarian literature betrays a fundamentally different orientation. This noteworthy change requires explanation.

Given the larger milieu of these writings, its discourse should be analyzed against the backdrop of contemporary attitudes toward Hasmonean rule.[171] Several scrolls expressly or implicitly criticize the priestly monarchy of the Hasmoneans, which likely informed the conceptions of sovereign power prevalent in this corpus. For instance, 4Q390, which censures the sinful reign of the sons of Aaron during the Second Temple period and compares their shortcomings to the failures of earlier Israelite kings (4Q390 1:1–5), probably refers to the Hasmonean dynasty.[172] This passage specifically faults the priestly kings for abandoning the law over the course of their reign (4Q390 1:6–8, 2:5–10). 1QpHab 8:8–13 (cited above) betrays a similar sentiment, attributing the downfall of the "Wicked Priest" to his arrogance upon becoming a ruler over Israel, abandoning God, and betraying the laws for his own enrichment.[173] From another vantage point, the deliberate stress in 4Q252 (cited above) on the ascendancy of Davidic rule has often been read as seeking to undermine non-Davidic rule.[174] Likewise, the plurality of messianic figures according to the twofold or threefold messianic schemes may imply dissatisfaction with the Hasmonean conflation of roles.[175] The cumulative criticism of Hasmonean rule may have in time aroused a broader distrust of royal power,[176] which in turn spawned an alternate political-juridical ideology focused upon priests and law, the primary concerns of Qumran writings.

The totality of this evidence suggests the following reconstruction: In the earliest stratum, reflected in both the TS and 4QMMT, and perhaps elsewhere,[177] the king is assumed to be the leader. Many scholars date these materials to the mid-second century BCE—overlapping with the Hasmonean dynasty—which helps explain why a royal constitution is axiomatic.[178] While these texts acknowledge royal sovereignty, they also demand the king's proper observance of religious laws.[179] Significantly, these texts also qualify their notions of kingship relative to idyllic models found in various biblical and apocalyptic works, as they present a king whose rule is conditional, potentially corrupt, and in need of guidance from righteous priests.

As the Qumran community coalesces into a distinctive sect that espouses an oppositional ideology, however, it evidently rejects monarchic rule. Monarchy is likely deemed an unstable institution, prone to political excesses and grave spiritual failures. Priesthood, by contrast, can be defiled and corrupted, but as an institution its sanctity is inherent and inviolable. The failure of Aaron's descendants, according to the Qumran sectarians, began when they usurped regal power, sacrificing their rarefied spiritual status by focusing on earthly concerns.[180] As the Hasmonean rulers become increasingly absorbed with political matters, consolidating their sovereignty through bold, and at times ruthless, policies,[181] the Qumran sect disengages from contemporary affairs.

Sequestered from the realpolitik of Hasmonean kings, the sect envisions, and partially constructs, an alternative community established upon the foundations of sacral law, led by pure, righteous priests and dedicated quorums. What remains of monarchy in the sectarian ideology is mostly deferred to a future, utopian age. Even Qumran eschatology reflects this conceptual transformation, as the priestly messiah is elevated above the royal messiah, and the latter figure is allotted only a nebulous, secondary role, in the sectarian imagination.

Seeking to forge a covenantal community, the sect pledges to adhere to the highest normative standards. Accordingly, the sect places a premium on deriving and transmitting the true revealed laws, and devising judicial arrangements and mechanisms for enforcing them.[182] Already in early works like the TS, the priests or councils exercise legal authority along with the monarch, and in later works their authority expands, while the king's influence declines. Texts such as 4Q174 and 4Q161 divert aspects of the royal judicial role to priests. Others, including CD and the Rule of the Community, assign this vital responsibility exclusively to nonroyal figures, including priests, masters of the (revealed and esoteric) Torah, a variety of councils, and the community. The multiplicity of figures and bodies disperse legal authority ever more widely.[183]

The broader trend that can be discerned in the Qumran turn toward forms of legalism returns to the concluding observations of earlier chapters. The tension between priestly law and royal power, which can already be detected in an early Hecataeus excerpt (see Chapter 1), emerges as a pervasive theme throughout much of Qumran literature. Gradually abandoning the idea of a sovereign crown as they isolate in the Judean desert, Qumran sectarians instead establish a different kind of society upon the foundation of sacral, priestly law.

Chapter 4 considers a parallel turn toward (priestly) legalism in the writings of Josephus. Whereas the shift in Qumran jurisprudence is engendered by internal disillusionment from within the Judean world, Josephus's political and legal theory is informed by daunting challenges that are mounted from the outside. Both ideologies alike identify sacral law as the ultimate substitute for political power.

4

Josephus on Kingship, Theocracy, and Law

In an important study of varieties of power in late antiquity, Brent Shaw describes Josephus as being caught "in a severe conflict" between two cultures with disparate notions of power: Roman formal-institutional power versus Judean informal-personal power.[1] When Josephus evaluates Roman power, he assimilates it into conventional Judean tropes: individual personalities loom large, diplomatic ties are seen as friendships, governmental grants are depicted as favors, and so on. Absent from Josephus's assessment, Shaw underscores, is a description of Rome's "constitution" (*politeia / politeuma*), in contrast with the writings of Polybius and others. Blind to the institutional dimension of politics, Josephus recognizes only the personality of the emperor as a familiar locus of power.

Shaw's provocative thesis mischaracterizes Josephus's writings. While Shaw rightfully points to the importance of power and politics for Josephus, his analysis overlooks a crucial dimension of Josephus's discourse. Notions of formal power and reflections upon the ideal "constitution" pervade Josephus's writings—not in his description of the Romans,[2] but in his portrayal of the Jews.[3] For Josephus, an optimal Jewish polity is constructed solely on the rule of law. This stable form eclipses the mercurial rule of men, which destabilizes classical regimes, including the Roman Empire.

This chapter reconstructs Josephus's legal-political philosophy, which grows out of his positive or ideal account of legal authority.[4] This differs substantially from Josephus's descriptions of the actual mechanics of justice,[5] which refract a turbulent reality where power is asserted, contested, and negotiated. Josephus's programmatic writings, by contrast, plot the foundations of legal authority and reimagine the potential social impact of the legal system. Centered upon the rule of law, Josephus's political vision builds upon Deuteronomy's jurisprudence. In fact, an embryonic version of Josephus's unique conception of the role of law in the "Jewish Republic" can already be discerned in the *Jewish Antiquities* restatement of Deuteronomy 17,[6] introduced in Chapter 1 and expanded upon below.

Similar themes reverberate in other sections of Josephus's oeuvre. Crystalizing over several decades following the destruction of the Temple—a pivotal context which I will argue informed his ideas— Josephus's philosophy leaves thin traces in the *Jewish War* and visible imprints in *Antiquities;* and receives a robust formulation in his final work *Against Apion.* Orienting his biblical exegesis, as well as his commentary on current affairs, Josephus's political theory becomes even more pronounced in the notions of constitutionalism and theocracy that structure much of his later writings.[7]

Restating Deuteronomy 17, and Josephan Antimonarchism

Josephus's restatement of Deuteronomy's sections on the judiciary (Deut 16:8–11, 17:8–13) and monarchy (Deut 17:14–20) in nearby passages in *Antiquities* (4.214–218, 4.223–224) reveals the primacy of legal authority in his political thought. Paraphrasing Deut 16:18 ("place judges and officers in your gates"), *Ant.* 4.214 states that each city should be ruled (*archetosan*) by seven men trained in virtue and the pursuit of justice (= "judges"), and two Levite assistants (= "officers"),[8] subtly conflating legal and political authority.[9] Drawing on the adjacent verses Deut 16:19–20,[10] *Ant.* 4.215–217 underlines the honor due to judges, the ban on bribery, and the duty to judge with integrity, because "God's strength is justice."

Immediately after, Josephus skips over Deut 16:21–17:7, which addresses unrelated topics, and proceeds to describe in *Ant.* 4.218 the central judiciary of Deut 17:8–13. In Josephus's rendition of these verses, the municipal judges (presumably along with the Levites) present unresolved cases to the higher judges who preside in Jerusalem:[11] "If the judges do not understand how to decide about matters that are lined up before them . . . let them send the case up intact to the holy city and let the high priest and the prophet and the *gerousia* [council of elders] come together and decide what seems best." In place of "the levitical priests and judge" of Deut 17:9, Josephus lists the high priest,[12] prophet,[13] and *gerousia*[14] as the supreme adjudicators—a significant elaboration. This triad, as Sara Pearce has persuasively argued, parallels the successors of Moses described elsewhere in *Antiquities:*[15] Eleazar the High Priest, Joshua the Prophet, and the *gerousia.*[16] So the central judiciary is composed of leading officials (just as the municipal tribunals rule locally). Glaringly absent from this list is the king. The reason for this omission becomes apparent in Josephus's treatment of monarchy a few paragraphs later.[17]

Ant. 4.223–224 cover the kingship verses of Deut 17:14–20. Strikingly, Josephus prefaces this section with a sweeping declaration that the optimal regime is non-monarchic: "Now aristocracy and the life therein is best. Let not a longing for another form of government take hold of you" (*Ant.* 4.223).[18] A related passage recorded later on in *Antiquities,* elaborating on Samuel's rebuke of the Israelites for choosing a king (discussed below), confirms the deep roots of this motif in Josephus's thought.

Josephus's strident opposition to kingship has received much scholarly attention since the nineteenth century.[19] Wellhausen understood Josephus's ideology as stemming from a loss of Jewish sovereignty, much as he identified antimonarchic materials in the Bible with the postexilic period.[20] One could also attribute Josephus's critique to the dismal record of many Israelite and Judean kings; the classic Roman antipathy to kingship; or a principled opposition to the monarchic form on democratic or republican grounds. While some or all of the above factors may be relevant, Josephus's antimonarchism largely arises from different concerns, as becomes apparent from his preferred political arrangement.

From among the three classical constitutional forms—monarchy, aristocracy, and democracy—Josephus privileges an aristocracy.[21] Still, his precise intention with this preference is also subject to scholarly debate.[22] Compounding the uncertainty is an *Apion* passage addressed below where Josephus proclaims that the "Jewish constitution" advances a unique fourth approach. In the present context, one should note Josephus's particular characterization of an aristocracy: "having the laws as your masters do each thing according to them, for it is sufficient that God is your ruler." On this account, aristocracy surpasses monarchy in its fealty to God's rule through law. This characterization also hints that the deeper source of Josephus's monarchic problem is that a ruler's powerful will threatens the normative order, and may undermine the kingship of God. In contrast with the standard explanation of Josephus's antimonarchism, which focuses exclusively on his assault on kingship, Josephus's high regard for law is also paramount. His objection to monarchic rule is fueled by his normative ideology.

Josephus's broader normative orientation can be discerned in his subsequent remarks on kingship. Notwithstanding his staunch opposition to this institution, Josephus must acknowledge the long history of Jewish kingship.[23] Thus, Josephus registers Deuteronomy's recognition of a monarchic constitution as follows:

> If, however, you should have a passion to have a king, let him be a compatriot, and let him always have a concern for justice and the other virtues. Let him concede to the laws and to God their superiority of wisdom and let him do nothing apart from the high priest and the advice of the elders [*gerousia*], and let him not have many wives, nor pursue an abundance of money or horses, since if he obtains them he will be full of contempt for the laws. If he should have a zeal for any of these, let him be prevented from becoming more powerful than is beneficial for you. (*Ant.* 4.223–224)

This restatement is in part rooted in the underlying verses. The notion that monarchy constitutes an inferior form of government, one that is adopted only if demanded by the popular will, builds on the conditional formulation of Deut 17:14.[24] The next verse stipulates that the king must be a compatriot. The prohibitions of the king amassing multiple wives, much wealth, and many horses are listed (in a different order) in Deut 17:16–17. Other clauses probably also trace to Scripture. Thus, Josephus's statement that the king should "always have a concern for justice" likely derives from the command that the king must transcribe, and perpetually read, the summary of the Torah (Deut 17:18–19); that he should "concede to the law and to God their superiority of wisdom" presumably follows from the imperative that the king fear God and observe the Torah's decrees (Deut 17:19–20); that he should "do nothing apart from the high priest and the advice of the elders" evidently stems from the mandate that the king transcribe the Torah before the "Levitical priests" (Deut 17:18),[25] as well as the injunction that the king should not rise above his brethren (Deut 17:20).

Buttressed by Scripture, *Ant.* 4.223–224 nevertheless rearranges or reorients the verses, and advances a distinctly Josephan political vision grounded in the rule of law. Thus, Josephus highlights the motifs of justice and the superiority of God's laws, which are expressed in the latter verses (Deut 17:18–20), before addressing the injunctions on the king. Likewise, Josephus casts all three injunctions (Deut 17:16–17) as forbidding practices that will lead to contempt of the laws.[26] Because Scripture raises this concern only with respect to a king who weds multiple wives, Josephus reorders the prohibitions and commences with the marital ban in order to underscore this rationale (and he omits the alternate rationale for the cavalry injunction as a measure for preventing a return to Egypt).[27]

Moreover, Josephus inventively draws on Deut 17:18–20 to place the king, more or less, within the confines of an "aristocratic" scheme: "Let him concede to the laws and to God their superiority of wisdom." The king's power is subsidiary to the true sovereign. In a similar vein, the king must solicit the counsel of the high priest and elders before acting.

Given that Josephus identified these figures as among the supreme judges (see *Ant.* 4.218), he is encoding here the king's deference to legal authorities, and their interpretation of God's will.[28] Read in sequence, the critical inferences from Josephus's remarks are that the high priest and the elders serve as proxies for God and mediate God's laws; and that the king's political action ought to be guided by divine laws filtered through these agents. Josephus's overall scheme subordinates the king to the legal regime.[29]

The larger implication of this passage becomes apparent when it is juxtaposed with the prior passage on the judiciary. Recall how in *Ant.* 4.214–218 Josephus emphasizes the importance of administering law but excludes the king from his expanded list of supreme judicial officials. Josephus's preference for (his version of) an aristocracy and opposition to a monarchy in *Ant.* 4.223–224 relates to this judicial arrangement. A surface reading of the nexus between these passages begins with Josephus's ardent opposition to monarchy, and then concludes that Josephus excludes the king from the coalition of supreme judicial officials by design. A more penetrating interpretation also notes the causal relationship that runs in the opposite direction: commencing with Josephus's elevation of the rule of law and then perceiving how this informs his evaluation of constitutional regimes. Conceiving of law as the foundation of political authority, Josephus deems monarchy to be an inferior constitutional form (which must be limited, or preferably, rejected). The ascendant value for Josephus is a veneration of law rather than a derision of kings.

Biblical Exegesis Shaped by Political Philosophy

A survey of several exemplary passages in Josephus's biblical restatement in *Antiquities* reveals that he adapted certain (normative and narrative) sections of Scripture in a systematic manner to reflect his distinctive political philosophy.[30] Various essential tropes about leadership are stressed by Josephus in these segments, including a preference for aristocratic (or republican) government, a devaluation of monarchy, and a promotion of the judicial role of the high priest and *gerousia*. Moreover, Josephus expounds in these contexts upon the dangers of unbridled power and the threat of lawlessness undermining a polity, and repeatedly upholds the rule of law as the sole remedy.

Samuel: Judges as Rulers

In recounting Samuel's vehement opposition to the popular call for monarchy, Josephus echoes the earlier themes of *Ant.* 4.224:[31]

> The people ... resented the outrages that the prophet's sons were committing against their earlier form of government and constitution.... They asked and begged him to appoint someone as their king.... Their words greatly grieved Samuel on account of his innate justice and hatred of kings. For he delighted intensely in aristocracy as something divine that renders blessed those who use it as their constitution. (*Ant.* 6.35–36)

Prior paragraphs provide further background. Samuel concluded his leadership tenure before his children's abortive stint (*Ant.* 6.31).[32] While the Bible reports that Samuel would judge the people by rotating among various locales (1 Sam 7:15–17), according to Josephus, Samuel set up several municipal venues for local hearings and circulated among them as judge, and thus established over time "much in the way of a sound legal system" (ibid.).[33] When Samuel aged, he transferred responsibility to his two sons, assigning to each a municipal venue and jurisdiction over a sector of the people. However, Samuel's sons perverted justice for gain, which aroused the opposition of the people (*Ant.* 6.32–34).

Christopher Begg argues that Josephus interpolates this extra-biblical material to highlight another dimension of Samuel's leadership, as a supreme legal authority.[34] But the purpose of this supplemental information seems more consequential. Samuel's political success is achieved by way of his judicial achievements, according to Josephus. Conversely, Samuel's sons fail as political heads because they are corrupt judges, and therefore inept leaders. When Josephus refers in this passage to the "outrages" of Samuel's sons against the earlier form of government and constitution, he has this corruption in mind. Perverting justice undermines the foundations of an aristocratic polity.

Notwithstanding the gravity of his sons' political offenses, however, Samuel grieves when the people agitate for constitutional change, for reasons one can infer. While the failure of the legal system has triggered a genuine crisis, the popular solution is profoundly misguided. Rather than restoring an upright aristocracy that embodies the rule of law, the people recklessly demand a king. But a monarch will prove even more damaging to the political and normative order. Only a government built on a sturdy legal foundation will flourish as a polity.[35]

Judges: Political Anarchy and Its Solution

The importance of constitutionalism and the vital role of law in constituting the ideal polity are also manifest in Josephus's stunning exegesis of the book of Judges. To be sure, many read Judges through a political lens, as a commentary on monarchy. Martin Buber famously interprets it as an antimonarchic work, and several passages in Judges have this connotation.[36] Other scholars demur,[37] arguing that the tumultuous closing chapters (17–21) impart a forceful, opposite message.[38] They adduce support from the ringing refrain that is sounded throughout this unit (Judg 17:6, 18:1, 19:1, 21:25)—"in those days there was no king in Israel; each man doing what was right in his own eyes"—which proclaims that the solution to anarchy is monarchy.[39] Josephus devotes much of *Ant.* 5 to Judges, especially its final chapters, but completely transforms their message. For Josephus, these chapters underscore a different political motif that substantiates his broader legal-political vision.

Introducing this biblical period, Josephus describes a state of political deterioration and lawlessness:[40] "After these things the Israelites became inactive with regard to their enemy ... they thought little of the order of their constitution and no longer paid attention to the laws" (*Ant.* 5.132). Josephus then clarifies what he means by neglecting the constitution: "Aye, even that aristocracy of theirs was now becoming corrupted. No more did they appoint councils of elders [*gerousia*] or any other of those magistracies beforetime ordained by law" (*Ant.* 5.135). In other words, according to Josephus, much of the turbulence at the outset of Judges is due to a constitutional failure, including the breakdown of the rule of law.[41]

By pointing to political and judicial collapse as the reasons for anarchy at this stage, Josephus is glossing over the causes catalogued in the biblical text: the impartial conquest, stressed in Judg 1:27–36; the failure to heed the divine call to sever any ties with the indigenous population, underscored in 2:1–5; and the sins of idolatry and intermarriage, emphasized in 2:11–3:6. Here, as elsewhere in Josephus, it is not idolatry, but the abandonment of the Jewish constitution, that is considered to be the cardinal sin of the Jews.[42]

Following this background description, Josephus begins his restatement of Judges by skipping to its chaotic final chapters, deferring his account of the interim chapters until later on.[43] At first blush, highlighting the analogous themes of the last chapters would seem to undermine Josephus's case for aristocratic rule, since they emphatically stress the indispensability of kingship for restoring civic order. Recall the ringing refrain of the final chapters, which offers monarchy as the antidote to mayhem. Josephus carefully sidesteps this implication, and projects the latter chapters in a different light. By monitoring Josephus's additional editorial moves, one can reconstruct his bold exegesis, which omits the pro-monarchic agenda of these biblical chapters and instead reinforces his own political philosophy.

Josephus commences his narration of the final chapters with a restatement of Judges 19, but he omits the opening pro-monarchic refrain, "in those days there was no king . . ." (Judg 19:1).[44] He likewise hardly cites any of Judg 17–18, thereby not only downplaying the idolatrous sin of the Micah episode but also eliminating two more citations of the pro-monarchic refrain (Judg 17:6, 18:1). Similarly, he never cites the final pro-monarchic refrain capping the episode (Judg 21:25), and instead inserts his own statement about the rise of the Benjaminites. After next recounting the fate of the Danites (excerpting Judg 18),

Josephus again returns to the tropes of constitutional failure and abandonment of law as the sources of the tribulations of the book of Judges (*Ant.* 5.174–179).

By opening his retelling of Judges with the chaos of its final chapters, which unfolds as a consequence of an inadequate political infrastructure, Josephus validates his political reading of this entire period. But he overrides the specific political message of the latter unit of Judges. Constitutionalism established through an aristocracy, judicial councils, and the rule of law emerges as the solution to anarchy, in Josephus's retelling, silencing the Bible's campaign for kingship.

In the midst of describing the turmoil of Judges 19–21, Josephus hints at this political panacea. *Ant.* 5.150–152 describes how the *gerousia* tempered the visceral rage of the tribes that were seeking to avenge the Gibeah atrocity,[45] cautioning them to heed the law and demand the surrender of the culprits.[46] The key to restoring order, then, is to abide by the rule of law, as administered by the council,[47]—that is, to adopt once again the framework that existed at the end of Joshua's lifetime.[48]

In the remainder of his restatement of Judges, Josephus returns several times to his own revised political refrain, something to the effect that in those days there was no lawful aristocracy in Israel, in order to explain repeated political lapses.[49] He likewise continues to hail his constitutional vision as a lasting solution in subsequent sections (see, e.g., *Ant.* 5.186, 5.234, 5.255, and 6.84-85). This enables Josephus to easily segue into *Antiquities* 6, where he recounts the strident antimonarchic (and pro-aristocratic) themes of the opening chapters of Samuel (a transition that is far more difficult to explain for traditional biblical commentators who accept the pro-monarchic material in Judg 19–21 at face value).

Moses's Successors

When Josephus describes the leadership that will succeed Moses, he noticeably pronounces the role of law in steering subsequent generations. The context of Moses's appointment of his successors is his valedictory address. Moses instructs the people to abide by the law and fulfill God's commandments, and thereby achieve ultimate happiness as a result of divine benevolence (*Ant.* 4.178–184). Moses then exhorts them: "Only obey those [rules] that God wishes you to follow, and do not value more highly another arrangement more than the present laws, and do not scorn the piety that you now have with regard to God and change it for another way" (*Ant.* 4.181). The temptation to pursue another path includes adopting a different constitution.[50] Similarly, Moses promises, future world renown is in store "if you will listen to and guard the laws that I arranged upon God's dictation to me, and if you will study their understanding" (*Ant.* 4.183). Moses feels confident about the future welfare of the people, as he relies on "the moderation of the laws and the orderliness of the constitution and the virtues of the generals" who will lead them.

According to *Ant.* 4.186, the future "generals" are "the high priest Eleazar and Joshua, the council of elders [*gerousia*], and the leading men of the tribes." This same cadre of leaders also accompanies Moses at his death, according to *Ant.* 4.324 (according to Deut 34:1–4, Moses dies alone), marking the transition in leadership. As we have seen, Sarah Pearce observes that they mirror the list of supreme judges enumerated in *Ant.* 4.218. This correspondence reflects a more fundamental point: Moses's successors are legal authorities, who will uphold the normative foundation of the constitution and implement its laws.[51]

Zimri's Complaint

Another *Antiquities* 4 section that Etienne Nodet links to *Ant.* 4.186 is Josephus's surprising elaboration on the sin of Zimri with the Midianites (*Ant.* 4.129–155). Josephus seizes on this episode as an opportunity to further meditate on similar themes of leadership and law.[52] Notably, rather than follow Scripture's emphasis on the heroic role of Phineas, Josephus focuses upon the nature of Zimri's challenge to Moses.

The background to Zimri's transgression is the adulterous and idolatrous behavior of the Israelites and the Midianites. Instigated by the wicked counsel of Balaam the prophet, the Mideanite women seduce the Israelites, who stray from their ancestral laws. While the Israelites are entrapped by the allure of hedonic pleasures, according to Josephus's rendition Zimri launches a more substantive assault on the ancestral laws. Accusing Moses of tyrannically imposing his own will under the cover of norms, Zimri depicts Moses as thwarting the self-determination of individuals. In essence, Zimri presents an indictment of legalism, or the specter of laws being used to mask power.

When Moses hears Zimri's scathing attack, he perceives a perilous threat to the lawful structure of the ancestral system. Zimri's purported call for freedom dangerously translates into a crusade for lawlessness. Phineas therefore decides to intervene, acting decisively to quell the unrest sparked by Zimri's confrontation.

Yet if Zimri's anarchic rally is destructive, the concerns Josephus raises through his voice about the potential abuse of law remain weighty. A tyrannical regime can manipulate laws to serve the personal ambitions of the leader (*Ant.* 4.149). An illegitimate, or incomplete, system of laws is subject to despotic abuse. Only by limiting personal clout can the rule of law be effective and enduring. For Josephus, the Mosaic Constitution, which enshrines the rule of law and marginalizes powerful political actors, is uniquely fashioned for this purpose.[53]

Deuteronomy 13: Political Idolatry

A last example of Josephus's political philosophy shaping his exegesis is found in a striking paragraph near the end of *Ant.* 4. The context is monumental: Josephus is in the midst of restating the last section of Moses's valedictory speech, which concludes the Pentateuch and, more particularly for Josephus, acts as a coda for his summary of Pentateuchal laws that fill books 3 and 4. In Josephus's rendition of this part of the speech, which loosely tracks the latter chapters of Deuteronomy, Moses speaks of "putting together the laws, and assisting in providing the arrangement of the constitution," and then adjures the people to observe the laws. But here Josephus boldly veers from the scriptural sequence, and incorporates into Moses's speech a paragraph based on a discrete pericope from earlier in Deuteronomy (Deut 13:7–17).

These charged verses describe the exacting punishment meted out against a relative, or some members of a town, who incite or drive others toward idolatrous worship:

> If anyone secretly entices you—even if it is your brother . . . saying, "Let us go worship other gods," whom neither you nor your ancestors have known. . . . Show them no pity or compassion and do not shield them. But you shall surely kill them. . . .
>
> If you hear it said about one of the towns . . . that scoundrels from among you have gone out and led the inhabitants of the town astray, saying, "Let us go and worship other gods," whom you have not known, . . . you shall put the inhabitants of that town to the sword, utterly destroying it and everything in it.

As biblical scholars have noted, these verses are laden with covenantal significance: harshly punishing flagrant violations of the most foundational loyalty of the Pentateuch—the exclusive worship of God. By relocating this pericope to the denouement of the Pentateuch, Josephus further highlights its centrality; but along the way he completely transforms its message:

> But even if one of their blood relatives should undertake to confound and abolish *the constitution* based upon them [the laws], or indeed a city should do so, [they declared that] they would defend them [the laws] both in common and individually: after prevailing, they would themselves pull it [the rebellious city] down from the foundations and not leave behind the ground of those who had run mad, if that were possible. (*Ant.* 4.309–310; emphasis added)

The ultimate transgression of the Torah, according to Josephus, is not a defiant act of idolatry but instead a systematic attempt to undermine the constitution and laws.[54] Accordingly, Josephus's exegesis substitutes the sin of idolatry with the offense of revolution, and calls for the utter rejection (destruction!) of an alternative political order that is not based on the laws.

Historically, Jews would repeatedly abrogate their Mosaic oath and alter their constitutional framework, as *Antiquities* illustrates again and again.[55] Likewise, individuals such as Zimri would also lead insurrections against the constitutional order.[56] In Josephus's estimation, such movements undermine the Jewish polity, and lead to the demise of the Jews. Only by safeguarding the laws and constitutional order will the Jewish polity be secure and flourish.

In sum, a selection from Josephus's rewritten Bible in *Ant.* 1–10 highlights several themes that lie at the core of his legal-political thought.[57] According to Josephus's retelling: When Samuel prefers aristocracy to kingship, he also intends to promote the rule of law; the primary message of Judges is that political anarchy can only be surmounted by a legitimate aristocracy that achieves lawful rule; the ideal successors of Moses are officials who govern by executing the laws; Zimri's protest against the tyrannical rules of whimsical leaders dissolves when laws are applied evenly; and the cardinal sin of idolatry translates into a traitorous rejection of the constitutional order. Throughout these passages, Josephus signals a profound commitment to the rule of law and conveys a deep skepticism about the reign of powerful men.

Josephus's Commentary on Contemporary Events

Josephus's political ideals, especially his promotion of an aristocracy, the priesthood, and the rule of law, also color his reflections on contemporary affairs.[58]

Josephus in Galilee

Josephus's conviction that legal order serves as the cornerstone of political success evidently influenced his personal conduct as a Galilean leader, at least according to his own narrative. When he became military commander and governor of the Galilee during the revolt against the Romans (in 66 CE), he also assumed the role of a regional judge. Eager to cultivate loyalty among the local authorities, Josephus designated them as amici to assist him, especially in adjudicating legal matters (*Life* 79).[59] While these initiatives may have a pragmatic thrust, in a parallel description in the *Jewish War* (an earlier work) they seem scripted to follow his political vision.[60]

In *J.W.* 2.566–568, Josephus describes his selection as a general in the Galilee, and the steps he took to bolster his appointment. He decides to win over the native population by including local leaders in his administration (*J.W.* 2.569–571). The specific administrative structure he implements is a judicial one: Josephus selects a council of seventy persons to serve as regional magistrates over the entire Galilee. Operating underneath the council, a cluster of municipal courts, each composed of seven judges, are assigned jurisdiction over lesser matters, and are instructed to refer more important ones to the council. Thus, Josephus's most basic administrative strategy is to establish a judicial network that foreshadows elements of the two-tiered arrangement of *Ant.* 4.214–218. In this account, Josephus describes the allocation of judicial responsibilities to others, less as a way of currying favor with them, and more as a way of integrating them into the governing structure. Already in his early autobiographical summary, Josephus intimates that legal order constitutes the foundation of a durable regime.

The Fourth Philosophy

An important illustration of Josephus's political philosophy inflecting his assessment of contemporary affairs is the surprising ambivalence discernible in his mature treatment of the "Fourth Philosophy" in *Antiquities* (see 18.4–25), which differs from his earlier disparagement of the "Zealots" in *J.W.* (2.118). In *J.W.*, Josephus describes how Judas the Galilean incited his countrymen to revolt against the Romans (in 6 CE). Scorning their willingness to pay a tribute to Rome and thereby bow before mere mortals, Judas impresses upon them that only God is their true master. In a derogatory comment, Josephus characterizes Judas as a sophist who founded a (presumably marginal) sect that shares nothing in common with the three Jewish philosophies that he proceeds to describe—the Pharisees, Sadducees, and Essenes.[61]

Returning to this event at greater length in *Antiquities* 18, Josephus provides a similar account which he embellishes with additional details, and likewise segues into a summary of the various philosophies of Judaism.[62] What distinguishes Josephus's latter report most is not his revised factual record but instead his characterization and evaluation of Judas's viewpoint. In this context, Josephus labels Judas's attitude and the following it spawned as a fourth school of philosophy, alongside the three main sects (or schools). By branding this approach for the first time as a significant fourth alternative philosophy of Judaism (in contrast with his descriptions of three Jewish philosophies in *J. W.* 2.119–166 and *Ant.* 13.171–173), Josephus elevates its stature and importance, even as he levels sharp criticisms against its founders and followers for their "innovation and reform in ancestral traditions."[63]

When Josephus proceeds to summarize the tenets of the Fourth Philosophy, he offers the following conspicuous characterization: "This school agrees in all other respects with the opinions of the Pharisees, except that they have a passion for liberty that is almost unconquerable, since they are convinced that God alone is their leader and master."[64] By associating their ideology with the Pharisees, the guardians of the ancestral tradition, Josephus links the Fourth Philosophy with his favored sect.[65] Moreover, accenting the Fourth Philosophy's passion for liberty, total subservience to God, and willingness to die for their creed, Josephus underscores positive values of this movement that resonate with central virtues and commitments promoted by the Jewish tradition according to *Antiquities* and *Apion*.

Yet precisely because Josephus now classifies this group as a competing philosophy, and not just a marginal offshoot,[66] he also criticizes the temerity of their staking out a new position, as well as certain specific emphases in their thought. Presumably, an aspect of their philosophy that offends Josephus according to *Antiquities* is its radical rejection of human agency. This would seemingly even preclude an administering body from mediating God's will by implementing legal norms, which Josephus sees as indispensable. Further, the Fourth Philosophy operates on the brink of lawlessness, which can easily deteriorate into violent civil strife. For Josephus, such disarray undermines liberty, and defeats the laudatory aspirations of the Fourth Philosophy. Nevertheless, as Josephus's political theology matures from the *Jewish War* through the latter sections of *Antiquities,* his overall identification with aspects of the Fourth Philosophy increases,[67] culminating in his formulation of a substantially similar fourth constitutional form in his final work, *Apion,* elaborated upon below.[68]

Crisis in Imperial Rome

Almost three-quarters of *Antiquities* 19 is devoted to describing Caligula's assassination and Claudius's rise to power.[69] Considering the almost complete irrelevance of this narrative for Jewish history, Josephus's inclusion of this lengthy excursus is highly puzzling.[70] Josephus offers his own rationale, explaining that Caligula's death was of the greatest importance for saving Judeans from ruin (*Ant.* 19.15–16). Louis Feldman points to Agrippa's role in facilitating Claudius's ascension, according to Josephus's rendition of this affair.[71] Others have assumed that Josephus is merely filling his work, stretching to reach the Dionysian twenty.[72]

All of these reasons fail to adequately explain this elaborate digression. While the disproportionate size of this and other sections rightfully engenders scholarly skepticism that Josephus had a polished master plan for these latter books,[73] the assumption that he haphazardly collected disparate material seems frivolous. More appealing is the recent inclination of a few scholars to attribute Josephus's aim in including certain *Antiquities* 18–20 sections to various ideas he wished to accent about power and leadership.[74]

In this vein, it is worth drawing attention to one particular moment that Josephus spotlights in *Antiquities* 19, despite its seeming remoteness from the subject matter of *Antiquities:* the fleeting effort by the Roman Senate to restore the Republic (or aristocracy, according to the parallel in *J. W.*),[75] following the assassination of Caligula. Josephus even includes parts of the senatorial "transcript" in his account. Further proof that this attempt was of interest to Josephus is his earlier reference to it in his cursory treatment of the Caligula affair in the *Jewish War*.[76]

At first blush, the fact that Josephus harps on this moment is particularly perplexing. Aside from its utter irrelevance for Jewish history, the import of this passing phase for Roman history is negligible. Indeed, Arnaldo Momigliano dismisses this moment as a blip in the Caligula affair, because "this comic opera republic survived little more than twenty-four hours."[77] And this aborted initiative left no obvious mark; it was the first and last time when the abolition of the Principate was openly contemplated.[78] Classical writers therefore devote little attention to it: Cassisus Dio references it in a short paragraph, Tacitus not at all, and Seutonious refers to it twice, but briefly.[79] Yet Josephus, living well after the Principate had been restored, chooses to preserve this episode twice in his writings, including a long-winded *Antiquities* account.[80] Moreover, given the radical thrust of the senatorial opposition to the imperial scheme following Caligula's assassination, which in Suetonius's brief rendition amounted to a desire to eradicate all traces of the caesars, recording this event while residing in Imperial Rome is not just odd, but brazen (perhaps even foolhardy or dangerous). What is its lasting legacy for Josephus?[81]

By highlighting this episode in the Caligula affair, Josephus presumably accomplishes something akin to what K. R. Bradley describes as the general effect of Suetonius's *Lives:*

> To write a work assessing previous regimes was in itself something of a political act, because by holding up to scrutiny the power of the Caesars, Suetonius was constantly reminding his readers that the Principate was an autocratic form of rule totally at odds with ancient Roman traditions of free government and capable of disintegrating into despotism of the worst kind at any moment. . . . The *Lives* have a certain critical, perhaps even subversive, dimension to them . . . any reflective reader of Suetonius might well have . . . *wondered about those in the past who,*

as Suetonius reminded them on several occasions, had thought (if not more) of restoring the old ways. (emphasis added)[82]

Bradley mostly alludes in this last line to the senatorial debate following the assassination of Caligula.[83] In a similar sense, Josephus's "political act" in describing this historic moment underscores to his readers in the late first century CE that even though an emperor replaced the senatorial Republic—and here Josephus's message has a unique slant that speaks not just to the Roman condition, but to political life at large—*libertas* remains elusive as long as it relies on powerful men (whether they convene in the constitutional form of the Republic or the Principate), rather than the rule of law.[84]

Reviewing the impassioned Senate speech of Sentius Saturninus recorded by Josephus (*Ant.* 19.167–184) takes on new meaning in this light. Sentius hails the realization of *libertas* as the ultimate political achievement. In hyperbolic, almost utopian, language he describes how even a brief taste of freedom "to think as we please, in a country that is subject to its own sense of right, and that regulates itself by the laws under which it once became a flourishing state" has brought complete fulfillment to the lives of those who seek it out.[85] Opposing *libertas* is tyranny, which "frustrates all the virtues, robs freedom of its lofty mood, and opens a school of fawning and terror." Most offensive about tyranny is the manner in which it undermines the rule of law: "inasmuch as it leaves matters not to the wisdom of the laws, but to the angry whim of those who are in authority."[86]

The entire drama of this historic episode, and Sentius's speech specifically,[87] accent themes that permeate Josephus's writings and are essential for his political thought.[88] By recording this event, Josephus signals that both republican and imperial governments can deteriorate into tyrannical forms because they rely on men rather than the stable and inviolable rule of law. This episode becomes emblematic for Josephus of a more sweeping ideological revolution that was transpiring in his thought regarding the Jewish polity, as he laid the groundwork for a fourth constitutional construct.

Constitutionalism and Theocracy

Josephus's writings on the judiciary and monarchy in *Antiquities* 4 implicate his broader vision of the rule of law, where law serves as a locus of political power. Echoes of this theme are ubiquitous for Josephus, pervading his interpretation of various seminal biblical episodes, and influencing his commentary on certain contemporary events. His systematic political thought is most fully developed in his "constitutional" writings in *Antiquities,* and especially *Apion.*[89]

In a retrospective comment, Josephus characterizes *Antiquities* as a detailed account of the laws and the constitution of the Jews, which demonstrates their special nature (see *Ag. Ap.* 2.287). Both the opening and the closing paragraphs of *Antiquities,* in fact, capture the centrality of the constitutional framework for this book.[90] Commencing with a programmatic statement, Josephus sets out his agenda to describe the history and constitution of the Jews, and refers several times over the course of these opening paragraphs to the laws (*Ant.* 1.5, 11–20). The concluding passages, which delineate all of the high priests who officiated since Aaron, twice enumerate changes in the governmental constitution at various stages of Jewish history (see *Ant.* 20.229, 234, 251, and 261), and likewise stress the centrality of the laws.

Moreover, throughout the legal sections of *Antiquities* 3 and 4, which restate many of the commandments of the Torah, Josephus repeatedly invokes the Jewish constitution. For example, his account of Sinai depicts Moses proclaiming that God has prescribed a well-ordered constitution for the people (*Ant.* 3.84). Subsequently, Josephus divides the laws into two parts[91]—and deliberately employs constitutional language in framing each set of norms (see, e.g., *Ant.* 3.84, 322; 4.181–184, 193–198, 302, 309–312). In particular, Josephus emphasizes the importance of the latter set of laws (which includes the judiciary and monarchy sections), which forms the "constitution" of the Jews and is vital for their political welfare in perpetuity.[92] Here Josephus begins a sustained political-theological argument, which he perfects in *Apion,* that the Torah's laws constitute the foundation of the successful polity of the Jews.[93]

Josephus's ultimate statement of political theology is recorded in his final work, *Against Apion.* In the words of Martin Goodman, *Apion* comes "as close as a Jew ever came to political theorizing about the nature of . . . a perfect state."[94] This work also emerges as the most proudly Jewish of Josephus's writings, presenting Josephus's fully developed reflections on the role of law and the Jewish constitution in the (ideal) Jewish polity.[95]

The utopian nature and ahistorical tone of *Apion* can be detected throughout this work.[96] Instead of the fracturing sectarianism, civil unrest, and religious disobedience of the *Jewish War, Antiquities,* and *Life,* Josephus depicts a united and devout Jewish people. By flattening the past and projecting toward an inexorable future, Josephus's Judaism emerges as steadfast, able to transcend the fluctuations of temporal affairs and stand impervious to historical setbacks. In presenting this idealized portrait, *Apion* ambitiously elaborates upon the political-theological motifs of Josephus's earlier works, and underscores their profound societal implications, which particularly resonate for post–70 CE Jews.

Extolling the virtues of the Jewish constitution in the latter part of *Apion* (2.145–186),[97] Josephus focuses substantively on the character, supremacy, and achievement of the legal system. When Josephus describes the role of the priests in this context, he transitions from their administrative role in the ideal polity to their specific juridical responsibilities. Serving under God who governs the universe, the priests are assigned "management of the most important matters" (2.185) and are appointed as "general overseers" (2.187). Detailing the mode of priestly rule, Josephus primarily highlights their supreme legal authority (he only refers to the priests in this context, with no mention of the prophet and *gerousia*):[98] the priests supervise the law, judge legal disputes, and punish convicts (*Ag. Ap.* 2.187, 194).[99] His almost seamless transition between politics and law reflects the blurring of these categories in Josephus's mature political theology.

The strong nexus between these spheres finds its most profound expression in this section as well. Rejecting the time-honored threefold constitutional schemes of the Greco-Romans (monarchy, oligarchy, and democracy) he relied upon in *Antiquities,* Josephus now introduces a fourth alternative to characterize Judaism:[100] "Some have entrusted the power of government to monarchies, others to the rule of the few, others again to the masses. But our legislator took no notice of any of these, but instituted the government as what one might call . . . a 'theocracy,' ascribing to God the rule and power." While Josephus does not explicitly address the manner in which God governs, this becomes eminently clear from the wider context: through God's comprehensive laws, as stated by Moses the legislator, and as administered by God's priests.[101] Unlike the classical three forms of government, which rely upon men, the governance of God relies upon just and lasting laws.[102]

Tracing back to the peerless legislator Moses who heeded the divine will,[103] Jewish law's ancestry surpasses all other legal traditions, according to Josephus, and its corpus remains constant throughout Jewish history. Despite dramatic changes in circumstances—military defeats, loss of autonomy, and diasporic dispersion—Jews maintain absolute fidelity to their laws. Contrasting the approach of the early Greeks, who obeyed the wishes and whims of their kings (*Ag. Ap.* 2.154–155), and the Spartans who betrayed the laws of their constitution,[104] the Jews have always upheld their laws and conducted themselves with stalwart devotion: "As for us, although we have undergone countless different fortunes, thanks to the changes among the kings who ruled Asia, we have not betrayed the laws even in the most extreme crises" (*Ag. Ap.* 2.228). Later on Josephus describes the courageous nature of this ongoing commitment: "We have trained our courage not for undertaking wars of self-aggrandizement but for preserving the laws. While meekly enduring defeat of other kinds, whenever people force us to alter our regulations then we undertake wars, even when it is beyond our capacity, and we hold out to the bitter end" (*Ag. Ap.* 2.272).

In highlighting the antinomy between executing laws and wars (of self-aggrandizement), Josephus clearly also intends to distinguish the Jews from the Romans.[105] While Romans enlarge their empire through triumphant battles, Jews bravely safeguard their laws. And their unswerving loyalty extends to all sectors of Jewish society, which differs markedly from other nations who entrust the laws solely to a jurist class. The stark contrast between Jewish and Roman civilization is likewise reflected in the fundamentally different ways they each achieve an orderly state. Whereas the meticulous organization of Roman civilization, as perceived by Josephus,[106] is especially evident in the proficient operation of its military camps and expeditions, the methodic structure of Jewish civilization is most apparent in its people's disciplined adherence to their laws.

Josephus amplifies this distinctive quality of the Jews one more time toward the end of *Apion:* "For most people, by now, transgressing the law has become a fine art! But certainly not among us. Rather, even if we are deprived of wealth, cities, and other good things, at least the law endures for us immortal" (*Ag. Ap.* 2.276–277). Josephus's larger message, in the aggregate, is even more emphatic. The only polity that will perpetually achieve lawfulness, order, and *libertas* is one governed by a theocracy—the inviolable rule of an ideal, sacred law.

Three aspects of Josephus's argument in this context resonate with themes from his earlier works discussed above. First, Josephus promotes law over power, especially monarchic power. In this vein, he taps into the antimonarchic sentiment of the Roman Republic that persists even during the Principate, recalling the post-Caligula interregnum attack on imperial rule for its tyrannical (i.e., monarchic) tendencies. By contrast, Josephus portrays the theocratic system of the Jews as authentically rejecting monarchy, and thereby embodying the pure Roman ideal in a way that Imperial Rome only complies with in form. Second, Josephus represents the Jewish legal system as a stable political structure. That is, he deliberately distinguishes his portrait of the ideal polity from the risks of anarchy or reckless innovation that undermine other political arrangements. It was precisely these latter deficiencies that plagued the Israelites during the period of the Judges or the Romans under despotic rulers, and that fundamentally undermined the Fourth Philosophy. Finally, Josephus focuses attention on the singular merit of Jewish law—whose content he described in *Antiquities* and whose essence he captures in

Apion—that continues to flourish in his lifetime. Indeed, according to Josephus, the Jewish commitment to law eclipses that of all other civilizations, including Rome.

Contextualizing Josephus's Legal-Political Philosophy

By these successive arguments Josephus not only portrays the Torah as promoting an ideal polity, but even succeeds in restoring contemporary Jewry to a dignified political position, despite its having suffered a catastrophic blow to its sovereignty in 70 CE.[107] In the aftermath of this tragedy, Jews were relentlessly subject to their enemies' taunts, including the blistering charge that recent political events signal the divine rejection of the Jewish people.[108] A revealing paragraph in *Apion* captures a similar animus: "For he [Apion] says that it is evidence of the fact that we do not employ just laws or worship God as we should that [we do not govern,] but are subservient to other nations, one after another, and that we have experienced some misfortunes affecting our city" (*Ag. Ap.* 2.125).

Reeling from a crushing defeat, Josephus (and most Jews) confronted daunting theological and political questions such as why the chosen people were spurned, and whether sovereignty and territorial control are the sole barometers of political success.[109] For Josephus the ultimate answers to these theological and political questions intersect and find their fullest expression in his mature writings: the essence of the Jewish polity lies in its legal supremacy, which continues to flourish in contemporary circumstances. In other words, Josephus successfully propounds a political-theological vision of Judaism that can be sustained even in a dramatically transformed landscape. As Josephus states at the end of *Antiquities*, the chain of Jewish leadership has led from a monarchy to a priestly aristocracy, and therefore currently approximates the form of an ideal government.[110] Among the primary responsibilities of the priestly aristocracy is administering a legal system, a function that continues to be as relevant as ever in Josephus's lifetime. Moreover, the juristic advances of post-destruction Jewry reflect their perpetual commitment to legal excellence. All of the above implies that a modern Jewish polity—a theocracy—can be constructed on the foundation of law.

In wrestling with these political-theological themes in the shadow of the Roman defeat of the Jews, Josephus anticipated, in a certain sense, the famous challenge that Saint Augustine faced three centuries later in his *City of God*.[111] After the sacking of Rome in 410 CE by the Goths, Augustine grappled with the importance of worldly power according to Christian theology. In response, he formulated his famous distinction between the "City of God" and the "City of Man," which constitutes one strategy for confronting this quandary. Josephus, centuries earlier, championed an entirely different approach. On the Jewish wasteland left behind by the Romans, Josephus builds the edifice of a new political-theological construct.

Apion, then, offers a paean to, and a petition for, the primacy of the ideal law of the Jews and the theocracy it sustains.[112] If the seeds of Josephus's thought can be found in his restatement of Deuteronomy's jurisprudence and its separation of powers, Josephus's crowning statement advances a stronger version of this jurisprudence, which seeks to eliminate sovereign power altogether.[113] Here Josephus undertakes an audacious rethinking of the political enterprise. Animated by a profound distrust of political authority that perpetually threatens to undermine justice, he boldly declares the autonomy and sufficiency of law, and in *Apion* he reconstitutes the entire polity upon the foundation of law—perhaps the most dramatic ideal of early Jewish jurisprudence recorded in the entire oeuvre of Second Temple literature.[114] The rule of law constitutes the essence of Jewish institutional power for Josephus, which is superior to the Roman variety that is wielded at the mercy of strong men. Contra Shaw, conceptions of the formal power of sacral law and reflections upon the ideal "constitution" of a theocracy pervade Josephus's biblical exegesis and political commentary, and dominate the mature political theology of his later works.

Part Two

Rabbinic Literature

5

Kingship and Law
in Tannaitic Literature

Part One (Chapters 1–4) analyzed select passages within Second Temple writings that portray the administration of justice and illuminate the relationship between legal and political authority. Building upon the dominant biblical strand of royal justice, and an anomalous Deuteronomic strand that separates judicial administration from royal power, postbiblical literature also reflects both paradigms, albeit with a crucial shift in emphasis. Several prominent writers and texts privilege Deuteronomy as a foundational source, and elaborate novel theories of jurisprudence in its wake. Philo closely tracks Deuteronomy's verses, but promotes a monarchic ruler and even projects him as a leading embodiment of the law (alongside the high priest, who is a distinct legal authority). Moving beyond the particulars of Deuteronomy while echoing some of its core themes, Qumran scrolls map a world of priests and legal councils, mostly relegating the royal prince to a secondary position or an eschatological role. Josephus understands Deuteronomy to be principally opposed to monarchy because an empowered ruler jeopardizes the rule of law. The superior constitutional form he outlines centers on God's sovereignty, with divine norms serving as the sole durable foundation of a lasting polity. While all of these postbiblical writings expand on Deuteronomy, each grapples in its own way with the relationship between kingship and law, and more broadly, the dynamic intersection between power and justice.

Part Two (Chapters 5–7) examines analogous issues as they arise in rabbinic literature. Beginning with the Mishnah, this chapter evaluates the rabbinic monarch, and the relationship of royal authority to judicial administration. A cursory treatment in Chapter 1 already indicated that Mishnah Sanhedrin—also formulated against the backdrop of Deuteronomy—elevates the role of the king, but recognizes the separate jurisdiction of an independent judiciary. In order to support this characterization of the Mishnah, and elaborate upon its implications for early rabbinic perspectives upon law and power, it is imperative to analyze the Mishnah's broader conception of kingship, as well as the ways it delimits the relationships among the king, the high priest, and the legal order. Along the way, this chapter will also examine tannaitic traditions recorded in the Tosefta (a parallel work of early rabbinic literature), and utilize them as a foil for understanding the Mishnah. After outlining the primary administrative template of the Mishnah alongside the Tosefta parallels in the first section, the second section will evaluate an alternate scheme that is preserved in rabbinic literature. Beginning with a Talmudic revisionist interpretation of Mishnah Sanhedrin,[1] this latter section will review rabbinic sources that express certain aspects of the royalist strand.

Expanding upon the foundation of this chapter's analysis of kingship and jurisdiction, Chapter 6 will provide a broad overview of early rabbinic conceptions of judicial authority, which also reflect an overarching aim to shield justice from power, as well as contrary perspectives that combine these forces. Chapter 7 will move beyond the fixed administrative schemes that are reconstructed in the prior chapters, and explore the dynamic interaction between law and politics that can be discerned in successive strata of rabbinic literature. Throughout, the same tension between power and justice that was palpable in Part One recurs in Part Two, and shapes rabbinic discourse in manifold ways. Most notably, a leading voice in tannaitic literature echoes certain Second Temple writings in amplifying Deuteronomy's jurisprudence, while also spawning novel ideas about the moderate version of separation of powers (described in this chapter) and the internal dissemination of powers (described in Chapter 6), which add significant new dimensions to early Jewish jurisprudence.

Royalty and Judicial Authority in Tannaitic Literature

The controversial status of the king in early rabbinic literature emerges from various passages in the Tosefta, Midrash Halakha, and Jerusalem and Babylonian Talmuds. In contrast with their portrayal of the Sanhedrin (the judiciary) and high priest as cornerstones of the Jewish administrative edifice, these writings equivocate about the stature of the monarchy.[2] Accordingly, they accent the alien nature of kingship, dispute the scope of royal prerogatives, and emphasize the need to limit the king's powers.[3] Further, in a stunning passage, the Tosefta and Sifre even openly debate the very desirability of the royal office.[4]

A survey of the Mishnah's selective treatment of kingship, however, reveals a different orientation altogether, which has particular relevance for this book's inquiry.[5] Evidence from the Mishnah strongly suggests the following conclusions: (1) the king is projected as a leading political figure, with broad powers, who is granted singular license to function independently from the law and other institutions; (2) by repeatedly drawing parallels between the king and the high priest, the Mishnah intimates that they stand on par in terms of their rank as leaders; (3) nevertheless, the king and the high priest diverge in their relationship with the Sanhedrin and courts and, more generally, with the broader, normative system; and (4) the above themes are significantly more pronounced in the Mishnah than in the Tosefta, as the latter contains mixed evidence about the standing of the king and does not explicitly draw a comparison between him and the high priest.

In order to highlight these points, this section will examine the main passages in the Mishnah and Tosefta discussing the monarchy alongside the high priesthood, in the juridical context and beyond (there are only a few such passages in the Mishnah).[6] In addition to focusing exclusively on their content,[7] this section will also consider the Mishnah's rhetorical emphases, which are especially manifest when contrasted with parallel sources in the Tosefta.[8] An analysis of mishnaic formulations proves particularly enlightening, as these are largely uncontested, anonymous passages that have been crafted by a strong editorial hand and reflect a remarkably consistent tone and style.[9] After examining these passages, this section will return to the juridical context to further evaluate the king's relationship to the judiciary.

Mishnah Sanhedrin 2:1–2

Tractate Sanhedrin, chapter 2, contains the most elaborate treatment of monarchy in the Mishnah.[10] An initial comparison of this corpus with analogous Tosefta materials reveals several striking discrepancies. Unlike *t. Sanh.* 4:5 which, as stated, openly debates whether there is an obligation to appoint a king, the Mishnah treats the position of the king as axiomatic. Similarly, whereas the Tosefta (ibid.) disputes whether the king is allowed the various entitlements described in 1 Sam 8, the Mishnah plainly affirms the king's sweeping powers, including his right of eminent domain:[11] "He [the king] may force a way, and none may oppose him. There is no limitation to the king's way. The plunder taken by the people [in war] must be given to him, and he receives the first choice" (*m. Sanh.* 2:4). Overall, the Mishnah is noteworthy in its enumeration of positive privileges and prerogatives of the king—such as waging a voluntary war[12]—that are entirely absent from Deut 17:14–20, which only imposes limits.[13]

The careful editorial strategy of *m. Sanh.* 2 is evinced in its opening passages that address the high priest and the king, respectively:

> The high priest may judge and be judged, testify and be testified against, perform *halitsa* and have *halitsa* performed for his wife. . . .
>
> The king may neither judge nor be judged, testify nor be testified against, perform *halitsa* nor have *halitsa* performed for his wife.[14]

Before discussing various aspects of kingship, the Mishnah commences with a suggestive pair of symmetric passages that capture the stark contrast between the high priest and king by drawing attention to the high priest's involvement in the judicial process,[15] which differs from the king. These paragraphs take on additional significance in light of the placement of chapter 2 within the tractate. Whereas the majority of tractate Sanhedrin discusses the judiciary—led by the Sanhedrin, the primary rabbinic institution that is afforded wide jurisdiction over legal and administrative matters[16]—*m. Sanh.* 2 relates to two other leaders: the high priest and the king. Given the principal role of the judiciary, the Mishnah frames its discussion of these two officials by considering their opposite relationships with it.

M. Sanh. 2:1–3 proceeds to significantly amplify the distinction between these two figures by stating that the high priest is governed by standard halakhah, such as levirate marriages and mourning rituals, which do not pertain to the king.[17] In taking this step, the Mishnah suggests that the king's distance from the judiciary is symptomatic of his broader autonomy from standard law. Conversely, the Mishnah establishes the judiciary's independence from the king (a theme that will be elaborated upon below, and in Chapter 6). Even though the Mishnah presumably recognizes limits on the king's autonomy, rhetorically it chooses to focus on his halakhic exemptions, in contrast with the high priest.[18] Conceiving of a leading official who stands beyond the grasp of the law is extraordinary within the context of tractate Sanhedrin (and Rabbinic Judaism at large), which depicts a comprehensive legal system.[19]

The Mishnah boldly establishes the king's extralegal standing without any sound biblical source, which sharply differs from the high priest, who is subordinated to the standard legal order despite contrary indications in Scripture. Consider the Mishnah's striking regulation that a king cannot attend a funeral—absent scriptural support[20]—in contrast with the high priest who, according to the primary tannaitic position (Rabbi Meir), must join a burial procession (albeit in an attenuated manner). The latter requirement overrides the biblical proscription that the high priest not leave the Temple (Lev 21:12), and overlooks the significant concern lest he defile himself by coming into contact with a dead body (Lev 21:11).[21] Evidently the Mishnah assumes that the high priest must conform to standard legal norms, including participating in funeral rites,[22] while the king has a supererogatory status.

In relaying this tradition, the Mishnah also borrows suggestive nomenclature that lays bare the novelty of its position. Labeling the royal palace with a Greek loan word (*palterin*),[23] the Mishnah demarcates a space for the king that mirrors the Temple (*miqdash*) where the high priest resides, thereby establishing a discrete base for each official.[24] Moreover, the Mishnah's topography has normative consequences: The king must remain within the royal palace,[25] unlike the high priest, who can exit the Temple, notwithstanding the biblical prohibition. Occupying his royal chambers, the king inhabits an extralegal sphere where he resists the gravitational pull of the normative order and the social network that it regulates. Overall, the king resides apart from the people, whereas the high priest engages with them.[26]

The Mishnah's continuation focuses on monarchy, and further projects the king in a favorable light. Mishnah Sanhedrin 2:4–5 (a form of midrash halakhah) delineates the king's special powers and prerogatives and the unique restrictions (i.e., the three royal prohibitions of Deut 17) that circumscribe his actions.[27] By presenting these prohibitions in a positive context, the Mishnah defangs these laws and their deep distrust of royalty, and it also substantively modifies them.[28] In addition, the mishnaic chapter reshuffles the order of these prohibitions and the neighboring verses (relative to Deut 17:14–20) in order to conclude with the citation and exegesis of an initial verse that calls for heightened reverence for the sovereign.[29] Thus, the final Mishnah enumerates various modes of displaying heightened respect for the king that are derived from the rabbinic interpretation of the biblical verse "'Thou shall surely set over thee a king (Deut 17:15)'—that his awe may be over thee." For the Mishnah, this respect is mandated exclusively for the king (not the high priest) and likely bespeaks his unique stature.[30]

Later rabbinic writings debate how to assess the singular autonomy and extralegal status granted to the king by the Mishnah, particularly his separation from the judicial system. The later Bavli (analyzed below) clearly marks it as negative, describing the king's independence reflected in the Mishnah as a reluctant concession to the insolence of non-Davidic kings of Israel, and therefore concluding that upright kings from the Davidic dynasty (who are not the subject of the Mishnah according to the Bavli) participate in the normative order and can likewise adjudicate.[31] Aside from the obvious strain involved in limiting the Mishnah's generic teaching ("The king may neither judge . . .") to non-Davidic kings, the Talmud's reading undermines the Mishnah's sweeping contrast between the king and the high priest, as well as the pro-monarchic tone of the entire mishnaic chapter.[32] Moreover, although the Mishnah primarily employs the generic designation "king," it draws support for several of its non-anonymous rulings from the life of King David.[33] The Mishnah's "king" plainly includes members of the Davidic dynasty.

An alternative understanding of the Mishnah can be traced in several Palestinian sources. Deuteronomy Rabbah explains the king's exemption from judgment ("the king may . . . [not] be judged") as follows:[34] "Our rabbis have taught us: Why may a king not be judged? R. Jeremiah said: Because of King David who wrote, 'Let my judgment come forth from Thy presence' (Psalms 17:2). Hence no human being may judge the king, only God." According to the midrash, the king (exemplified by David) is granted a kind of sovereign immunity in court, not as a concession, but on principle, because he is subject only to God's jurisdiction. Undoubtedly, this is also closer to the simple sense of the Mishnah.[35] Other Palestinian rabbinic sources likewise understand the opening clause of the Mishnah that precludes the king from judging in its literal sense.[36] Thus, rabbinic interpreters who were more chronologically and geographically proximate than the Bavli confirm that the plain sense of the Mishnah's statement that "the king may neither judge nor be judged" is the correct one (*pace* the Bavli).[37]

The Mishnah's statement does not necessarily reflect the king's superiority,[38] but his distinctive political role that requires substantial autonomy, coupled with the need to preserve the independence of the judiciary.[39] In contrast, the high priest's role as a spiritual leader demands his compliance with standard halakhic norms, and he is best integrated into the judiciary. Accordingly, the high priest's responsibilities are closely linked with those of the Sanhedrin, as accentuated by the Mishnah's rhetoric.[40]

In all, the Mishnah separates the king from legal affairs, and instead vests legal authority in the judiciary and high priest. In this vein, the citation of verses from Deut 17 in *m. Sanh* 2:4–5 should be underscored. The Mishnah echoes Deuteronomy's allocation of judicial responsibility to officials other than the king. At the same time, the Mishnah affirms the king's leadership role and buffers him from judicial intervention. Adapting Deuteronomy's template (which subordinates the king to the priesthood), the Mishnah emerges as more pro-monarchic than this biblical foundation.

The significance of these mishnaic passages can be better appreciated by contrasting them with the Tosefta's parallel teachings. The Tosefta does not draw a symmetric opposition between the king and the high priest; it generally treats both officials the same. Adopting a single formulation for both, the Tosefta places them within the constraints of the halakhah as "ordinary people" (despite several exemptions that apply to each): "if he [the king / high priest] violates a positive or negative commandment or any other commandment, he is treated like an ordinary person [*hedyot*] in all respects" (*t. Sanh.* 4:1–2).[41] In this vein, the Tosefta emphasizes that the high priest is subject to homicide laws, notwithstanding his unique function in facilitating atonement in cases of accidental manslaughter.[42]

Treating the king and high priest as "ordinary people" suggests that they are both subject to the jurisdiction of the courts. This may be corroborated by another somewhat ambiguous Tosefta passage—"one does not summon (or appoint) a king, nor a high priest, except before a court of seventy-one" (*t. Sanh.* 3:4)—which perhaps relates to summoning these officials before a court.[43] Moreover, the Tosefta differs from the Mishnah in apparently ruling that both the king and the high priest can participate in the judiciary and are subject to its jurisdiction. To wit, the Tosefta never declares that the king cannot be summoned to court, nor records the rule precluding the king from (delivering or being the object of) testimony.[44] Further, the fact that *t. Sanh.* 2:15 only bars the king from joining the Sanhedrin and the court of intercalation implies that he can function as a lower-level judge.[45] *T. Sanh.* 4:4 may even envision the king serving as a leading judicial authority when it establishes his special prerogative to sit in the Temple chamber,[46] although the meaning of this passage is far from certain.[47]

Addressing the largely parallel laws of the high priest and king sequentially, the Tosefta (mostly)[48] classifies them in the same normative category. This is further reinforced by the Tosefta's commanding forms of reverence for both (*t. Sanh.* 4:1, 2). Finally, *t. Sanh.* 4:10 may stipulate a novel rule that a king's wife must be of priestly lineage.[49]

Notwithstanding the profound differences between these synoptic sections of Mishnah and Tosefta, it is plausible that they share a textual base. Arguably, the carefully crafted mishnaic laws present a revision of earlier Tosefta materials.[50] The following is a possible reconstruction of the Mishnah's redaction: It expands (and essentially changes) the principle of *t. Sanh.* 2:15—prohibiting the king from joining the Sanhedrin—to bar the king from participating in the judiciary altogether (perhaps based upon the same underlying rationale).[51] In a similar vein, the Mishnah omits, or even rejects, *t. Sanh.* 3:4's ruling that the court of seventy-one has responsibility for summoning (or appointing) the king.[52] In contrast, the Mishnah preserves, and underscores, the association between the high priest and the Sanhedrin (see also *m. Sanh.* 1:5, which states that the high priest is judged by the Sanhedrin). In order to amplify the dichotomy between the king and the high priest, the Mishnah relocates to other tractates the punishment for manslaughter (which presumably applies to both leaders) and the king's role in augmenting the Temple courtyard (which blurs his role with that of the high priest).[53] Instead the Mishnah presents a symmetric contrast, which summarily captures the fact that the high priest is subject to the court's jurisdiction and bound by standard law, while the king is not.

Finally, as described above, the Mishnah expands upon the powers and privileges of the king, unlike the Tosefta. It concludes by trumpeting the special reverence owed to the king ("that his awe may be over thee"). Notably, this mishnaic teaching is formed by concatenating two distinct sources from the Tosefta—one pertaining to the high priest (*t. Sanh* 4:1), the other to the king (*t. Sanh* 4:2).[54] For the pro-monarchic Mishnah, such respect is reserved for the king alone.

In sum, two main features distinguish *m. Sanh.* 2 from the arguably earlier Tosefta passages. First, the Mishnah rephrases or omits restrictive positions about the monarchy that are recorded in the Tosefta and embellishes the king's authority and prestige. Second, the Mishnah employs a parataxis absent from the Tosefta, wherein the king is projected as equal to (or greater than) the high priest in stature, but opposite in relationship to the normative order. These two points might be connected, as the Mishnah's positing extensive royal power implies a high degree of independence.[55] Importantly, the Mishnah presents the king's autonomy as a positive defining feature of royalty.

At the same time, by removing the king from the legal sphere and subsuming the high priest within an established judicial framework, the Mishnah enables the formation and ascendancy of an independent judiciary, a central point for this book. The Mishnah projects the Sanhedrin as the supreme institution bearing responsibility for all judicial affairs and certain ancillary matters. In the mishnaic scheme, the judiciary stands atop the administrative hierarchy. These latter points, which require separate analysis, will be discussed in Chapter 6.

The leadership structure of the Mishnah, accordingly, consists of a kind of triangular setup composed of a primary judicial institution, with two subordinate offices: the high priest, who serves adjacently to the court, and the king, who operates at arm's length, being granted autonomy to achieve distinct aims. Similar dual arrangements between the king and the high priest recur in a couple of other contexts, reinforcing the impression that the Mishnah has adopted a deliberate design (especially when contrasted with related Tosefta materials).[56] These mishnaic passages likewise promote the monarchy, emphasize the parallel standing of the king and high priest, and shed light on additional aspects of their respective responsibilities.

Mishnah Sotah 7:7–8

Rabbinic literature designates the king as the official who publicly reads the Torah at the post-Sabbatical *Hakhel* ceremony (see Deut 31:9–13), in contrast with Josephus and other Second Temple interpreters who identify the reader as the high priest. While this divergence has been often noted, the precise nature of rabbinic tradition on this matter has been misunderstood by modern scholarship.[57] Beyond the general significance of assigning the king the *Hakhel* recitation, the particular presentation of this rite in Mishnah Sotah further highlights the king's vital religious role.

The context of the Mishnah's treatment of this topic is a chapter that catalogs ritual recitations based upon whether they must be recited in Hebrew, or any language is acceptable. The listing of Hebrew-language recitations, *m. Sotah* 7:2, enumerates "the portion read by the king [*Hakhel*]" alongside the "benedictions of the high priest." Upon examination of the subsequent paragraphs that fill in details about these recitations, the deliberateness of the Mishnah's juxtaposition becomes eminently clear. In its substantive teaching and literary construction, the Mishnah draws a strong parallel between the ritual recitations assigned to these respective officials.[58]

M. Sotah 7:7 defines the "benedictions of the high priest" not merely as a blessing, but instead as the high priest's public Torah reading on Yom Kippur (a ritual with no biblical source), which is followed by a series of special blessings. The Mishnah vividly depicts the ceremonial procession in which a lineup of officials transport the Torah scroll to the high priest, who then reads from the scroll while standing:

> What is [the procedure regarding] the benedictions of the high priest? The synagogue attendant takes a Torah scroll and hands it to the synagogue president. The synagogue president hands it to the deputy, and he hands it to the high priest. The high priest stands, receives [the scroll], and reads from it while standing . . . and he pronounces eight benedictions in connection therewith.

The very next Mishnah (*m. Sotah* 7:8) defines the "portion read by the king [*Hakhel*]" as including not just a public reading but also a series of special blessings. The Mishnah intentionally invokes the same imagery of a procession as in the previous passage:

> What is [the procedure regarding] the portion read by the king? . . . The synagogue attendant takes a Torah scroll and hands it to the synagogue president. The synagogue president hands it to the deputy, and he hands it to the high priest, and he hands it to the king. The king stands, receives [the scroll], and reads from it while sitting. . . . The same benedictions that the high priest pronounces, the king also pronounces.

The concluding line confirms the deliberate comparison between these two ceremonial recitals.[59]

What emerges is a pair of mishnaic passages that are fashioned through a kind of cross-pollination process. In one direction, *m. Sotah* 7:7 grafts upon the high priest the kingly role of reading the Torah. Conversely, *m. Sotah* 7:8 grafts upon the king the priestly role of reciting blessings.[60] The result is that both the high priest and the king conduct a public Torah reading followed by a series of blessings, accompanied by the same impressive procession.

While most scholars characterize Mishnah Sotah as assigning the public Torah recital to the king,[61] in fact it records two distinct, public ceremonies where the Torah is read and blessings are recited. Even as Mishnah Sotah diverges from Second Temple traditions in assigning the post-Sabbatical *Hakhel* reading to the king, it deliberately sets the description of this ritual alongside the Yom Kippur public Torah reading and benediction ceremony led by the high priest (described in *m. Yom.* 7:1, and deliberately duplicated here). This dual assignment to the king and high priest corresponds to the other mishnaic passages that pair these figures.

By comparing the ritual recitation of the king at *Hakhel* to the high priest's service on Yom Kippur, the Mishnah elevates the king's role.[62]

Further, the Mishnah depicts the king as officiating in the Temple court-yard, and includes the high priest in the hierarchy of personnel that transport the Torah scroll to the king, implying that in some sense the high priest is subordinate to the king. Similarly, while the high priest is enjoined to read while standing, the king is afforded the privilege of sitting.[63]

Unlike the Mishnah, Tosefta Sotah does not link the ritual readings and blessings conducted by the king and high priest,[64] nor accent a par-allel, dual distribution of leadership responsibilities to the king and high priest. Further, *t. Sotah* 7:13–14 invokes the biblical figure Ezra, a priest, as a paradigm for the king's *Hakhel* reading. This runs counter to the Mishnah's depiction of two distinct occasions for royal and priestly rituals, as Ezra emerges as a kind of priestly monarch. Tosefta Sanhedrin likewise hails Ezra as a model monarchic figure.[65]

Moreover, the Tosefta includes two statements that are absent from the Mishnah, which, at least in effect, reduce the ritual sanctity of the *Hakhel* reading and the significance of assigning the king this responsi-bility. First, it records the position of R. Judah that the king's *Hakhel* reading would take place outside on the Temple Mount, and not within the sanctum of the courtyard.[66] Second, it preserves R. Tarfon's testi-mony (*t. Sotah* 7:8) that even priests with blemishes participated in the priestly ensemble that accompanied the *Hakhel* assembly.[67]

The most arresting discrepancy between the Mishnah and Tosefta lies in their differing reactions to a recollection of a past *Hakhel* reading that was led by Agrippa, a king of inferior lineage.[68] The Mishnah records his exemplary behavior: "King Agrippa stood, received it [the Torah scroll], and read from it while standing, for which the Sages praised him." The mutual respect and admiration between the king (displaying rever-ence for the Torah) and the Sages (recognizing his upstanding behavior) informs the continuation of the Mishnah's account as well: "When he reached, 'you are not permitted to put a foreigner over you (Deut 17:15),' his eyes ran with tears. They said to him, 'Fear not, Agrippa, thou art our brother, thou art our brother.'" By contrast, *t. Sotah* 7:16 never records that King Agrippa respectfully stood during his reading, and harshly condemns those who meekly reassured him despite his alien lineage: "[The people of] Israel made themselves liable to extermination because they flattered Agrippa."[69] King Agrippa's rule was illegitimate, and the people of Israel should have denounced him.

These polar reactions to Agrippa's *Hakhel* reading are consistent with the Mishnah and Tosefta's different orientations toward monarchy. The Tosefta, which preserves positive and negative perspectives, openly rebukes a problematic regime. The Mishnah, on the other hand, consistently presents a positive slant toward the monarchic institution. Instead of disparaging Agrippa, it depicts him glowingly.[70] *M. Bikk.* 3:4 likewise presents him as a an exemplar of religious practice, unpretentiously leading the ceremony of the first fruits.[71] This may conform with a broader pro-monarchic historical revision that is reflected in the Mishnah.[72]

In sum, Mishnah Sotah employs a deliberate rhetorical construct to present another facet of the dual distribution of leadership responsibilities to the king and high priest. The Tosefta, by contrast, does not appear to register this symmetric scheme. Conceiving of Ezra the Priest as a model monarchic figure, the Tosefta does not promote a division of leadership responsibilities. Elevating the king's standing, the Mishnah's distinctive orientation can also be discerned in its discussion of the *Hakhel* laws and the "historic" recitation of Agrippa. As opposed to the checkered material recorded in the Tosefta, the Mishnah presents a uniformly positive portrait.[73]

Mishnah Horayot, Chapters 2–3

A third set of passages recorded in Mishnah Horayot deepens the imprints of the above motifs. Here again one finds a positive account of kingship as well as a deliberate comparison with the high priest. Moreover, like Mishnah Sanhedrin, Horayot depicts the central court as a leading institution. Further echoing Sanhedrin, Horayot aligns the priest with the judicial role, in contrast with the king, who acts autonomously. All three are cast as leading authorities.

The overall subject matter of Horayot is the special sin offerings that are obligatory for the atonement of leaders in certain circumstances (based on an exegesis of Lev 4 and Num 15). The Mishnah offers a schematic presentation of these sacrificial laws.[74] Chapter 1 discusses the special sin offering that must be brought by the high court (the "bet din") after declaring an erroneous ruling.[75] Chapter 2 discusses the offering of the high priest after an erroneous ruling, which is comparable to that of the court. Its latter half introduces the king (referred to as "*Nasi*")[76] as the third official who must bring a special sacrifice. His obligation is triggered by a misdeed rather than a mistaken ruling.

While the overt purpose of these passages is to analyze subtleties in sacrificial laws, they more broadly outline the different foci of power according to rabbinic tradition. Significantly, the Mishnah thereby includes the king among the nation's leaders, even as it treats him discretely in certain respects.[77] Parenthetically, Mishnah Horayot confirms that all three institutions are fallible, and responsible for repairing their own failures. Evidently, notwithstanding a kind of principle of sovereign immunity that precludes the king from being judged in court (*m. Sanh.* 2:2, reiterated in *m. Hor.* 2:6, but see 2:8), the king remains accountable for his own transgressions.[78]

The elevated stature of the king (*Nasi*) alongside the high priest is highlighted in Horayot's final chapter. *M. Hor.* 3:1–2 juxtaposes the laws applicable to both (with the details omitted):

> An anointed [high] priest who committed a sin ... and likewise a *Nasi* who committed a sin. ...
>
> an anointed [high] priest who vacated his appointment, who then committed a sin, and likewise a *Nasi* who vacated his position, who then committed a sin. ...

Notably, the Mishnah pursues this comparison, notwithstanding the fact that the high priest bears greater similarity to the court in the realm of these sacrificial laws. Moreover, the comparison presented here between the king and the high priest is an original creation of the Mishnah, and does note derive from Scripture. Thus, the Mishnah, invoking the dual structure also evident in tractates Sanhedrin and Sotah, emphasizes the parallel standing of the king and the high priest.[79]

The climactic statement regarding monarchy in Horayot likewise appears in chapter 3. In a pointed exegetical comment, *m. Hor.* 3:3 dispels in one stroke any possible sign of monarchic inferiority to the other leadership positions. Justifying the rabbinic identification of the *Nasi* as the king, the Mishnah explains, "Who is the '*Nasi*'? The king, for it is stated in Scriptures: 'and he did any of all the things which the Lord his God hath commanded (Lev 4:22),' [referring to] *a Nasi, above whom there is none but the Lord his God*" (emphasis added).[80] This mishnaic teaching constitutes one of the most positive characterizations of monarchy recorded in all of rabbinic literature.[81]

An evaluation of analogous Tosefta passages again captures distinctive dimensions of the Mishnah's presentation that are absent in what is arguably the raw material of the Tosefta.[82] First, the Tosefta does not record any comparison between the king and the high priest.[83] Second, while *t. Hor.* 2:2 identifies the *Nasi* as the "*Nasi* of Israel," presumably a reference to the king, it does not cite the resounding exegesis of the Mishnah to explain this identification. Moreover, the next Tosefta passage—addressing a scenario not discussed in the Mishnah[84]—states that when a "*Nasi* of Israel" (i.e., of non-Davidic lineage) and a "*Nasi* of the House of David" share power, they both offer special sacrifices.[85] In contrast, the Mishnah, which identifies the "*Nasi*" as the king who has no superior other than God, may deny that this title can be divided.[86]

The conclusion of Tosefta Horayot explicitly ranks the monarch relative to other leaders (presumably for the purpose of sequencing their respective sacrifices, if they coincide). In a passage with a mixed message, the Tosefta states: "A sage takes precedence over the king, since if a sage dies there is no replacement, but if the king dies all [the people] of Israel are worthy of being kings. The king takes precedence over the high priest."[87] Even as the Tosefta elevates the king over the high priest, it stations him beneath a sage, who is considered truly unique.[88] Not surprisingly, the Mishnah never records this partially dismissive statement.[89] Indeed, *m. Hor.* 3:3, which emphasizes the singular stature of the monarch, runs counter to this sentiment.

In sum, by structuring the underlying biblical verses as an elaborate tripartite scheme, and by comparing the various officials with one another, Mishnah Horayot presents the court, high priest, and king as a triad of leaders who warrant special rules for achieving atonement under certain circumstances. In addition, by specifically comparing and contrasting the king's regulations with those that apply to the high priest (especially in *m. Hor.* 3:1–2), the Mishnah again signifies that it conceives of these two dignitaries as occupying parallel offices. At the same time, Mishnah Horayot invokes the fundamental dichotomy of Mishnah Sanhedrin that associates the high priest with the court (i.e., both are depicted in the role of adjudication),[90] as opposed to the king. Finally, by employing certain rhetorical devices, the Mishnah spotlights the preeminent stature of the monarch, despite his limitations. The Tosefta omits much of this material and instead records rulings and statements about monarchy that are of a more equivocal nature.

Other Mishnaic Passages

Various other mishnaic passages confirm the monarch's prominent role and standing: *M. Abot* 4:13 famously identifies three forms of authority in Jewish society, stating plainly what was implicit in the various passages surveyed above: "Rabbi Simeon says there are three crowns—the crown of Torah, the crown of priesthood, and the crown of royalty."[91] Other suggestive sources include *m. Yoma* 7:5 (registering the king's special prerogative to consult with the priestly *Urim* and *Thummim*); *m. Yoma* 8:1 (singling out the king for a leniency in a normative context); *m. Yoma* 3:10 and *m. Naz.* 3:6 (celebrating the conduct of King Munbaz and Queen Helena);[92] *m. Yeb.* 6:4 (recording the king's appointment of a high priest);[93] *m. Shebu.* 2:2 (enumerating the king first among an assembly of officials that are collectively authorized to expand the zoning of Jerusalem, including the Temple area); and *m. Sanh* 10:2 (listing kings who have forfeited their share in the "World to Come").[94] Underlying this rare negative final passage is a recognition of the stature of monarchs, which lends gravity to the statement that some have forfeited their share in eternity.[95]

Evaluating the Mishnaic Juridical Scheme

In all, the various passages in the Mishnah addressing kingship reflect a pro-monarchic[96] orientation,[97] in contrast with the Tosefta.[98] Beyond shedding light on the nature of kingship in early rabbinic literature, the above sources bear important implications for juridical themes that are the focus of this book. *M. Sanh.* 2:2, alongside other mishnaic passages that reinforce its underlying arrangement, illuminates the relationship between the king and the judiciary in the rabbinic system, and the distribution of power between them.[99] It contains two propositions that invite a comparative legal analysis.

The seemingly straightforward notion that a king cannot be judged codifies something akin to the doctrine of sovereign immunity, a staple of early legal systems. But its justification in the context of the Mishnah clearly differs from other contexts. The doctrine is usually thought to grow out of the ancient conception of the king as the head of the legal system.[100] As such, it takes a small step to assert that he stands beyond the reach of the law. In contrast, mishnaic law emphatically denies the king's legal authority. Moreover, mishnaic law operates with the axiom that all are bound by halakhic norms, and accordingly leaders are generally under the jurisdiction of the law.[101] Therefore, the Mishnah's affirmation of the king's "immunity" is far from obvious. Not surprisingly, other rabbinic voices, such as Tosefta and Bavli Sanhderin cited above, refute this principle or limit its scope.[102] In a similar vein, a rabbinic passage openly rejects the Greek adage *para basileos nomos agraphos* (lit. about the king the law is not written, i.e., not applicable).[103] Even according to the Mishnah, sovereign immunity does not imply a doctrine of infallibility, as seen in the analysis of Horayot.

The other proposition of *m. Sanh.* 2:1–2, that the king cannot judge, is far more anomalous from a comparative perspective, and must be traced to its Deuteronomic roots. Denying a venerated assumption of royal justice that was prevalent through late antiquity, the Mishnah asserts that a king may not preside as a judge,[104] and he certainly does not oversee the judiciary. In the words of Robert Cover, the Mishnah here is stating a startling "rule of sovereign judicial incapacity."[105] Only when situated against the backdrop of Deuteronomy 17, and alongside its Second Temple amplifications, can the Mishnah's teaching be rightly perceived as an iteration of this distinctive line of jurisprudence. Nevertheless, the Mishnah goes further in two respects. First, it explicitly precludes the king from a juridical role, while other sources do so only indirectly by vesting legal authority elsewhere. Second, it denies the king's jurisdiction even though it elevates the stature of the royal office. Moreover, the Mishnah's willingness to endorse Deuteronomy's scheme wholesale is especially conspicuous in light of the particular milieu of its redaction, Roman Palaestina of the early third century CE.

Imperial Rome hailed the emperor as the supreme legal authority.[106] In sharp contrast, the Mishnah envisions an independent judiciary by design. While Greco-Roman political thinkers developed theories of a mixed constitution in which powers are distributed among different constituents,[107] none suggested that legal authority be separately administered. Thus, the Mishnah's promotion of an autonomous judiciary, and its emphatic exclusion of the king from the administration of justice, breaks with prevalent jurisprudential assumptions, and joins the postbiblical sources that follow the Deuteronomic trajectory.[108] Not surprisingly, other rabbinic writings resist the juristic scheme of the Mishnah, as discussed in the next section.

Rather than advancing the independent propositions of sovereign immunity and sovereign judicial incapacity, Mishnah Sanhedrin couples them. Other Jewish writings affirm one or the other proposition, but not both.[109] The logic of these alternative approaches seems clear: sovereign immunity frequently attaches to the supreme legal authority, and, conversely, one who is not privileged to judge is presumably still subject to the law. Nevertheless, the Mishnah stakes out a novel position that links these propositions and thereby establishes a buffer between the king and the judiciary. Depicting the courts (and high priest) as fully responsible for legal tasks, the Mishnah carves out space for the king to rule.[110]

The Contrary Rabbinic Position: A Royal Judiciary

Despite the categorical separation of the Mishnah, later rabbinic tradition encountering this corpus rejects this framework. Refracted through the prism of the later Bavli (introduced above), Mishnah Sanhedrin has thus been interpreted in a very different sense, which dominates subsequent discussions of rabbinic law. Below I will analyze the Bavli's dramatic revision of the Mishnah, and then attempt to account for its transformative hermeneutic by placing it in a wider context.

The Bavli's Interpretation of Mishnah Sanhedrin

Responding to the mishnaic rule that "the king may neither judge nor be judged," the Bavli significantly qualifies its scope and impact.[111] Citing the teaching of Rabbi Pappa,[112] *b. Sanh.* 19a–b elaborates: "This refers only to the kings of Israel; kings of the house of David, however, both judge and are subject to judgment. For it is written, 'O House of David, thus said the Lord: Render just verdicts, morning by morning (Jer 21:12).'" According to the Bavli, the Mishnah's teaching records a secondary rule that pertains to non-Davidic kings.[113] The primary rule, applicable to Davidic kings, maintains by contrast that kings participate in, and are subject to the jurisdiction of, the judiciary. Here the Bavli invokes a distinction that originated in the biblical schism between the Northern kingdom (i.e., non-Davidic kings) and the Judean kingdom (the Davidic dynasty).[114] In later biblical legacy, non-Davidic rule is often associated with corruption and catastrophe.[115] Accordingly, various rabbinic traditions portray Davidic kings as ideal rulers, and non-Davidic ones as inferior in stature.[116]

Next, the anonymous Talmud introduces the story of a capital trial involving (the non-Davidic) King Jannaeus[117] in order to provide an etiology for the secondary rule of the Mishnah:[118] "But why this prohibition of non-Davidic kings [judging or being judged]? Because of an incident which happened with a slave of King Jannaeus who killed a man. Simeon b. Shetah said to the sages: Be bold and let us judge him." Reluctantly answering the sages' summons, Jannaeus defies their jurisdiction in various ways, until Simeon commands him: "Stand on your feet, King Jannaeus, so witnesses may testify against thee. For you do not stand before us but before He who spoke and the world was created." Jannaeus, then, shrewdly turns to the feeble associate judges for a verdict, aiming to drive a wedge between them and Simeon:

> The king replied, I will not act by your word but upon the words of your colleagues. He [Simeon] then turned to the left and to the right, but all looked at the ground. Then Simeon b. Shetah said to them, Are you wrapped in thought? Let the Master of thoughts come and call you to account. Instantly, Gabriel came and smote them all and they died.

Capping this bloody episode, a new jurisdictional rule is announced: "Then it was stated: The king may neither judge nor be judged, testify nor be testified against."

According to the Bavli, the Mishnah's secondary rule, then, originates as a response to an ugly encounter between King Jannaeus and the sages. To avoid future confrontations, it was decided that non-Davidic kings[119] may not be judged, and, evidently should be distanced from the judiciary altogether.[120] Nevertheless, Davidic kings, who are not defiant, continue to be regulated by the primary rule authorizing a king to judge and be judged.

In his "Folktales of Justice," Robert Cover underscores the formative role the trial narrative plays in this Bavli passage.[121] While the Mishnah records perhaps the only pragmatically viable setup (the alternate secondary model), the Bavli makes it clear that Simeon courageously pushed for a different kind of solution (the ideal primary model). In Cover's words "the gesture of courage is conjoined with pragmatic concession" in the Bavli, and "still the gesture of courage is the aspiration." The Talmudic myth inspires us to transcend power, and specifically here, emboldens judges to "speak truth to power" and not elect for "prudential deference . . . the great temptation, and the final sin of judging."[122] In a fuller sense, building upon Cover's reading, the Bavli conveys the aspirational value of the ideal model wherein the king judges and is judged.[123] The juridical vision of the Bavli thus integrates the various branches of leadership.[124]

Like Cover, later interpreters of the Mishnah tend to read the mishnaic text through the lens of the Bavli. They interpret the Mishnah as presenting a secondary rule that applies only to non-Davidic kings.[125] According to this understanding, the ideal model—that is, the integrated scheme of the Bavli—remains the preferred juridical scheme; which is, of course, contrary to the plain sense of Mishnah Sanhedrin.

The Bavli in Context

By marginalizing the Mishnah's scheme (i.e., relegating it to a secondary rule) the Bavli succeeds in harmonizing (to some extent) rabbinic tradition with widespread biblical and contemporary notions about a king's judicial role. In other words, one can map both the Mishnah and the Bavli's revision against the pivotal biblical tension encountered in the previous chapters. The Mishnah, as well as other postbiblical writings analyzed in the first part of this book, elaborate upon the Deuteronomic tradition that separates kingship from the judiciary; the Bavli resists this anomalous position and partially restores the regnant form of judicial administration (while also mandating that the king submit to the court's jurisdiction).[126]

Similarly, the Yerushalmi overtly challenges the Mishnah's dictum: "'[The king] can neither judge'—Has it not been written: 'And David administered justice and equity to all his people (2 Sam 8:15)' and yet you say so [that the king cannot judge]?!" Unlike the Bavli, the Yerushalmi does not revise the mishnaic teaching, but instead countermands it on the basis of clear biblical precedent, which establishes that a king can surely judge.[127] While presumably neither Talmud endorses an absolutist model where the king commands all legal affairs,[128] they each call for an integrative model where the king can serve as a judge on the court.

There are, in fact, multiple antecedents to the Talmudic approach in early rabbinic literature, and some even inch closer to an absolutist model:

MISHNAH SANHEDRIN: If the principal arrangement of Mishnah Sanhedrin separates the monarchy and judiciary, a secondary voice within the same mishnaic chapter erases this division.[129] Emphasizing the comprehensive scope of the imperative that the king must always carry his Torah scroll with him (based on Deut 17:18–19), the Mishnah specifies various royal activities where this duty is incumbent (*m. Sanh.* 2:4): "And he shall write in his own name a Torah scroll. When he goes forth to war he must take it with him. . . . *When he sits in judgment it shall be with him.* . . . As it is written, 'It shall remain with him and he shall read in it the days of his life' (Deut 17:19)" (emphasis added). Presiding in judgment is here enumerated as a prototypical royal function, which evidently conflicts with the rule of *m. Sanh* 2:2.[130]

TOSEFTA SANHEDRIN: Recall the Tosefta material surveyed in the first section that points to the king's potential involvement in the judicial process, which is at variance with the Mishnah's separation between the crown and the courts. *T. Sanh.* 2:15 only precludes the king from serving on the intercalation court and Sanhedrin, but implies that he can adjudicate in other settings.[131] *T. Sanh.* 4:4 may even envision the king serving as a leading judicial authority. These Tosefta passages suggest that the king has a judicial role, at least in some capacity (and also that he is judged, as discussed above).

SIFRE ZUTA/*BARAITA*: Another tannaitic source explicitly identifies the king as a judge. Interpreting the scriptural terms "elders" and "judges" (in Deut 21:2), a rabbinic teaching renders them as follows:[132] "R. Eliezer b. Jacob said: 'your elders' refers to the Sanhedrin, 'and your judges' refers to the king and high priest."[133] Although the underlying biblical verse has a particular context (i.e., leaders conducting an expiation ritual upon the discovery of an unidentified cadaver), the general formulation of this source suggests a broader application. Enumerating the king alongside the supreme court and high priest, this tradition portrays them as three leading judicial bodies, perhaps with each one exercising discrete authority. This source plainly diverges from the Mishnah's principal scheme in which only the courts and high priest exercise judicial power.[134]

MEKHILTA RABBI ISHMAEL: Certain aggadic passages depict a juridical scheme where the king's authority is paramount.[135] A vivid example is a Mekhilta passage that describes Moses's judicial role (see Exod 18) in royalist terms. When Jethro observed Moses administering justice, the Mekhilta elaborates upon what he saw:[136] "'And when Moses's father in law [Jethro] saw ... (Exod 18:14)'—What did he see? He saw that he [Moses] was as a king, sitting on his throne, and all stand before him. He said: 'What is this that you do to the nation, why do you preside alone (ibid.)?'"[137] The midrashic Moses acts as a king when he dispenses justice, which should be contrasted with another rabbinic tradition that describes Moses as a proxy for the court of seventy-one.[138] Encapsulated in this latter tradition is a very different notion of judicial authority being entrusted to an autonomous legal institution. Consonant with the main juridical scheme of the Mishnah (i.e., the plain sense of *m. Sanh.* 2:1–3), this institutional model will be evaluated in Chapter 6.

In the Ancient Near East, the king is the lawgiver and its final arbiter. Throughout much of the Bible, the king administers justice. The Roman emperor overshadows the legal system. Likewise, certain salient rabbinic texts summarized in the latter section endorse (all, or aspects of) the construct of a royal judiciary. Yet, in marked contrast, the plain sense of the Mishnah analyzed in the first section assigns legal authority to an independent judiciary and distances the king from the legal process.

While the Mishnah echoes other postbiblical texts analyzed in previous chapters that expand upon the anomalous biblical strand of Deuteronomy by locating justice outside of the royal precinct, it also recalibrates the Deuteronomic scheme in important ways. Unlike Deuteronomy (and the expansions of the Temple Scroll and Josephus), which situates the king beneath the priests and other judicial officials, the Mishnah refuses to demote the king. Instead, the Mishnah envisions a king who is granted singular autonomy to lead, without being constricted by the broad reach of the judiciary. The king cannot judge, but in certain respects the court cannot govern either.[139]

Accordingly, the slogan of the Mishnah—the king may neither judge nor be judged—is a reciprocal statement that not only divides between kingship and the courts, but gestures at a more sweeping separation between the spheres of politics and law. The rationale behind this partition may be better understood in light of the historical context. Living under Roman rule after the failed Jewish revolts of 66–70 and 132–135 CE, the rabbis were stripped of political authority, and mostly invested their energies in developing their own legal system, and preserving its integrity and autonomy. Nevertheless, in confronting imperial success, they may have selectively assimilated certain political ideas from the Romans.[140] Accordingly, the rabbinic conception of kingship assumes certain trappings of Roman power, a point Azzan Yadin emphasized in analyzing *m. Sanh.* 2.[141] Reflecting on power from their distinctive perspective, however, the rabbis likely filtered this conception to conform with their broader normative commitments.[142] Their vision of the ideal Jewish leadership scheme (as recorded in the Mishnah), therefore, erects a barrier between the king and the judiciary, thereby affirming the king's sovereignty and protecting the independence of the court.[143]

As seen in the second section, the Mishnah's firm separation is not sanctioned by other early rabbinic texts, and engenders direct resistance in later Talmudic glosses. Corresponding to varying degrees with the dominant biblical template, these passages uphold forms of royal justice. While certain of them place the king at the head of the judiciary (*Mekh.*, arguably *t. Sanh.* 4:4, and perhaps *y. Sanh.* 2:3), others refer to a distinct judicial role for the king (*m. Sanh.* 2:4), or place the king alongside other officials, or within, a larger tribunal (*t. Sanh.* 2:15 and the Sifre Zuta / *baraita*). Just as noteworthy is the Bavli, which transforms the Mishnah's teaching through a revisionist interpretation that reinserts the king into the judicial forum according to its ideal scheme. These latter texts (the Bavli, *t. Sanh.* 2:15, and the Sifre Zuta / *baraita*) adhere to the Mishnah's scheme in one respect—by affirming the notion of "institutional justice" (see Chapter 6)—but clearly differ in also assuming that there is a prominent role for a king within the legal institution. All of the rabbinic sources cited in the second section thus advance alternative viewpoints that are at odds with the Mishnah's original position. Throughout these latter sources, then, one can discern a phenomenon that will resurface in various forms in Chapter 7: the merging of power and justice, or at least the inability to keep rulers out of, and away from, the judiciary. Surely, a strong drive animates the powerful to monopolize justice. It is precisely this impulse that the dominant model of rabbinic jurisprudence aims to resist, as will be seen in Chapter 6.

6

Juridical Models
in Tannaitic Literature

Chapter 5 analyzed a leading strand in early rabbinic literature that locates judicial authority outside of the monarchy. Recognizing the partition erected between royalty and legal authority provides an essential
backdrop for understanding rabbinic jurisprudence, but offers little in
the way of expounding its conception of legal administration. Having
established the king's lack of jurisdiction, this chapter aims to provide a
positive account of legal authority, as reflected in early rabbinic literature. It will explore several fundamental questions about rabbinic jurisprudence, including: Who controls judicial authority in the rabbinic
worldview? How is justice to be administered according to rabbinic ideology or ideologies? What are the juridical and theological values advanced by these constructs?[1]

At first blush, the answers to these questions seem straightforward.[2]
An entire mishnaic tractate is devoted to describing the Sanhedrin and
lower courts, delineating the various tiers of judicial tribunals, the distribution of subject matter jurisdiction among these tiers, the precise
number of judges in each tribunal, and their requisite qualifications and
disqualifications. Other mishnayot provide rich details about court procedures, including the protocols for announcing verdicts and administering
punishments. Even the precise venue of the Sanhedrin is specified.

Such a summary account, however, obscures the revolutionary dimension of a rabbinic jurisprudence that elevates the Sanhedrin atop the judiciary, in lieu of alternate schemes that leave traces in this corpus. While the most renowned rabbinic scheme revolves around the Sanhedrin and lower courts (this model will be labeled "institutional justice" throughout this chapter), other secondary models abound. For instance, a number of rabbinic texts encountered in the latter section of Chapter 5 affirm a construct of royal justice. Likewise, a survey of rabbinic literature reveals other modes of organizing justice, including arrangements led by priests and individual sages. Just as the prominence of the legal sphere in Qumran precipitated a swelling interest in the nature and modes of judicial administration, this topic also receives ample attention, and differentiated treatment, throughout rabbinic literature. Simply asserting the role of the Sanhedrin without registering the plurality of judicial models does not accurately capture the varieties of rabbinic jurisprudence.

Moreover, the fuller significance of institutional justice emerges from the bold manner in which it promotes a distinctive form of judicial leadership that supplants other alternatives, in part by directly challenging the basic premises underlying their notions of legal authority. Understood in this vein, institutional justice emerges as a counter construct to the schemes of royal, priestly, and individual justice. The fact that institutional justice constitutes the primary judicial model within rabbinic jurisprudence—as is evident in the elaborate portrayals of this scheme, as well as the dearth of criticism leveled against it—means that it is embraced by rabbinic sages in place of other well-known alternatives. Thus, unlike Qumran writings which propagate a number of judicial arrangements, rabbinic literature mounts significant opposition to each alternative scheme, and simultaneously privileges one model—institutional justice—over and against the others.[3]

Evaluated alongside these other juridical models, another crucial feature of institutional justice becomes evident. The alternative schemes are all extensions of older judicial arrangements. For instance, ample biblical, Second Temple, and classical literature affirms the leading role of the king as a legal authority. Promoting the king as the chief judge, then, grows organically out of early Jewish traditions. In contrast, the notion of institutional justice is mostly alien to pre- and extra-rabbinic legal traditions. When rabbinic sources anchor the legacy of the Sanhedrin in biblical materials, they largely override the plain sense of these texts. Accordingly, the notion of institutional justice constitutes an innovation of rabbinic jurisprudence. While rabbinic accounts of other forms of judicial administration can be mostly attributed to the vestiges of earlier systems, their portrayal of institutional justice should be understood as deliberate and purposeful. By espousing this model beyond more conventional schemes, rabbinic literature offers a meaningful polemic against earlier models.

This chapter will survey various models of justice that one can discern in early rabbinic literature, culminating in an analysis of institutional justice. The first section will examine a few representative rabbinic texts that exemplify royal, individual, and priestly justice. Each one of these schemes also elicits an opposing reaction within rabbinic literature. Accordingly, the next section proceeds to evaluate the formidable criticism lodged against royal and individual justice, and the more layered response to the model of priestly justice. Amplifying these counter voices underscores a more sweeping rejection of these familiar schemes within rabbinic literature, which paves the way for a new juridical construct that overcomes the deficiencies of these other schemes and becomes the preferred rabbinic model.

The third section analyzes the dominant model of institutional justice led by the Sanhedrin. Evaluating the jurisdiction of the Sanhedrin and the subsidiary tribunals refers here, not to the thorny question of the historicity of the rabbinic court system, but instead to the ideal of institutional justice, wherein a permanent, independent institution of rabbinic sages serves as the ultimate legal authority.[4] This section demonstrates how a novel rabbinic exegesis mapped this model onto biblical verses, reorienting them away from powerful, individual, or cultic leaders, and toward a permanent, centralized, and plural institution of justice. After reviewing this hermeneutic breakthrough, the remainder of this section surveys a selection of texts that depict the institutional design of rabbinic justice; despite noteworthy differences, these texts share a common juridical template. What emerges from them is a distinctive model that becomes the mainstay of rabbinic jurisprudence. The conclusion of this chapter will explore the reasons for this preference.

A prefatory note about the methodology of this chapter is in order. Throughout, I employ a taxonomy of several models to analyze rabbinic representations of the administration of justice. Although these classifications are not native to rabbinic literature, they function as a heuristic device (along the lines of the Weberian typology of legal systems)[5] that helps conceptualize and articulate distinct juridical trends within this corpus. Still, several caveats are worth delineating at the outset. The underlying rabbinic material is not entirely consistent, and does not always adhere to coherent divisions. Likewise, certain rabbinic texts illustrate more than one tendency, and could be analyzed from various vantage points. The broader distinction among these categories is not absolute, and several of them converge in certain respects. Ultimately, the ascendant model of institutional justice does not entirely efface the other alternatives. Finally, this chapter employs (as does Chapter 7) developmental language advisedly in describing the ascendancy (and unfolding) of institutional justice. One can discern a conceptual progression, or an arc of development (or adaptation), among the schematic materials, but this does not necessarily map onto a diachronic timeline.

Most of the rabbinic statements analyzed below do not reflect legal structures that were fully operative in rabbinic society. When these texts were authored or redacted in late antiquity, rabbis had little authority to implement these ambitious juridical visions, as their jurisdiction was under considerable limits imposed by Roman rule. In a certain sense, though, it is precisely their confined circumstances that inspired rabbis to freely imagine how to construct legal power (see Chapter 8). Some of the models they envisioned elaborated on schemes that operated in elemental form in rabbinic society, and others obviously varied from, and responded to, the legal realities of late antiquity.[6] Either way, the abundant energy these rabbis invested in this conceptual enterprise demonstrates the importance of legal order for their ideology. That their writings tended toward one typology of administering justice in particular—institutional justice—is especially noteworthy, and forms the central thesis of this chapter.

Alternative Models of Judicial Administration

The contours of several ancillary models of judicial administration can be discerned within rabbinic literature, especially the Mishnah.[7]

Royal Justice

One alternative model was already analyzed in Chapter 5. After describing the dominant mishnaic position, which separates the king from the judiciary, the latter section evaluated a secondary stance that affords the king judicial responsibility. For instance, R. Eliezer b. Jacob interprets Deut 21:2's words "and your judges" as (also) referring to the king. Other rabbinic sources discussed above likewise envision a significant judicial role for the king, albeit in various guises. These passages portray the king as a leading judge, as a participant in the judiciary, or as a co-equal judicial authority. In all of these capacities, the sovereign joins political clout with judicial authority, and figures prominently within the legal system.

Individual Justice

Another juridical model attested to in rabbinic literature attributes judicial authority to the charismatic leadership of individual sages, often operating locally and outside of a formal framework. In fact, H. P. Chajes, in a classic study of the judicial process in rabbinic literature, demonstrated that rabbinic *ma'asiyot* (anecdotes of legal cases) do not tend to describe the operation of permanent courts.[8] Instead, most rulings are issued extemporaneously by individual rabbis who command varying degrees of legal authority.[9] According to Chajes, this indicates that during the rabbinic period there were no established rabbinic courts.

While little noticed at the time,[10] Chajes's thesis is now widely accepted among scholars, who have adduced additional evidence on its behalf and elaborated upon its implications.[11] His insight makes a great deal of sense given the sociopolitical reality within Roman Palaestina during the rabbinic period, when Romans presumably prevented Jews from establishing an autonomous judicial system.[12] From a juridical perspective, his thesis attests to the prominence of individual justice (as well as informal and local justice) within rabbinic literature.[13]

Certain prescriptive statements have a similar implication. *M. B. Bat.* 10:8 offers a prime example: "R. Ishmael said: He that would become wise let him occupy himself with monetary laws . . . and he that would occupy himself in monetary laws, let him serve [as the pupil of] Simeon b. Nanos." Tutelage under a single sage provides the best legal training.

Other rabbinic texts, likewise, authorize individual judges. A sequence of passages in tractate Bekhorot describes a lone sage's capacity to determine the halakhic status of a firstborn animal. *M. Bek.* 4:4 expands this authority to other legal subject matters (the Mishnah also addresses the question of liability for an erroneous ruling): "If [a layperson] gave a legal decision, declaring the guilty exempt or declaring the innocent culpable, or declaring the clean unclean or declaring the unclean clean, what he has done cannot be undone, but he must compensate [the wronged litigant] from his own means. But if an [authorized] expert approved by the court [erred], he is exempt from having to make restitution." While differentiating between an expert and lay judge in terms of liability for an erroneous ruling, the Mishnah explicitly identifies the decisor as a sole figure.[14] Similarly, *b. Sanh.* 5a cites an ostensibly earlier source[15] to establish that a reputable expert (a *mumheh lerabim*) can adjudicate civil (i.e., monetary) disputes alone.[16] Likewise, *t. Sanh.* 1:1 establishes that a single judge can arbitrate (*bitsua*) civil disputes.[17] Other rabbinic passages similarly confirm the tradition that a single person may render verdicts or issue rulings.[18]

Priestly Justice

A third judicial scheme portrayed in various early rabbinic sources involves Levites, priests, and the high priest (this model will be labeled "priestly justice"). While rabbinic literature contains several perspectives on the relationship between the priesthood and the judiciary, a selection of sources plainly affirm the leading judicial role of priests.[19] Certain passages, in fact, describe the independent standing of priests as adjudicators, and even the jurisdiction of an autonomous priestly court.

An emphatic rabbinic teaching, which proclaims the exclusive legal role of the Levites and priests, elaborates on Moses's valedictory blessing to Levi (*Sifre Deut.* 351):

> "They [the Levites] shall teach Jacob thine ordinances (Deut 33:10)." *This shows that all instructions [horayot] must issue from their mouths alone,* as it is said, "And according to their word shall every dispute and every stroke be (Deut 21:5)," "dispute" refers to any disputes concerning the (red) heifer, the broken-necked heifer, and the woman suspected of adultery, "stroke" refers to plagues affecting both men and houses. (emphasis added)

Appealing to two Deuteronomy verses (21:5 and 33:10), and five biblical legal rituals (the red heifer, the broken-necked heifer, the woman suspected of adultery, and leprosy of men and houses), the Sifre offers a panoply of sources establishing the legal supremacy of Levites and priests. More, the Sifre induces from these instances that the Levites and priests monopolize legal authority—"*This shows that all instructions [horayot] must issue from their mouths alone.*"[20]

Likewise, the jurisdiction of the priests is affirmed in tractate Horayot.[21] *M. Hor.* 2:1–2 addresses an erroneous ruling by the (anointed) high priest, which obligates him to bring an atonement sacrifice:[22] "An anointed high priest who made a decision for himself. . . . If [he] gave [an erroneous] decision alone and acted [accordingly] alone, he makes his atonement alone. If he gave his ruling together with [the court of] the congregation and acted accordingly together with the congregation, he makes his atonement together with the congregation." The first scenario involves a high priest who rules alone,[23] reflecting his judicial autonomy vis-à-vis the court (*m. Hor.* 2:1 concludes: "for the ruling of the priest to himself is equivalent to the verdict of the court").

Elsewhere, rabbinic sources refer to what appears to be an autonomous judicial body called the "court of priests."[24] For example, *m. Ketub.* 1:5 states that this tribunal would increase the financial commitment of a man who marries a virgin: "The court of the Priests used to levy 400 *zuz* for a virgin."[25] Other sources containing explicit or more oblique references to the judicial role of priests have been collected by scholars.[26]

In sum, all three models (royal, individual, and priestly justice) are reflected in rabbinic literature. Significantly, these models correspond to juristic schemes that were prevalent throughout the biblical and Second Temple periods, as well as in Roman legal practice. In the Bible, a king (e.g., David) or leader (e.g., Moses) exercises judicial authority. Likewise, various biblical sources indicate the leading judicial role of priests (both in theory and in practice). Numerous Second Temple texts portray the king administering the law, describe individual sages resolving legal matters, and proclaim the jurisdiction of the high priest and priesthood. Finally, Roman law authorizes a single *iudex* (magistrate) to preside over legal procedures, installs a praetor to oversee legal affairs, and operates under the emperor's command of the entire legal enterprise. Both antecedent and parallel legal systems, accordingly, invest judicial authority in a leader, a lone figure, or the priestly caste.[27] Assimilating earlier or contemporary juridical constructs, rabbinic jurisprudence likewise recognizes these models.[28]

While the preservation of these models derives from a conservative aspect of rabbinic jurisprudence, the manner in which they are challenged, and eclipsed, proceeds from its revolutionary thrust. The next section examines the explicit rabbinic critique of royal and individual justice recorded in later rabbinic literature (which expresses notions that seem to inhere in the juridical preferences of the earlier strata), and then the more subtle, but unmistakable, reworking of priestly justice. Ultimately, this cumulative opposition clears the ground for constructing the novel juridical template of institutional justice.

Criticism of Alternative Models

Royal Justice Opposed

As argued in Chapter 5, rabbinic opposition to royal justice underpins the administrative scheme of Mishnah Sanhedrin chapter 2, even if it is not overtly stated. Later rabbinic writings are more candid about challenging this juridical scheme. A pair of Talmudic texts express outright distrust of royal power intervening in the administration of justice. Elaborating on a single tannaitic teaching, the Yerushalmi openly challenges the place of the king in the judicial process, while the Bavli, in a subtle and original hermeneutic that requires some unpacking, offers an even more daring assault on royalty.[29]

Both Talmuds are elaborating upon the Tosefta ruling (*t. Sanh.* 2:15) cited in Chapter 5 that prohibits the king from joining the Sanhedrin. The Yerushalmi (*y. Sanh.* 2:1) adds a rationale: "A king may not preside with the Sanhedrin—out of suspicion [*mipne he-hashad*]."[30] Presumably, the Yerushalmi refers to the risk that a powerful king will obstruct the impartial operation of the court.

A parallel Bavli passage (*b. Sanh.* 18b) likewise explains the Tosefta's exclusion of the king from the Sanhedrin, but formulates the idea differently, with the aid of Scripture: "A king may not preside with the Sanhedrin—because it is written, 'Do not speak [*lo taaneh*] in a legal dispute [*rib*] (Exod 23:2),' [meaning], Do not speak against the master of the judges [*rab*]." In order to appreciate the novelty of this exegesis, and its resistance to the specter of royal power invading the court, it is necessary to briefly digress and consider the evolution of the rabbinic hermeneutics on this verse.

Exod 23:2 reads: "Do not side with the multitude to do wrong; do not speak in a dispute [*lo taaneh al rib*] so as to pervert it in favor of the multitude [*lintot akhare rabim lehatot*]." The latter clause prohibits the fabrication of testimony to support the false position of a majority of judges (or something to that effect).[31] Rabbinic traditions, however, tease out from its several clauses various rules regulating lawful trials.

Thus, the primary tannaitic interpretation derives the principle of majority rule in capital trials from this verse.[32] A secondary exegetical teaching (*t. Sanh.* 3:8) understands the verse in an alternate manner that pertains to the relationship between authority and justice: "Another teaching, *lo taaneh al rib lintot akhare rabbim lehatot* (Exod 23:2), do not state at the moment of the verdict, it is sufficient that I will appear like (i.e., I will follow the opinion of) my master [*rebbe*], rather say what your own opinion is." Interpreting the word "*rabim*" [multitude] as the plural form of the word "*rab*" [a master with legal authority], the Tosefta alters the meaning of this verse. Enjoining the less experienced judge not to mimic ("*lintot*," lit. to lean after) the judicial ruling of his master, the Tosefta expresses a concern, amplified in the later Bavli, that the hierarchy among the judges will distort the independent judgment of each judge, and thereby undermine the integrity of justice.

In the early amoraic period, this same verse[33] is likewise understood as addressing the relationship between the ruling of a superior and an inferior judge, but this hermeneutic arises out of a different concern. Rather than safeguarding the independence of the lesser judge, the Yerushalmi reads this verse as protecting the dignity of the more eminent one. The launching point for the amoraic discussion is the first clause of *m. Sanh.* 4:2: "In civil suits and in cases of cleanness and uncleanness, we begin with [the opinion of] the *gadol* [most eminent of the judges]; whereas in capital cases, we commence with those on the side [benches]." Both Talmudim base the protocol that judges announce their legal opinions in a set order on an exegesis of Exod 23:2.[34] The Yerushalmi records a debate revolving around this verse: "Rabbi says, 'Do not speak in a *rib* [legal dispute] (Exod 23:2)'—It is written '*rab* [master]': One should not speak after the master but before him. R. Yose b. Haninah said . . . one should not speak before the master but only after him."[35] Referring to the order in which judges announce their verdicts in non-capital matters,[36] the two views debate whether the master judge must speak first (as stated in the Mishnah) or last. Both alternatives are apparently ways of conferring honor upon him.[37]

Returning to the Bavli, it likewise construes this verse as an injunction against contradicting the judicial opinion of the master—which in this context refers to the king, were he to join the Sanhedrin.[38] But here the Bavli switches gears, and reaches a startling conclusion as a result.[39] Sharing the Tosefta's concern that the subordinate judge will not speak freely before a royal superior propels the Bavli to expel the king from the supreme court.[40]

In sum, several rabbinic interpretations of Exod 23:2 address the role of a powerful judge (whether he is a master sage or royalty), with significantly different emphases worth noting. While the earlier sources seek to preserve the autonomy of the inferior judges in the presence of the master judge (the Tosefta), or compel respect for the latter figure (the Yerushalmi), the Bavli radically transforms this exegetical motif by invoking it to expel the king from the Sanhedrin. By endorsing this exclusionary principle, rather than adopting a softer rule that would prescribe that the king must speak last as the final arbiter, the Talmud betrays a deep distrust of muscular judges.[41] A similar, if unspoken, distrust seems to pervade much of rabbinic jurisprudence, which endorses institutional justice over the powerful rule of a royal judge.

Individual Justice Opposed

Implicit in the rabbinic opposition to royal justice is a broader skepticism about single, powerful judges. Other rabbinic sources challenge the model of individual justice directly. Despite the clear authorization for an individual judge recorded in the rabbinic citations above, each source is debated, qualified, or revised in subsequent rabbinic literature.[42] A later Talmudic analysis (*b. Sanh.* 6a; see also *y. Sanh.* 1:1 below) of the jurisdiction of a single judge described in *m. Bek.* 4:4 severely limits its application.[43] Seeking to harmonize this Mishnah with a teaching of R. Abahu that defines the minimal judicial quorum as three judges, the Bavli qualifies the scope of the former: "Here [*m. Bek.* 4:4] we are dealing with a case where the parties accepted the judge. If so, why make him pay indemnity [if he errs]?—Because they had said to him: We agree to abide by your award on condition that you give a decision in accordance with the Torah." In other words, a single judge may adjudicate only if the litigants have explicitly agreed to heed his decision (just as they may agree to be bound by the ruling of a relative or three herdsmen).[44] As a reading of the Mishnah, this is surely forced (this is particularly evident in the Talmud's being compelled to introduce a conditional stipulation in order to justify the indemnity rule). Advancing this reading, notwithstanding this strain, the Talmud evidently seeks to constrict individual justice.

In terms of the sanction of a single judge to adjudicate civil matters, a rabbinic source quoted above (*b. Sanh.* 5a) limits this allowance to a "reputable expert," while ordinarily three judges are required. Further, another Bavli passage explicitly precludes even a "reputable expert" from proclaiming the new lunar month. Elaborating upon the mishnaic ruling that "an individual is not authorized by himself [to make a proclamation]," *b. Ros. Has.* 25b adds: "There was no more universally recognized expert in Israel than Moses, and yet the Holy One, blessed be He, said to him, [Do not sanctify the month] until Aaron is with thee, as it is written. 'And the Lord said unto Moses and Aaron in the land of Egypt saying, This month is to you (Exod 12:1).'" This exegetical tradition about Moses not judging alone has parallels in other rabbinic teachings where single figures are depicted as presiding alongside a quorum or a legal council.[45]

Beyond these various qualifications, a significant voice in rabbinic ideology openly rails against individual justice. This stance reflects how essential a plurality of judges is for the emergent rabbinic jurisprudence of institutional justice (and dovetails with a broader phenomenon in which rabbinic discourse remaps aspects of the largely individualistic world of the sages onto an institutional ideal that is focused on the collective).[46] A survey of such sources reveals the high stakes of this polemic.[47]

M. Abot 4:8 employs overtly theological language:[48] "He [R. Ishmael] used to say: Judge not alone, for none may judge alone save One."[49] The act of judging alone is itself a form of spiritual effrontery.[50]

Underlying this spiritual concern may be a secondary apprehension about the risks of human error, corruption, or arrogance, which increase when a single judge presides. *T. B. Qam.* 8:14 likewise censures this mode of jurisprudence in stark terms, "R. Shimon Shezuri said: The household of my father was among the homeowners in the Galilee. Why was it [his property] destroyed? Because they adjudicated civil matters alone." Rhetorically charged, this passage expresses intense opposition to individual justice, depicting it as a grave sin that elicits divine wrath. Both sources are undoubtedly reacting to an actual contemporary practice.

The most extensive polemic surrounding individual justice—which builds upon *m. Abot* 4:8—is an elaborate Yerushalmi passage. Beginning with the apparent authorization of a single judge described in *m. Bek.* 4:4 (even as the judge is held liable under certain circumstances), *y. Sanh.* 1:1 (like *b. Sanh.* 6a, cited above) limits this Mishnah to a case where litigants have explicitly accepted the judge's lone decision. Yet the Yerushalmi differs from the Bavli in its remarkable explanation of the judge's financial liability: "He must nevertheless pay compensation, because he brazenly judged on his own. For we have learned, 'Judge not alone, for none may judge alone save One (*m. Abot* 4:8).'" Meaning, even though litigants can validate the ruling of a lone judge, the judge is still held liable for his error because he breached the requirement of presiding with a plurality of judges.[51] By invoking *m. Abot* 4:8 in this context, the Yerushalmi transforms it from an exhortation to a statutory regulation with legal consequences.

In the continuation, the Yerushalmi intensifies its polemic against individual justice by employing rhetoric that even surpasses Mishnah Abot. Humans should not judge alone, because even God does not judge alone: "Said R. Judah b. Pazzi, Even the Holy One, blessed be He, does not give a decision all by himself.... Said R. Yohanan, Under no circumstances does the Holy One do a thing in his world without consulting with the heavenly court.... Said R. Eleazar, Each passage in which it is stated, 'And the Lord,' means that at hand are He and His court." For a monotheistic tradition to project such a pluralistic image of divine justice is no simple matter[52] (and tellingly the following lines record an opinion that affirms the singular role of God at least in the execution of truthful verdicts).[53] That the tradition nevertheless insists upon God's being accompanied by a celestial assembly speaks to the importance of plural justice. Obviously, the crux of the opposition to individual justice here is not theological (since even God does not judge alone), but likely arises from a concern about the risks of allowing a single judge to preside.

The latter half of this lengthy Yerushalmi passage has two more sections. The first records a couple of cases where the validity of legal decisions made by single judges are contested or questioned. In response, the Yerushalmi upholds these verdicts by asserting that an expert may judge alone, as may a judge who is accepted by the litigants (their assent can even be implicitly inferred when they appear before a single judge).[54] The final section lists a number of rabbis who unabashedly judged alone, without any limitations or preconditions. In other words, one group of rabbis forcefully rejects individual justice; a second group embraces a general rule of plural justice, but recognizes circumstances when a lone judge can preside; and a third group proclaims the authority to judge alone.[55]

The main thrust of rabbinic jurisprudence, however, marginalizes individual justice, notwithstanding its scriptural and extra-rabbinic foundations. The dominant institutional scheme advanced in rabbinic literature thus relies upon a plurality of judges.[56] Presumably this collective structure aims to displace the widespread practice of judging alone.[57]

Responses to Priestly Justice

Relative to the frontal critiques of royal and individual justice, rabbinic texts do not openly contest priestly justice. Nevertheless, various sources seek to limit, amend, or override this template. These texts express a tacit, wide-ranging, criticism of, and challenge to, priestly justice, and can be subdivided into several kinds of responses.

CONTAINING PRIESTLY JUSTICE: After *m. Ketub.* 1:5 (cited above) registers a ruling of the priestly court, it concludes with the following gloss: "and the Sages did not reprove them." This exemplifies a first set of rabbinic responses to priestly justice, where the judicial decisions of priests are recorded along with the reaction (whether positive or negative)[58] of rabbinic sages to their verdicts.[59] For instance, *m. Roš. Haš.* 1:7 details the evidentiary standards that were accepted by the priests, but subsequently rejected by the rabbinic court: "R. Jose said: Once Tobiah the Physician saw the new moon in Jerusalem, together with his son and his freed slave; and the priests accepted him and his son but pronounced his freed slave ineligible. And when they came before the court they accepted him and his slave but declared his son ineligible." A couple of passages near the end of tractate Ketubbot present rabbinic debates about whether to affirm or overrule a legal decision reached by prominent priests. *M. Ketub.* 13:1 reads: "If a man went abroad and his wife claimed maintenance, Hanan says she must [only] take an oath at the conclusion. . . . But the sons of the high priests disputed with him. . . . R. Dosa b. Harkinas decided according to their opinion. R. Johanan b. Zakkai said: Hanan said well. . . ." The next Mishnah has a similar structure. In both sources, the legal opinion of the priests is assessed under the rubric of rabbinic law.[60] Other passages even expose priestly resistance to rabbinic rulings.[61]

INCORPORATING PRIESTLY JUSTICE: A second set of sources incorporates priestly justice into a broader juridical framework. Consider the structure of Horayot. This tractate, which affirms the high priest's legal authority, projects the rabbinic court as supreme. Only after establishing the court's principal role in Mishnah Horayot, chapter 1, does it discuss the priest's jurisdiction in relationship to this institution in chapter 2.[62] Contrast this with *Sifre Deut.* 351 (cited above), which relies solely on Levites and priests for legal instructions (*horayot*).

A similar hierarchy is evident in the redaction of *m. Sanh.* 2:1 (examined in Chapter 5). Read as a discrete unit—"The high priest may judge and be judged"—this source may suggest an independent priestly judicial role, similar to *m. Hor.* 2:1. Yet, as redacted within tractate Sanhedrin, the Mishnah's apparent intent is that the high priest will judge as a member of the tribunals described in the tractate's opening chapter.[63] Likewise, the Mishnah's teaching that the high priest is judged links up with a corollary teaching in *m. Sanh.* 1:5.[64]

The transfiguration of the legal role of priests from autonomous judicial authorities to fixtures within the rabbinic court system is more explicit in other rabbinic sources.[65] Commenting on Deut 17:8–9, "If a legal matter is baffling for you . . . then you shall go up to the place that the Lord your God will choose, where you shall immediately come to the Levitical priests," *Sifre Deut.* 153 states, "'where you shall come'—to include the Yavneh Court (i.e., a leading institutional court) . . . 'to the Levitical priests'—it is preferable [*mitsvah*] that the court include priests and Levites among its members." While the underlying verses assign jurisdiction to the Levitical priests, the Sifre directs the matter to the court, which ideally contains priests and Levites among its judges. Further, the Sifre concludes, the court is legitimately constituted even without their participation. Rabbinic exegesis thus substitutes the Levitical priests of Scripture with a rabbinic court, and converts them into potential members of the latter institution.[66]

A synoptic analysis of several related rabbinic texts reveals additional nuances in the mode of integrating the priests into the rabbinic court. After reiterating the Sifre's statement that it is preferable that the court include priests and Levite judges, Midrash Tannaim adds, "to teach that every Sanhedrin that has three divisions (i.e., priests, Levites, and Israelites) is praiseworthy." The threefold division evokes a somewhat similar setup envisioned by the Tosefta (describing the several courts that edit the Torah scroll which the king transcribes): "He (the king) writes a Torah scroll in his name . . . and its version is corrected in the court of the priests, the court of the Levites, and the court of Israelites who are eligible to marry priests" (*t. Sanh.* 4:7). Here, however, the tribal divisions form three discrete courts (including a priestly court). A parallel Yerushalmi source has a noticeably different formulation regarding the identity of the court: "and it [the king's Torah scroll] is corrected from the scroll that is in the Temple courtyard according to the court of seventy-one."

Gedalyahu Alon, who evaluated these sources as historical data, struggled to harmonize them with one another.[67] But it seems preferable to view these sources as variants of a judicial scheme that aim to incorporate priestly justice into the rabbinic court system. Certain rabbinic sources retain traces of discrete priestly and Levitical courts (Tosefta). But the wider trend absorbs priestly justice into a single rabbinic court, where an even threefold distribution within the court remains an optimal quota (Midrash Tannaim); or morphs into an ideal of cross-representation (of any size) from all three tribal groups (Sifre); or dissolves into an institution of anonymous members (Yerushalmi).

A last parallel text, *m. Sanh.* 4:1–2, is best understood in light of this conceptual approach as a final variant scheme. Discussing the heightened lineage qualifications that are requisite for a judge to serve on a capital court,[68] the Mishnah states: "All [of the family stocks] are qualified to try civil cases; but all are not qualified to try capital cases, but only *priests, Levites, and Israelites who are eligible to marry priests*" (emphasis added). The Mishnah thus invokes the same three groups as *t. Sanh.* 4:7 (including Israelites who are eligible to marry priests), but rather than segregating them into discrete tribunals, or even aiming for a quota, the Mishnah deems individuals from any of these three sectors as equally qualified to preside as a member of a capital court.[69]

APPROPRIATING PRIESTLY JUSTICE: A third and final current that can be detected in rabbinic sources relating (implicitly or explicitly) to the priesthood and the judiciary involves rabbinic sages and courts not just absorbing priestly judges or assuming their judicial role, but even appropriating clear-cut priestly responsibilities. Consider the supervision of the rituals enumerated in the resounding, pro-priestly *Sifre Deut.* 351 passage quoted in the previous section. All five rituals—the red heifer, the broken-necked heifer, the woman suspected of adultery, and leprosy of men and houses—are explicitly led by priests, according to Scripture (and the Sifre).[70] Yet it is particularly telling that other tannaitic sources list all five rituals as falling under the exclusive or joint jurisdiction of the leading institutional court.[71] Just as the priestly orientation of this Sifre is unmistakable, a contrary proclivity of other rabbinic writings—notwithstanding the biblical evidence—is equally pronounced.

Moreover, other texts also encroach on priestly jurisdiction by the kinds of matters they assign to the supervision of rabbinic sages and courts. For instance, the opening sequence of Mishnah Sanhedrin, which describes the various subject matters administered by the courts, refers to various Temple procedures. *M. Sanh.* 1:3 states that Temple valuations are conducted by tribunals of different sizes: "The assessment of consecrated objects for redemption purposes is made by three; valuations of movable property by three, according to R. Judah one of them must be a priest; in the case of real estate by ten including a priest, in the case of a person by the same number." Parenthetically, a decimal tribunal deviates from the other tribunal sizes listed in this mishnaic chapter, and likely derives from a separate mishnaic source listing quorums of ten.[72] As a redacted passage, however, it highlights the sweeping judicial vision advanced by the opening of tractate Sanhedrin, which even assigns priestly duties to the institutional courts. In a similar vein, *m. Sanh.* 1:5 declares, "they may not add to the [Temple] city or the courtyards save by the decision of the court of seventy-one." Augmenting the Temple city and courtyards of course has implications for the execution of cultic rituals.[73]

Several descriptive passages in tractate Sheqalim have a similar connotation. *M. Seqal.* 7:6–7 records seven decrees of the (rabbinic) court concerning the Temple (one is explicitly treated as an internal priestly matter elsewhere).[74] Although this source ostensibly details historical legislation,[75] the administrative hierarchy it depicts affirms the court's role in supervising Temple regulations.[76] Other early rabbinic sources likewise describe a rabbinic court administering what would seem to be priestly or Temple affairs.[77]

Another striking manifestation of the court directing Temple affairs is evident in tractate Yoma.[78] The Mishnah describes rabbinic judges instructing and training the high priest, and warning him to comply with cultic regulations. Although the biblical source for the special cultic rituals of the Day of Atonement refers exclusively to the high priest (see Leviticus 16), *m. Yoma* 1:3–5 privileges judicial elders with the primary responsibility of overseeing these sacred rites:[79]

They delivered to him [the high priest] some elders of the court,[80] who read to him concerning the ceremonial of the day, and say to him: "My lord the high-priest, say it aloud, lest thou hast forgotten, or not studied this." On the morning of the day preceding the Day of Atonement, he is placed at the eastern gate, and bulls, rams, and sheep are passed before him, that he should get a knowledge of the service.

In the Mishnah's rendition, the court elders first mentor the high priest, and only afterward transfer him to the care of the priestly elders. The Mishnah's description of their parting words takes matters a step further:

The elders of the court transfered him to the attendance of the elders of the priesthood ... [they] made him swear, took farewell, and went away. They said to him: "My lord the high-priest, we are delegates of the court, and *thou art our delegate and the delegate of the court;* we conjure thee by Him who has made His abode in this house, that thou shalt not alter one thing about which we have spoken to thee." (emphasis added)

Projecting the court as the guardian of Temple laws and traditions, this passage astonishingly recasts the high priest as a proxy of the court, which essentially implies that it is the court that administers the Temple service. Other rabbinic passages about the Temple and its rituals may have a similar connotation, albeit in less dramatic terms.[81]

Perhaps the apex among the sources that assert the ascendancy of the court in Temple matters is *m. Sanh.* 11:2 (and its parallels). Locating the Sanhedrin and two secondary courts at various stations on the Temple Mount, the Mishnah describes the Sanhedrin as occupying the Chamber of Hewn Stone inside the Temple.[82] Citing Deut 17:9, which designates the Temple as the place where superior priestly rulings are issued, the Mishnah identifies this situs as the judicial headquarters of institutional justice. A similar sketch of rabbinic instruction being issued from the Chamber of Hewn Stone is recorded in *m. Pe'ah* 2:6.[83]

This rabbinic topography requires further interrogation in light of other rabbinic sources which indicate that the Chamber of Hewn Stone is a priestly chamber.[84] According to *m. Tamid* 2:5, after the priests concluded their preparatory work for the daily offering, they "came down and betook themselves to the Chamber of Hewn Stone." There, they cast the second of four lots in order to ascertain who would conduct the cultic services (*m. Tamid* 3:1). They proceeded to cast other lots there (*m. Tamid* chapters 3–4), and then entered and exited, returning "to the Chamber of Hewn Stone to recite the *Shema* (*m. Tamid* 4:4)," and other prayers (*m. Tamid* 5:1). Finally, they cast more lots there (*m. Tamid* 5:2), and the priests who were not selected disrobed from their Temple vestments (*m. Tamid* 5:3). In total, three lots, the prayers, and the changing of garbs all transpired in the Chamber of Hewn Stone, leading one scholar to rename it the "Chamber of the Priests."[85] Considered against this backdrop, the rabbinic tradition recorded in *m. Sanh.* 11:2 (and *m. Pe'ah* 2:6) apparently appropriates this space,[86] designating it as a supreme judicial chamber.[87] Moreover, the stunning conclusion of Mishnah Midot (5:4),[88] which likewise describes the Chamber of Hewn Stone as the venue of the high court, significantly expands the court's cultic role:

> "The Chamber of Hewn Stone"—there the Great Sanhedrin of Israel used to sit and judge the priesthood; and if any priest was found to be blemished he clothed himself in black and veiled himself in black and departed and went his way; and he in whom no blemish was found clothed himself in white and veiled himself in white, and went in and ministered with his brethren the priests.

The Sanhedrin emerges as the principal guardians of the Temple, qualifying (or disqualifying) the priests for Temple service.[89]

Overall, various sources describe the court as presiding in the Temple, managing Temple finances, regulating Temple practices, qualifying Temple officials, supervising the cultic head, and holding him accountable. Together, these sources constitute the conceptual culmination in a succession of responses that one can identify in early rabbinic literature.

Certain sources depict autonomous priestly judges. In response, one set of rabbinic texts express rabbinic evaluations of priestly justice; a second set incorporates the priests into a larger judicial framework, or relegates their participation in the judicial process to an optimal or optional choice; and a third set expands the jurisdiction of the (rabbinic) courts to encompass vital aspects of Temple and priestly affairs. Crossing from the former to the latter, one witnesses the prominence of priestly justice in certain rabbinic texts give way to its displacement or usurpation in other ones, especially those oriented toward institutional justice.

Institutional Justice

The above survey of royal, individual, and priestly justice documents the ample attestations of these well-established juridical schemes in rabbinic literature. At the same time, each one of these constructs confronts substantial pushback—whether by direct polemic, implicit opposition, or even subtle subversion—within this same corpus (sometimes in later strata). In the aggregate, the opposing materials point toward a different juridical scheme that overcomes the deficiencies of the three alternate models, or incorporates certain of their elements in a qualified manner.[90]

Institutional justice exemplifies such a juridical scheme. Undermining the power bases inherent in the constructs of royal, priestly, and individual justice, institutional justice limits or strips the judicial influence of these leaders. Instead of powerful, cultic, or charismatic individuals, institutional justice authorizes an autonomous panel of judges to head the legal system. Consider in this regard the account of the rabbinic judiciary in the opening chapters of Mishnah Sanhedrin. Tribunals are composed of multiple judges, and the size increases for higher ranking tribunals (see *m. Sanh.* 1:1–6), thereby repudiating the template of individual justice. Likewise, the tractate announces early on that the jurisdiction of the supreme tribunal extends to proceedings against a high priest—"the high priest may not be tried save [i.e., he is only tried] by the court of seventy-one" (*m. Sanh.* 1:5). Given that in much of pre-rabbinic literature the high priest was seen as the foremost judicial authority, holding him under the authority of the leading institutional court constitutes an assault on priestly justice. Finally, and most explicitly, Mishnah Sanhedrin eviscerates the paradigm of royal justice. In an astounding ruling (analyzed extensively in Chapter 5), *m. Sanh.* 2:2 declares, "A king may [not] judge." In all, Mishnah Sanhedrin advances a comprehensive vision of institutional justice in place of other alternative juridical schemes.

By promoting this model, rabbinic jurisprudence moves decisively in a new direction. In contrast with the alternate schemes, which carry forward various biblical and Second Temple judicial paradigms, institutional justice introduces a novel conception of rabbinic jurisprudence. Sharing loose analogs with the biblical elders (*zeqenim*) and assemblies (*edah*),[91] Second Temple and classical councils (*gerousia*), contemporary rabbinic circles,[92] and even the Roman Senate, the rabbinic notion of a Sanhedrin (a loan word from Greek)[93] or a *bet din* (likely a Hebraic form of a borrowed term)[94] is an original construct of *per curiam* justice that eclipses all these forerunners. Populated with anonymous sages of equivalent stature, the Sanhedrin (or, an alternately named, leading court) operates at the helm of the legal system, with secondary tribunals (sometimes dubbed "minor Sanhedrins") functioning underneath its watch. Invested with consummate jurisdiction, the Sanhedrin even acts as a kind of kritarchy. Notably, this robust juridical vision is advanced with scant biblical support, yet nowhere in rabbinic literature is the Sanhedrin's central role ever challenged.

To underscore the novelty of institutional justice, it is worth revisiting a couple of elementary biblical texts about the administration of justice, and observing how they are interpreted in rabbinic hermeneutics. Deuteronomy 16:18 states, "you shall appoint judges and officers throughout your tribes, in all your towns," requiring the installation of individual judges throughout the land of Israel. Yet in *Sifre Deut.* 144 this verse is understood in an institutional manner: "From where do we know that a court [*bet din*] is to be appointed for the whole of Israel? It is taught, 'you shall appoint Judges (Deut 16:18).'" The continuation of the Sifre (cited below) likewise refers to the establishment of institutional courts in each city and tribe of the land of Israel. Single judges are replaced in this rabbinic reading by judicial panels.

Moreover, an "institutional" orientation is manifest in the rabbinic interpretation of key verses from Deut 17:8–13.[95] ("If a legal matter is baffling for you ... then you shall immediately go up to the place that the Lord your God will choose, where you shall consult with the Levitical priests and the judge ... they shall announce to you the decision in the case. Carry out exactly the decision that they announce to you from the place that the Lord will choose.") While the legal authorities enumerated in Scripture are the priestly leaders and a leading judge,[96] various rabbinic sources (including several cited above) refer to a supreme tribunal or tribunals. Thus, *m. Sanh.* 11:2 renders these verses differently from their plain sense:[97]

> It is written "If a legal matter is baffling for you ... (Deut 17:8)."
> Three courts of law were there, one situated at the entrance to the Temple Mount, another at the entrance of the courtyard, and the third in the Chamber of Hewn Stones. They went to the court which is at the entrance to the Temple Mount ... [then to the courtyard ... then]. If not [yet answered], they all proceed to the Great Court of the Chamber of Hewn Stones whence instruction (Torah) issued to all Israel, for it is written "from the place that the Lord will choose." (Deut 17:10)

What stands out vividly in this description is the institutional architecture of justice. Canvassing the landscape of the Temple Mount, one encounters a triad of judicial tribunals, culminating in the pinnacle institution of the Sanhedrin.[98] Instead of priestly or individual justice, rabbinic interpretation erects an institutional edifice.

A similar hermeneutic tendency is manifest in rabbinic interpretations of the opening clause of these verses ("If a legal matter"). Rather than construing this as describing a legal difficulty of a local sage or disputants, rabbinic sources portray an institutional breakdown. According to one rabbinic exegesis, this verse refers to a local court's uncertainty about a legal tradition concerning a given issue (see *t. Sanh.* 7:1), whereas another interpretation depicts inner dissension among the members of a lower court, spawned by the recalcitrance of a "rebellious elder" (see *m. Sanh.* 11:2). Both readings tellingly assume that the basic juridical entity is an institutional court.

Likewise, an analogous phenomenon transpires in the rabbinic appeal to Exodus 18 / Deuteronomy 1 as a partial source for the opening sequence of Mishnah Sanhedrin (as expounded by *y. Sanh.* 1:4, *b. Sanh.* 17a).[99] The mishnaic judiciary arguably emulates the idea of a hierarchy and centralized structure evident in the Mosaic paradigm. Yet the Mishnah adapts the biblical arrangement in one vital respect. Calculating the minimal population of a city that can host an intermediate tribunal of twenty-three judges, the Mishnah cites an opinion that sets the bar at 230 people. It provides the following justification, "to correspond to the chiefs of ten,"[100] alluding to the final numerical category listed in Exod 18:25–26 / Deut 1:15–17 ("Moses chose capable men out of all Israel, and appointed them heads over the people—chiefs of thousands, hundred, fifties *and tens*"; emphasis added). While Scripture clearly refers to a network of individual judges,[101] the Mishnah converts this category into an institutional arrangement, where a tribunal of twenty-three judges presides over 230 people, at a ratio of 1 to 10. Similarly, the head of the judicial hierarchy in the rabbinic paradigm is not a single chieftain such as Moses, but instead the supreme institution of the Sanhedrin. To adopt the formulation of a Talmudic gloss on this Mishnah, "Moses acts as a proxy for the seventy-one [judges of the Sanhedrin]."[102]

Through such transformative readings, rabbinic exegesis replaces the priestly and individual judicial schemes of Scripture with an institutional construct which is the design of rabbinic jurisprudence. From a structural perspective, the institutional model differs profoundly from the alternate schemes, and in significant ways overcomes their inherent deficiencies. Rather than bowing to powerful rulers, justice is meted out autonomously; instead of leaning on charismatic sages, justice is widely diffused; in lieu of seeking priestly guidance, the law is rationally deliberated and decided. Institutional justice eclipses the other alternatives.

Rabbinic Sources on Institutional Justice

Analyzing several rabbinic depictions of institutional justice will further illuminate the distinctive nature of this template.[103] Despite the discrepancies among these accounts, which should be noted, they all share a common typology. Its essential features will be delineated following an overview of these sources.

As stated, *m. Sanh.* 1:1–6 depicts a hierarchical, centralized court system, composed of three tiers, each having original jurisdiction over different subject matters. The lowest tier courts of three judges have jurisdiction over civil disputes, as well as other subject matters. The middle tier courts of twenty-three judges have jurisdiction over capital cases.[104] The highest-tier supreme council of seventy-one (or seventy) judges (the exact figure is the subject of a tannaitic debate) presides over issues or figures of national import. The expansive responsibilities of the courts extend beyond legal matters to officiating at various rituals and cultic rites and managing certain "affairs of the state."[105]

A second source, *Sifre Deut.* 144, also describes a three-tiered system, but with a different structure:

> From where do we know that a court [*bet din*] is to be appointed for the whole of Israel? It is taught, "you shall appoint judges" (Deut 16:18).... And from where do we learn that a court is to be appointed for every city? It is taught, "judges in all your gates" (ibid.).... And from where do we learn that a court is to be appointed for every tribe? It is taught, "judges for your tribes" (ibid.).[106]

This threefold scheme envisions a court system that is divided not by size but by geographical terrain.[107] Developing the blueprint of Deut 16–17,[108] the Midrash's scheme incorporates local courts of justice into a central framework. While the source provides no explicit information about the jurisdiction of the respective courts, a plausible conjecture is that they are not differentiated according to subject matter. Instead, they likely form a hierarchy, wherein the higher courts have supervisory responsibility over lower ones.[109]

A third source, *M. Hor.* 1:5 (along with the fourth and fifth source),
focuses on instruction rather than judgment. It operates with an alternate arrangement composed of a Great Court (also called "the court")
and tribal courts, whose rulings are followed by the broader congregation or the respective members of a tribe:[110] "If the court gave a decision and all the congregation or a greater part of them acted at their
word.... If the court gave a decision, and seven tribes or the greater part
of them acted at their word.... If the court of one of the tribes gave a
decision, and that tribe acted at their word." The hierarchical scheme
depicted here partially corresponds to the Sifre which also speaks of
these two tiers, but has no obvious relationship to the structure delineated in the opening of tractate Sanhedrin. According to Horayot, the
court's responsibility is to provide authoritative instructions (*horayot*) to
the public, rather than to adjudicate legal disputes.[111]

A fourth source, *m. Sanh.* 11:2 (cited above)—which expands upon
Deuteronomy 17—focuses on a network of leading courts clustered on
the Temple Mount, which supports the basic municipal courts. Unresolved legal questions are presented to the Temple-area courts following
a set protocol. A dissenting municipal judge (literally and figuratively)
ascends the Temple Mount and consults with the court at the entrance
of the Temple Mount and, if necessary, the court at the entrance to the
courtyard, and ultimately the "Great Court" presiding in the Chamber
of Hewn Stone. So higher tiered tribunals are only consulted if lower
ones cannot resolve the matter (in contrast with the scheme in *m. Sanh.*
1:1–6, which describes the distinct original subject matter jurisdiction of
the courts in each tier).

M. Sanh. 11:2 thus presents an arresting image of revelation of the
law descending from the sacred mountain.[112] The courts perched at different elevations on the slope serve as guardians of religious traditions,
while the lead court at its pinnacle announces authoritative rulings. Torah
is "issued [*yotset*] to all Israel" (*m. Sanh.* 11:2) from the Temple Mount,
in fulfillment of Deut 17:10–11 ("Carry out exactly the decision that they

announce to you from the place that the Lord will choose, diligently observing everything they instruct you ...") and its echo in Isaiah 2:1–5 ("For instruction [Torah] shall come forth [*yetse*] from Zion, The word of the Lord from Jerusalem").[113] If *m. Hor.* 1:5 depicts a fallible court (mis) leading the populous,[114] *m. Sanh.* 11:2 (and the next source) presents a portrait of ironclad justice.

A parallel passage, *t. Sanh.* 7:1[115]—a fifth rabbinic source—partially harmonizes *m. Sanh.* 11:2 with *m. Sanh.* 1:1–6, by stating that the lead Temple court consists of seventy(-one) judges, while the other Temple courts are composed of (twenty-) three judges (depending on different recensions). In addition, the Tosefta arguably overlaps with *Sifre Deut.* 144 when it maintains that the municipal courts (of twenty-three judges) first attempt to resolve the matter locally, before turning to the superior Temple tribunals.

Beyond these specific insertions, the Tosefta recasts the image of justice encountered in the Mishnah:

> Said R. Yose, At first there were dissensions in Israel only in the court of seventy[116] in the Chamber of Hewn Stone in Jerusalem. And there were other courts of twenty-three in the various towns of the land of Israel, and there were [two] courts of (twenty-) three judges each in Jerusalem,[117] one on the Temple Mount, and one on the Rampart. [If] someone needed to know what the law is,[118] he would go to the court in his town. . . . If they had heard the law, they told him. If not, he and the most distinguished member of that court would come up to the court on the Temple Mount.[119] If they had heard the law, they told them. If not [they go] . . . to the court on the Rampart. . . . If not, these and those would go to the Great Court which was in the Chamber of Hewn Stone . . . even though it consists of seventy-one members, (it) may not fall below twenty-three. . . . And there they remained in session from the time of the daily offering. . . . On Sabbaths and on festivals they came only to the study house. . . . [If] a question was brought before them, if they had heard the

answer, they told them. If not, they stand for a vote. . . . From there did the law go forth and circulate in Israel. From the time that the disciples of Shammai and Hillel who had not served their masters so much as was necessary became numerous, dissensions became many in Israel.[120]

Describing the general mechanics of resolving a legal inquiry, the Tosefta offers a stunning portrait of a towering supreme court overseeing a highly integrated legal system.[121] Combining the quantitative and regional hierarchies encountered above, municipal courts function concentrically around the axis of the Temple courts.[122] Legal questions are submitted to the local, smaller courts, and if they remain unresolved, they are systematically transferred up the hierarchical ladder until they are settled. The law then spreads back down into every town, and all uncertainties are dispelled. In a similar vein, the continuation of the passage describes the procedure for promoting judges that also follows a strict rank and order.[123]

Most strikingly, the Tosefta describes the legal system as arriving at a uniform declaration of the law. To reach this result, the Tosefta privileges the supreme tribunal in a manner that surpasses all prior sources. Lower courts are limited to ruling according to ancient traditions that have been transmitted to them. Only the leading court can address matters of first impression. After an internal deliberation and vote, it announces a binding ruling, which is then widely disseminated.[124] The lead court's role is also educational. Therefore, it is not just the litigant who seeks clarification but a member of the lower court. Likewise, the lead court continues teaching, or instructing on Sabbath and holidays, even when it presumably does not address specific inquiries.[125]

Considered alongside one another, these five portraits of institutional justice arguably contain substantial differences: whether justice is organized by size or geography; and if the latter option, whether to plot the districts according to tribes, municipalities, or Temple zones; whether jurisdiction is assigned based upon the original subject matter or the difficulty of the issue at hand; whether the court's function is to adjudicate disputes, preserve traditions, offer instructions, teach, conduct rituals, or shoulder administrative responsibilities; whether the high court oversees the operation of the lower courts; whether it has unique authority to interpret, innovate, or even legislate; whether justice is inspired from above, or arises from below; and whether the high court speaks on behalf of God or the people. Notwithstanding these significant variations, all of these passages adopt the same institutional template of legal authority.

Several salient characteristics are markers of "institutional justice." Most obviously, a panel of judges presides collectively and shares legal authority.[126] The administration of justice is thereby widely diffused, epitomizing the internal mode of separating power described in the Introduction. Moreover, these judges enjoy full autonomy over legal affairs, operating independently of other officials or powerful figures. In addition, institutional justice has a permanent quality, rather than tending to legal disputes when they arise in an ad hoc manner. In certain versions, the institutional courts expand their role beyond adjudication to dispensing religious instruction, promoting justice, and overseeing certain public affairs.[127] Finally, institutional justice has a centripetal impulse. Eschewing a provincial approach to administering justice, this scheme envisions a wide network of courts operating around a judicial epicenter.[128]

In aggregate, then, these formative rabbinic texts introduce a distinctive model of legal authority. The fact that they adopt a common framework, which in many ways serves as a counterpoint to other alternatives, signals the import of this jurisprudential choice. A pioneering mode of administering justice thus becomes the preferred template of rabbinic jurisprudence.

Contextualizing Institutional Justice

The allure of institutional justice for the rabbis must also be understood in its sociopolitical context. In a recent survey of the rabbinic period, Seth Schwartz points out that a distinguishing characteristic of rabbinic stories about the past is that they think in institutional terms.[129]

He offers the specific example of rabbinic accounts of the Sanhedrin. Indeed, it is not just rabbinic stories but their juridical schemes that employ institutional terminology and conceptualization, in lieu of other alternatives of which the rabbis were well aware. The institutionalization of justice is a carefully wrought construct.

Elaborated over the second century CE when the rabbinic movement began to coalesce, institutional justice was designed to serve an important social role. Schwartz argues that institutionalization offered the rabbis "the strongest possible assertion of their own legitimacy."[130] The force of this argument comes into sharper relief when one considers the alternate templates. Royal and priestly justice would offer no foundation for rabbinic authority. Even individual justice would just validate the decisions of "a largely unintegrated, scattered group of sub-elite informal experts."[131] Institutional justice, by contrast, relies upon the integrity and pedigree of an institution, which endures in perpetuity. Moreover, it ostensibly advances, not an assertion of power, but a claim of its inherent legitimacy. By embracing this juridical construct, and committing to its underlying values, the rabbinic movement better secures its foundations.

This juridical arrangement also contributes to the inscription of other signature characteristics of rabbinic law. Laying the groundwork for a legal bureaucracy, institutional justice assigns judicial power not to outstanding individuals but to those who occupy influential offices (a kind of Weberian transformation)—in the rabbinic idiom, "Jephtah in his generation is like Samuel in his generation."[132] A related development is the formalization of judicial appointments, as well as the professionalization of the judiciary.[133] Likewise, this model erects a permanent judicial infrastructure that supports an elaborate normative edifice that sustains rabbinic society.[134] Moreover, this normative structure influences the nature of law. Rather than tailoring judicial decisions to particular circumstances, judges are called upon to articulate and implement general laws.[135] Finally, this paradigm's endorsement of the collective viewpoint over individual authority resonates with the preference in (at least certain strands of) rabbinic discourse for achieving broader consensus. Tannaitic teachings are frequently anonymous (implying widespread assent), and when debates arise among sages, the majority viewpoint often prevails.

Endorsing this juridical model also influences the political vision of the rabbis. Vesting legal authority in an independent entity encourages the expansion of the organs of justice. A sprawling institution can incorporate other judicial agencies (e.g., tribal courts, priestly judges, individual judges, reputable experts, and ad hoc courts), and assume additional responsibilities such as legislating, instructing, and directing public affairs. The blueprint of a grand judiciary anchors the rabbinic "state,"[136] and fortifies the contemporary rabbinic movement.

A final noteworthy dimension of institutional justice touches on tensions between law and power that have surfaced throughout this book. Inherently, this model aims to shelter justice from power, limiting its impact as an external pressure on the legal system, and as an internal force that erodes its operation. In this vein, institutional justice not only divides the judicial and political branches, but also tries to erase the accumulation of power from within the court. An egalitarian streak within the institutional template even aims to distribute legal authority uniformly among the members of the court through several mechanisms in order to achieve an internal dissemination of powers (see Chapter 7).

Yet the relationship between law and power in this scheme is manifestly more complex. Ironically, institutional justice creates hierarchies of a different sort by elevating certain tribunals within the judicial branch, thereby supplanting one power structure with another. Further, although institutional justice aims to curb the individual and consolidate the corporate entity, its sources remain inconsistent about the degree of parity that exists among the members of a judicial panel. Finally, beyond the internal dynamic of the judiciary remains the open question of the relationship between the judiciary and the political branch. As much as a fundamental rabbinic impulse aims to separate between these realms, the viability and desirability of this division remains contested throughout rabbinic discourse. Chapter 7 will elaborate on the egalitarian and hierarchical dimensions of institutional justice, and what they reveal about the fraught relationship between justice and power.

7

The *Nasi* and the Judiciary in Rabbinic Literature

A thread running through Part Two is the rabbinic aspiration to separate the administration of justice from sovereign rule, and even purge the courts from a concentration of power, thereby preserving the autonomous rule of law. Chapter 5 analyzed the dominant approach of the Mishnah that envisions the king as a political head but assigns broad jurisdiction to an independent body. Chapter 6 explored institutional justice, the primary juridical scheme of the Mishnah, led by the flagship institution of the Sanhedrin along with a network of subordinate courts. This template extends values discerned in Chapter 5 by consigning justice to a panel of (anonymous) judges, rather than to prominent individuals (i.e., a king, high priest, or a single sage). Distributing authority among members of the court further shields it from being overwhelmed by powerful forces. A corporate institution controls justice.

Yet certain depictions of the operation of institutional justice, examined below, arguably run counter to this design. A set of texts describes a hierarchy among court members, led by a chief judge (the *Nasi*). These texts distinguish gradations of authority within the court's internal structure. Another set defies the deliberate division between the ruler and the court by identifying the Patriarch (also titled *Nasi;* more on both uses below) as being in charge of judicial appointments. Controlling this external authority affords the political head substantial influence over the court.

The disjuncture between these texts and the ideal of institutional justice exposes a meaningful fault line. Careful spade work reveals earlier or alternate strata that fit better with the model of institutional justice. Conversely, certain hierarchical accounts reflect a material revision of an institutional arrangement that was relatively or completely nonhierarchical. Meanwhile, the notion of patriarchal appointments represents only one (arguably later) approach within rabbinic literature. So texts that rework the institutional template evidently represent subsequent phases (or secondary accounts) of rabbinic jurisprudence.

Focusing on these modified forms of institutional justice, however, is illuminating in its own right. The emergence of vertically inflected constructs serves as a critical addendum to the previous chapters. Pushing beyond the elemental administrative architecture of prior chapters, which neatly splits law from politics,[1] this chapter explores the unresolved tension between these realms that persists in rabbinic literature, which is increasingly manifest in the context of unfolding historical developments.[2] To paraphrase the words of a leading legal historian, the early rabbinic division between law and power is an imaginative construct that is "historically contingent and perpetually contested and renegotiated."[3] By charting the rabbinic discourse on legal and political authority, this chapter aims to uncover different ways this arrangement is contested and renegotiated.

One mode of renegotiation that transpires in the face of contesting political forces is to absorb a degree of political infiltration into the courts. The institutional scheme of the courts is thus restructured to accommodate a limited hierarchy or an external actor, as discussed in the first and second sections.[4] Another type of judicial response, explored in the final section, confronts the political threat head on. Thus, various Yerushalmi passages abandon the measured equilibrium of the separation of powers of *m. Sanh.* 2, and (at least threaten to) invoke penal sanctions in order to contain the absolutist leader. Ultimately, the clash between justice and political power even spawns a turn to the stronger version of early Jewish jurisprudence encountered previously in several Second Temple texts.

Before turning to the rabbinic passages below, one clarification is in order. Whereas the rabbinic texts surveyed in previous chapters mostly focus on the king as the political figurehead, the ones analyzed below involve a contemporary official (an actual or a theoretical figure) labeled the *Nasi* (this label came to be associated—through a murky process that is much disputed among scholars—with a prominent Jewish notable and local dynastic figure, who began to claim and accumulate a quasi-royal status at some point between 70 and 200 CE).[5] Nevertheless, a meaningful continuum links these leading figures within rabbinic ideology. In fact, various rabbinic texts (albeit from a slightly later period) portray the present-day leader as a scion of the Davidic dynasty, or even as a prefiguration of the messianic king.[6]

Yet if the political profile of the ruler is fairly stable in rabbinic literature, the ruler's role in the legal sphere is anything but constant.[7] Texts involving the *Nasi* inaugurate a noticeable change in the relationship between the political and legal domains. This transformation is due, in part, to a basic distinction between rabbinic references to the king and the *Nasi*. Whereas the label "king" appeals to an idyllic office from a rarefied past, the title "*Nasi*" is informed by contemporary dynamics (in the rabbinic mindset, there is an actual figurehead, at least from the time of Judah the Patriarch onward, who acts as the *Nasi*). This difference influences the position of the political leader within the legal sphere. In theory, the paradigmatic ruler can be kept apart from judicial affairs, but in reality the present-day leader intervenes in legal matters. The *Nasi* texts reflect this consequential fact.

Nevertheless, the legal role of the *Nasi*, as depicted in the texts below, is not simply reducible to any set of empirical facts that may have involved actual leaders interceding in legal affairs. Most of these texts are not descriptive in nature. Rather, they are programmatic accounts of institutional justice formulated in the crucible of changing historical circumstances. This chapter concludes the Part Two analysis of rabbinic jurisprudence by examining various ways it is revised in light of an evolving reality.

Nasi as Chief Judge: A Reappraisal

Even as early rabbinic jurisprudence mostly shields the judiciary from powerful influences, the inner hierarchy of the court or *yeshiva* (the academy or council),[8] as represented in several texts, surprisingly elevates a single figure within its ranks. Officiating at the head of the Sanhedrin is a chief justice, bearing the title *Nasi* (lit. exalted one). *T. Sanh.* 8:1 describes the seating arrangement of the Sanhedrin surrounding the *Nasi:* "The Sanhedrin was arranged like [half an arc] . . . the *Nasi* sat in the middle, with the elders sitting to his right and left." Another well-known source affirms the *Nasi*'s primary position among the sages, alongside an associate *Ab Bet Din* (lit. father of the court). Recording a long-standing debate on a cultic matter between successive pairs of leading sages (the *zugot*),[9] *m. Hag.* 2:2 concludes by referencing these roles: "Jose b. Joezer says [he] may not lay hands [on a sacrifice] . . . Joseph b. Johanan says he may . . . Shammai says he may not . . . Hillel says he may. The first [of each pair] were the *Nesiim*, and those second to them were the *Abot Bet Din.*" Later rabbinic sources present a similar scheme where the *Nasi* heads the academy, and the *Ab Bet Din* serves as his deputy.[10]

Promoting a leading sage seems to conflict with a principal aspiration of institutional justice: constructing a relatively level judiciary. In fact, this section will argue that the original institutional arrangements reject or constrict any hierarchy. Depictions of the *Nasi* heading the Sanhedrin apparently reflect a later development that grows out of a political incursion into the court, which alters the shape of rabbinic jurisprudence.

The Meaning of the Term Nasi

A spate of recent scholarship on the Patriarchate has led to a reexamination of the title *Nasi* in early rabbinic literature,[11] but studies have mostly focused on this term as a political label for the Patriarch. Scholars have mainly assumed that another meaning that surfaces in legal contexts—*Nasi* as head of the Sanhedrin or academy—is dissimilar and immaterial for a study of the Patriarchate. Thus, Sacha Stern dismisses two early references to the term *Nasi* because they pertain to its juridical meaning.[12] However, as Shmuel Safrai argued more than fifty years ago,[13] a study of the term *Nasi* must critically assess the roots of this latter usage as well, without making any prior assumptions about the term's connotation.[14] Rather than positing two distinct meanings of *Nasi* (a political and a juridical meaning), the analysis below proceeds with an a priori assumption that they are interrelated unless proven otherwise.

Although a comprehensive study of the term *Nasi* is beyond the scope of this book,[15] in the present context it is only necessary to gain a better understanding of its (range of) definition(s) within rabbinic literature, including within juridical settings. By way of background, consider briefly the term's semantic in pre-rabbinic literature.[16] Biblical and Second Temple sources invoke this label to signify a form of political leadership. In the Bible, *Nasi* refers to a king (e.g., Ezek 37:25), tribal leader (e.g., Num 1:4), a clan head (e.g., 1 Chron 4:38), or a regional head (e.g., Num 25:18).[17] During the Second Temple period, the term appears more frequently (especially in Qumran; see Chapter 3) and is used to denote a prince or a messianic figure.[18] According to Rofe, the ample use of this term in this period is intended to signify a less powerful ruler.[19] In late antiquity, this label gains currency as a marker of sovereignty, and is famously used as a title by Bar Kochba (in letters, documents, and coins dating to the second century CE) in his quest for royal stature.[20] Throughout biblical and postbiblical writings, then, this term has political undertones, referring to assorted leadership positions. Nowhere in pre-rabbinic literature is it used to describe a chief judge.

Turning to early rabbinic literature, the term *Nasi* appears only sporadically. Certain passages conform to pre-rabbinic usage. Elaborating upon the sin-offering of the *Nasi* (see Lev 4:22–26), *m. Hor.* 3:3 explicitly defines the term: "Who is meant by '*Nasi*'? A king . . ."[21] Given that the underlying verses do not mention a king,[22] this definition reveals the default rabbinic understanding of this term.[23] Additional early sources addressing these verses presumably interpret "*Nasi*" in the same way.[24] Several other sources that invoke this term refer more generally to a ruler, who is contrasted with a commoner. For instance, *t. Sanh.* 4:3 speaks of the honorable disposal of the property of deceased kings and *Nesiim,* as opposed to the treatment of a commoner's property.[25] In later rabbinic literature, "*Nasi*" serves as the common designation for the Patriarch, and perhaps by extension other political leaders. Thus, the Talmud queries whether the Patriarch or Exilarch are required to bring the sin-offering of the *Nasi.*[26] Moreover, specific leaders bear this title (e.g., Judah the *Nasi*).[27] Employing this label in this manner draws on its political roots.

Several other more ambiguous sources likely remain in this same semantic field.[28] They seem to cite this term as a title for a leadership position. Discussing the assignment of property in order to bypass encumbrances that were generated by a pledge, *m. Ned.* 5:5 states: "Yet one may assign his share [in property] to the *Nasi.* R. Judah says, It is all one whether he assigned it to the *Nasi* or a commoner." Distinguishing the *Nasi* from a commoner (as in *t. Sanh.* 4:3), the Mishnah apparently refers here to a political leader. Likewise, the Mishnah's continuation implies that the *Nasi* is a communal head who controls public property and can serve as a trustee for the private property of others.[29]

Another somewhat obscure tannaitic passage arguably conforms to the above characterization. Mekhilta (*Neziqin, Parsha* 5 = *Sifra Kedoshim, Parsha* 10) evidently interprets the biblical "*Nasi*" as an official other than a judge. In the course of deriving a general rule not to curse one's parents from Exod 22:27—"*Elohim* thou shalt not curse, nor curse a *Nasi* of thy people"—the Midrash Halakha parses the italicized words of this verse:

> Now, if your father is a judge, then he is included in the warning, "*Elohim* [a judge] thou shalt not curse." If he is a *Nasi,* then he is included in the warning, "Nor curse a *Nasi* of thy people." But

suppose he is neither a judge nor a *Nasi*, but an ignorant person (*bor*)? Behold you reason and establish a general rule on the basis of what is common to both. The peculiar aspect of the case of a judge is not the same as the peculiar aspect of the case of the *Nasi* (and vice versa). . . . What is the common feature of both? They are great and "of thy people" and because of their greatness you are warned against cursing them.

The Mekhilta differentiates between the "great" positions of *Elohim* and *Nasi,* as each have distinct "peculiar aspects." Given that the term *Elohim* refers to a judge, one can surmise that *Nasi* refers to a leader.[30]

This brief survey establishes that various rabbinic passages that speak of the *Nasi* have a political semantic—either explicitly defining him as a king, or openly or tacitly depicting him as a political leader, or indicating that his role is distinct from that of a judge—which leads one to question the roots of the juridical semantic of this term.[31] Moreover, there is a more basic reason to question whether chief judge is a primary definition of the term *Nasi* in early rabbinic literature. An examination of relevant sources casts doubt on whether such a position ever existed according to the early strata of this literature, and certainly about whether there was a formal title for this office. Several tannaitic sources about judicial administration depict the operation of a collective and egalitarian institutional court. Other sources that introduce a hierarchy only hint at the position of a chief judge, and hardly recognize a titular head of court. The next paragraphs will substantiate these skeptical claims. Afterward, the texts where the term *Nasi* is used in a juridical context will be examined, in order to attempt to reconstruct how this term acquired a legal connotation.

Leveling the Court

The rabbinic portrayals of the courts cited in Chapter 6 show few traces of an internal hierarchy among the judges who preside on the Sanhedrin or lower courts, and arguably no indication of a chief judge.[32] They mainly speak about an institution,[33] or the sum figure of its constituents,[34] where the weight of authority emanates from the body of the court, an elect assembly of nameless sages. This is also the thrust of an *m. Ros. Has.* 2:9 homily concerning the biblical elders—a scriptural archetype for the Sanhedrin in rabbinic literature,[35] and by extension other satellite tribunals—which amplifies their collective, institutional voice:[36] "For it is written, 'Then went up Moses and Aaron, Nadab and Abihu, and seventy of the elders of Israel (Exod 24:9),' and why are the names of the elders not expressly set forth if not to teach that every three [judges] which have risen up as a court over Israel are like the court of Moses." Glossing over the names of individual luminaries (Moses, Aaron, or a contemporary sage like Rabban Gamliel),[37] the Mishnah focuses on the unnamed elders and judges and their corporate authority in proclaiming parity among all tribunals, whether they are headed by Moses, Gamliel, or anyone else.[38] The authority of the Mosaic Court and the Gamliel Court is due, not to their eponymous figureheads, but to their anonymous members.

Indeed, rabbinic jurisprudence operates with rules and regulations that arguably reflect, and even reify, an egalitarian structure in the court.[39] Ranging from substantive to ceremonial, they level the court by recruiting judges of a similar stature, bolstering each judge, or assimilating all of them into a unified judicial body. A number of such protocols and procedures will be considered below.

JUDICIAL QUALIFICATIONS: Several sources enumerate specific (ethical, intellectual, and spiritual) characteristics that qualify somebody as a judge.[40] Drawing on the traits of the Mosaic judges (see Exod 18:21, 25; Deut 1:13, 15), for example, rabbinic protocol enlists officials with similar characteristics to serve on the court.[41] A later Talmudic passage vividly captures the aspiration of such a policy:[42] "'And they shall bear the burden of the people with thee (Num 11:17)'—'with thee' intimates that [the judicial elders must] be like thee [Moses]." Rather than a single figure, such as Moses, pronouncing judgment, the judicial "burden" should be carried by a court of peers. According to such sources, all judges (at least of a given tier) ideally have similar qualifications, strengths, and attributes, suggesting that they all serve in analogous roles.[43]

VOTING PROCEDURES: Another aspect of the operation of the courts that promotes parity among the judges is distinctive voting regulations. Consider the cardinal principle of majority rule.[44] By assigning equal weight to each judge's vote, this method of reaching a verdict treats all the judges on the court *pari passu*. Moreover, a striking revote procedure conducted by an expanded panel, mandated by the Mishnah when even a single judge abstains—although a clear majority exists irrespective of his vote—highlights the importance of each judge's opinion.[45] According to this protocol, a verdict cannot be reached without the full participation—including a definitive vote—of all of the court's members.[46]

FORM OF VERDICT: Even though majority rule weighs each judge's decision, it is of course the cumulative votes that steer the court. One rabbinic opinion even requires the verdict to be announced as the uniform ruling of the court.[47] Not divulging the identity of the judges in the majority and dissent (which may be due to prudential or religious considerations)[48] further preserves the court's institutional integrity.[49] Amplifying the institutional voice blunts the impact of any single judge[50] and flattens any hierarchy among the judges.

MINIMUM QUORUM: *T. Sanh.* 7:1 (and parallels) establishes that the high court (of seventy-one judges), can exercise full institutional authority with a minimum quorum of twenty-three members present. Notably, any subset of twenty-three can speak on behalf of the court, and no particular judge(s) need be present. Evidently all judges have the same standing, and as long as a critical mass convenes, they can represent the court.[51]

THE LIMITS OF DEMURRAL: Against this backdrop, the rabbinic interpretation of the "rebellious elder" as an insubordinate judge who continually defies the high court's instructions by advancing a contrary ruling makes a great deal of sense.[52] The court's institutional authority precludes the legitimacy of a perpetual demurral. Rabbinic justice relies on the consensus of all, rather than the singular conviction of a lone voice.

SEATING CONFIGURATION: A protocol about the seating configuration of the judges of the Sanhedrin relates to the inner dynamic within the court.[53] According to the Mishnah's version of this protocol, the positioning of the judges affirms their identical stature, and fosters open and balanced deliberations among them. A second protocol relating to the seating (and voting) order on all tiered courts, however, may signal a limited hierarchy. These protocols will be considered below.

The above procedures advance the vision of *m. Ros. Has.* 2:9, which concentrates judicial authority in the institution of the court, irrespective of its members. These rules assemble a group of like judges; secure each judge's vote;[54] combine the judges into a cohesive body; recognize any quorum of high court judges; nullify anti-institutional dissent; and seat court members so that they engage with one another in reaching a joint verdict.[55] In structure and procedure, institutional justice envisions a profoundly egalitarian and collective judicial process, which would seem to be in tension with promoting any meaningful hierarchy among the members of the court, let alone a distinguished role for a chief judge.

Thin Traces of a Hierarchy, and the Ab Bet Din

The above offers a reconstruction of an ideal institutional template of a level court. Certain sources, however, seem to register a limited hierarchy within the composition of the court. Consider the following passage that describes a strict rank among the judges in terms of their seating and voting order: "In civil suits . . . we begin with [the opinion of] the *gadol* [most eminent of judges];[56] whereas in capital cases, we commence with those on the side [benches]" (*m. Sanh.* 4:2).[57] Another Mishnah describes the meticulous arrangement of the student apprentices who accompany the Sanhedrin: "And three rows of students sat in front of them, each knowing his own place. In case it was necessary to appoint [another judge], he was appointed from the first [row] in which case one from the second [row] moved up to the first. . . . He did not sit in the place vacated by the first but in the place suitable for him [i.e., at the end of the row]" (*m. Sanh.* 4:4).

Notably, parallel Tosefta teachings arguably betray a more elastic design.[58] Evidently a strictly stratified judiciary is borne out only by certain rabbinic texts.[59] A similar duality of perspectives may be reflected in other tannaitic sources that discuss the size of the high court, and a leading body.[60]

Moreover, even sources that depict a vertical ordering of the court only loosely point to a chief judge,[61] and never invest him with enhanced authority. Nor do they clearly record a fixed title for this position. Surveying tannaitic literature, the following terms (aside from *Nasi*) are arguably used to describe the supreme figure: (1) *gadol*,[62] (2) *rosh bet din*,[63] (3) *mufla*,[64] (4) *rosh yeshiva*,[65] (5) *ehad memuneh al gabei kulan*,[66] and (6) *Ab Bet Din*.[67] These multiple designations are a sign of indeterminacy, reflecting the inchoate nature of a position that has not yet attained any formal recognition (perhaps mirroring the historical reality).[68]

The one item on this list that may be a nominative title is *Ab Bet Din* (lit. Patriarch of the Court). To the extent that early rabbinic literature recognizes the post of a chief judge, the official title is likely *Ab Bet Din*, not *Nasi*. This appellation plainly designates a head of the court, not a secondary figure, as it came to be understood later on in rabbinic literature.[69] Indeed, several tannaitic sources corroborate the primacy of the *Ab Bet Din* among the judges of the court. For instance, *m. Ed.* 5:6 records the sages' plea to an iconic sage to rescind his controversial halakhic opinions: "Akabya b. Mahalalel testified to four opinions. They said: Akabya, retract these four opinions that you have given and we will make you *Ab Bet Din* in Israel." One can hardly imagine Akabya being swayed by an offer to assume a secondary role within the court. Rather, he is being promised the foremost position of *Ab Bet Din* "in Israel."[70] Likewise, a *baraita* (*b. Sukkah* 29a) employs hyperbolic language to emphasize the unique stature of the *Ab Bet Din*. "Our rabbis taught, On account of four things is the sun in eclipse: On account of an *Ab Bet Din* who died and was not mourned fittingly."[71] According to one recension of *m. Yoma* 7:5,[72] the *Ab Bet Din* is the only judicial official who can consult with the high priest wearing the *Urim* and *Thummim*.

Likewise, certain later sources reflect the supremacy of the *Ab Bet Din,* which may be a vestige of an early rabbinic conception.[73] A passage in Sifre Zuta cited in Yalkut Devarim[74] describes the bequeathal of the office of *Ab Bet Din* from father to son, a hereditary system befitting a senior position; *b. Hag.* 13a discusses teaching the "Matter of the Chariot" to the *Ab Bet Din,* thereby singling him out for this exclusive knowledge; *Exod Rab., Parsha* 15 portrays the *Ab Bet Din* leading the intercalation of the calendar; and a couple of later midrashim depict God as the *Ab Bet Din* of a future apocalyptic court (*Exod Rab., Parsha* 5), and Eli the Priest as the *Ab Bet Din* in biblical times (*Tanh. Shmini* 2). In all these sources, the *Ab Bet Din* is represented as a principal figure.

Reviewing early rabbinic literature for descriptions of the chief judge, then, reveals significant ambiguity about whether there originally was such a role altogether. Rabbinic jurisprudence projects a comprehensive vision of an evenly constituted court, which leaves little room for such a position. Certain rabbinic sources that nevertheless introduce a vertical construct must be weighed against the contrary evidence. Further, even the hierarchical sources that point to a leading judge imply that this was an informal or de facto position (i.e., a leading sage often headed the assembly). To the extent that there was a judicial head, he was likely referred to as the *Ab Bet Din.* All of this evidence, weighed alongside the terminological analysis in the prior section, suggests that the title *Nasi* originated outside of the legal context.

Nasi *Entering the Court*

In order to test this hypothesis, however, it is necessary to evaluate rabbinic sources that nevertheless seem to cast the *Nasi* in a legal role. Certain references have an uncertain connotation. For instance, *m. Ta'an.* 2:1 describes a fast-day ritual, which involves both the *Nasi* and the *Ab Bet Din:* "They used to bring out the Ark into the open space in the town and put wood-ashes on the Ark and on the heads of the *Nasi* and *Ab Bet Din.* . . . the eldest among them uttered before them words of admonition." While the *Nasi* officiates at this ceremony, there is no indication that he acts on behalf of the court. Arguably, he arrives as a political head, while the *Ab Bet Din* represents the court.[75]

Another passage in the Mekhilta (*Kaspa, Parsha* 1) contains conflicting signals about the meaning of *Nasi*.[76] Similar to the Mekhilta passage cited above, this passage interprets the term *"Nasi"* in Exod 22:27 as a discrete, presumably political, designation, which is distinct from the term *"Elohim* [a judge]."[77] Certain recensions of the Mekhilta even align the *Nasi* with a biblical king.[78] Nevertheless, this source also contemplates a person bearing both titles of *Nasi* and *Elohim* simultaneously, and one line in this passage even seems to assume that a *Nasi* is a judge. Perhaps this source reflects a blurring of definitions, as the meaning of the term *Nasi* begins to evolve.

In any case, other sources plainly present the *Nasi* in a juridical setting. *M. Hag.* 2:2 (cited above) depicts the successive pairs of *zugot* who debated legal matters as composed of a *Nasi* in the principal role and the *Ab Bet Din* as second in line. A well-known *t. Pesah.* 4:11 passage, describing Hillel's public ruling that a Passover sacrifice may be offered on the Sabbath, has a similar implication.[79] After Hillel guided the masses, they appoint him *Nasi,* and he continues to instruct them. In other words, Hillel's outstanding legal expertise secured for him this distinctive title. Likewise, *Semahot* 10:13[80] discusses the intensive mourning practices that are to be observed by members of the rabbinic academy after the death of the *Nasi,* the *Ab Bet Din,* or a *hakham* (sage).[81] A few other rabbinic sources also invoke the term *Nasi* in a juridical context.[82]

To evaluate the significance of these sources, however, one has to consider their provenance. While these sources represent the *Nasi* as a leading sage and legal authority, and some even elevate him above the *Ab Bet Din* and other sages, they may well belong to a later stratum of rabbinic literature. Thus, the pivotal line in *m. Hag.* 2:2—the only mishnaic source that unquestionably invokes a legal semantic of the term *Nasi*[83]—is a concluding (and arguably later) gloss that caps the list of the *zugot,* offering a retrospective characterization of figures from an earlier period.[84] Likewise, the Hillel narrative has long been understood by scholars to be a literary account of an earlier event, and the conferral of the title *Nasi* upon Hillel is especially considered to be anachronistic.[85] Similarly, *Semahot* 10:13 and related Talmudic passages are presumably later sources, and may well reflect a modified rabbinic conception of the *Nasi* and other rabbinic legal authorities.

The possibility that a secondary sense of *Nasi* surfaces in these texts is noteworthy. For this would suggest that the legal connotation is secondary to the primary semantic; a conclusion that is strongly reinforced by the cumulative evidence presented above. Thus, rather than assuming that the term *Nasi* has an original semantic of chief judge or sage, or a generic head that can apply across different realms, it is more plausible that the term's initial definition was political, and that the juridical title only materialized afterward.

Valuable insight into the evolution of the term *Nasi*—from functioning as a political label, to signifying a position with legal authority, to constituting the title of the chief judge—can be gained from a synoptic study of three sources that depict the seating configuration of the high court. *T. Sanh.* 8:1 (cited at the beginning of this section) describes the *Nasi* positioned at the center of the Sanhedrin, with the judicial elders seated in an arc formation around him:

> The Sanhedrin was arranged like the half of a round threshing-floor [*hatsi goren*] so that they all might see one another, and the *Nasi* sat in the middle, with the elders sitting to his right and left . . .

A parallel source, *m. Sanh.* 4:3,[86] only overlaps in part:

> The Sanhedrin was arranged like the half of a round threshing-floor [*hatsi goren*] so that they all might see one another . . .

Although its first clause is identical (regarding the seating plan of the Sanhedrin), the Mishnah does not contain the Tosefta's latter clause spotlighting the *Nasi*. It seems likely that the Mishnah in fact preserves the original description of the court's seating arrangement, and the

Tosefta adds a later interpolation that inserts the *Nasi* into this distinctive formation.[87] According to this hypothesis, the *Nasi*, in effect, "invades" the tribunal.

A third version of this teaching, found in *y. Sanh.* 1:6, makes sense in light of this conjecture and reflects a further adaptation of this rabbinic tradition:

> The Sanhedrin was arranged like the half of a round threshing-floor [*hatsi goren*], and the *Nasi* sat in the middle, with the elders sitting to his right and left, *so that they all might see the Nasi*. (emphasis added)

Notice that in the Yerushalmi's formulation not only is the *Nasi* mentioned alongside the Sanhedrin, but the purpose of the seating plan has changed. According to the Mishnah and Tosefta, its aim is to construct a horizontal setup where the judges see one another; but the Yerushalmi depicts this as a vertical arrangement, a way of enabling all the judges to observe the *Nasi* at the center.[88] By the Talmudic phase, the *Nasi* has not only become completely integrated into the Sanhedrin, he has become the focal point of the judiciary.[89]

Following the literary trail of these synoptic sources, then, suggests the following possible reconstruction (which may mirror a historical transformation as well): Originally, the Sanhedrin is envisioned as an even panel of judges who openly deliberate and ideally reach consensus on legal issues. The very configuration in which the judges sit emphasizes the parity among them. This vision is preserved in *m. Sanh.* 4:3.[90]

The intermediate phase,[91] *t. Sanh.* 8:1, reflects the insertion of the *Nasi* into this scheme.[92] Presumably the *Nasi* is a political leader, who officiates along with the court at certain rituals (e.g., *m. Ta'an.* 2:1), and perhaps also participates in adjudication. Notably, one can still discern a disjuncture in the Tosefta between the court and the *Nasi:* the court elders look at one another, even as the *Nasi* sits in their midst. The Tosefta dates this passage to the times of Gamaliel II (of Yavneh), but it is likely that this is a somewhat later literary construction.[93] Finally, *y. Sanh.* 1:6

indicates a third phase where the *Nasi* takes charge of the judicial tribunal, as the ruler coopts the court.[94] One can surmise that only after this phase does the term *Nasi* assume a distinct juridical connotation.[95]

A Shifting Semantic

The above analysis can be synthesized and filled out as follows: early rabbinic sources perpetuate the political semantic of the term *Nasi* found in pre-rabbinic literature, utilizing it to refer to the king, and as a label for a political leader. While there may not have been an actual figure known by this title during the early rabbinic period,[96] tannaitic writings formulate an archetype of this office, possibly based on the recent history of the leadership of Bar Kochba, or maybe the burgeoning of the Patriarchate.[97] The political role of the position of the *Nasi* is suggested by sources such as *t. Sanh.* 4:3 that group him alongside the king, or Mekhilta (*Neziqin, Parsha* 5), which distinguishes between the *Nasi* and a judge. In addition, the spare mishnaic sources that mention the *Nasi*, including *m. Ned.* 5:5 and perhaps *m. Ta'an.* 2:1, refer to a political figure. Over time this label also has a contemporary resonance, as it becomes associated with a leading notable in Jewish society. At the end of the tannaitic period, this title becomes affixed to Judah the Patriarch, and his progeny become known as *Nesiim.*

Thus, early rabbinic sources (especially the Mishnah) primarily depict the *Nasi* as a political, not a legal, authority. Considering the broader administrative vision of the Mishnah described in Chapter 5, the distance between these roles is considerable. The Mishnah promotes the formation of an independent judicial body, the autocratic rule of a political head, and an ideal of separation. Moreover, the template of institutional justice further reduces the internal influence of powerful forces by constructing a level court, with no fixed, titular head. Accordingly, the *Nasi*, a political leader, has no judicial responsibility in early rabbinic literature.

Changes in late second-century-CE Judean society, however, alter the balance of law and power. Judicial practice increasingly revolves around leading sages and notable figures. Echoing this reality, the juridical vision of rabbinic literature adopts a more vertical structure, with an ascendant role for the Patriarch.[98] At this stage, rabbinic sources (the earliest being *t. Sanh.* 8:1) exhibit the *Nasi*, first as functioning alongside the court and subsequently as commandeering judicial power. With the *Nasi* seated at the head of the judicial assembly, the juridical model begins to resemble a royal judiciary.

Rabbinic discourse, however, evidently reappropriates or assimilates this title in a final transformation that may respond to, or result from, this encroachment. Shedding the political cast, a last layer of *m. Hag.* 2:2 designates the principal sage as the *Nasi,* and a legal semantic is born.[99] The *Ab Bet Din* in turn is demoted to a secondary rank, reflecting the full absorption of the *Nasi* into the rabbinic circle.[100] Several other rabbinic texts suggest a similar pattern, supporting this overall reconstruction.[101] In other words, a complex process, perhaps following loosely along the trajectory sketched above, leads from the term's primary political definition to the emergence of a secondary legalistic title.[102]

Notice how the institutional model is thereby restored through this final recalibration. Rather than having the political leader dominate judicial affairs, this deliberate or organic revision reestablishes an independent juridical construct. Yet lingering imprints are evident in the internal hierarchy that now shapes the court. Institutional justice is once again autonomous, but legal authority is no longer evenly distributed within the court. As will be seen presently, a loosely analogous process transpires not just within the court but without.[103]

The *Nasi's* External Authority: Judicial Appointments

A second set of rabbinic texts that seem to undermine the independent nature of institutional justice relates to appointment powers. While a step removed from the direct command of legal authority, this capacity still affords a substantial means of navigating legal affairs. By carefully selecting judges, the person who exercises this power can determine much about the orientation of the court. Moreover, its potential exercise (which often includes the right to dismiss judges) can exert considerable pressure on the court's jurisprudence from a distance.[104] Several passages identify the *Nasi*—in these contexts clearly referring to a political leader, presumably the Patriarch—as commanding this power, thereby encroaching on the autonomy of the courts.

The section below will argue that in fact political control of this power is highly contested in early rabbinic literature. Certain sources describe internal modes of selecting judges, which cohere with the autonomy of institutional justice. Nevertheless, a clear line of sources identifies the *Nasi* as wielding this consequential power. The politicization of the appointment process evident in these texts likely echoes historical developments, as the Patriarch (or a Judean notable) apparently began to exercise such powers in practice. Similar to the pattern detected in the first section, rabbinic literature registers this transformation even in programmatic texts, which changes the balance of its jurisprudence. But a seminal Yerushalmi passage also attempts to reconfigure rabbinic jurisprudence in light of these developments to better preserve its commitment to judicial autonomy. In short, rabbinic jurisprudence here, too, is inflected by a rise of political clout. The trail of writings on appointment power captures this dynamic.

Whereas most prior scholarship on appointment powers has focused on the complex historical questions of the existence, and jurisdiction, of rabbinic courts within an imperial world, and who, if anyone, actually made (informal or formal)[105] appointments,[106] scholarship has hardly analyzed this material from a jurisprudential perspective,[107] nor considered what it reveals about rabbinic notions of law and power. Numerous passages in rabbinic literature, which invoke terms such as *semikhah, minuy, reshutah, hoshiv ba-yeshiva, mumheh, zaqen,* and *hakham,* arguably relate to the subject of judicial appointments.[108] Although an exhaustive study of these terms, and their knotty interrelationship, is beyond the scope of this work, a select examination of several programmatic sources on judicial appointments sheds light on these neglected dimensions.

A Self-Constituting Court

Several tannaitic texts (some of which were encountered above and in Chapter 6) depict an autonomous process wherein the court appoints its own judges, which complements the rigorous separation of powers advanced by early rabbinic jurisprudence. Describing a scenario where the Sanhedrin needs to make an appointment (*semikhah*), the Mishnah delineates the strict protocol that is followed: "And three rows of students sat in front of them [the Sanhedrin]. . . . In case it was necessary to appoint [*lismokh*] [another judge], he was appointed [*somkhin*] from the first [row]" (*m. Sanh.* 4:4). According to *t. Sanh.* 7:1, the Sanhedrin oversees the nomination of judges beginning at the ground level (i.e., staffing local courts) based on their evaluation of the candidate's qualifications, "And from there [the Chamber of Hewn Stone] they [the Sanhedrin] send for and examine everyone who is wise and prudent . . . they make him a judge in his town. Once he has been made a judge in his town, they promote him." Another passage, *t. Sanh.* 1:1, similarly consigns the authority to appoint judges to the judiciary, albeit even to smaller tribunals—"an appointment [*semikhah*] is administered by three [judges]."[109] In the Bavli, this same term, *semikhah,* is invoked to signify rabbinic ordination that includes authorization to conduct certain judicial procedures, which is bestowed by a rabbinic court or individual sages.

Another source with a similar implication employs different terminology, designating a qualified judge as a *mumheh,* a judicial expert. While this label may have initially indicated specialized competence in a specific area (i.e., identifying animal blemishes), it morphed into a general designation for a certified expert judge. Delineating the rules of liability in the case of a judicial error, *m. Bek.* 4:4 differentiates between a lay judge and one "who is an expert [*mumheh*] of the Bet Din." Only the judicial expert, who has official stature, is exempt from a duty to indemnify.[110] Perhaps originally experts certified other experts. The Mishnah, however, operates with an institutional arrangement wherein the expert receives his designation from the rabbinic court.[111] Elsewhere, rabbinic sources employ the terms *mumheh* and *mumheh le-rabim* without a direct reference to an authorizing court, but the latter may be implied.[112]

A third phrase that in certain sources suggests a self-constituting body is the verb and object pair, *hoshiv ba-yeshiva* (to seat in the rabbinic council or academy). Recorded in passing in several passages involving the leading council of seventy-two elders, who are depicted as guardians of ancestral traditions on legal matters,[113] this phrase describes the installation of a new member into the council.[114] Thus, the oft-repeated tannaitic statement of R. Simeon ben Azai, "I have it as a tradition from the mouths of seventy-two elders, on the day they seated R. Elazar ben Azariah in the academy (*hoshivu . . . ba-yeshiva*)." The elders are the ones who inducted R. Elazar into their council.[115]

Political Control of Appointment Power

By contrast, numerous passages depict appointment power as being the prerogative of a patriarchal figure, especially Judah the Patriarch. Most of these passages are descriptive in nature, and scholars generally presume that they are historically credible. More relevant in the present context are a couple of programmatic passages (which are likely informed by this historical reality) that affirm, or even celebrate, the political source of judicial appointments.

Sifre Deut. 346 highlights the authority of the *Nasi* (Patriarch) to appoint elders to the yeshiva,[116] and dramatizes the celestial reverberations of such an act:

> "And there was a king in Jeshurun (Deut 33:5)" . . . when the *Nasi* seats the elders [*moshiv zeqenim*] in the yeshiva below, His [God's] great name is praised above, as it is said, "And there was a king in Jeshurun (ibid.)." When? "When the heads of the people were gathered (ibid.)," "gathering" implies the elders, as it is said, "Gather unto Me seventy men of the elders of Israel" (Num 11:16).

Note how the passage evokes the model of a royal judiciary, as the council of elders convening below is associated with the majestic rule of the "king in Jeshurun" presiding above. While the latter phrase refers most directly to the divine sovereign, the *Nasi* assumes the derivative role of appointing elders to the "royal" court.[117] Convening the council is thus a royal task. In other words, this programmatic passage recognizes the political leader as in charge of appointments, and also appeals to an alternate jurisprudential model of royal justice that coheres with this arrangement.

Sifre Deut. 17 also depicts the act of "seating"—the passage refers explicitly to judges—as a prerogative of a political functionary.[118] Far from glorifying this act, however, this source betrays skepticism about the politicization of appointments, and remonstrates against the selection of inept judges: "'You shall not favor persons in judgment (Deut 1:17),' This refers to him who is appointed to authorize judges (*ha-memuneh le-hoshiv dayanin*). You might say, So and-so is a fine man ... I will appoint him judge. The result might be that such a judge might free the guilty." Other rabbinic sources collected by Gedalyahu Alon (especially *y. Bikk.* 3:3) record scathing criticisms of (patriarchal) corruption in the appointment process.[119] In any event, from a normative perspective the capacity to appoint judges is portrayed here as a matter of political discretion that the rabbis can only hope to influence by religious rhetoric.

Locating judicial appointments in political hands, the above passages veer from the template of institutional justice. In the first passage this shift is pronounced. Advancing an alternate jurisprudential construct, this passage employs royalist rhetoric and ideology. The second passage, on the other hand, averts the conceptual issue, focusing instead on the practical pitfalls engendered by a politicized process. A third, more elaborate passage from the Yerushalmi offers a different kind of response. Explicitly registering the political turn in judicial appointments, the Talmud also attempts to restore the role, and integrity, of the court.

Jerusalem Talmud

A famous *y. Sanh.* 1:2 passage on judicial appointments employs an alternate key term, *minuy*.[120] The passage explicates this term upfront:[121]

"There [in Babylon] they call appointment to a court [*minuy*] [by a different term, i.e.,] ordination [*semikhuta*],"[122] implying that these are interchangeable labels for the appointment of a rabbinic judge. Nevertheless, the change in terminology seems telling. Whereas the Babylonian word *semikhah* connotes a designation that a sage or tribunal confers upon a qualified student (as seen in the sources cited above), the Palestinian term *minuy* evidently signifies a formal appointment (to an office, or perhaps a status), likely associated with whomever is in power.

The heart of the passage describes three different phases in the "legislative history" of the *minuy* process, a passage that Hayim Lapin aptly describes as "highly schematic in both its periodization and its referents" and "cover[ing] over a more complicated history."[123] By reframing these historical processes in terms of set normative arrangements, the passage also offers insight into the jurisprudential vision of the rabbis. The passage reads as follows:

> R. Abba: At first, each one would appoint [*memaneh*] his students. For example, Rabbi Yohanan b. Zakkai appointed Rabbi Eliezer and Rabbi Joshua, and Rabbi Joshua [appointed] Rabbi Aqiba....
>
> They changed the system and bestowed honor on this [i.e., the Patriarch's] house. They said, a court[124] that appointed without the approval of the Patriarch [*Nasi*], its appointments are not valid, and a Patriarch who appointed without the approval of the court, such appointments are valid.
>
> They changed the arrangement and enacted that a court could not make any appointments without consent of the Patriarch, and the Patriarch could not appoint without consent of the court.

R. Abba, who presents this teaching, is a third-century Palestinian sage. By this period, scholars concur, Patriarchs (i.e., Judah and his progeny) controlled appointment power. R. Abba's account responds to this reality. Registering the central role of the Patriarch, this passage also notably restores the authority of the sages, at least to a certain extent. It strikes this delicate balance by delineating a multiphased scheme.

The first phase harkens back to an earlier period when (individual) sages would draw their leading students into the rabbinic circle. These students would then presumably begin to serve as judges or rabbinic authorities among the masses. Presented through the lens of the passage, however, this process is depicted in formal terms as an official appointment, a *minuy*, which encompasses "official" responsibilities. By asserting the primary role of the rabbinic sages in controlling appointments, the passage distinguishes them as the original source of legal authority.[125]

Similarly, a significant, if subtle, terminological shift in the second phase further enhances the standing of the rabbinic circle. Now the sages are labeled a "court," rather than a cadre of leading rabbis. This institutional language exposes the particular jurisprudence that undergirds R. Abba's tripartite scheme. All appointments on this account relate back to the institutional authority of the court. Thus, the second phase crucially represents the Patriarch's control of appointment power not as a function of the Patriarch's prerogative and dominant sociopolitical standing, but instead as emanating from the rabbinic court—an honor bestowed by the court upon the Patriarch. In other words, rather than conceptualizing the Patriarch's external appointment power as a breakdown in judicial independence, the passage proclaims that the ultimate source of authorization, at least in theory, remains with the court.[126]

In the third phase,[127] which despite being formulated in the past tense probably should be understood as a rabbinic aspiration, the court is (re)positioned as an actual partner in making appointments (a similar sharing of appointment power, referred to as *reshuta*, is discussed elsewhere in rabbinic literature).[128] Building upon the legal foundation of the first two phases, the court of sages (re)claims its rightful role in this process. This way appointment power is not fully ceded to the political arm, but (re)structured as a joint authority.

The passage thus acknowledges, but also recasts, the political intervention in legal affairs.[129] An analogous pattern was encountered in the

first section: the programmatic passages that proclaim the leading juridical role of the *Nasi,* which breach the egalitarian structure of institutional justice, were likely formulated in light of an actual intrusion of
Judean notables into the court. Over time, however, the institutional
framework is remolded in rabbinic discourse around a rabbinic head,
now labeled the *Nasi* (with a secondary *Ab Bet Din,* etc.). So too, here,
after first relying on an organic or internal appointment process that is
well aligned with the institutional template, schematic passages recognize the emerging prerogative of an external political actor, which likely
reflects a historical assertion by the Patriarch of this capacity. The
Yerushalmi, though, formulates a response to this development that partially restores the core design. It conceptualizes the political control of
appointment power as part of a jurisprudence that is rooted in the court.
But here too, the profile of the court is transformed. Appointment power
is now depicted as a discrete formal authority that is (at least partially)
assigned to the ruler. In both instances, power dynamics reconfigure the
court and modify its institutional jurisprudence.[130]

Law as a Check on Power, Law that Eradicates Power

The relationship of the political head to the legal establishment, according to certain salient rabbinic materials surveyed in Part Two, can
be summarized as follows: The political leadership of the king is separated from the judiciary (i.e., the basic version of separation of powers),
which operates as an independent and egalitarian institution (i.e., the
internal version) (Chapters 5 and 6); the *Nasi* as the political leader, in
due course presides over a more hierarchical rabbinic court (Chapter 7);
and the *Nasi* as the Patriarch, according to numerous sources, exercises
remote control over the court (ibid.). The latter rabbinic sources that describe the *Nasi* (as leader or Patriarch) directing certain facets of the
judiciary considerably alter the balance of power between the political
and judicial branches envisioned by the tannaitic sources examined in
Chapters 5–6. Overcoming the foundational separation principle that

"the king may [not] judge . . . (*m. Sanh.* 2:2)," a political head participates in, and even tries to take over the reins of, the administration of
justice.

One kind of response encountered in the first two sections of this
chapter is to try to absorb this shock to the integrity of institutional justice and revise the scheme accordingly (i.e., operating with a more vertical structure within the court, or adopting a joint-appointment mechanism). A second type of response, which will be examined presently, is
to withdraw the firm partition that separates the judicial and political
spheres. If the ruler appropriates judicial powers, he must conversely be
held legally accountable (at least in theory). A series of homiletic texts
from the next strata of rabbinic literature therefore overrides the second
part of the separation principle, "the king . . . [cannot] be judged," and
asserts jurisdiction over leadership figures. Mirroring the arc of the texts
described above, where political power commandeers the sphere of law,
these texts envision the rule of law extending to political actors.

A final response examined herein adopts the elements of a stronger
form of jurisprudence, which moves beyond the moderate and internal
modes that characterized rabbinic jurisprudence thus far. Without an
adequate partition separating law and politics, the threat of muscular
rulers looms large. In several passages where the clash between justice
and power comes to a head, a final jurisprudential impulse can be discerned that hails the rule of law, and forecasts the demise of absolutist
rulers. This chapter closes with an exemplar of such a text.[131]

Notably, these texts are all recorded in the Yerushalmi's commentary
on *m. Sanh.* 2. Perhaps more than any other rabbinic pericope examined in this book, this mishnaic chapter advances the basic separatist
principle of rabbinic jurisprudence by dividing the political and judicial branches. While preserving the immunity of the ruler, the Mishnah
also safeguards judicial independence and carefully structures the institutional configuration of the court, a profound expression of the internal
dissemination of power. Yet a series of Yerushalmi texts responding to
the Mishnah deliberately rescind its separation by representing political
rulers—archetypical kings and Patriarchs—as subject to the rule of

law.[132] And in a final thrust, the Yerushalmi even aspires to impeach the rule of autocratic leaders, a pointed expression of the stronger version of early Jewish jurisprudence that seeks to eliminate political power.

The new responses evident in these Talmudic writings are informed by historical dynamics, similar to the materials in the first two sections. As the material moves from depicting the idyllic relationship between a theoretical king and the judiciary to the actual interaction between the political leader and the courts, the normative vision is also renegotiated. As present-day leaders intervene in legal processes, an expansive notion of the rule of law is necessary to try to constrain, or potentially depose, political actors.

Judging the Ruler

Explaining the mishnaic principle that the king is not judged, *y. Sanh.* 2:3 (see Chapter 5) cites the Davidic prayer, "Let my judgment come forth from Thy presence (Psalms 17:2)." That is, because the king is judged directly by God, he is exempt from the jurisdiction of human courts. The Yerushalmi, however, continues with a somewhat surprising addendum, "R. Isaac in the name of Rabbi: The king and people are judged before Him every day," and supports this tradition with a proof-text (1 Kgs 8:59). What arguably began as a declaration of the king's special status and partial sovereign immunity is thus reformulated as a statement about his escalated accountability.[133] This homiletic teaching stresses that the powerful ruler is bound by the law and subject to a higher form of penal control.

Another Yerushalmi passage discussing the *Nasi*, who is depicted as having a royal status, goes a step further by undercutting the sovereign's immunity from the jurisdiction of a human court. In association with the ruling of *m. Sanh.* 2:1–2 that "the high priest ... [can] be judged," while the king cannot, the Yerushalmi cites traditions that address what happens when a high official violates the law. Following the first clause of the Mishnah, the Yerushalmi affirms that a high priest receives lashes.[134] Next, the Talmud considers the treatment of a political official who violates the law. Here it records an account of a provocative teaching of Resh Laqish concerning a *Nasi*'s violation, which infuriates the contemporary Patriarch (*y. Sanh.* 2:1): "Resh Laqish said, A *Nasi* who sins—they administer lashes to him by the decision of a court of three judges. What is the law as to restoring him to office? Said R. Haggai, By Moses! If we put him back into office, he will kill us! R. Judah (II) Nesiah heard this ruling and was outraged. He sent Goths to arrest Resh Laqish. [He] fled to the Tower."

Segueing from the Mishnah's law concerning the king to Resh Laqish's ruling regarding the *Nasi*, the Yerushalmi seamlessly shifts the focus from the king to the Patriarch (see *y. Hor.* 3:1).[135] Yet, read against its backdrop of the Mishnah, Resh Laqish's teaching that a guilty Patriarch is punished with lashes subverts the underlying mishnaic rule that a king is not judged.[136] Whether Resh Laqish's ruling presents a substantive challenge to the Mishnah or should just be understood as a contemporary polemic against the corruption of political leaders,[137] this passage clearly presents a rabbinic voice that protests against the dangers of shielding powerful men from legal accountability.[138]

In fact, it is precisely the change in subject from the king to the *Nasi* that may explain the Talmud's resistance to the mishnaic rule. Facing the potential defiance of an unbridled *Nasi*, especially after he has arrogated to himself legal authority (as described above), the principle of separation is no longer sustainable. The political leader must be placed under the court's jurisdiction, at least in theory.[139]

Deposing the Ruler

A similar story recorded in *y. Sanh.* 2:6 also emphasizes the culpability of the king / *Nasi*—this time in the heavenly court—and culminates with a stronger version of early Jewish jurisprudence.[140] Delivering a scolding homily concerning venal rulers, a Tiberian sage forcefully rebukes the Patriarch in its climactic lines:

> Yose of Ma'on expounded in the Tiberian synagogue: "Hear this, priests (Hos 5:1)"—Why do you not study Torah? Have you not been given the twenty-four priestly gifts? They replied: Nothing

at all has been given to us. "Pay attention, House of Israel (Hos 5:1)"—Why have you not given the twenty-four priestly gifts which you have been commanded at Sinai? They replied: The king has taken everything.[141] "Hearken, house of the king, for is judgment [*mishpat*] upon you? (Hos 5:1)"—Was I referring to you when I spoke of, "The judgment [*mishpat*, i.e., allotment] of the priests (Deut 18:3)"? In the future I will judge you, condemn you, and destroy you from the face of the earth. R. Judah (II) Nesiah heard [about this] and became enraged. [Yose] panicked and fled.

According to the homily, the king has confiscated priestly entitlements[142]—here considered to be a special subsidy to support learning Torah (the laws)[143]—and thereby trespassed over the boundary dividing the monarchic and priestly offices of *m. Sanh.* 2:1–2. Arguably the seizure of these subsidies signals the ruler's plan to usurp legal authority from the priests, an even more egregious flaunting of the separation of roles. Although formulated as decrying the transgressions of the king (in this recension),[144] Yose's sermon obviously targets the Patriarch, the modern-day leader, who clearly understands his intent.

Confronting this corrupt state of affairs, the entire homily is presented as an inquisitorial trial that seeks to uphold the Torah's laws. God acts as an investigating magistrate who enforces *mishpat* (demanding compliance with the priestly obligation to study the Torah, and the Israelite obligation to support the Priests in this endeavor) and executes *mishpat* (rounding up the suspects, identifying the true culprit, and punishing him).[145] When the political leader is found to be guilty of raiding the priestly domain, the homilist announces God's resounding declaration, which has a double entendre: "Hearken, house of the king, for is judgment [*mishpat*] upon you? [alt. upon you is judgment!] (Hos 5:1)." Read as a rhetorical question (the primary translation), the ruler is informed that the priestly allotment (*mishpat*) is not his; and read as a declaration (the alternate translation), the king is told that he will be convicted in a trial (*mishpat*). Lastly, notice the legalistic formulation of the concluding peroration, "In the future I will judge you (*lesheiv imahen bedin*), condemn you, and destroy you from the face of the earth." Notwithstanding the Mishnah's pronouncement that the king has immunity from legal proceedings, here he is condemned by trial, and told that in the future he will face a final judgment.[146]

Taken together these Yerushalmi passages challenge the autonomy of the king, and by extension, the *Nasi,* and protest against the immunity of the sovereign. Warranting heavenly and corporal punishment, the king / *Nasi* is said to be bound by the law.[147] Yet the particularly severe concluding line of Yose's homily sounds another note, revealing a climactic turn in rabbinic discourse on the intersection of law, power and politics. God sentences the king to a devastating last punishment: "In the future I will judge you, condemn you, and destroy you from the face of the earth." The absolutist king is not just being punished for a particular transgression, but for eroding the normative roles and commitments of all sectors of society, and being the root of anomie.[148] The looming punishment is final and fatal.

More than declaring the culpability of a sinful king / *Nasi,* then, the passage encapsulates a sweeping response that is necessary to avert a normative breakdown that is triggered by unbridled power.[149] There is no longer any possibility of dividing or balancing between domains, or reining in the king. The critical partition between the political and legal sphere is no longer effective; a mere punitive check is no longer viable. Facing the stark choice of a society led by either a boundless sovereign will or a regime of norms—an alternative that traces all the way back to Hecataeus—the passage unequivocally champions the rule of sacral law and calls for the elimination of royal power.[150]

In all, a series of texts from *y. Sanh.* 2 caps a progression of responses that can be discerned within rabbinic writings to an evolving relationship between law and politics. Previous chapters described how the Mishnah formulates a basic jurisprudence that separates legal and political authority, and disseminates power within the court. Certain rabbinic traditions encountered in this chapter, however, challenge the stasis of this division. Due to the increasing clout of the political leader, both inside and outside of the court, the integrity of the legal order begins to erode. Several responses to this political infiltration can be discerned in rabbinic literature, including ways of recalibrating the institutional scheme, analyzed in the first two sections; and checking the political leader with (actual or the threat of) legal restraints, analyzed in the final section. But the hovering prospect of an unfettered leader may foreclose these options. An epic conflict could erupt between political absolutism and law's empire.[151] Ultimately, Yose's homily propounds a stronger version of rabbinic jurisprudence, which resonates with several Second Temple jurisprudential accounts analyzed in Part One. The final part of this book will elaborate upon this convergence, and more broadly explore the historical, legal-philosophical, and comparative dimensions of early Jewish jurisprudence.

Part Three

Roots, Theory, Afterlife

8

Formative Factors

Second Temple and rabbinic works contain rich, even revolutionary, insights into the nature of legal authority. Building upon the biblical foundation, an array of passages offers vivid depictions of the administration of justice. Some early works echo the absolutist orientation dominant in antiquity and pervasive in the Bible, and elevate the king's role (e.g., Psalms of Solomon). Other writings present a more syncretistic account of "royal justice" (e.g., Philo), or contain multiple voices, supporting a monarchic model alongside alternate arrangements (e.g., rabbinic literature). Chapter 7 demonstrated that even writings that resist a royalist scheme can be refashioned around the commanding presence of a political leader (e.g., the *Nasi*).

Yet the most striking finding in this book relates to the manner in which various influential writings break with the regnant paradigm. A clear alternate arc can be discerned spanning across early Jewish texts discussing the nature of legal authority, beginning with Deuteronomy 17 and ending with Talmudic writings. In contrast with a prevalent conception that locates law in the province of rulers, these writings collectively project law's independence.[1] Moreover, the width of the arc thickens with the passage of time from antiquity through late antiquity. What began as an exceptional jurisprudence recorded in a discrete biblical passage became the nucleus for some of the most formative legal writings of the Second Temple and rabbinic periods.

One cluster of texts, including certain Qumran and rabbinic passages, expresses a moderate version of this jurisprudence. While upholding royal authority in the political sphere, these writings assign legal authority to independent officials, and either subordinate or join the king's judicial role to their authority, or separate the king from the legal domain altogether. Some of these texts further advance internal constraints on power. Disseminating legal authority among a panel of officials, they envision a legal regime that functions by administering broadly applicable laws in a consistent manner. The prinicipal template in rabbinic literature especially limits the role of powerful, charismatic, or individual judges, and elevates the institutional role in the administration of justice.

A stronger version of this jurisprudence is manifest in another set of texts that hails the ascendancy of law over the rule of powerful men. Hecataeus already alludes to a fundamental antinomy between (Jewish) priestly legal authority and (non-Jewish) monarchic rule, and the gap between these two modes of authority widens in later Jewish writings. Sundry Qumran texts exalt priests and councils alongside the community, while they marginalize the role of the king. More sweepingly, Josephus rejects monarchy, and instead champions a theocracy structured around the supernal rule of law. A later Talmudic passage even dramatizes the epic triumph of justice over sovereignty.

Amplifying the Deuteronomic legacy, these writings collectively articulate a jurisprudence of legal autonomy. Further, keenly sensitive to the corrosive impact of power, they share a deep commitment to securing justice from its pervasive reach. The chapters above describe the remarkable turn to legalism and the promotion of an expansive rule of law in these foundational Jewish writings. Yet several basic questions follow in their wake: Why does the early Jewish jurisprudence reflected in these writings follow this surprising trajectory? What are the theoretical underpinnings of this jurisprudence, and how does it compare to modern notions of separation of powers? Finally, what is the legacy of early Jewish jurisprudence in later periods (at least in broad strokes)? The chapters in Part Three will examine each of these respective questions in turn.

This chapter evaluates several formative factors that contributed to the surprising influence of Deuteronomy's anomalous jurisprudence on post-biblical literature. The initial three factors—the historical reality of dis-empowerment, canonical status of Deuteronomy (and the Pentateuch), and theological conceptions of kingship—are unquestionably relevant, but they are also only partial explanations. A more careful assessment of each points to a fourth factor that is arguably most decisive—the cen-trality of law in the discourses of Sinai and beyond, which is integrally connected to the ideal of law's autonomy and independence.

The Historical Factor: Disempowerment and Its Responses

Jewish ideas about the centrality of law are often dismissed as apolo-getic responses to Jewish disempowerment, and a similar charge can be made about claims of its independence. Stripped of political clout, the argument would go, Jews sought to reclaim authority by promoting the supremacy and autonomy of law. On this reading, the Jewish turn to legalism does not constitute a bold innovation, or even an authentic expression of organic Jewish values. Instead it reflects a necessary solu-tion to a coerced reality. Masking a lack of political alternatives, a legal-istic ideology enables maintaining authority in the only form possible, so there is little that is genuinely groundbreaking here.

This kind of criticism, which traces back in some form to Wellhausen (perhaps even to Tacitus),[2] not only commits a genetic fallacy by im-pugning mature concepts due to their ostensibly dubious origins, but also represents a gross simplification of the source of these ideas. Even though most of the postbiblical writings analyzed throughout this book were authored during periods of (varying degrees of) Jewish disempower-ment, the kernel of their jurisprudence traces back to a biblical era of

empowerment, and their programmatic tone points forward to an anticipated age of restored political power. Undermining Wellhausen's influential characterization of biblical laws as a postexilic priestly creation, ancient covenantal chapters exalt the role of law,[3] and materials that scholars
date to a monarchic period depict an elaborate judicial network.[4] In other
words, biblical traditions emerging from a world of political strength emphasize an autonomous legal scheme. A backdrop of political vitality
likewise informs various Second Temple texts written through the Hasmonean period,[5] which articulate similar notions about the role of law.

From the Persian period onward, however, Jews generally wielded
reduced sovereign powers, and by the late Second Temple and beyond,
the deteriorating political condition and eventual loss of political autonomy certainly altered the milieu in which various Jewish works were
produced.[6] Authors writing in such settings were likely responding *in
part* to this reality. Nevertheless, it is crucial to realize that varying degrees
of disempowerment generated a range of reactions, and advancing an
overly determined reading of these writings fails to adequately appreciate their subtle nature or significance.

To wit, the selections examined in this book contain diverse viewpoints about legal authority and its relationship to political power.
Alongside the late Second Temple and post-destruction writings that
embrace the Deuteronomic model, other works espouse a royalist model
(see Chapter 1). In rabbinic literature, in fact, both the Deuteronomic
and the royalist forms of jurisprudence find expression (see Chapters 5
and 6). Diverse interpretive and axiological perspectives are reflected
in writings from these periods.

Even the Deuteronomic trajectory within postbiblical jurisprudence
cannot be characterized merely as an apologetic response to (forms of)
disempowerment that champions judicial supremacy and downgrades
political authority. The postbiblical schemes in this tradition are more
varied than that. Consider, for example, the various mishnaic passages
(see Chapter 5) that advance a robust, if ill-defined, portrait of monarchic power, separate from the jurisdiction of the courts. Attributing the
Deuteronomic contours of such writings to disempowerment simply

ignores their specific content. Other writings that more plainly privilege law over political power are also not adequately explained as deriving solely from political conditions, because the inevitability implied in this characterization is misleading.

Certain early Christian writings provide an important foil for assessing political and juridical theories spawned from an inferior position within the Roman Empire of antiquity and late antiquity.[7] Although formulated under similar conditions, they did not generally advance the rule of law as a solution for their sociopolitical predicament.[8] Even the later writings of Augustine, which explicitly address how political setbacks correlate to religious supremacy, offer an altogether different (i.e., extralegal) reply.[9] What these divergent approaches demonstrate is that circumstances alone do not dictate a specific response. If anything, it is the particular reaction of various Jewish jurists and thinkers to their encounter with specific historical conditions, especially their predilection toward legal expansion, as well as the range of juridical constructs that they advanced as a result, which makes their writings noteworthy.

In contrast with those who impugn Jewish political discourse due to the historical context of its origins, modern thinkers, ironically, have been increasingly drawn to such writings for very similar reasons. Legal and political theorists, such as Robert Cover and Michael Walzer, have deliberately focused upon them in order to gain important, and unpredictable, insights into law and politics from the vantage point of those who are disempowered.[10] Moreover, the absence of sovereignty that limited the practical ramifications of Jewish political thought, also carved out more freedom for its leading thinkers to conceive of new legal and political ideas unencumbered by the constraints of their immediate feasibility. To analogize from another period, Bernard Bailyn has emphasized that the political genius of the American founding fathers was fostered precisely due to their "provincialism." Living across the Atlantic, far from the epicenter of Western civilization, spurred these creative thinkers to generate monumental political ideas (which they eventually found ways to implement).[11] In the case of early Jewish political writings, a very different set of "provincial" conditions similarly nurtured a more capacious imagination that introduced a striking and varied jurisprudence of judicial independence.[12]

Rather than positing an inexorable link between conditions of disempowerment and Jewish legalism, therefore, a more constructive approach is to analyze the ways thinkers represent legal authority in the relative absence of power, and respond to a range of historical challenges.[13] Drawing on past traditions, they also cultivate new ideas and concepts, and gradually devise several models of separation. The impetus behind legal expansion reflected in these writings can hardly be reduced to even a variable state of disempowerment, although undoubtedly sociohistorical circumstances from the Persian period onward were a contributing factor.[14] The trajectory discernable among various early Jewish jurisprudential writings was certainly driven by other factors as well, especially the centrality of law.

The Source Factor: Deuteronomy and the Pentateuch

A different kind of a factor that gradually elevated the significance of what originated in the Bible as a secondary template of legal authority traces to its scriptural address: Deuteronomy. By a certain stage in postbiblical history, legal traditions found in Deuteronomy and the rest of the Pentateuch, irrespective of their specific content, carried greater significance for most Jews than alternative traditions recorded elsewhere in Scripture. For this reason, Deuteronomy's jurisprudence arguably looms larger for many postbiblical interpreters than mainstream ideas recorded elsewhere in Scripture.

Reconstructing the early history of privileging the Pentateuch as a source of law goes beyond the scope of this book, but one can adumbrate its broad contours. The notion of assigning different normative weight to the divisions of the Hebrew Bible is firmly rooted in later rabbinic literature. A thrice repeated Bavli dictum asserts, "words of Torah cannot be deduced from words of *Kabbalah* [other Scriptural traditions],"[15] to conclude that binding laws cannot be derived from non-Pentateuchal Scripture. Such a categorical rule might not apply across rabbinic literature,[16] but it is certainly true that the Pentateuch constitutes the primary scriptural source for halakhic teachings.[17] Thus, midrash halakhah only systematically expounds the Pentateuch.[18] The rare instance where a non-Pentateuchal passage is seen as contradicting a Pentateuchal norm calls into question its very (canonical) legitimacy.[19] Other rabbinic sources, especially from a later period, reinforce a distinct hierarchy among the Bible's divisions.[20]

While in pre-rabbinic literature this division is not as sharply demarcated, traces of the Pentateuch's unique stature can be found much earlier.[21] Late biblical books—Ezra, Nehemia and Chronicles—cite phrases such as "*Torat Moshe* [Torah of Moses]" or "*Sefer Moshe* [Book of Moses]" that refer to a distinct Mosaic corpus,[22] which likely corresponds to something akin to Deuteronomy or the entire Pentateuch.[23] These designations are invoked to distinguish the Mosaic corpus as a foundational normative source.

Over the next centuries, the primacy of the Pentateuch became ever more apparent in certain circles. The Samaritans adopted only the Pentateuch as sacred literature.[24] Among the Judeans, who gradually canonized the Bible into a tripartite division at later stage(s),[25] the relative superiority of the Pentateuch as a formative corpus was arguably reinforced in a more nuanced manner. The chapters that frame the Prophets and Writings call for an intensive meditation upon the Pentateuch as a cardinal imperative.[26] Likewise, the third-century-BCE Septuagint translation of the Pentateuch into Greek likely reinforced its unitary status and signaled its priority over other divisions (which were only translated later), especially for communities of the Diaspora.[27] Although the Pentateuch's normative status was not directly at issue in any of the above, its elevation readily followed from these developments. Still, the exact standing of the Pentateuch relative to other sacred books (whether eventually included in the scriptural canon or not) was likely contested throughout this period.[28]

With this general background, it is instructive to consider the relevance of the source factor for the writings addressed in this book. In the case of rabbinic literature, this factor clearly plays a role in privileging Deuteronomy. Its impact on the jurisprudence of the other postbiblical works also seems probable, but requires some unpacking. Although certain of these writings betray more complex attitudes toward the relative authority among the divisions of the Bible than rabbinic literature, they all notably single out the Pentateuch in their exegesis. Even so, discerning the underlying reasons for their respective preferences ultimately points to what is arguably the most salient factor that shaped early Jewish jurisprudence—the centrality of law.

Qumran Literature

The primacy of the Pentateuch in Qumran is manifest in numerous ways. Many manuscripts of Pentateuchal books were found in the Qumran caves. Its library includes various works of rewritten Pentateuch (e.g., the Temple Scroll or 4QReworked Pentateuch) or of individual books (e.g., Genesis Apocryphon). Countless passages draw from, or expound upon, Pentateuchal verses (including writings grounded in non-Pentateuchal books).[29] Several scattered references refer explicitly to "*Sefer ha-Torah / Moshe* [The Book of the Torah/Moses]."[30]

At the same time, non-Pentateuchal Scripture figures prominently in Qumran,[31] and has particular relevance for the apocalyptic aspirations of the sectarian community. About a quarter of the biblical manuscripts are prophetic literature. Works of rewritten Bible and *pesharim* build upon non-Pentateuchal books, as do the liturgical *Hodayot*. The central sectarian works are likewise shaped by all of Scripture. CD is thus filled with non-Pentateuchal references.[32] The Rule of the Community also contains such references,[33] and opens with an explicit appeal to act justly as God commanded Moses and the prophets (1QS 1:2–3).

Significantly, this opening directive situates the prophets in a normative role, an association that recurs elsewhere.[34] For instance, 1QS 8:15–16 interprets "a path to God (Isa 40:2)" as "the study of the law wh[i]ch he commanded through the hand of Moses, in order to act in compliance with all that has been revealed from age to age, and according to what the prophets have revealed through his holy spirit."

Notice how the divine path converges with actions prescribed in the Pentateuch and the prophetic (and ongoing revelatory) traditions. CD likewise invokes Moses and the holy anointed ones (5:21–6:1), and the Torah and prophetic books (7:15–18), when decrying the abandonment of commandments. Similarly, the epilogue of 4QMMT (4Q397 Frags. 14–21:9–10) arguably appeals to the Pentateuch as well as other parts of Scripture in a normative context.[35]

Complementing the heightened role of prophetic traditions in Qumran is the pivotal concept of ongoing revelation.[36] Alongside Mosaic teachings, Qumran writers exalt the revelatory words of David, Isaiah, and other early prophets; the inspired traditions of the sect; the declarations of the Teacher of Righteousness; and the (imminently) anticipated guidance of the eschatological prophet. This dynamic scheme would seem to unsettle the notion of a singular revelatory moment or a closed canon.[37]

Evidently a cross section of sacred writings influences sectarian ideology. Nevertheless, the Pentateuch and its norms still occupy a focal position in Qumran.[38] A vivid illustration of this is a particular reference to the "*Sefer ha-Torah*" interpolated within a selective citation of the by-now-familiar Deuteronomic verses on the judiciary. Restating Deut 17:10–11's description of the supreme judgment announced by the Levitical priests and judge, the Temple Scroll (11Q19 56:3–4) appends this interpolated reference at the end, "And you shall act according to the law which they explain to you and according to the word which they say to you *Blank* from the *Sefer ha-Torah*." As reformulated, the verses mandate that the judges' rulings derive specifically from the Torah.[39] More generally, Qumran literature presents a world where punctilious observance of pentateuchal-based religious laws is of paramount significance.[40] Among the Pentateuchal books, Deuteronomy particularly stands out.[41] Its manuscripts abound, and it plays a distinct normative role in various Qumran works.[42]

In fact, the status of prophetic and other revealed works in Qumran should be correlated to the Pentateuch and its laws, and understood as an outgrowth of Mosaic revelation.[43] Casting prophetic figures in a legal role extends the Mosaic model; and affirming the notion of ongoing revelation offers a way of continuing Mosaic revelation. Moreover, for the community at Qumran, who self-consciously inhabit a world without active prophecy,[44] divine inspiration is arguably generated by an exegesis of the legal norms of the Torah.[45] This hermeneutic process also seems crucial for achieving the community's eschatological aspirations.

Josephus

By the late Second Temple period the singular stature of the Pentateuch is widely accepted, and both Josephus and Philo endorse this viewpoint, albeit each in his own way. In both *Antiquities* and *Apion,* Josephus highlights the laws taught by Moses the lawgiver,[46] and in the former work he recounts them in detail.[47] Already in the introductory paragraphs, Josephus proclaims their importance, and Moses's singular standing (*Ant.* 1.15–20). This section underscores the principal motifs that Josephus aims to amplify throughout *Antiquities.*

Even earlier in the introduction, however, Josephus adduces the famous translation of the Pentateuch (*Nomos*) commissioned by Ptolemy II as a precedent for teaching about Judaism to a Greek audience, while stressing that he will enlarge the scale of his work to retell all of Scripture (*Ant.* 1.12).[48] Accordingly, after restating much of the Pentateuch in the initial four books of *Antiquities,* Josephus dedicates the next six or so books to summarizing the rest of Scripture. For the leading chronicler of the Jewish past, using a larger library has obvious appeal. The rest of Scripture preserves a vast trove of material that is relevant for the historical record.[49] Moreover, Josephus also draws profound lessons from the entire Bible. For instance, when Josephus wishes to learn about the optimal constitution (see Chapter 4), he derives insights from the Pentateuch as well as the rest of Scripture (e.g., Judges and Samuel). In this vein, Josephus extends the demand for exactitude, which originally applies only to the Pentateuch (see Deut. 4:2, 12:32), to all of Scripture, avowing that in his biblical restatement he will neither add nor subtract from Scripture (see *Ant.* 1.17).[50]

In order to better grasp the interrelationship of the Pentateuch to the rest of Scripture for Josephus, another introductory passage from *An-*

tiquities is illuminating. Linking the substantive content of all of Scripture, *Ant.* 1.14 emphasizes the surprising salience of Mosaic laws for the great Jewish historian of antiquity. Foremost among the numerous lessons one learns from the historical record of Scripture, Josephus avers, is that those who follow God's will and obey the laws will flourish and avoid the misfortunes that beset those who transgress them. Similarly, by evaluating scriptural history, Josephus insists, one realizes how profoundly Moses the lawgiver comprehended God's nature, and the veracity of the Mosaic account of God's deeds (*Ant.* 1.15–17). In short, according to Josephus the remainder of Scripture reinforces the Mosaic laws and affirms the Pentateuch's vital teachings. Notably, by the latter part of *Apion* (2.145–286), his final work, Josephus focuses exclusively on the Pentateuchal laws of Moses in summarizing the essence of Judaism.

Philo

Philo underscores the superlative quality of Moses and Mosaic laws in many different works, extolling Moses as the optimal lawgiver, and Mosaic edicts as ideal laws.[51] Consistent with his own evaluation, he cites the Pentateuch frequently throughout his oeuvre.[52] Notably, Philo always refers to the entirety of the Pentateuch as a unit, which he attributes to Moses.[53] He further emphasizes the uniformity of Pentateuchal laws by describing the Decalogue as an encapsulation of the principal legal themes of the Pentateuch.[54]

In contrast to Josephus, Philo focuses on the Pentateuch to such an extent that scholars wonder to what degree he was even familiar with the rest of Scripture.[55] Indeed, Philo's citations of non-Pentateuchal books are sporadic and infrequent. Moreover, Philo notably attributes these non-Pentateuchal sources to a Mosaic circle.[56]

What emerges is that Philo's larger hermeneutic enterprise revolves around the Pentateuch and Mosaic teachings. This emphasis is far from obvious, and critical for understanding Philo's interpretive agenda. At first blush, Philo's allegorical exegesis, which accentuates philosophical tropes, seems more suited for non-Pentateuchal books.[57] Even within the Pentateuch, Philo devotes much space to the creation account, narratives, and personalities of Genesis and Exodus. Such an emphasis would seem to easily extend beyond the Pentateuch. Yet Philo's exposition on the relationship of Genesis to the rest of the Pentateuch offers an important clue as to why this does not follow. The creation account supplies a necessary backdrop for understanding the essence of the Mosaic laws, according to Philo, and similarly the patriarchal narratives exemplify the laws as animated.[58] At the same time, Mosaic laws "point the way to the ideal life—life according to nature."[59] Even Philo's Hellenistic allegorical worldview merges into his account of the laws of the Torah, or in the words of Hindy Najman, participates in a "Mosaic discourse."[60] So Philo's naturalistic-philosophical ideology is embedded in his exegesis of the Pentateuch and its laws.[61]

In sum, the formative and normative significance of the Pentateuch can be discerned in late biblical literature, and finds fuller expression in Second Temple literature, including the writings of Qumran, Josephus, and Philo. Even though one cannot categorically separate the Pentateuch from the other scriptural divisions in these writings (indeed, prophetic books maintain an important role in Qumran and Josephus), the exalted status of the Pentateuch is incontrovertible. The very placement of a tradition (especially concerning a normative matter, such as the structure of legal authority) within the Pentateuch affords it greater import for the writings of Qumran, Josephus, Philo, and of course rabbinic literature.

But concluding the analysis of the source factor here may actually obscure matters more than it explains them. Even if traditions from Deuteronomy have heightened stature, this does not determine how they should be balanced alongside other teachings from the Pentateuch or even the rest of Scripture. For instance, Philo and rabbinic literature draw on Deuteronomy 17 as well as Exodus 18 as sources for their respective accounts of legal authority,[62] and the Bavli, for example, culls from Jeremiah 21 (see Chapters 2 and 5). Thus, Deuteronomic pericopes may be aligned with other Pentateuchal or biblical passages. Moreover, any teaching of the Pentateuch is subject to interpretation, and privileging the Pentateuch divulges little about how to construe its verses. Recall how Philo expands upon Deuteronomy 17, and yet locates a ruler at the head of the judiciary (see Chapter 2).[63] Only certain amplifications of Deuteronomy's account of legal authority will lead to the particular jurisprudence that is recorded in these postbiblical works. Or, to formulate this differently, only an exegete with a certain juristic orientation will turn to Deuteronomy and use it as a springboard for developing robust notions of legal autonomy and a separation of powers.

In truth, the very notion of privileging the Pentateuch derives from such an orientation. While the heightened stature of the Pentateuch was described above as an incidental factor that may have contributed to the influential afterlife of Deuteronomy's jurisprudence, on deeper reflection the question of the status of the Pentateuch, and its normative significance, are intimately connected. A basic reason the Pentateuch is distinguished from other scriptural divisions involves its function as the repository of most laws.[64] The title "Torah,"[65] or its Greek translation *nomos,* accentuates this dimension.[66] As the normative commitment intensified among Jews from the Persian period onward, and as the Pentateuch increasingly came to be understood as a legal charter, it eclipsed other sacred works as a source of authority.

This brief excursus sketched the normative stature of the Pentateuch for postbiblical works as diverse as the writings of Qumran, Josephus, and Philo. These authors offer three divergent reconceptualizations of the biblical and Jewish tradition—the apocalyptic, the political-historical, and the naturalistic-philosophical—and yet they all strikingly accent the normative dimension of the Pentateuch, and share in common a deep commitment to the legal principles of Judaism. One could easily imagine how these various remappings of Judaism would clash with a legalistic emphasis,[67] but the opposite is true. James Kugel commented on this point in reference to Philo and Josephus:[68]

> Even Philo, whose love of the allegorical interpretation of biblical narrative hardly requires glossing, and his younger

contemporary Josephus, who says that his two principal motives in writing a history of his people were to put the events in
which he himself had participated in their broader historical
context as well as to publish an account of events so as to combat
the Greek-speaking public's general ignorance of them—both
these writers nevertheless devote a hefty part of their rewriting
of the Pentateuch to a review of its law and their proper interpretation. This is certainly a significant fact.

This insightful summary should be sharpened in two respects. First,
it is worth emphasizing that Philo's allegory and Josephus's historiography would seem a priori to be incongruous with a normative account
of Judaism. Second, notwithstanding the logic behind this presupposi-
tion, not only do Philo and Josephus devote much attention to law, they
remarkably view their allegorical and historical projects as integrally
connected to the laws.[69] Josephus's history affirms the necessity of abiding
by God's laws, and his political vision promotes the rule of sacral law;
and Philo's naturalism mirrors the perfect laws of Moses. Likewise,
Qumran's eschatology demands exact normative interpretations and
punctilious observance of the revealed laws. Their writings thus constitute formative expressions of the normative bias of early Jewish thought,
which is also captured in the exceptional jurisprudence they each advance. Within rabbinic writings, legalism becomes so pronounced that
the Pentateuch assumes an unparalleled normative stature. Tracing back
to the Sinaitic discourses, and reverberating across the centuries, this
legalistic orientation perhaps most accounts for the particular jurisprudential turn that is manifest among these prominent postbiblical works.

The Theological Factor: Conceptions of Kingship

Another factor driving the juridical shift described throughout this book
intersects with theological conceptions of kingship in biblical and postbiblical literature. A profound tension in this body of writings concerns

the very legitimacy of kingship in a theocratic system, and this has important secondary implications for the monarch's position within the judicial scheme. While the Bible contains sundry materials relating to kingship, scholars have discerned three overarching perspectives.[70] These can be briefly summarized, after which I will examine their impact on the nature and form of legal authority.

A pronounced royalist theology in antiquity conceives of the king as a quasi-divine figure, a kind of earthly embodiment of, or intermediary for, celestial powers. Numerous Mesopotamian and Egyptian texts speak of rulers and Pharaohs, mutatis mutandis, in terms of deification.[71] In a similar vein, select biblical passages depict the filial relationship between the king and God. Psalms 2:7 announces God's declaration to the anointed king, "you are my son, today I have begotten thee," and Psalms 89:27–28 records a reciprocal affirmation of the familial bond between the king and God, "He [the king] shall cry to me, You are my Father, my God, and the Rock of my salvation. I [God] will make him the first-born, the highest of the kings of the earth."

An emphatic voice in biblical and postbiblical literature rejects this royalist theology, perceiving human kingship to be an affront to divine authority. The most crucial expression of this motif appears following the Israelites' initial bid for a king to govern like "all the nations" (1 Sam 8:4–5, verses which overlap to a degree with Deut 17:14–20). Met with palpable disapproval by the prophet Samuel, the petition elicits an even more pointed rebuke from on high. Deeming this request to be a kind of idolatrous rejection of divine rule, God exclaims, "they have rejected Me, that I should not reign over them. Just as they have done to me from the day I brought them up out of Egypt to this day, forsaking me and serving other gods" (1 Sam 8:7–8).

The biblical responses to the idolatrous threat posed by a temporal king are varied. A concessionary stance makes room for a mortal ruler of limited jurisdiction but insists that "the king is not a god."[72] This is exemplified by the continuation of 1 Samuel, where, despite the theologically problematic nature of monarchy, God proceeds to sanction the appointment of Saul and future kings as political rulers in accord with the popular request, but does not invest them with sacral authority. Even with a limited mandate, the king's capacity to abuse whatever political powers he obtains is bluntly outlined (1 Sam 8:11–18), and the king and his nation are deliberately enjoined to obey God's commandments (see 1 Sam 12:14–15).

A more strident biblical response does not narrow the scope of kingship, but renounces the institution entirely. Hosea (13:4–11) records the furious words of God expressing the profound betrayal of divine sovereignty inherent in human kingship. Other biblical passages echo a similar sentiment. Reacting to the popular demand that he become a dynastic ruler, Gideon flatly declines. "I will not rule over you, neither shall my son rule over you, the Lord shall rule over you" (Jdg 8:23), Gideon insists, proclaiming the exclusive legitimacy of a theocracy. The Sinaitic discourses, which will be considered further below, arguably epitomize this model.

The various conceptions of kingship—a royalist theology, a limited monarchy, and a theocracy—seem to generate, or correlate with, distinct notions of legal authority. Under a royalist theology, dispensing the highest form of justice is one of the outstanding attributes of the sacral king.[73] In this spirit, the Psalmist entreats God to designate the king as the mediator of divine justice. "Give the king your justice, O God, and your righteousness to a king's son. May he judge your people with righteousness, and your poor with justice" (Ps 72:1–2). Similarly, elaborate biblical accounts of royal justice display a divinely inspired king, such as Solomon, or an exalted messianic ruler, such as the "Shoot of Jesse," exercising supreme legal authority.

The second conception, which opposes the royalist theology and instead envisions a limited monarchy, likely also influences the configuration of legal authority, albeit in a slightly more complex manner. With a weakened monarchic institution—the king being a pale shadow of an absolutist or divine figure—a void in leadership arises, raising basic "constitutional" questions about the delegation of powers.[74] The king will retain certain sovereign functions, but whether this encompasses legal authority is debatable.

To appreciate the reason for this disjuncture, one must consider the orientation toward limited kingship reflected in the conclusion of the 1 Samuel 8 narrative. Moshe Halbertal has described this compromise position as premised on an understanding that "the king is not a god."[75] Halbertal continues, "According to this understanding, God does not monopolize politics as his exclusive realm; instead, he sets limits on the claims that politics can make." Struggling "against the transformation of the political into the cosmological," this biblical tradition cuts the king down to size. This is achieved, according to Halbertal, by limiting the king to the political role of "a warrior, a *legislator,* or a *judge*" (emphasis added).

Halbertal's account rightly characterizes 1 Samuel, but his inclusion of legal authority among the king's "political" responsibilities touches on a crucial issue that is contested in Scripture. Whereas 1 Samuel presumably considers legal authority to be a standard administrative power (akin to military leadership or collecting taxes),[76] the thrust of Deuteronomy 17, and its extensive postbiblical elaborations, suggests otherwise.[77] Thus, Deuteronomy 17, like 1 Samuel, describes the king in tentative language and reduces his role so as to not undermine divine sovereignty, but differs in its assignment of legal authority to the priests and judge, who are proximate to God, and not the political ruler who is bound by divine laws.[78] Legal authority in Deuteronomy does not fit within the political, temporal sphere.[79]

Finally, the theocratic vision that insists upon God's exclusive sovereignty may animate the stronger version of jurisprudence reflected in early Jewish writings. Although in Chapter 4 this juridical model was described as championing the supremacy of the rule of law (mediated through sacral priests) to the exclusion of a monarchic figure, one can also reconceptualize it as a unique variant of royal justice, where law issues from the commandments of the divine king.[80] A theocracy arguably enables, or even to a certain extent drives, this form of Jewish jurisprudence.[81] Similarly, one can reconceptualize the previous paradigm (i.e., the more moderate opposition to a royalist theology) by thinking of two realms: a human king administering temporal, nonlegal matters, and the divine king overseeing supernal justice. Framed in this manner, sacral law falls under the domain of the divine sovereign.

It should be apparent by now that in addition to a possible causal relationship there is a deep structural resemblance between the distinctive models of Jewish jurisprudence traced throughout this book and the constructs of kingship described in this section. The basic and stronger versions of postbiblical jurisprudential writings correspond to the two alternative biblical responses to a royalist theology.[82] Just as the basic jurisprudence seeks to limit the role of the king to political matters and separate him from legal affairs, so too the first response to a royalist theology seeks to restrict the king to political matters and separate him from divine affairs. Similarly, just as the stronger jurisprudence insists that the rule of law requires the complete elimination of royal power, so too the second response insists that the kingdom of God cannot brook human kingship of any kind.

Yet the structural affinity between these templates should not be mistaken for an inherent identity. A theocratic conception does not necessitate rule by sacral law. Various biblical texts that trumpet the kingship of God do *not* emphasize God's rule through laws. Even passages that adopt a robust vision of a theocracy may intend to espouse an ideal of spiritual anarchy.[83] Likewise, a limited monarchy can arguably include administering legal affairs among the monarch's political responsibilities. God need not rule through laws, and laws need not be overseen by a spiritual authority.[84]

Accordingly, the decisive idea that transforms the jurisprudence of certain early Jewish writings, especially in its stronger form, is that theocracy is tantamount to divine rule *through* sacral law.[85] Moreover, with a growing association of God's rule with legal norms the convergence of these notions is increasingly manifest. The focus gradually shifts from the divine king commanding edicts to the people upholding sacred laws. The identification of God's dictates with sacred laws becomes so profound over time that in later rabbinic discourse the legal order is understood to be an immutable expression of divine will that is beyond divine repeal or elaboration—for the Torah "is not in Heaven."[86] This gives rise to the ubiquitous notion of the ancestral laws in Josephus or the even more all-encompassing account of the halakhah, and its institutional guardians, in rabbinic literature.[87] Only such a prodigious concept of law can assume so central a role within Jewish religion and society.[88] Its flourishing in the postbiblical period (and beyond) arguably derives from a fourth and final factor—the primacy of law and its autonomy within Judaism, beginning with its covenantal foundation as represented in the Bible.

The Covenantal Factor

Beyond focusing on a historical factor (disempowerment), a source factor (Deuteronomy's canonical status), and a theological factor (early conceptions of kingship) to explain the rise of an alternate arc within Jewish jurisprudential writings, it is instructive to revisit its biblical roots.[89] Certain of its constitutive elements trace back to the Bible in a much more profound manner than articulated thus far. Discerning these elements helps capture the core ideals that animate this jurisprudence.

In mapping out the trajectory of this jurisprudential strand, this book began with the foundation of Deuteronomy 17, which records a relatively anomalous administrative scheme that separates legal authority from royal power. Characterizing this biblical chapter in this manner, however, should not obscure its congruence with the rest of Deuteronomy. Moreover, Deuteronomy's jurisprudence—to invoke Steven Fraade's formulation—reworks and amplifies covenantal rules found earlier in the Pentateuch, especially in the Covenant Code,[90] in order to provide the rudiments of a "constitution."[91] Among numerous adaptations,[92] Deuteronomy expands upon several components of the Sinai Covenant, the legal nucleus of the Pentateuch.[93] It is the enduring traction of these cluster of tropes in formative biblical and postbiblical sources that offers a final, and perhaps most profound, explanation for the evolution of the early Jewish jurisprudence examined in this book.

Exodus's Sinaitic Covenant famously resembles the form of an Ancient Near Eastern suzerainty treaty, but contains several distinguishing features relating to the normative order. One relates to the remarkable way law comprises the primary substance of the covenant, and forms the content of the treaty's stipulations.[94] Several others flow from the striking identification of the suzerain and vassal with God and Israel, respectively (the royal metaphors are of much significance here). God, the suzerain king, directly reveals the law to Israel, a "kingdom of priests" (Exod 19:6), thereby widely diffusing responsibility among the people;[95] assigning divine law (the Torah) to human hands; and refusing an intervening role of a monarchic figure in this process.[96] To recapitulate, the Sinaitic discourse underscores the centrality of law, depicts God charging the people with its custody, emphasizes the human recipients of divine law, and precludes a powerful figure from commandeering legal authority.

Deuteronomy elaborates upon all four of these Sinaitic motifs. The primacy of law (theme one), and its pervasive role throughout all sectors of Israelite society (theme two)—from the widows and orphans to the priests and elders—and in all regions—from peripheral towns to the center—are critical themes in Deuteronomy.[97] The middle section of Deuteronomy (12–28) presents a lengthy code,[98] which is introduced by a hortatory prologue narrating an episodic history of the Israelites, including revelation at Horeb (Sinai) and the Decalogue, and capped by a renewal of the covenant. Moreover, in a host of ways Deuteronomy reinforces Israel's sweeping normative commitments: charging the people to transcribe God's laws; recite, study, and teach them; serve God by fulfilling the laws; and cleave to God by upholding them.[99] In its normative landscape, the central Temple is cast as the situs of supreme legal instruction, and all towns throughout the land of Israel are meant to host judges and officers.[100] Alongside priests, elders, and judges who exercise legal authority, ordinary Israelites are charged with obedience to divine law as the primary form of piety.[101] Beyond the supremacy of law and its expansion to all segments of society, Deuteronomy's jurisprudence also advances the human role in administering God's laws (theme three) by establishing judicial mechanisms for receiving testimony, examining legal matters and enforcing verdicts.

Chapter 17, a pivotal chapter in Deuteronomy's normative framework, reinforces similar motifs, and incorporates a final Sinaitic element. Designating a leading venue to complement the local magistrates, this chapter consolidates the judicial system (theme one). It also elevates the role of law in the sacral center, and announces a capital offense for those who disregard supreme legal instructions. In terms of the scope of legal responsibility (theme two), this chapter appoints Levitical priests and a judge whose rulings resolve the most vexing of legal questions, thereby maintaining legal order throughout the land. As for the human role in adjudication (theme three), Moshe Weinfeld has argued that Deuteronomy incorporates notions of "wisdom" into its jurisprudence by relying upon human reason to analyze rules, issue instructions, and dispense justice.[102]

Perhaps most significantly, this same chapter also amplifies a fourth Sinaitic motif. As described in the Introduction, Deuteronomy 17 noticeably marginalizes the king from the legal process, and nominates judges who preside outside his realm.[103] While the assignment of divine laws to the Israelites at Sinai could theoretically accommodate different forms of legal administration[104] (including priestly judges or sages), enthroning a royal persona at the helm of the judiciary would subvert the Sinaitic scheme (and clash with the tenor of much of the Pentateuch).[105] In this sense, Deuteronomy 17's jurisprudence offers a profound realization of Sinaitic (and Pentateuchal) values.

Rather than viewing the above as discrete Sinaitic legal themes that are magnified and institutionalized in Deuteronomy, they are best understood in concert. An enduring transmission of sacral law to human hands calls for its secure entrustment, which is shielded from the domineering will of a powerful sovereign. Formulated in the pattern of the Sinaitic template, Deuteronomy expands the scope and reach of sacral law and installs independent judges who can supervise just administration. Or to articulate this point in jurisprudential language: a particular conception of the source (= God) and ontology (= divine) of the law dictates a preferred mode of its administration (= judicial independence).[106]

A similar coalescence of motifs recurs in the postbiblical jurisprudence examined in this book. Indeed, the very manner in which Deuteronomy reworks covenantal themes stimulates a parallel hermeneutic process, well described by Fraade, where Deuteronomic innovations provide "the interpretive foundations for a variety of postbiblical Jewish reconceptions of Israel as a covenantal people with a divinely revealed polity."[107] The interplay of covenantal ideas that is discernible in both Deuteronomy and its postbiblical expansions exposes cumulative layers of a particular jurisprudence in the early Jewish imagination.

The centrality of law is manifest in Qumran, Josephus, and Philo, despite their widely disparate conceptualizations of Judaism. Qumran's sectarian community is devoted to legal obeisance; Josephus's theocracy revolves around the rule of law; and Philo's naturalism mirrors the embodiment of the perfect laws of Moses. In rabbinic discourse, the normative dimension of Judaism looms largest. As Moshe Halbertal has argued, even if there is much legalism in pre-rabbinic literature, the rabbinic idea of halakhah as the epitome of religious life remains unprecedented.[108]

A clear intensification of the primacy of law (theme one), therefore, pervades these postbiblical writings, along with a sense that law is the repository of the entire community (theme two), even if leading sages or priestly figures stand at the fore. The human role in the adjudicatory process is likewise pronounced (theme three), especially in rabbinic literature which develops a religious doctrine that the "Torah is not in heaven." Indeed, as Hayim Shapira has argued, rabbinic discourse develops an almost paradoxical notion that God is most manifest in halakhah when human decisors assume heightened responsibility for legal rulings.[109]

These three jurisprudential themes in postbiblical literature all contribute toward, and are reinforced by, the various modes of separation advanced by these writings (theme four). Thus, the Mishnah, and in a different sense Qumran writings, divide between royal power and the administration of justice. Rabbinic jurisprudence further erases vertical hierarchies from within the court. Finally, Hecataeus hints at an abolition of royal power, and Josephus's theocracy articulates a grand vision of the rule of sacral law in lieu of the classical forms of government. All of these templates promote the autonomy and independence of law.[110]

A durable regime of law requires its administration to be assigned to loyal jurists, certain biblical and postbiblical works assert, not powerful actors. In this manner, it is law—mediated through jurists—that rules, and shapes a society that is ennobled by its values. The postbiblical writings that follow the remarkable jurisprudential arc examined in this book offer thick elaborations of this core concept. Inscribed in elementary form upon biblical foundations, a flourishing jurisprudence materializes across the centuries, reflecting a sustained commitment to the centrality of law and its profound potential to structure society.

9

Ancient and Modern Jurisprudence

Parts One and Two presented a thick account of a distinct trajectory within early Jewish jurisprudential writings. Now it is possible to evaluate its nature from a comparative jurisprudential perspective. A preliminary comparison in the Introduction accented the separatist orientation of Deuteronomy's jurisprudence by drawing a sharp contrast with certain ancient and premodern traditions, which in different ways bind law to power, and a more measured contrast with others. In order to further illuminate the conceptual underpinnings of the postbiblical amplifications of Deuteronomy's jurisprudence, it is helpful to also bring them into conversation with more familiar legal traditions that share their separatist impulse, which they inevitably evoke from a contemporary vantage point: modern constitutional and continental jurisprudence.

Acknowledging the inescapable pull of a presentist perspective, after the extensive analyses of the prior two parts, also demands engaging in a more nuanced appraisal of the various affinities that we discern. As stated in the Introduction, we cannot but help see the ancient schemes as precursors of modern constitutional structures, for obvious reasons enumerated below. But a comparative analysis is most illuminating when it pushes beyond this surface and examines underlying differences as well as less recognizable parallels. Moreover, particular jurisprudential ideas that were conceived in a distant past may linger in ways that are elusive and obscure, and bringing them to the fore may also shed new light on contemporary and familiar structures. A potential contribution of this study is to probe ancient and modern discourses with these goals in mind, which is the aim of this chapter.

Comparative Constitutionalism

In ancient Jewish jurisprudential writings one discerns loose analogs to concepts that would become, many centuries later, the cornerstones of early modern and modern jurisprudence, including the separation of powers, an independent judiciary and the rule of law (the idea of a theocracy also has a different kind of modern currency).[1] This apparent convergence invites a closer comparison between the juristic concepts that lie at the core of these two legal traditions, notwithstanding the obvious chasm that divides them. Whether or not these early modern and modern constitutional notions derive in any meaningful way from ancient Jewish writings (a counterintuitive proposition that would require independent investigation),[2] a general correspondence between several of their foundational juristic concepts stands out. Even as ancient Jewish writings were authored against the grain of prevailing ideas while modern discourse tracks a larger, paradigm shift in Enlightenment thought, they both underscore the centrality of law in society. Further, they both promote the autonomy of law, and assign its discrete administration to independent judicial institutions. Finally, and perhaps most notably, both sets of writings separate power, by assigning supreme legal authority to a different address than the locus of political authority.

Two Paths toward Separation of Powers

Despite these structural resemblances, there are profound differences between these respective schemes, especially in their conceptions of separation of powers. What distinguishes the ancient Jewish incarnation of this principle is not just that it breaks with, and revises, regnant paradigms, in contrast with the early modern doctrine that conforms with wide-scale transformations.[3] The respective genealogy of, and justification for, separation in each of these traditions reveal fundamentally distinct traditions and concerns.

The modern formulation of this constitutional doctrine arises out of a profound story of rights and democracy that traces back to the dawn of the era of the Enlightenment. Beginning in the seventeenth century, a sustained assault on monarchic powers culminated in the Glorious Revolution of the latter half of the century. In its aftermath, a constitutional monarchy was devised that shifted much power to Parliament and the people, and thereby reshaped the nature of law and government. During this century, an early version of the notion of separation of powers found expression in the writings of Locke, alongside the actual restructuring of Parliament and the burgeoning of judicial independence in England. Over the course of the more violent transformations of the eighteenth century, these changes took even deeper root. A revolution in France buried the ancien régime, and a very different one that transpired across the Atlantic launched a new experiment in nation building. At the heart of these spectacular revolutions was a demand for sovereignty by the people. In the United States, the founding fathers heeded the clarion call of Montesquieu and constructed their new republic on the pillars of three branches of government, whose powers were deliberately separated from one another in order to protect and fulfill the will of the people.[4]

The modern separation of powers is born out of these circumstances, although its principal justification in early discourse is not always easy to discern. Locke's rationale relates to notions of representation and accountability. Montesquieu's own justification turns on the theme of tyranny,[5] although, as Jeremy Waldron has pointed out, this argument is more asserted than explained.[6] A similar theme is famously amplified by Madison in *Federalist* 47 and 51, where he contends that the rights of individual citizens are best safeguarded (in a "government which is to be administered by men over men") by having "ambition counteract ambition." Madison's influential account has been oft-repeated in Western jurisprudence ever since.[7]

In contemporary constitutional discourse, a variety of reasons for separation of powers have been cataloged, although they tend to cluster around related themes. For instance, Bruce Ackerman openly probes the question "Why separate?" and answers by enumerating three aims of separation: enhancing popular self-government; achieving greater professional competence (in implementing laws); and protecting fundamental rights. All three are grounded in democratic concerns.[8] Other approaches explain the way separation of powers advances the rule of law, likewise understood as a vehicle of democracy, which serves to check and limit governmental powers.[9] In sum, the various justifications for separation of powers that have been posited usually revolve around themes of rights and democracy within the context of popular sovereignty.

In contrast, the postbiblical separation of powers plainly does not emanate from principles of democracy or individual rights. These early modern and modern values are no doubt alien to the ancient Jewish mind-set,[10] which underscores obligations rather than rights, and primarily focuses upon the corporate entity.[11] Instead, an ancient Jewish notion of separation is grounded in an entirely different rationale revolving around the centrality and autonomy of law, and the need to preserve its integrity from the encroachment of those who wield power. Evidently, separation of powers need not serve democratic goals, but can derive from an altogether different genealogy related to the autonomy and integrity of law.

Revisiting the Western Notion of Judicial Independence

Yet in light of the above, it is worth reconsidering the nature of separation of powers as it arises in the modern polity, particularly with respect to the distinct role of the judicial branch, in order to interrogate whether it is in fact solely grounded in a theory of rights and democracy. As we have seen, the rationale behind separating powers is not adequately articulated in certain early modern works, and this is especially true of the individuation of the judicial branch.[12] Whereas the initial forms of separation of powers in the early modern period were focused on a binary division between the king and parliament, rather than a tripartite separation,[13] it was only Montesquieu's misunderstanding of the English form of government, and then the framers' deliberate constitutional structure which it inspired, that carved out a discrete judicial branch.[14] Even then, the original aim of the framers was presumably to add the "weakest" of the branches (see *Federalist* 78). It was only following the influential jurisprudence of the Marshall Court, and especially its avowal of the doctrine of judicial review, that a powerful third branch gradually emerged.[15] Thus, the autonomy of the sphere of law, and its supreme adjudication, did not arise in a straightforward manner from the elemental forms of separation of powers. Moreover, from a certain vantage point independent judicial authority is the most puzzling of these powers.

The standard approach to evaluating judicial power in modern constitutional theory is to view the court within the framework of statecraft, as an engine of democracy[16] (a further extension of this idea has been called "legal constitutionalism").[17] But this perspective is far from obvious. Whereas the executive and legislative branches at least ostensibly trace back to the democratic will of the people (filtered through their representation), the judicial branch has a far more attenuated relationship to them.[18] Moreover, the substantial independence and authority of the judiciary poses difficult questions concerning its very legitimacy on democratic grounds (what Alexander Bickel famously labeled as the "counter-majoritarian difficulty").[19] While important democratic defenses of judicial power have been advanced by scholars such as Ely and Ackerman, other commentators, including Bickel, Kramer, Tushnet, and Waldron, have accepted such criticisms to varying degrees, and accordingly have called for greater judicial restraint and a return to popular sovereignty.[20]

In addition, other hallmark features of the modern exercise of judicial power raise further challenges when evaluated under the lens of democratic theory, including fundamental rights jurisprudence, the doctrine of *stare decisis* (and more generally the judicial obligation to follow precedent), and the enshrinement of constitutional norms. These well-established principles and practices elevate and entrench legal norms, seemingly even when they are at odds with the democratic will of the people. Here, too, significant democratic justifications have been formulated in defense of these doctrines (akin to theories that ground the rule of law in democratic justifications, and seek to advance democracy through the judicial branch),[21] but one wonders whether they are commensurate to the force and stature of these juristic concepts in Western democracies.[22]

Rather than evaluating the above doctrines and practices as arising (exclusively) from democratic concerns, then, it may be constructive to (also) view them as deriving from the unique stature of law, and the distinctive standing of legal norms, within Western society.[23] Indeed, perhaps the above-enumerated doctrines reflect a deeply embedded intuition in the West that associates law with an autonomous sphere of justice, irrespective of particular democratic considerations. Returning to the origins of judicial independence in the Anglo-American tradition helps capture this point. The rising power of the judiciary in England emanated, not from a separation of the governing branches, but through a very different process that built upon the cumulative (and idiosyncratic) traditions of the common law, which represented a distinct kind of (intellectual and societal) enterprise.[24] Justice Coke famously described this singular enterprise, and the need to keep it beyond the sovereign's reach, from an intellectual and disciplinary standpoint (as only the court can apply "artificial reasoning," in contrast with rational thought).[25] But perhaps a more fruitful way to frame this dichotomy is to distinguish between law and politics. This division may have carried over into the new republic, which further demarcated a distinct province of law.

Consider especially the landmark 1803 US Supreme Court decision in *Marbury v. Madison*,[26] where Chief Justice John Marshall—in a carefully wrought opinion that sidestepped a direct confrontation with President Jefferson—established the unique position of the judiciary as the ultimate arbiter of constitutionality. As Paul Kahn shrewdly observes, the essence of the court's ruling revolves around what it signifies about legal—not political—authority:

> Ironically, modern legal interpretations of *Marbury* locate its brilliance in the assertion of a political strategy that accomplishes its end of empowering the Court while avoiding any command to the executive.[27] . . . On this view, governance by the courts must be defended on political grounds, just like any other assertion of political authority. The significance of *Marbury*, however, lies in the other direction, that is in the distinction of law *from* political action.[28]

Kahn rightly locates the magnitude of *Marbury* in the crucial boundary that it draws between law and politics. As Kahn argues, these realms have fundamentally different natures, and their separation has enduring implications for American constitutionalism.[29]

Various features distinguish the sphere of law. According to Kahn, law constitutes the realm of reason, in contrast with politics that represents the realm of will and action.[30] For Ronald Dworkin, law embodies and advances moral principles.[31] Harold Berman identifies tradition and authority as inherent aspects of law.[32] Other salient characteristics of legal reasoning include interpretation, analogical and analytical arguments, and collective deliberations. Some, or perhaps even all, of these features seem to single out the judicial task, the practice of law, and the role of legal doctrines.[33] It is this distinct nature of law that requires safeguarding and delimiting; which is achieved by separating powers.

Here is where the account of early Jewish jurisprudential writings analyzed throughout this book offers an illuminating critical perspective on the doctrine of separation. As the legal sociologists Nonet and Selznick have argued, the fuller meaning of jurisprudential principles emerges when they are located within their social context.[34] In this vein, early Jewish prototypes of separation expose a core sociological tension between law and power that underlies this doctrine.[35] Several postbiblical works demonstrate how an ideal of separating the administration of justice from political power can grow organically out of a society that cherishes the legal order. Experiencing a heightened need to conserve and maintain the integrity of law and the pursuit of justice from the corrosive impact of political power spawns such a separation.[36]

In early Jewish discourse the exalted status of law derives from its hallowed nature (as the Torah's norms are perceived of as an expression of the divine will). While Modern society may have more varied commitments, peeling beneath the layers of modern jurisprudence one may still be able to discern a transfigured form of this sacral discourse, a kind of secularized legal theology (pace Weber). Berman and others have written extensively about the religious sensibility that shapes the nature of law in the West.[37] Pointing to foundational elements of jurisprudence such as ritual, tradition, authority, and universality, Berman has argued that their origins are grounded in law's religious ancestry.[38] One need not fully concur with his argument to consider the intriguing proposition that the singularity of the domain of law is due to its religious roots, or alternatively the manner in which law supplants (and thereby fills) the social role of religion. Even without making as bold a claim, a more moderate account along the various lines articulated above would still recognize the unique realm of law as the sphere of morality, tradition, and reason, and it is this "hallowed" ground that requires safekeeping.[39]

In sum, notwithstanding the marked differences between the origins of the notions of separation of powers in Western and ancient discourses, the above analysis suggests a greater affinity between them than appears at first blush. Not only are they structurally similar, but perhaps their underlying rationales also overlap to a degree. In fact, the conceptual resemblance between certain strands of American and rabbinic jurisprudence runs deeper and extends to the second iteration of separation of powers as well (the "internal version—dissemination of powers").[40] Elaborating on the concept of the "reign of law" inaugurated by *Marbury*, Kahn emphasizes that this notion denies the authority of powerful actors to the point that it cannot even brook the empowerment of the judge as a particular subject. Accordingly, from the time of *Marbury* onward, constitutional decisions are pronounced as the "opinion of the Court" (i.e., a legitimate form of legal authority), not just the sole ruling of a powerful judge (which, in Kahn's taxonomy, would be a form of political authority).[41] In a structurally similar manner, various rabbinic writings from late antiquity (examined in Chapter 6), which seek to evenly distribute power within the court, display a similar shift in emphasis away from powerful, individual judges and toward a *per curiam* judicial institution (i.e., the Sanhedrin).[42]

The Stronger Version of Separation in Modern Western Jurisprudence

The third iteration of separation of powers (the "stronger version— elimination of powers" described in the Introduction and Chapter 4), however, exceeds the postulates of modern Western jurisprudence by advancing a more daring thesis about the relationship between law and power, with an even bolder implication or undercurrent. Whereas the basic model that surfaces within certain early Jewish writings locates political power in a distinct realm apart from the judiciary, a stronger version asserts that a commitment to legalism requires vanquishing political actors even from an alternate arena. Here the autonomy of law necessitates not just the segregation of the political sphere but its abolition. Instead of reliance on political actors, the polity should rest entirely on the rule of law, through the mediation of an autonomous legal body (a kind of kritarchy or nomocracy). Therefore, what is at stake in espousing this model of legal authority is the very viability of the political system, or at least its conventional forms.

According to this viewpoint, the democratic tenet of "a government of laws, and not of men,"[43] is necessarily incomplete so long as men and women have any role in governance. The rule of law demands the absolute and total rule of law.[44] This is the heart of what Josephus signifies by "theocracy," notwithstanding the violence done to this term in modern times (as explained in Chapter 4).[45] Likewise, the Talmud also expresses a similar theme through its piercing homiletics (see Chapter 7). Grappling with the relationship between justice and sovereignty, these texts expose an irresolvable clash between these spheres. Moreover, they invert prevalent assumptions by positing that, instead of the powerful controlling the law, those with legal authority should command power.

This stronger variant within early Jewish jurisprudential writings mounts a formidable challenge to modern Western legal regimes that advance the notions of the rule of law and an independent judiciary as an adjunct to a more accommodating notion of separation of powers. In modern templates,[46] the judiciary operates alongside one or more political branches populated by people who govern. In contrast, the stronger jurisprudence proposes that a genuine commitment to legalism requires the dissolution of political institutions that are led by influential officials.[47] Thus, the stronger version presses the notion of the rule of law well beyond its ordinary expression in modern Western jurisprudence, toward a more ambitious and far-reaching formulation.

While the claim that the rule of law compels the complete removal of sovereign actors has no obvious analog in contemporary discourse, the notion of predicating the polity on a foundational rule of law does resonate with aspects of modern jurisprudence. For instance, the US Constitution, which establishes different branches of federal government, has traditionally been understood as a statement of the "fundamental and paramount law of the nation." In a more sweeping sense, arguably the entire design of the US Constitution aims not just to affirm the "rule *of* law," but to achieve "rule *by* law."[48]

Moreover, whether to view law as underpinning political power represents a foundational inquiry in modern jurisprudence. A vigorous debate about the parameters of the rule of law among Continental jurists in the early part of the twentieth century turned on the question of the essential balance between law and politics. Their exchange remains vital to contemporary jurisprudence almost a century later.

During the Weimar Republic, leading Continental theorists, including Hans Kelsen and Carl Schmitt, disagreed fundamentally about the nature of German constitutional law and the legitimacy of liberal democratic government.[49] A vocal critic of the Weimar Republic, Schmitt repeatedly assailed its liberal parliamentarianism which governs through democratic pluralism safeguarded by legal procedures. Underlying his opposition was a wholesale rejection of modern liberalism's conception of the state as a neutral institution under the rule of law. Instead, Schmitt advanced an alternate political model in which a strong-willed sovereign decisively governs the state without the constraints of universal normative principles. Through the declaration of absolute decisions, an administration asserts its legitimacy against any divisive opposition from within the state. All dimensions of the state, including the legal system, grow out of the political will of the sovereign. By expanding the scope of the political sphere (already in his early landmark essay "The Concept of the Political"),[50] Schmitt maintains throughout his writings that a constitution depends on a prior political decision or action of the governing entity.[51]

Opposing Schmitt and other critics, Hans Kelsen was a staunch defender of the Weimar Republic and the German Constitution. For Kelsen, both of these Weimar institutions embodied a liberal democracy that promoted individual freedom, the central objectives of a political system. As scholars have persuasively argued,[52] Kelsen's political ideology intersects with, and is sustained by, his ambitious legal theory, generally considered to be his primary legacy.[53] A form of Kantian and positivist jurisprudence, Kelsen's legal theory helps realize, to use his youthful formulation, "the idea of the rule of law state."[54]

Sketching a universal, positive theory of law, Kelsen defines its core as a normative system whose rules are enforced. The validity of the specific norms derives from a *grundnorm*, the system's foundational norm. That is, the basic norm grounds the entire legal framework, and is a precondition to its validity. This very construct is crucial for Kelsen's political ideology as well. For this *grundnorm*—the basis of the whole legal edifice—also constitutes the foundation of the entire polity. Ultimately, the governmental entity derives its authority from a legal source.

In contrast with dualist theories of the relationship between law and the state, Kelsen's general theory proclaims their identity. Whereas the dualists conceptualize the political authority of the state as preceding the law, and consider the capacity to act without legal authorization as an essential element of statehood, Kelsen envisions a political system where people are subject as far as possible to the rule of law, not of people. Kelsen thereby achieves a "utopia of legality" (a term coined by Lars Vinx), where all acts of the state conform to legal norms.[55]

Divergent conceptions of the role of law and politics animate the opposing theories of Schmitt and Kelsen. While Schmitt and Kelsen both contend that the legal and political spheres intersect, they dispute the nature of their interrelationship. Schmitt contends that the legal order emerges from a decisive sovereign will, so law represents the expression of a powerful political force. Conversely, Kelsen understands the polity to be authorized by the rule of law, so that a legal base sustains the political entity.[56]

Returning to early Jewish jurisprudential writings, the stronger variant, like Kelsen, contemplates politics from a legal vantage point. But beyond Kelsen, this approach demands the total suspension or substitution of political rule by the legal order. More than situating the political branch within a legal frame, the stronger thesis proclaims the realm of law to be absolute.

Conclusion

Formative early Jewish writings discussing the nature and form of legal authority advance an extraordinary jurisprudence. In contrast with a popular conception that locates law in the province of rulers, these texts project a profound commitment to an autonomous and independent rule of law. What began as an anomalous strand in Deuteronomy 17, becomes amplified through a series of postbiblical writings extending into late antiquity.

Certain works express a moderate version of this idea. Even as they uphold monarchic rule, they aim to shield law from the intervention of the ruler and assign legal authority to independent officials. Further, these texts tend to disperse legal authority among a panel of judges and envision an autonomous legal system that functions by administering broadly applicable laws in a consistent manner. The dominant template in rabbinic literature especially seeks to limit the role of royal, priestly, and individual judges, and to elevate institutional justice. A stronger version, expressed in other texts, including Qumran writings, Josephus, and the Talmud, hails the supremacy of law and its ascendancy over the rule of powerful men. Although these writings from Jewish antiquity and late antiquity vary in their emphases and historical backgrounds, their overall orientation converges. They considerably expand the province of law and assert its independence. Collectively, these writings establish, and loudly proclaim, law's empire.

The legacy of this distinctive orientation was highly influential.[1] But it also evolved in unexpected ways. Although this topic requires discrete study, it is worth highlighting a few milestones in the post-Talmudic afterlife of this formative jurisprudence.

In the medieval world, Jewish law served a crucial role in preserving the Diasporic community. Living as a minority group in Christian and Muslim lands, with minimal political power, Jews relied upon their robust legal tradition to maintain social cohesion.[2] Medieval Jewish writings, accordingly, expounded upon the centrality of law. In this context, the question of the relationship of law to politics also arises, most famously in the eleventh homily of Rabbi Nissim Gerondi.[3] Surveying portions of Deuteronomy and rabbinic literature, Gerondi brilliantly posits that Jewish jurisprudence ideally operates with a binary system of judicial authority: the Sanhedrin upholds eternal principles of (divine) justice, while the king renders pragmatic verdicts.

The content of this fascinating homily has been analyzed extensively,[4] but its relationship to early rabbinic jurisprudence deserves further consideration. Distilling the variegated rabbinic material into a binary scheme, Gerondi's homily advances a novel configuration of the distribution of legal authority in light of the objectives of a legal system, which has a complex relationship to rabbinic jurisprudence. Its account of the Sanhedrin constitutes a stunning elaboration upon major rabbinic tropes. Emphasizing the primacy of the Sanhedrin's legal authority, Gerondi further proclaims that its institutional independence is indispensable for preserving the integrity of sacral law.[5] In articulating the Sanhedrin's exclusive commitment to deontological principles of justice, Gerondi also underscores the court's apolitical nature.[6] But in another respect, Gerondi's crucial reinsertion of the king into the juridical order grafts on a new element that sharply diverges from much prior jurisprudence.[7] Given the prevailing rabbinic opposition to the juridical role of powerful men, this innovative dimension of Gerondi's homily requires explanation.[8]

Some scholars suggest that the king's jurisdiction is merely supplemental for Gerondi, serving to correct failures in criminal procedure.[9] Rejecting this argument, Menachem Lorberbaum insists that Gerondi's thesis is bold and far-reaching.[10] Situating Gerondi within a wider medieval discourse, Lorberbaum describes his agenda as nothing short of delimiting a secular sphere for the political order, independent of the sacral-legal domain of the rabbinic courts. Moreover, Lorberbaum argues, much medieval Jewish jurisprudence shares this aspiration.[11] But even on a more moderate reading,[12] Gerondi's scheme opens up a space for the king to participate in the judicial process. Circumscribing the exclusivity of the court's jurisdiction, Gerondi thereby affirms the supplementary legal authority of the political organ, and the relevance of political considerations for certain legal decisions.

Gerondi thus expounds upon aspects of earlier rabbinic jurisprudence, but also introduces an opposite dimension. Whereas a primary aim of the dominant strand of rabbinic jurisprudence was to detach legal authority from the political sphere, now a contrary objective is also being pursued.[13] Gerondi's homily fosters the juridical legitimacy of the political sphere.

The reversal in direction makes much sense, however, given the distinct milieus in which these respective accounts were formulated. Much early rabbinic discourse resisted a regnant jurisprudence wherein a domineering ruler commandeered all judicial powers. Meanwhile, a sustained effort to secure and enlarge the authority of rabbis gradually succeeded. After centuries of this cumulative process, which was well suited to political conditions of limited empowerment, rabbinic law formed the backbone of medieval Jewish society (indeed, the first motif of Gerondi's homily trumpets the singularity of halakhah). Yet the exclusivity of rabbinic law also had its limits from the perspective of medieval Jewry, given the rigidity of religious rules, and the need for communal governance. Thus, medieval thinkers sought to construct a political or "secular" sphere, afford it legitimacy, and carve out its space within the halakhic system.[14] Moreover, they sought to elevate the role of human agency and enable the use of extra-normative considerations in the legal sphere as well. Accordingly, an opposite jurisprudential process unfolded that aimed to contract the sprawling normative system and allow it to accommodate necessary political interventions.

Turning to the early modern period, the influential afterlife of early Jewish jurisprudence (especially its stronger version) is manifest in different ways, which can be illustrated by a couple of instructive examples. The first involves the general predicament of Western European Jewry over the course of the pivotal seventeenth century. Even as the social conditions of early modern Jewish communities improved considerably, especially in centers like Amsterdam, the overall political odyssey of Diaspora life—where Jews lived under a host government—persisted.[15] Yet from the perspective of early modern political thought, new questions were being raised about the legitimacy of Jewish communities, along with an increasing call for sovereignty to be unitary.[16] In the words of Anne Oravetz Albert, "the political landscape had changed so as to make Jewish sovereignty both more necessary and more impossible to justify."[17]

In a revealing hermeneutic shift that surfaces in a polemical work from Amsterdam (highlighted by Albert), one can discern a jurisprudential expression crafted for this new historical moment, which also echoes certain early Jewish jurisprudential traditions. Grappling with the perpetual exegetical challenge that Gen. 49:10 ("The Scepter shall not depart from Judah") poses to Jews with minimal political clout, Isaac Orobio de Castro, a former Converso, vigorously defends Jewish sovereignty by advancing a "novel" interpretation wherein the "Scepter" refers not to kingship but to the rule of law.[18] According to Albert, "Orobio in one striking passage . . . locates . . . rule in the hands of judges, i.e., rabbis, who possess absolute, God-given authority in a distinctly governmental sense."[19]

Albert points to partial medieval antecedents for Orobio's teaching. But in truth, his position is an implicit[20] revival of a very old tradition.[21] Evaluated against the backdrop of early sources, especially Josephus, Orobio's hermeneutic should be recognized as a renewed formulation of the stronger strand of early Jewish jurisprudence. The devastating reality confronted by post-destruction Jewry—who struggled to define themselves politically under the rubric of classical notions of government—spawned a conception of law as the foundation of the polity in antiquity. And the burgeoning stature of seventeenth-century Jewry—who nevertheless had to contend with changing early modern notions of sovereignty—awakened a similar legal-political theory. There is enduring traction to this jurisprudential model well over a millennium later.

Another early modern incarnation of the strong version of Jewish jurisprudence, however, pivots in a very different direction. In the periods of the Enlightenment and Emancipation, the reach of Jewish legal-political ideas extended beyond ethnic boundaries and helped shape Western political discourse. For example, Eric Nelson traces the rise of seventeenth-century "republican exclusivism" to the Protestant reception of antimonarchic Jewish writings, including Josephus and rabbinic literature.[22] Nelson likewise demonstrates the profound influence of Josephus's theocracy on shaping other aspects of early modern Western thought.[23] Given that this is the most dramatic exemplar of the strong thesis of law's empire, the potential for this idea to be repercussive is beyond doubt. Yet it is precisely in following this trail that matters take a counterintuitive, and even ironic, turn.

As Nelson explicates, Josephus's notion of a theocracy paved the way for supporting, of all things, a doctrine of religious toleration in the early modern period. Explaining this effect, Nelson states that early modernists understood that, according to Josephus's ideal, the head of the Israelite *politeia* was the civil sovereign, who was entrusted with the administration of Mosaic laws. Because those laws encompass both civil and religious affairs, what emerges is that the civic authority (as opposed to the sacral authority, e.g., the high priest) also administers religious laws.[24] Adopting this model in early modern times, however, leads to a paradoxical result, for the only religious laws that a civic authority would support in practice are those that serve a civic purpose. Therefore, the early modern version of theocracy mandates a divinely ordained emptying of religious laws (i.e., a divinely ordained notion of toleration).

Beginning with a comprehensive mosaic legislation crammed with religious laws, and ending up with a blank set that tolerates all religious practices, is difficult to fathom. Yet this transformation can be traced to a crucial inversion that the concept of theocracy undergoes when it passes through the filter of early modern political thought. While sixteenth- and seventeenth-century writers understood the Josephan doctrine to assign jurisdiction over religious laws to the civic authority, the essence of Josephus's theocracy emphasizes the opposite idea. In a theocracy, religious jurists order the polity; or, more accurately, the immutable sacred laws of God, which are mediated through priestly jurists, constitute the polity.[25]

Thus, the appropriation of theocracy by early modern political thinkers to establish religious toleration is deeply ironic.[26] The irony is not merely a function of translation, which is an inevitable feature of the extension of Jewish jurisprudential ideas to a universal context,[27] but is manifest in the particular political doctrine that emerges, in which the leading civic authority erases (religious) legal dictates in order to make room for religious toleration. A modern version of a theocracy that would be more consistent with the Josephan doctrine would contemplate a diametrically opposite arrangement, where law guides the polity by operating independently of the civic authority, or perhaps in lieu of one (similar to Orobio's position above). In other words, it would envisage an independent judiciary, or even a more comprehensive vision of law's empire.[28]

In sum, a glimpse into the afterlife of the early Jewish jurisprudence described in this book reveals its enduring influence. It achieves heightened significance in a medieval world that relies on religious norms to achieve social cohesion. From a different vantage point, it becomes even more consequential in an early modern world, when it transcends the walls of the ghetto and enters into a broader Western discourse. At the same time, this jurisprudence is radically transformed through the crucible of law, power, and politics of these subsequent phases. In the medieval period, the intersection among these forces engenders a surprising reversal in the jurisprudential design as rabbinic discourse now seeks to restore the royal position in the administration of justice. In the early modern period, the stronger form of jurisprudence is overhauled and then repurposed in favor of an aggrandized civic authority. Advancing the legacy of early Jewish jurisprudential writings, certain post-Talmudic works also adapt the core ideas of its most distinctive traditions, and thereby perpetuate the enduring struggle over how to represent, or even control, legal authority.

Abbreviations

Writings of Philo

Abraham	*On the Life of Abraham*
Contempl.	*On the Contemplative Life*
Creation	*On the Creation of the World*
Decalogue	*On the Decalogue*
Good Person	*That Every Good Person Is Free*
Hypoth.	*Hypothetica*
Moses 1, 2	*On the Life of Moses* 1, 2
Spec. Laws 1, 2, 3, 4	*On the Special Laws* 1, 2, 3, 4

Qumran Texts

The different caves at each site are denoted with sequential numbers (1Q, 2Q, etc.).

1QHa	Thanksgiving Hymns
1QM	War Scroll
1QpHab	Pesher Habakkuk
1QS	Rule of the Community
1QSa	Rule of the Congregation
1QSb	Rule of Benedictions
4QMMT	Miqsat Ma'ase ha-Torah
4Q159	Ordinances

4Q161	Pesher Isaiah
4Q174	Florilegium of Eschatological Midrashim
4Q175	Testimonia
4Q246	Aramaic Apocalypse
4Q252	Patriarchal Blessings
4Q285	War Rule
4Q448	Prayer for the Welfare of King Jonathan
4Q491	Self-Glorification Hymn
4Q521	Messianic Apocalypse
CD	(Cairo) Damascus Document
LK	"Law of the King" (section in the Temple Scroll)
TS, 11Q19	Temple Scroll

Writings of Josephus

Ag. Ap.	*Against Apion*
Ant.	*Jewish Antiquities*
J.W.	*Jewish War*
Life	*The Life*

Rabbinic Literature

m.	Mishnah
t.	Tosefta
y.	Jerusalem Talmud
b.	Babylonian Talmud

Tractates Cited

Abod. Zar.	Avodah Zarah
Abot	Avot
B. Bat.	Bava Batra
B. Mesi'a	Bava Metzi'a

B. Qam.	Bava Qamma
Bek.	Bekhorot
Ber.	Berakhot
Bikk.	Bikkurim
Ed.	Eduyyot
Git.	Gittin
Hag.	Hagigah
Hor.	Horayot
Kelim	Kelim
Ketub.	Ketubbot
Mak.	Makkot
Meg.	Megillah
Menah.	Menahot
Mid.	Middot
Miqw.	Mikwa'ot
Mo'ed Qat.	Mo'ed Qatan
Naz.	Nazir
Ned.	Nedarim
Nidd.	Niddah
Ohal.	Ohalot
Parah	Parah
Pe'ah	Pe'ah
Pesah.	Pesahim
Qidd.	Qiddushin
Ros. Has.	Rosh Hashanah
Sanh.	Sanhedrin
Seqal.	Sheqalim
Shab.	Shabbat
Shebu.	Shevu'ot
Sotah	Sotah

Sukkah	Sukkah
Ta'an.	Ta'anit
Tamid	Tamid
Tem.	Temurah
Yad.	Yadayim
Yebam.	Yevamot
Yoma	Yoma
Zebah.	Zevahim

Midrashim

Deut Rab.	Deuteronomy Rabbah
Exod Rab.	Exodus Rabbah
Gen. Rab.	Genesis Rabbah
Lev. Rab.	Leviticus Rabbah
Mekh.	Mekhilta (Rabbi Ishmael, Rabbi Shimon Bar Yohai)
Midrash Tannaim Deut.	Midrash Tannaim on Deuteronomy
Num. Rab.	Numbers Rabbah
Pesiq. Rab.	Pesiqta Rabbati
Sifra	Sifra
Sifre Deut.	Sifre Deuteronomy
Sifre Num.	Sifre Numbers
Sifre Zuta Deut.	Sifre Zuta Deuteronomy
Sifre Zuta Num.	Sifre Zuta Numbers
Tanh.	Tanhuma

Notes

Introduction

1. The plain sense of the verse is that fulfilling God's commandment is within human reach. The rabbinic interpretation appears in *y. Mo'ed Qat.* 3:1; *b. B. Mesi'a* 59b. See also *b. Tem.* 16a.
2. See *b. Sanh.* 109a; *Gen. Rab.* 118:6; *Pesiq. Rab.* 25:2.
3. See *m. Abot* 1:1. The Mishnah famously omits priests. See Moshe David Herr, "The Continuity in the Chain of Transmission of the Torah" [Hebrew], *Zion* 44 (1979): 43–56.
4. The "mission" includes studying, preserving, transmitting, and, especially, executing the teachings and principles of the Torah. The latter is primarily achieved in the manner described in the next paragraph.
5. On the growing emphasis on the normative content of the Pentateuch, see Chapter 8.
6. Throughout this book, I will focus primarily on programmatic texts that portray the ideal operation of the administration of justice, rather than on descriptive texts detailing the actual mechanics of judicial administration. For example, in examining rabbinic literature, I explore ideal portrayals of the jurisdiction of the leading court, the Sanhedrin, even if in fact this institution did not operate during the rabbinic period and the jurisdiction of Jews was highly constricted within the Roman Empire (see Chapters 6 and 8). My aim is to recover aspects of Jewish ideology, theology, and jurisprudence, rather than to inquire into the actual clout of Jews in antiquity and late antiquity. Admittedly, the distinction between prescriptive and descriptive texts in biblical, Second Temple, and rabbinic literature is often not categorical. Occasionally I will present specific arguments about why an ambiguous text seems to be programmatic in nature. Beyond this, the most I can do is to be mindful of the methodological challenges for this study.
7. There are multiple biblical discourses on Sinai. See, e.g., Baruch J. Schwartz, "What Really Happened at Mount Sinai? Four Biblical Answers to One Question," *Bible Review* 13, no. 5 (1997): 20–30.

8. Numerous secondary works relate to aspects of this study, including recent studies by Steven Fraade, Christine Hayes, Beth Berkowitz, David Goodblatt, Aharon Shemesh, Mordechai Sabato, Hayim Shapira, and Moshe Halbertal.

9. The structure of legal authority can inform, or intersect with, other aspects of the Jewish legal system, including the nature of Jewish law (i.e., whether it is positivistic or naturalistic); the process of its elaboration (i.e., whether its development is formal or pragmatic); and the justification for its binding nature (i.e., whether its sanction is divine, rational, or political). Likewise, the source of judicial authority can influence the role of law within Jewish society (i.e., which sector of society shapes the legal system). Much of the material analyzed in this book touches (directly or implicitly) on these important juristic matters. See also note 88.

10. Studies addressing these issues usually use the famous eleventh sermon of Rabbi Nissim Gerondi (fourteenth century) as their point of departure. As important as this sermon is for understanding medieval rabbinic thought, its synthetic portrait of rabbinic jurisprudence hardly offers a critical analysis of the earlier material. Moreover, scholarship has underscored certain distinctly medieval dimensions of this work. Accordingly, this book returns to primary Second Temple and rabbinic sources to analyze them on their own terms. In the Conclusion, I will briefly address this sermon in the context of considering the medieval legacy of the materials analyzed herein.

11. The link between law and authority has been especially underscored in the jurisprudential writings of Joseph Raz. Raz has argued that a defining feature of every legal system is the claim that it possesses legitimate authority. Although the claim of legitimacy may be factually incorrect, the system at least must be of a kind that is capable in principle of possessing the requisite properties of authority. This leads Raz to articulate his "source thesis," which he contrasts with H. L. A. Hart's "incorporation thesis" and Ronald Dworkin's "coherence thesis." See Joseph Raz, *Ethics in the Public Domain: Essays in the Morality of Law and Politics* (Oxford: Oxford University Press, 1994); and Raz, *The Authority of Law: Essays on Law and Morality* (Oxford: Oxford University Press, 1979). For helpful recent discussions, see John Gardner, *Law as a Leap of Faith* (Oxford: Oxford University Press, 2012), 138–145; and Liam B. Murphy, *What Makes Law: An Introduction to the Philosophy of Law* (New York: Cambridge University Press, 2014), 85–88.

12. Even modern legal systems, which ostensibly disentangle the legal and political domains, must contend with the charge that they remain profoundly intertwined. A significant voice in modern jurisprudence known as "critical legal studies" underscores the inherently political nature of law in general, notwithstanding the claim of modern systems to separate law from politics. According to the "Crits," law constitutes a medium of politics, and legal rhetoric camouflages a deep discourse of power. See, e.g., Duncan Kennedy, *A Critique of Adjudication: Fin de Siècle* (Cambridge, Mass.: Harvard University Press, 1997); and Roberto M. Unger, *The Critical Legal Studies Move-*

ment (Cambridge, Mass.: Harvard University Press, 1986). While the primary focus of the "Crits" is on the function of law, they also critically evaluate legal rhetoric, the constructs of legal institutions, and even scholarly expositions. See, e.g., Duncan Kennedy, "The Structure of Blackstone's Commentaries," *Buffalo Law Review* 28 (1979): 205. Other perspectives note the extensive interaction between law and politics as a social phenomenon, and situate the nature of that relationship in a sophisticated sociological account of processes of state formation and political stability. See, e.g., Philippe Nonet and Philip Selznick, *Law and Society in Transition: Toward Responsive Law* (New Brunswick, N.J.: Transaction Publishers, 2001). Seen from these angles, heading the judiciary is an even more overt form of accumulating political clout or functioning as a tool of the state. Thus, modern law also arguably revolves around politics, and this is much more blatantly true in an ancient context.

13. Corresponding to this reality, one branch of classical jurisprudence, known as the "command theory of law," offers a positivistic characterization of legal systems altogether. According to this theory, law is defined as the commands of a sovereign reinforced by the threat of punishment. See Thomas Hobbes, "Of the Rights of Sovereigns by Institution" and "Of Civil Laws," in *Leviathan,* ed. C. B. Macpherson (Baltimore: Penguin Books, 1968), 107, 162; Jeremy Bentham, *Of Laws in General,* ed. H. L. A. Hart (London: Atholone Press, 1970); and John Austin, *The Province of Jurisprudence Determined* (Amherst, N.Y.: Prometheus Books, 2000), 14. For recent treatments, see, e.g., Gerald J. Postema, "Law as Command: The Model of Command in Modern Jurisprudence," *Philosophical Issues* 11 (2001): 470. Obviously there are more nuanced versions of positivism, but I deliberately refer to command theory because of its more obvious reliance on sovereign power. At the same time, even certain natural law theories have been deployed to justify the jurisprudence of the powerful.

14. The present survey relates to both the realities and the theories of ancient, classical, and Western jurisprudence, whereas my examination of Jewish materials concentrates mostly on the theories. The reason for the broader canvas in my survey is that early Jewish writers and thinkers mostly encountered the realities of other legal systems. In Chapter 9, I compare early Jewish jurisprudence with modern Western jurisprudence.

15. For an overview, see Raymond Westbrook, ed., *A History of Ancient Near Eastern Law* (Leiden: Brill, 2003); Pamela Barmash, "Ancient Near Eastern Law," in *The Oxford Encyclopedia of the Bible and Law,* ed. Brent A. Strawn, vol. 1 (Oxford: Oxford University Press, 2015), 13–23. The above generalization extends to Ephraim Speiser and his students, who underscored the development of an ancient legal civilization in Mesopotamia, but still of course recognized that it was anchored in royal authority.

16. ANE codes were not necessarily implemented. See Sara J. Milstein, "Making a Case: The Repurposing of 'Israelite Legal Fictions' as Post-Deuteronomic Law," in *Supplementation and the Study of the Hebrew Bible,* ed. Saul Olyan et al. (Providence, R.I.:

Brown Judaic Studies, 2017), 162–168. Still, they clearly project the central position of the king.

17. See generally Hans J. Boecker, *Law and the Administration of Justice in the Old Testament and Ancient East,* trans. Jeremy Moiser (Minneapolis: Augsburg Publication House, 1980).

18. See Raymond Westbrook and Bruce Wells, *Everyday Law in Biblical Israel: An Introduction* (Louisville, Ky.: Westminster John Knox Press, 2009), 35; and Moshe Greenberg, "Some Postulates of Biblical Criminal Law," in *Studies in the Bible and Jewish Thought* (Philadelphia: Jewish Publication Society, 1995), 28.

19. Ernest Hartwig Kantorowicz, *The King's Two Bodies: A Study in Mediaeval Political Theology* (Princeton, N.J.: Princeton University Press, 1997), 4, 13, referring to the king's public body (as opposed to his private body).

20. Although both ancient Mesopotamia and Egypt shared the notion of a powerful, quasi-divine ruler, there were important differences in their respective conceptions of kingship. See Henri Frankfort's classic study *Kingship and the Gods: A Study of Ancient Near Eastern Religion as the Integration of Society and Nature* (Chicago: University of Chicago Press, 1978).

21. See, e.g., *Cambridge Ancient History,* ed. F. Walbank et al., vol. 4 (Cambridge: Cambridge University Press, 2008), 94; vol. 7 (Cambridge: Cambridge University Press, 2008), pt. 1, 71–81; and vol. 7, pt. 2, 107–108; *The Cambridge History of Greek and Roman Political Thought,* ed. Christopher Rowe and Malcolm Schofield (New York: Cambridge University Press, 2000), 458–464.

22. See generally Adriaan Lanni, *Law and Justice in the Courts of Classical Athens* (New York: Cambridge University Press, 2006); Raphael Sealey, *The Justice of the Greeks* (Ann Arbor: University of Michigan Press, 1994); and John David Lewis, *Early Greek Lawgivers* (London: Bristol Classical Press, 2007).

23. See generally David Johnston, *Roman Law in Context* (Cambridge: Cambridge University Press, 1999), 3–7; Alan Watson, *Law Making in the Later Roman Republic* (Oxford: Clarendon Press, 1974) 6, 22; and H. F. Jolowicz and Barry Nicholas, *Historical Introduction to the Study of Roman Law,* 3rd ed. (Cambridge: Cambridge University Press, 1972), 80.

24. See Johnston, *Roman Law in Context,* 3–7.

25. Johnston, *Roman Law in Context,* 3–7. See generally Aldo Schiavone, *The Invention of Law in the West,* trans. Jeremy Carden and Antony Shugaar (Cambridge, Mass.: Harvard University Press, 2012); Bruce Frier, *The Rise of the Roman Jurists: Studies in Cicero's Pro Caecina* (Princeton, N.J.: Princeton University Press, 1985); and Jill Harries, *Law and Empire in Late Antiquity* (Cambridge: Cambridge University Press, 1999).

26. See Johnston, *Roman Law in Context,* 3–7.

27. See David Johnston, "The Jurists," in Rowe and Schofield, *The Cambridge History of Greek and Roman Political Thought,* 616–634.

28. See Tamar Herzog, *A Short History of European Law: The Last Two and a Half Millennia* (Cambridge, Mass.: Harvard University Press, 2018), 21–26.

29. Classical writings that seem to support the autonomous rule of law (e.g., Aristotle, *Politics* III: 16, and Herodotus, *The Histories* VII: 104) function within a monarchic system and never introduce a discrete judicial body. In a more general sense, a broad overview such as *The Cambridge History of Greek and Roman Political Thought* hardly touches on the construction or autonomy of the courts. See also Leo Strauss, *An Introduction to Political Philosophy: Ten Essays* (Detroit: Wayne State University Press, 1989), 31ff. Still, the tension between a rarefied conception of law and its human administration can be discerned in famous works such as Sophocles's *Antigone,* and various accounts of the trial of Socrates. Other classical works may sketch the rudiments of an autonomous juridical body. See, e.g., Xenophon's *Lacedaemonion Politeia,* chap. 8, or the "nocturnal council" in Plato's *Laws,* bks. 10, 12. The latter depends on how this highly contested platonic institution is understood. See the summary and references in Christopher Bobonic, "Plato's Politics," in *The Oxford Handbook of Plato,* ed. Gail Fine (Oxford: Oxford University Press, 2019), 596–604.

30. See Herzog, *A Short History of European Law,* 59. My summary in the next three paragraphs draws selectively on this illuminating work, but the focus on judicial independence (or lack thereof) is my own.

31. See Herzog, *A Short History of European Law,* 87.

32. See generally Harold Berman, *Law and Revolution: The Foundation of the Western Legal Tradition* (Cambridge, Mass.: Harvard University Press, 1997), 274–276; Manlio Bellomo, *The Common Legal Past of Europe: 1000–1800* (Washington, DC: Catholic University of America Press, 1995); and Peter Stein, *Roman Law in European History* (New York: Cambridge University Press, 1999).

33. On the theoretical side, there were lively medieval debates about the relationship between the king and the law. See the classic account of Franz Kern, *Kingship and Law in the Middle Ages:* vol. 1, *The Divine Right of Kings and the Right of Resistance in the Early Middle Ages;* vol. 2, *Law and Constitution in the Middle Ages,* trans. S. Chrimes (Oxford: Blackwell, 1939).

34. See Herzog, *A Short History of European Law,* 88–89.

35. See Berman, *Law and Revolution,* 165–173; James A. Brundage, *Medieval Canon Law* (London: Longman, 1995); and Kenneth Pennington, "The Growth of Church Law," in *The Cambridge History of Christianity: Constantine to c. 600,* ed. Frederick Norris et al. (Cambridge: Cambridge University Press, 2007), 386–402.

36. On English common law and the crown, see generally John H. Langbein et al., *History of the Common Law: The Development of Anglo-American Legal Institutions* (New

York: Aspen, 2009); J. H. Baker, *An Introduction to English Legal History*, 3rd ed. (London: Butterworths, 1990); and S. C. Milsom, *Historical Foundations of the Common Law* (London: Butterworth, 1969). For a somewhat alternate account, see Philip Hamburger, *Law and Judicial Duty* (Cambridge, Mass.: Harvard University Press, 2008).

37. See Langbein, *History of the Common Law.*

38. Herzog, *A Short History of European Law*, 134–148, describes this process as deliberate (a purposeful reimagining of common law as rooted in customary law that is the product of the community), whereas my description suggests a confluence of factors.

39. See, especially, Coke's description of the "artificial reason" of the common law, in *Prohibitions Del Roy*, 77 E. R. 1342 (1607).

40. See Chapter 9.

41. See Barmash, "Ancient Near Eastern," 19 (including the important corrective of Norman Yoffee). My references to biblical scholarship below are limited because my focus herein is on "the conception and discourses . . . *that would have been conveyed to the biblical text's earliest readers.*" Christine Hayes, *What's Divine about Divine Law? Early Perspectives* (Princeton, N.J.: Princeton University Press, 2015), 12–13.

    Studies of Jewish conceptions of kingship primarily focus on two major themes or tensions: the very legitimacy of the monarchy in a theocratic system (especially in the biblical period); and the relationship among kings and priests (an especially pressing issue during the Hasmonean period). A third fundamental theme involving the relationship between the king and the law has received far less scholarly attention. To a certain degree, this third topic converges with the first and second (see Chapter 8), but it requires discrete analysis.

42. This section briefly summarizes certain biblical portraits of the administration of justice, but may say little about actual practices. See, e.g., Michael Lefebvre, *Collections, Codes and Torah* (New York: Clark, 2006). But see note 51.

43. For a summary of scholarly theories about the compositional history of Exod 19–24, see Thomas B. Dozeman, *Exodus* (Grand Rapids, Mich.: Eerdmans, 2009), 411–568. Scholarly dating of this material ranges from the tenth to the seventh century BCE. See the summary of theories in John J. Collins, *The Invention of Judaism* (California: University of California Press, 2017), 22–27.

44. See Greenberg, "Some Postulates," 25–42. See also the criticisms of Bernard S. Jackson, *Essays in Jewish and Comparative Legal History* (Leiden: Brill, 1975), 25–63; and the response in Greenberg, "More Reflections on Biblical Criminal Law," in *Studies in Bible, 1986*, ed. Sara Japhet (Jerusalem: Magnes, 1986), 1–18. See also Pamela Barmash, *Homicide in the Biblical World* (Cambridge: Cambridge University Press, 2005), 142n63.

45. See Bernard M. Levinson, "Strategies for the Reinterpretation of Normative Texts within the Hebrew Bible," *International Journal of Legal Discourse* 3, no. 1 (2018): 5–6: "It was therefore not the legal collection as a literary genre but the voicing of publicly revealed law as the personal will of God that was unique to ancient Israel."

46. For a comprehensive collection, see Kenneth A. Kitchen and Paul J. N. Lawrence, *Treaty, Law and Covenant in the Ancient Near East*, 3 vols. (Wiesbaden: Harrassowitz, 2012).

47. On how this trope shaped the formation of the Pentateuch, see Todd P. Kennedy, "'To All the Children of Israel': The Formation of the Pentateuch as Scripture" (PhD diss., Union Theological Seminary, 2018).

48. See Collins, *The Invention of Judaism*, 24.

49. God is the exclusive king of Israel. Still, rather than subordinating the people to divine royal justice, the Exodus covenant elevates the status of all of Israel as a "kingdom of priests and holy nation" (Exod 19:6). As scholars have highlighted, the verse's implication is that all Israelites enjoy a priestly-royal status. Given the substantial legal role of priests and kings, I would add that they presumably also exercise a degree of legal authority. See, e.g., James Kugel, *How to Read the Bible: A Guide to Scripture Then and Now* (New York: Free Press, 2007), 233–249; and Chapter 8. On sacral law, see Max Weber, *Max Weber on Law in Economy and Society*, ed. Max Rheinstein (New York: Simon and Schuster, 1954), 224–255; and Remi Brague, *The Law of God: The Philosophical History of an Idea* (Chicago: University of Chicago Press, 2007).

50. Given the Sinaitic conception of God as the Suzerain, one might conceptualize biblical jurisprudence as a unique variant of royal justice, where God the King commands the laws. Alternatively, one might view the sacred laws of Sinai as a kind of embodiment of "nomos." (In the Sinaitic framing, both formulations may coexist or merge.) Either formulation may shed light on the displacement of the regnant model of royal justice in postbiblical jurisprudence: either because it has been superseded by divine royal justice (i.e., because of the source of the law), or due to the special stature of divine law (i.e., due to the law's ontology). (Parenthetically, the motif of God's sovereignty seems more pronounced in biblical writings, whereas in postbiblical writings the special status of divine law is more emphasized.) But both formulations are incomplete because they relate to the source or ontology of divine law, not to its preferred mode of administration, which is arguably a separate matter. The question I am investigating is "Who on earth?"—i.e., who administers justice? Here the Bible reflects different templates, with the standard form of royal justice being in fact dominant, and Deuteronomy's "independent" model being relatively anomalous. So the surprising expansion of Deuteronomy's jurisprudence in postbiblical literature is a crucial phenomenon that needs to be explored. Nevertheless, in Chapter 8 I propose linking the matter of law's source and ontology with its optimal mode of administration. See note 88.

51. For an account that considers how power dynamics, including monarchy, influence formal law and actual practices, see Douglas A. Knight, *Law, Power, and Justice in Ancient Israel* (Louisville, Ky.: Westminster John Knox, 2011).

52. See Ze'ev W. Falk, *Hebrew Law in Biblical Times: An Introduction*, 2nd ed. (Provo, Utah: Brigham Young University Press, 2001), 1–50.

53. The local population and the affected parties were involved in all aspects of the legal procedure: initiating legal claims, testimony, administering justice, and enforcing punishments. See, e.g., Ze'ev Weisman, "The Place of the People in the Making of Law and Judgment," in *Pomegranates and Golden Bells: Studies in Biblical, Jewish and Near Eastern Ritual, Law, and Literature in Honor of Jacob Milgrom,* ed. David P. Wright, et al. (Winona Lake, Ind.: Eisenbrauns, 1995), 407–420.

54. See Robert Wilson, "Israel's Judicial System in the Pre-exilic Period," *Jewish Quarterly Review* 74 (1983): 229–248.

55. See generally Keith W. Whitelam, *The Just King: Monarchical Judicial Authority in Ancient Israel* (Sheffield, UK: Journal for the Study of the Old Testament, 1979). Of course, this depends on the wider question of biblical attitudes toward monarchy. For a recent scholarly survey, see Galvin Garrett, *David's Successors: Kingship in the Old Testament* (Minnesota: Liturgical Press, 2016), 1–18.

56. The point is especially emphasized by Whitelam, *The Just King,* 13–16, 29–37, 207–220.

57. See Lyle M. Eslinger, *Kingship of God in Crisis: A Close Reading of 1 Samuel 1–12* (Decatur, Ga.: Almond Press, 1985), 254–258, 258n24. The fact that one word has both connotations is a further indication of the nexus between political and legal authority.

58. See Exod 21:12–13, Num 35:9–29, Deut 19:1–10.

59. This episode may be part of a process of centralization. See Elizabeth Bellefontaine, "Customary Law and Chieftainship: Judicial Aspects of 2 Samuel 14, 4–21," *Journal for the Study of the Old Testament* 38 (1987): 47–72 (who also discusses Absalom).

60. On the influence of Hittite motifs relating to the king as supreme judge, see Meir Malul, "Absalom's Chariot and Fifty Runners (II Sam 15,1) and Hittite Laws § 198 Legal Proceedings in the Ancient Near East," *Zeitschrift für die Alttestamentliche Wissenschaft* 122 (2010): 44–52.

61. See Gary N. Knoppers, "Rethinking the Relationship between Deuteronomy and the Deuteronomistic History: The Case of Kings," *Catholic Bible Quarterly* 63 (2001): 404.

62. See also 1 Kgs 7:7 and 10:9.

63. On the composition, dating, and redaction of the royal psalms, see Mark W. Hamilton, *The Body Royal: The Social Poetics of Kingship in Ancient Israel* (Leiden: Brill Academic, 2005).

64. See also Isa 16:5 and 42:1.

65. See, e.g., various references in *King and Messiah in Israel and the Ancient Near East,* ed. John Day (Sheffield, UK: Sheffield Academic Press, 1998).

66. See, e.g., 1 Sam 30:23–25; 2 Sam 8:15, 12:1–6; 1 Kgs 3:9–28, 7:7, 10:9; 2 Kgs 15:5; Jer 21:12, 22:1–5, 15–17, 23:5–6, 26:16–24; Isa 9:6, 11, 16:5, 42:1–4; Ps 72:2, 122:5; Prov 16:10; 2 Chr 26:21.

67. For a summary of scholarly theories about the compositional history of Deuteronomy and its dating, see Jack R. Lundbom, *Deuteronomy* (Grand Rapids, Mich.: Eerdmans, 2013), 6–92.

68. See Bernard Levinson, "The Reconceptualization of Kingship in Deuteronomy and the Deuteronomic History's Transformation of Torah," *Vetus Testamentum* 4 (2001): 511–534; and Norbert Lohfink, "Distribution of the Functions of Power: The Laws concerning Public Offices in Deuteronomy 16:18–18:22," in *A Song of Power and the Power of Song: Essays on the Book of Deuteronomy*, ed. Duane L. Christensen (Winona Lake, Ind.: Eisenbrauns, 1993). See also David Zvi Hoffmann, *Sefer Devarim*, vol. 2 (Tel-Aviv: Netsah, 1959–1961), intro.; and Milstein, "Making a Case," 172–177.

69. On the scholarly dating of this pericope and its relationship to Deut 16:21–17:7, see Bernard M. Levinson, *Deuteronomy and the Hermeneutics of Legal Innovation* (New York: Oxford University Press, 1997), 98–143.

70. The scholarly dating of this pericope is much debated, ranging from the inauguration of the Israelite monarchy until the fifth century BCE. Some contend that verses 18–19 are a postexilic interpolation. See Nili Wazana, "The Law of the King (Deut 17:14–20) in the Light of Empire and Destruction," in *The Fall of Jerusalem and the Rise of the Torah*, ed. P. Dubovsky et al. (Tübingen: Mohr Siebeck, 2016), 176.

71. The Levitical priests and a judge operate at the helm of a network of municipal judges and officers. See Deut 16:18–20. The Levitical priests are further described in Deut 18:1–8.

72. See Levinson, *Deuteronomy and the Hermeneutics*, 130–133; Jeffrey H. Tigay, *Deuteronomy: The Traditional Hebrew Text with the New JPS Translation* (Philadelphia: Jewish Publication Society, 1996), 164–165; and Moshe Weinfeld, *Deuteronomy and the Deuteronomic School* (Oxford: Clarendon Press, 1972), 235.

73. See Levinson, "The Reconceptualization of Kingship," 520–523.

74. The connotation of Deut 17 is that the king is subordinate to the judicial officials. Postbiblical interpreters respond to this in different ways.

75. The subordinate role of the king in the legal process corresponds with the overall tone of Deut 17's monarchy section. Although this passage incorporates monarchy within Deuteronomy's administration, it casts the king in a dubious position in several respects. Nowhere does the chapter imbue the king with any cosmic, or even sacral, significance. On the contrary, it employs discernibly tentative language (see Deut 17:14), and has stridently antimonarchic intertexts (1 Sam 8, 1 Kgs 4). Accordingly, various interpreters conclude that Deuteronomy's preference is to avoid kingship altogether. Further, Deuteronomy's register of prohibitions relating to the monarchy challenges its very viability. Banning the king from acquiring horses for a cavalry, wedding wives for diplomacy, and amassing wealth for a treasury undermines the king's sovereign capacities. Finally, Deuteronomy does not assign the king any positive powers and privileges, other than transcribing and reading the law (Deut 17:18–19). The latter mandate humbles the king before God (and God's laws) and his subjects (who are treated as equals), further reflecting a deep skepticism about monarchy. A chapter that restricts, rebukes, or opposes monarchy will certainly not assign the king legal authority. Only

the Levitical priests (and judge) who are proximate to God—residing in God's Temple—can interpret God's law. The king, in turn, is subordinated to the Levitical priests. See also the references in note 68; Gary N. Knoppers, "The Deuteronomist and the Deuteronomic Law of the King: A Reexamination of a Relationship," *Zeitschrift für die Alttestamentliche Wissenschaft* 108 (1996): 329–346; Wazana, "The Law of the King," 169–194.

76. On 2 Chron 19, see Chapter 1, note 1. The complex formulation I employ here is due to the fact that in a much larger sense, the Pentateuch hardly refers to a king, and locates legal authority outside of the monarchic institution. See generally James L. Kugel, "Some Unanticipated Consequences of the Sinai Revelation: A Religion of Laws," in *The Significance of Sinai: Traditions about Sinai and Divine Revelation in Judaism and Christianity,* ed. George J. Brooke, Hindy Najman, and Loren T. Stuckenbruck (Leiden: Brill, 2008), 1–13; and Simeon Chavel, "Legal Literature in Scripture" [Hebrew], in *The Literature of Scripture: Introduction and Studies,* ed. Zipporah Talshir, vol. 1 (Jerusalem: Yad Ben Zvi Press, 2011), 227–272. See Chapter 8.

For another possible echo of Deut 17's approach, see Ezekiel 44:23–24 regarding the priests (contrast this with Ezekiel 45:9–10 regarding the *Nasi*). The priestly legal role is well attested in other passages, including Exod 28:29–30, Deut 19:17 and 21:5, and Mal 2:6–7. See Chapters 3 and 6.

77. See 1 Kgs 21.

78. This right is implied in 1 Sam 8:14–15.

79. As Nahum Sarna has noted, in Scripture Ahab evidently has no power to impose his will upon his subjects. Instead, he is restrained by law. In contrast, Akkadian and other legal documents demonstrate the absolute royal powers that he commanded. See "Naboth's Vineyard Revisited (1 Kings 21)," in *Tehillah Le-Moshe: Biblical and Judaic Studies in Honor of Moshe Greenberg,* ed. Mordechai Cogan (Winona Lake, Ind.: Eisenbrauns, 1997), 119–126.

80. On the broader theme of the subservience of even absolutist kings to at least the form of the rule of law, see the important formulation in Berman, *Law and Revolution,* 9.

81. The Deuteronomic strand contains the seeds of the notion of an independent judiciary: Levitical priests and a judge operating collectively, separately from the primary locus of political power, the king. Further, in Deuteronomy the role of the priests and the cult is secondary to individual service to God, so it is difficult to view them as an especially exalted or empowered group (instead they serve the people). See Kugel, *How to Read the Bible,* 313. See also David Flatto, "The Historical Origins of Judicial Independence and Their Modern Resonances," *Yale Law Journal Pocket* 117 Part 8 (2007), http://yalelawjournal.org/forum/the-historical-origins-of-judicial-independence-and-their-modern-resonance. Both of these biblical strands differ from the ANE conception of the king as the giver of the law, the bearer of supreme judicial intuition, and often the exclusive judicial authority. See references cited in notes 15–18.

82. See Collins, *Invention of Judaism*, 82; and Chapter 8.

83. Philo leans heavily on Deut 17, even though he also embraces aspects of royal justice. See Chapters 1 and 2.

84. To be sure, not all postbiblical works operate with this assumption. See David C. Flatto, "Constructing Justice: The Selective Use of Scripture in Formulating Early Jewish Accounts of the Courts," *Harvard Theological Review* 111, no. 4 (2018): 493n19.

85. These iterations resonate with certain aspects of Western jurisprudence. See Chapter 9.

86. Hanina Ben-Menahem argues that the Talmud affords a surprising degree of latitude to rabbinic judges to deviate from laws on the basis of extralegal considerations: *Judicial Deviation in Talmudic Law: Governed by Men, Not by Rules* (Chur, Switzerland: Harwood, 1991). These arguments are not necessarily incompatible. The focus of this book is on early rabbinic literature, whereas Ben-Menahem primarily focuses on Talmudic material. Indeed, I will argue in Chapter 7 that one can discern an erosion of the rabbinic scheme in later strata. Moreover, the argument of this book focuses on the marginalization of (political) power that threatens to corrupt the administration of justice, whereas Ben-Menachem refers to internal modes employed by rabbis to reach their decisions.

87. This is how the schemes are structured and envisioned as functioning on their own terms. What the underlying motivation of their authors were in formulating these schemes, and whether the visions themselves can be debunked, are separate questions. See below.

88. The themes of Sinai relate to the source (= God) and ontology (= divine) of law, but do not directly address how it should ideally be administered. See note 50. It is arguable that the former and latter are separate questions—indeed, from the perspective of a history of ideas, they did not emerge at the same time. Thus, the historical overview suggests that in the classical world there was much reflection on the source and ontology of law, but far less thought about its optimal mode of administration. Nevertheless, these topics may well intersect. To offer an illustration from modern jurisprudence, Ronald Dworkin's account of the source and ontology of law (a version of natural law theory) privileges the jurisprudence of the Herculean judge. See *Law's Empire* (Cambridge, Mass.: Harvard University Press, 1986). Likewise, I argue in Chapter 8 that the particular conception of the source and ontology of law thematized in Sinaitic discourses leads to, necessitates or privileges, its independent administration—i.e., Deut 17 and its afterlife. See also note 91.

89. Tony Honoré, *About Law: An Introduction* (Oxford: Oxford University Press, 1995), 14.

90. With all their nascent achievements, certain scholarly endeavors tend to simplify the material analyzed and insufficiently explore the range and subtlety of the legal and political issues that they encompass, in contrast with the exemplary studies listed in this paragraph. In the present book I aspire to similarly make a meaningful contribution to these growing fields by mining the biblical and rabbinic material in a nuanced manner,

teasing out distinct strands from a variety of Jewish writings, and evaluating the significant diachronic development of jurisprudential ideas, especially during the Second Temple and rabbinic periods.

91. Hayes's thesis about divine law's ontology may have a more intimate link with this book's thesis about law's administration. She argues that the rabbis amplify the human role in their conception of divine law, which may illuminate my claim that the rabbis stress its independent administration. A heightened human dimension of divine law may call for an independent body of (human) jurists to administer law. What is fascinating is that one might have thought the opposite to be the case—i.e., that the more rarefied a conception of divine law, the more crucial that it be administered in a distinctive or independent manner. Indeed, Philo and certain Qumran writings espouse notions of divine law's ontology that differ from those of the rabbis, and they also reach notable conclusions about law's administration: Philo's natural law is administered by multiple bodies (see Chapter 2), and Qumran's revealed law is administered by priests, councils, and the community (see Chapter 3). Lastly, Josephus's notion of sacral law leads to an even more sweeping reimagining of the polity (see Chapter 4).

92. Hayes, *What's Divine about Divine Law?*; Aharon Shemesh, *Halakhah in the Making: The Development of Jewish Law from Qumran to the Rabbis* (Los Angeles: University of California Press, 2009); Beth A. Berkowitz, *Execution and Invention: Death Penalty Discourse in Early Rabbinic and Christian Cultures* (New York: Oxford University Press, 2006); Devora Steinmetz, *Punishment and Freedom: The Rabbinic Construction of Criminal Law* (Philadelphia: University of Pennsylvania Press, 2008); Michael Walzer, *In God's Shadow: Politics in the Hebrew Bible* (New Haven, Conn.: Yale University Press, 2012); Steven D. Fraade, *Legal Fictions: Studies of Law and Narrative in the Discursive World of Ancient Jewish Sectarians and Sages* (Leiden: Brill, 2011); Gerald Blidstein, *Political Principles in Maimonidean Thought* [Hebrew], 2nd ed. (Ramat Gan: Bar-Ilan University, 2001); Yair Lorberbaum, *The Disempowered King* [Hebrew] (Ramat Gan: Bar-Ilan University, 2009).

93. See, e.g., Bernard Bailyn, *The Ideological Origins of the American Revolution* (Cambridge, Mass.: Harvard University Press, 1992). But see Eric Nelson, *The Royalist Revolution: Monarchy and the American Founding* (Cambridge, Mass.: Harvard University Press, 2014).

94. See, e.g., Gordon S. Wood, *The Purpose of the Past: Reflections on the Uses of History* (New York: Penguin, 2008), 293–294.

95. See, e.g., the sundry rabbinic sources on kingship and justice in Chapter 5.

96. See, e.g., the variant juridical schemes in Qumran literature in Chapter 3.

97. See, e.g., the reevaluation of Philo's royalism in Chapter 2.

98. See, e.g., Lynn Hunt's call for converting the historiographical challenge of presentism into a "fruitful tension." Hunt, "Against Presentism," *Perspectives on History*, May 1, 2002,

https://www.historians.org/publications-and-directories/perspectives-on-history
/may-2002/against-presentism.

99. Aspects of this process are powerfully captured in Caroline Walker Bynum, "Why Paradox? The Contradictions of My Life as a Scholar," *Catholic Historical Review* 98, no. 3 (2012): 433–455.

100. Hayes, *What's Divine about Divine Law?*, 1.

101. This touches on the Weberian definition, because power is legitimately monopolized. It also touches on Arendt's definition, since politics is conceived of as a sphere of action that is based on the exercise of will. See also Roger Scruton, *Dictionary of Political Thought*, 2nd ed. (London: Macmillan, 1996), 48, 530, 535. Nevertheless, in the early Jewish sources examined here this sphere remains only vaguely defined.

102. In general, legal authority in premodern times tends to combine a number of different roles that would be differentiated in modern jurisprudence.

103. The body of norms are binding, but usually not fully enforceable.

104. Still, the concept of law in each set of texts likely varies. While aspects of this will emerge in the analyses below (see, e.g., the discussion of Philo's jurisprudence in Chapter 2), a full exploration of this rich theme is beyond the scope of this study.

105. Early Jewish writings contain relatively few metaphysical reflections, but they articulate rich legal (and to a lesser extent political) ideas relating to questions of adjudication, legal procedure, and the nature of legal authority.

106. See Gad Prudovsky, "Can We Ascribe to Past Thinkers Concepts They Had No Linguistic Means to Express?," *History and Theory* 36 (1997): 15–31.

107. The methodology employed in this book and the issues explored here dovetail to a degree with critical tools and subjects that arise in the fields of *mishpat ivri* and *makhshevet yisrael*, but also differ in important ways. I hope to elaborate on this methodological point in another forum.

108. For a classic study on the significance of context for understanding political-philosophical ideas, see Quentin Skinner, "Meaning and Understanding in the History of Ideas," *History and Theory* 8 (1969): 3–53.

109. An engagement with the text proves to be a fundamental exercise necessary for critique, deconstruction, or evaluation. In any event, critical inquiries do not drain the content of these texts, which have a life of their own. Consider an example from a different context: Charles Beard's trenchant criticisms of the staggering class interests that shaped the US Constitution do little (even if his argument is accepted) to change the legal, social, or ideational import or impact of what was produced.

110. The "culture of texts" that is forged is especially repercussive given the relatively scattered conditions of Jewish diasporic life over the centuries.

111. These approaches include much of what the "Crits" would say about the rhetoric, ideology, and coherence of these texts (e.g., Are judges less driven by power than rulers?); the underlying motives and agendas of their authors and followers (e.g., What are the

motives of sectarian priests in imagining an eschaton without a Davidic king?); and how the social realities measured up to the values espoused within the texts (e.g., How much was the influence of powerful individuals in fact constrained in rabbinic society?). I intermittently raise some of these issues in this book, but my general goal is to lay the groundwork for further inquiries along these lines.

112. See, e.g., the discussions of the social advantages of institutional thinking for the rabbis (Chapter 6); the relationship between recognizing a hierarchy within the courts and the growing power of the Patriarchate (Chapter 7); and the qualified significance of conditions of disempowerment in shaping early Jewish jurisprudence (Chapter 8).

113. See Judith N. Shklar, "The Liberalism of Fear," in *Political Thought and Political Philosophers,* ed. Stanley Hoffman (Chicago: University of Chicago Press, 1998), 3–20; Jeffrey Abramson, *Minerva's Owl* (Cambridge, Mass.: Harvard University Press, 2009), 43, 83.

114. Whereas Plato defines "justice" as everyone fulfilling their proper roles in a republic, and Aristotle defines it as the virtuous joining together in the best political arrangement, certain early Jewish writings may implicitly define it as a society led by an independent judiciary and an autonomous legal system. See David C. Flatto, "Justice in Rabbinic Judaism," in *Encyclopedia of the Bible and its Reception,* ed. Christine Helmer et al., vol. 14 (Berlin: De Gruyter, 2017), 1092–1096.

115. These notions were likely helpful in overcoming limitations in the power, jurisdiction, and enforcement mechanisms of Jews living in various phases of antiquity and late antiquity. But it would probably be a mistake to attribute their formulation to this factor alone. Consider, for example, the fact that Qumran writers no doubt had powerful social tools of enforcement at their disposal, so the lack of enforcement was not as pressing in the sectarian world. At the same time, rabbinic Judaism, which had fewer tools, did elaborate on penal themes, which would be odd if lack of enforcement was a primary challenge they were trying to overcome. Still, lack of enforcement relates to the broader theme of disempowerment, which was likely a contributing factor that informed the contours of postbiblical jurisprudence to a certain extent. See Chapter 8.

116. See Clifford Geertz, "Local Knowledge: Fact and Law in Comparative Perspective," in *Local Knowledge: Further Essays in Interpretive Anthropology* (New York: Basic Books, 1983), 173. I am indebted to Oscar G. Chase for this reference.

1. Postbiblical Jurisprudence

1. The earliest expansion on Deut 17 is 2 Chron 19:5–11, dated by some scholars to the late fourth century BCE. Drawing on Deut 17, the Chronicler conflates it with a royalist strand. He details the judicial reforms of King Jehoshaphat, who appoints judges in all the municipal courts in Judah, and also selects Levites, priests, and family heads

for the Jerusalem court. The latter are placed under the supervision of Jehoshaphat's delegates: the high priest, in charge of religious matters, and the governor of Judah, in charge of royal affairs. Finally, Jehoshaphat instructs the newly appointed judges about their judicial responsibilities. Thus, the king constructs the judiciary, which is a bold revision of Deut 17. This important pericope, and its possible Persian influences, requires separate analysis.

Eventually, Chronicles is included in the Hebrew Bible, exemplifying what Benjamin Sommer describes as a tradition that becomes Scripture due to the ongoing nature of the canonical process. See Sommer, *Revelation and Authority: Sinai in Jewish Scripture and Tradition* (New Haven, Conn.: Yale University Press, 2015), 166. In hindsight, one can characterize this as an example of an intrabiblical interpretation. Likewise, the term "postbiblical" writings can be usefully applied to refer to late Second Temple and rabbinic writings.

Throughout this book, I utilize translations from the *NRSV* (*New Revised Standard Version*) Bible, with my own modifications, for citations from the Hebrew Bible; the *Loeb Classical Library,* 10 vols. and two supplements, trans. F. H. Colson and G. H. Whitaker (Cambridge, MA: Harvard University Press, 1929–1962), for citations from the writings of Philo; the *Loeb Classical Library,* 10 vols., trans. H. St. J. Thackeray et al. (Cambridge, MA: Harvard University Press, 1997–), and *Flavius Josephus: Translation and Commentary,* ed. Steve Maison (Leiden: Brill, 2000–2008), for citations from the writings of Josephus; Garcia Martinez Florentino and Eibert J. C. Tigchelaar, *Dead Sea Scrolls, Study Edition,* 2 vols. (Leiden: Brill, 1997–1998), and various works of secondary literature cited in Chapter 3, with my own modifications, for citations from Qumran literature; and Herbert Danby, *The Mishnah* (London: Oxford University Press, 1958), Jacob Neusner, *The Talmud of the Land of Israel: A Preliminary Translation and Explanation* (Chicago: University of Chicago Press, 1982), and *The Babylonian Talmud,* trans. Israel Slotki et al., ed. Isidore Epstein, 18 vols. (New York: Soncino, 1961), with my own modifications and translations, for citations from rabbinic literature.

2. Numerous other Second Temple texts relate to aspects of this topic. For example, the *Letter of Aristeas* represents a complex model of political and juridical leadership. See David C. Flatto, *Between Royal Absolutism and an Independent Judiciary: The Evolution of Separation of Powers in Biblical, Second Temple and Rabbinic Texts* (Cambridge, Mass.: Harvard University Press, 2010), 90–95.

3. Hecataeus's opposition to monarchy thus exceeds Deut 17's skepticism toward this institution.

4. Several of these psalms clearly allude to the Roman Empire. See PS 2:1–2, 26–27; 8:15–21; and 17:12.

5. See also PS 18. For background, see Eberhard Bons et al., *The Psalms of Solomon: Language, History, Theology* (Atlanta: SBL Press, 2015).

6. Scholars debate about the relationship of the spiritual and the political and national dimensions of Psalm 17. Compare Joseph Klausner, *The Messianic Idea in Israel* (New York: Macmillan, 1955), 323, with John J. Collins, *The Scepter and the Star: The Messiahs of the Dead Sea Scrolls and Other Ancient Literature* (New York: Doubleday, 1995), 55. In support of Collins's perspective, Psalm 17 presents the king's supreme judicial authority as intrinsic to his spiritual role.

7. See the discussion below about the target(s) of Psalm 17.

8. Collins notes that there is no (indisputable) parallel to such a statement about the messiah elsewhere in Jewish literature. Collins, *The Scepter and the Star*, 55.

9. See Collins, *The Scepter and the Star*, 54.

10. Others read PS 17's messianic vision as support for Herodian rule. See Samuel Rocca, "Josephus and the Psalms of Solomon," in *Making History: Josephus and Historical Method*, ed. Zuleika Rodgers (Leiden: Brill, 2007), 313–333, and references in 324n40.

11. Collins importantly notes that PS is the earliest witness to the hope for a messianic Davidic king in the Hellenistic and Roman eras. Collins, *The Scepter and the Star*, 50–56; see also 166–167.

12. Sections of Hecataeus are preserved in Diodorus's *Bibliotheca Historica* (I, 28, and XL, 3), which is excerpted in Photius's *Bibliotheca*.

13. Bezalel Bar Kochva, *The Image of the Jews in Greek Literature: The Hellenistic Period* (Berkeley: University of California Press, 2010), 90–135; and Bar Kochva, "The Jewish Ethnography of Hecataeus of Abdera," *Tarbiz* 75, nos. 1–2 (2007): 51–94, esp. 83. The excerpt below comes from Menahem Stern, *Greek and Latin Authors on Jews and Judaism*, vol. 1 (Jerusalem: Israel Academy of the Sciences and Humanities, 1974–1984), 25–29.

14. For more on the unique perspective reflected in this passage, see Bar Kochva, "The Jewish Ethnography," 80–85.

15. See Erich S. Gruen, *Heritage and Hellenism: The Reinvention of Jewish Tradition* (Berkeley: University of California Press, 1998), 52.

16. See Gruen, *Heritage and Hellenism*, 52, for a catalog of various factual errors in this passage from Hecataeus, such as the claim that Moses founded Jerusalem and erected the Temple.

17. The continuation of this passage likewise accents the unique spiritual standing of the priests, "He . . . assign[ed] . . . greater ones [allotments of land] to the priests, in order that they . . . might be undistracted and apply themselves continually to the worship of God."

18. See Stern, *Greek and Latin Authors on Jews and Judaism*, 31; and Bar Kochva, "The Jewish Ethnography," 52, 83–84. Warren Harvey, however, points out that in the context of the Pentateuch—which hardly refers to the monarchy—Hecataeus's claim is less bizarre than may appear at first blush.

19. E.g., Daniel Schwartz argues that this passage was written by a Jewish pseudo-Hecataeus from the late Hasmonean period. See Schwartz, "Diodorus Siculus 40.3—Hecataeus or Pseudo-Hecataeus?," in *Jews and Gentiles in the Holy Land in the Days of the Second Temple, the Mishnah and the Talmud,* ed. M. Mor et al. (Jerusalem: Yad Ben-Zvi, 2003), 181–197.

20. Doron Mendels posits that material in this passage came from Jewish priestly circles in the late fourth century that deliberately diminished the status of the Davidic kingdom. "Hecataeus of Abdera and a Jewish *Patrios Politeia* of the Persian Period (Diodorus Siculus 40.3)," *Zeitschrift für die Alttestamentliche Wissenschaft* 95, no. 1 (1983): 96–110. For other theories, see Bar Kochva, "The Jewish Ethnography," 83–84.

21. Hecataeus's description of the Jewish administration also departs from classical alternatives to a monarchy, such as a democracy or an oligarchy. See also John J. Collins, *Between Athens and Jerusalem: Jewish Identity in the Hellenistic Diaspora* (New York: Crossroad, 1983), 156.

22. At a more basic level, Hecataeus's description of the manner in which the Jews obey the legal instruction of the priestly judges is noteworthy, because it captures the degree to which Jews appear even to outsiders to be a law-abiding people.

23. See Bar Kochva, "The Jewish Ethnography," 56–61.

24. This encounter is also recorded in Josephus's *Ant.* 14:41ff, and in Strabo, *Geogr.* XVI, 2:40, 762 (no. 115).

25. The degree to which this administrative system appeared anomalous to Diodorus and his audience is less clear. Considering the purported senatorial sanction of this leadership scheme and the wider Roman antipathy to kingship, the Jewish ancestral preference must have had some appeal. In another context, however, Diodorus lauds rule by kingship, and describes the high priest as aiding the king (I:70–75).

26. For possible explanations for this rise in prominence, see Chapter 8.

27. While works such as *Maccabees* and *Aristeas* provide obvious (albeit understudied) portals into Jewish reflections on power and politics, other roughly contemporaneous Jewish writings also contain significant, if less overt, political and juridical insights, which have been overlooked.

28. For a full analysis and references, see Chapter 2.

29. See Naomi G. Cohen, "Contemporary Political Overtones of Philo," in *Proceedings of the Tenth World Congress of Jewish Studies* (Jerusalem: ha-Igud ha-'Olami le-Mada'e ha-Yahadut, 1990), 253.

30. For present purposes, I use the terms "ruler," "king," and "monarch" interchangeably, but Philo may distinguish among them, as I discuss in Chapter 2.

31. See Edwin R. Goodenough, *The Politics of Philo Judaeus: Practice and Theory* (New Haven, Conn.: Yale University Press, 1938), 86–120. Although Philo supports monarchy, he also promotes democracy. See Chapter 2.

32. For more on Philo's political thought, see Goodenough, *The Politics of Philo Judaeus;* Harry A. Wolfson, *Philo: Foundations of Religious Philosophy in Judaism, Christianity, and Islam,* rev. ed., vol. 2 (Cambridge, Mass.: Harvard University Press, 1962), 325–337; Isaak Heinemann, *Philons Griechische und Judische Bildung: Kultur-vergleichende Untersuchungen zu Philons Darstellung der Judischen Gesetze* (Breslau: M. und H. Marcus, 1932), 182–202; and Ray Barraclough, "Philo's Politics: Roman Rule and Hellenistic Judaism," in *Aufstieg und Niedergang der Römischen Welt, II,* 21.1 (Berlin: W. de Gruyter, 1984), 417–553.

33. See Deut 16:19–20. See also Exod 23:6–8, Deut 1:17, and 1 Sam 8:3.

34. Philo's definition of governmental responsibilities encompasses administering justice, but is broader. See 4.170.

35. See, e.g., *Moses* 1.62, 148–149.

36. Interestingly, Philo's characterization of Moses (as a judge or teacher) and the advice of Jethro differs elsewhere in his writings. Moreover, as Louis H. Feldman points out, this biblical episode is absent from the *Life of Moses.* See Feldman, *Philo's Portrayal of Moses in the Context of Ancient Judaism* (Notre Dame, Ind.: University of Notre Dame Press, 2007), 132–136.

37. For a full analysis and references, see Chapter 3.

38. For further analysis, see A. M. Wilson and L. Wills, "Literary Sources in the Temple Scroll," *Harvard Theological Review* 75 (1982): 275–288; Lawrence H. Schiffman, "The King, His Guard, and the Royal Council in the Temple Scroll," *Proceedings of the American Academy for Jewish Research* 54 (1987): 237–259; and M. O. Wise, *A Critical Study of the Temple Scroll from Qumran Cave 11* (Chicago: Oriental Institute of the University of Chicago, 1990).

39. Deut 17:20.

40. See Johann Maier, *The Temple Scroll: An Introduction, Translation and Commentary* (Sheffield: Journal for the Study of the Old Testament, 1985), 126.

41. The scroll refers to judgment (*mishpat*), law / instruction (*torah*), anything (*kol devar*), and all his counsels (*kol etsah*).

42. See Yigael Yadin, *The Temple Scroll: The Hidden Law of the Dead Sea Sect,* vol. 1 (Jerusalem: Israel Exploration Society, 1985), 345.

43. By abiding by LK, the king apparently fulfills the charge of Deut 17:19 that the summary of the law shall "remain with" him, and he "shall read it."

44. For a full analysis and references, see Chapter 4.

45. See *Ant.* 6:36, 94.

46. *Ag. Ap.* 2:164–165.

47. See, e.g., *Ag. Ap.* 2.166–171, 190–217, and 291–295.

48. *M. Sanh.* 2 is the primary text that relates to the interplay between the two sections of Deut 17. In Part Two I will also analyze other relevant tannaitic passages.

49. For a full analysis and references, see Chapter 5.

50. See *m. Sanh.* I, II.

51. One can group *Hecataeus* with these latter three texts.

52. The emphasis on legal supremacy arises from Deuteronomy. An archetypical royalist model is more likely to stress the authority of the king than the laws (which may be inferior to, or even derive from, the king's will); but Deuteronomy, however interpreted, affirms the centrality of the laws.

2. Philo's Jurisprudence

1. Classical scholarship on this excursus includes Isaak Heinemann, *Philons griechische und Judische Bildung: Kultur-vergleichende Untersuchungen zu Philons Darstellung der Judischen Gesetze* (Breslau: M. und H. Marcus, 1932), 182–202; Edwin R. Goodenough, *The Politics of Philo Judaeus: Practice and Theory* (New Haven, Conn.: Yale University Press, 1938), 86–120; Harry Austryn Wolfson, *Philo: Foundations of Religious Philosophy in Judaism, Christianity, and Islam,* 2 vols. (Cambridge, Mass.: Harvard University Press, 1962), 2:325–337. More recent scholarship will be cited below.

2. Philosophical and political influences inform Philo's exegesis in this excursus, alongside his rich and subtle scriptural interpretations. Perhaps more than any other thinker analyzed herein, Philo creatively generates his political thought and jurisprudence through a reading of Deuteronomy 17.

3. See also John W. Martens, *One God, One Law: Philo of Alexandria on the Mosaic and Greco-Roman Law* (Leiden: Brill, 2003), 84, 104.

4. 4.133–238.

5. See also Sarah J. Pearce, *The Words of Moses: Studies in the Reception of Deuteronomy in the Second Temple Period* (Tübingen: Mohr Siebeck, 2013), 289–305.

6. Depictions of God's sovereignty abound in the Bible. See, e.g., Exod 15:18, Jdg 8:23, Isa 44:6, Ps 22:29, 29:10, 93:1, 97:1, 98:6, 99:1–3.

7. *Moses* 1.148–162. But see note 80.

8. Some commentaries cite the Deut 17:14 clause, "like all the nations that are around," to identify certain powers and privileges.

9. There are two plausible explanations for this omission, both of which may be true. First, Philo does not consider this to be a core royal power (see David C. Flatto, *Between Royal Absolutism and an Independent Judiciary: The Evolution of Separation of Powers in Biblical, Second Temple and Rabbinic Texts* [Cambridge, Mass.: Harvard University Press, 2010], 68–71). Second, Philo privileges the Pentateuch over the rest of the Bible (including Samuel) in his writings (see Chapter 8).

10. For Philo, legal authority converges with the ruler's broader sovereign powers. That Philo enumerates this as the ruler's dominant responsibility reflects both the primacy of law and the prominence of the royalist model of administering justice.

11. In *Moses,* the nexus between the king and law is even more pronounced. See below. Yet Philo omits Exod 18:13–27 from this work.

12. The latter is based upon, "justice, justice shall thou pursue" (Deut 16:20).

13. 4.66–69.

14. "For the Lord your God is God of gods and Lord of lords, the great God, mighty and awesome, who is not partial and takes no bribe, who executes justice for the orphan and the widow, and who loves the strangers, providing them with food and clothing."

15. This hermeneutic may derive from the verse's use of the term "countrymen [*be-amekha*]," which also appears in Exod 22:27 alongside the term *Nasi,* i.e., *archon.*

16. But see note 15.

17. *Spec. Laws* 4.160.

18. On the origins and history of this concept, see Martens, *One God,* 31–66.

19. See the references in Martens, *One God,* at 90–99, 103–130; Christine Hayes, *What's Divine about Divine Law? Early Perspectives* (Princeton, N.J.: Princeton University Press, 2015), 120–124. See below.

20. See Rofe's thesis cited in Chapter 3, note 86.

21. Philo mostly uses *archon* in this excursus, but in 4.164, 168, 176 he uses *basileos.*

22. My analysis loosely uses and interchanges the terms "king," "monarch," and "sovereign" for stylistic reasons, but my subject throughout is the Philonic ruler.

23. See *Philo of Alexandria: Writings* [Hebrew], 5 vols., ed. Suzanne Daniel-Nataf (Jerusalem: Bialik Institute and Israel Academy of Sciences and Humanities, 2000), 3:135.

24. Contrast with *Sifre Deut.* 157.

25. On dynasties in the Bible, see Tomoo Ishida, *The Royal Dynasties in Ancient Israel: A Study on the Formation and Development of Royal-Dynastic Ideology* (Berlin: W. de Gruyter, 1977).

26. 4.169.

27. Interestingly, Philo labels Moses in this passage as *basileos* (not *archon*), which may suggest either that the excursus is a more mature formulation of political thought that employs revised nomenclature or that, notwithstanding the structural affinities, ultimately only Moses serves as a king, and all others are lesser rulers. See Martens, *One God,* 93n27, 94. See also *Spec. Laws* 1.226–233.

28. See the subsequent section in the appendix about war, *Spec. Laws* 4.219–229, where the king is likewise strikingly absent. See also Philo's description of God as the "Prince of Peace," *Decalogue* 178.

29. See, e.g., *Moses* 2.49–51; *Decalogue* 176–177. Other sources suggest a more complex position. See, e.g., *Spec. Laws* 1.54–55.

30. See Martens, *One God,* 65.

31. See Martens, *One God,* 121–122. Recall, more generally, that the excursus comprises part of an expository work on the Mosaic laws.

32. See *Moses* 2.4.

33. See Martens, *One God,* 101, 127.

34. See Martens, *One God,* 122.

35. See Martens, *One God,* 105–110, 121–123.

36. See below. Compare Martens, *One God,* 94n33.

37. See, e.g., *Abraham* 3–6; *Moses* 2.11, 13, 48, 52; *Creation* 3, 69, 71; *Good Person* 72–91.

38. Other biblical figures, such as Joseph, are also depicted by Philo in a suggestive manner. See Martens, *One God,* 93n27.

39. See also *Spec. Laws* 2.13.

40. The exact relationship between written Mosaic law and "higher" forms of living, natural, and unwritten law is a subtle and critical issue in Philo. See Hindy Najman, *Past Renewals* (Leiden: Brill, 2010), 107–118; Hayes, *What's Divine about Divine Law?*, 11–124, 133–137; Martens, *One God,* 103–130.

41. In *Abraham* 60–61, Philo refers to the "clearer signs" of the commands that are manifest in nature and visible to those who are living laws (i.e., Abraham).

42. To a lesser degree, this mandate devolves on all individuals. See below.

43. See Martens, *One God,* 89, 125n38, 127. See also Hayes, *What's Divine about Divine Law?*, 135–137.

44. Recall Philo's omission of the conclusion of Deut 17:18.

45. See, e.g., *Abraham* 3–6: "For they were not scholars or pupils of others, nor did they learn under teachers what was right to say or do: they listened to no voice of instruction but their own"; *Abraham* 16; *Creation* 172.

46. *Abraham* 3–6. See also *Good Person* 72–91.

47. Philo sounds this theme immediately before the excursus: "Praise cannot be duly given to one who obeys the written laws, since he acts under the admonition of restraint and the fear of punishment. But he who faithfully observes the *unwritten* deserves commendation, since the virtue which he displays is freely willed" (*Spec. Laws* 4.150; emphasis added). This theme also resonates with the broader, noncoercive nature of law in Philo's account.

48. This process helps cultivate a kind of philosopher-king. See *Moses* 2.3–4.

49. The biblical paragons are a model for future generations. See, e.g., *Abraham* 3–6. In a similar vein, the ruler is a *living* model for his generation.

50. 4.164.

51. Internalizing the Mosaic laws affects the ruler's administration of justice. In modern jurisprudential terms, this approximates an ennobled form of legal realism, whereby the Torah shapes the king's orientation, disposition, and intuition in administering justice. I thank Paul Kahn for this insight.

52. See also *Moses* 2.51, which describes the interaction between the law and the polis, albeit on a cosmic scale.

53. See *Moses* 2.16, which states that law is durable and resilient, and impervious to kings and tyrants.

54. See *Moses* 2.44, which alludes to the way a stable, successful polity would enable laws to flourish.

55. Philo's reliance on Deut 16:19–20 in establishing the king's legal role magnifies the initial omission of Deut 17:8–13, given that the former verses about local justice are a prelude to the latter account of centralized justice. See Alexander Rofe, *Mavo le-Sefer Devarim* [Hebrew] (Jerusalem: Akademon, 1988), 75.

56. Both sections of Deut 17 could be read contrary to their plain sense to establish the king's judicial role. Deut 17:18, stating that the king transcribes the summary of the law "in the presence of the Levitical priests," could be read as incorporating the king into the judicial process. Also, "the judge" of Deut 17:9, could be interpreted as referring to the king (see Ibn Ezra). Notably, Philo advances neither of these readings.

57. See also 4.69.

58. An elaboration on the argument presented in the next few paragraphs is presented in David C. Flatto, "Constructing Justice: The Selective Use of Scripture in Formulating Early Jewish Accounts of the Courts," *Harvard Theological Review* 111, no. 4 (2018): 504–508.

59. Philo also differentiates between Deut 17:8–13 and Exod 18:13–27 / Deut 1:9–18 (linking the latter to Deut 17:14–20). See Flatto, "Constructing Justice."

60. This highly original scheme only has loose parallels: Within the Bible, see 2 Chronicles 19:11. In classical writings, Aristotle distinguishes between law and equity, the former demanding expertise, the latter calling for a different kind of decision making. A medieval version of this partition in England (which developed over time) locates these two kinds of matters in distinct tribunals, the Court of Common Pleas and the King's Bench. Roman law invokes other divisions, as both jurists (experts) and praetors (political appointees) are central to the administration of justice, and sometimes the emperor directly intervenes in legal affairs. In later Islamic law, the sages (*ulama*) are masters of the sharia, while administrative matters of the *siyasa* are the province of the caliphs. In modern jurisprudence, there are parallels in countries with distinct constitutional and standard courts. In a different sense, early American jurisprudence distinguishes between the learned decisions of appellate courts, and the commonsense decisions of trial courts. To this day, in the United States the Supreme Court exercises original jurisdiction for "great" matters (involving "great" litigants, such as government officials / states), and appellate jurisdiction for "difficult" matters.

61. See, e.g., *Spec. Laws* 4.1; see also 4.59–61, which prohibits judges from using hearsay testimony.

62. See Septuagint ad loc., which uses the term *hyperogkon* for "great" and *brachea* for "small" matters. In verse 26 it uses *hyperogkon* for "difficult" and *elaphron* for "small" matters.

63. The supreme authority is arguably most capable of enforcing the rule of law in such circumstances, for reasons described in the continuation. Philo's conception of supreme jurisdiction over "great" matters shares a loose analogy to modern constitutional doc-

trines of judicial review and "strict scrutiny," which emphasize the court's heightened mandate to protect vulnerable legal rights of minority groups.

64. See *Spec. Laws* 4.179.

65. An alternative translation of the biblical clause is "If you are baffled by a matter."

66. In other words, perhaps Philo contrasts the "baffling matter" of Deut 17:8 with the "great" matters referred to in Exod 18:22.

67. The distinction between these two terms is noted in certain later rabbinic texts. According to *b. Sanh. 16a* (citing earlier *braitot*), they are either interchangeable adjectives for difficult matters or refer to two distinct grounds for the Sanhedrin's jurisdiction, one for "difficult" matters, the other for "great" matters, understood, unlike Philo, as matters involving an eminent litigant. But Philo's further teaching about dividing the allocation of supreme jurisdiction has no rabbinic parallel. According to *b. Sanh. 16a*, the Sanhedrin has exclusive jurisdiction over supreme legal matters (whether there are one or two kinds of supreme matters).

68. A modern analogy is a litigation that is fraught with sociopolitical consequences, but where the actual legal issue in dispute is relatively straightforward.

69. See, generally, 4.55–58.

70. See Pearce, *Words of Moses*, 118–119.

71. "One and by no means an inconsiderable part of justice is that which is concerned with law courts and judges. This I have already mentioned."

72. Martens (*One God*, 124) argues for a unity of several forms of substantive law in Philo's thought. In a parallel sense, one can discern a unifying objective among its multiple administrators. So there are at least two main innovations in Philo's jurisprudence. The first, emphasized by Martens, is his unique blend of ideas about the ontology of substantive law. The second, emphasized here, is that the distinctive ontology of law requires a division or multiplicity in its mode of administration.

73. "The law tells us that we must set the rules of justice [*prodidaskéto dí tá díkaia*] in the heart and fasten them for a sign upon the hand and have them shaking before the eyes, etc." See also Naomi Cohen, "Philo's Place in the Chain of Jewish Tradition," *Tradition* 44, no. 2 (2011): 13; Sarit Kattan Gribetz, "The Shema in the Second Temple Period: A Reconsideration," *Journal of Ancient Judaism* 6, no. 1 (2015): 71–73.

74. In 4.143, Philo discusses how "nothing should be added or taken away, but all the laws originally ordained should be kept unaltered just as they were," making it clear that fulfillment of the laws of Moses is essential for executing justice.

75. "For there is no sweeter delight than that the soul should be charged through and through with justice, exercising itself in her eternal principles and doctrines and leaving no vacant place into which unjustice can make its ways."

76. In other words, the masses should also aspire to become a kind of living law. Similarly, they should emulate the ancients and the ruler who embody this quality. See also *Con-*

templ. 78 (where the literal and allegorical dimensions of the law are presented as resembling a "living creature").

77. For background, see John M. Barclay, *Jews in the Mediterranean Diaspora: From Alexander to Trajan (323 BCE–117 CE)* (Berkeley: University of California Press, 1996), 48–180.

78. The larger context is Philo's explanation for the Pentateuch's beginning with creation as a prelude to the Mosaic laws, rather than with the establishment of a polity.

79. *Moses* 2.51. Philo further describes the entire universe in political terms—the Stoic notion that the cosmos is a polis. See also *Creation* 3.

80. Note that the Philonic kingdom does not have an address, omitting Deut 17:14's reference to the land of Israel.

81. See *Moses* 2.44, which argues that under the right conditions all of humanity would follow the Mosaic laws.

82. A limited form of rulership also better fits the antimonarchic ideology prevalent in first-century-CE Roman Egypt.

83. For further background, see Daniel Leon, "The Face of the Emperor in Philo's Embassy to Gaius," *Classical World* 110, no. 1 (2016): 43–60; and Maren Niehoff, *Philo of Alexandria: An Intellectual Biography* (New Haven, Conn.: Yale University Press, 2018), 25–46.

84. See Ray Barraclough, "Philo's Politics: Roman Rule and Hellenistic Judaism," in *Aufstieg und Niedergang der Römischen Welt, II,* 21.1 (Berlin: W. de Gruyter, 1984), 417–553.

85. See, e.g., J. A. Crook, *Augustus: Power, Authority, Achievement,* in *Cambridge Ancient History,* 2nd ed., ed. Alan K. Bowman et al., vol. 10 (Cambridge: Cambridge University Press, 1996), 118–120.

86. Ptolemaic kingship was centralized, but under Roman rule governmental tasks were officially partitioned. Therefore, imperial concentration of powers engendered criticism. Although in his explicit rhetoric Philo mostly supports the Augustan solution (*Embassy,* 143–150), he underscores the differentiation of functions inherent in Roman political theory and probes whether a consolidation of roles is defensible or desirable. This may even underlie his conflicting writings on the relationship between kingship and the high priesthood, and whether they should ideally be consolidated or partitioned. See Flatto, *Between Royal Absolutism,* 71–79.

87. But see *Moses* 2.7 on certain advantages of consolidating power.

88. Philo's royalism informs his promotion of the ruler, notwithstanding the ambivalence of Deut 17; resourcefulness in locating other Pentateuchal sources to support this stance; identification of the ruler as a supreme legal authority, contrary to Deut 17's plain sense; and associating the ruler with the sovereignty of God.

89. Deut 17 thus substantiates the supremacy of law for Philo.

3. Qumran Literature on Kingship, Councils, and Law

1. Proximate sections of the TS are based on other pericopes in Deuteronomy. For 2 Chron 19's possible influence on the LK, see Dwight D. Swanson, *The Temple Scroll and the Bible: The Methodology of 11Qt* (Leiden: Brill, 1995), 171–172.

2. For background, see Lawrence H. Schiffman, *The Courtyards of the House of the Lord: Studies on the Temple Scroll*, ed. Florentino Garcia Martinez (Leiden: Brill, 2008); Casey Elledge, *The Statutes of the King: The Temple Scroll's Legislation on Kingship (11Q19 LVI12–LIX21)* (Paris: Gabalda, 2004); Michael O. Wise, *A Critical Study of the Temple Scroll from Qumran Cave 11* (Chicago: Oriental Institute of the University of Chicago, 1990); and Yigael Yadin, *The Temple Scroll: The Hidden Law of the Dead Sea Sect*, vol. 1 (Jerusalem: Israel Exploration Society, 1985).

3. The LK also cites Deut 16:18–19, which addresses judges, to admonish the king to adjudicate fairly (11Q19 57:19–20), and draws from the traits of Mosaic judges, Exod 18:21, in describing the royal guard (11Q19 57:8–9).

4. Yoav Barzilay, "The Law of the King in the *Temple Scroll:* Its Original Characteristics and Later Redaction" [Hebrew], *Tarbiz* 72 (2003): 59–84.

5. Moshe Weinfeld, "The Temple Scroll or 'The Law of the King,'" in *Normative and Sectarian Judaism in the Second Temple Period* (London: T and T Clark, 2005), 158–185.

6. Arguably, his judicial role can have an impact on the temple's sanctity. Biblical traditions, by contrast, often assign the king a cultic role. See, e.g., 1 Sam 21:1–6; 2 Sam 6:12–19; 1 Kgs 8; Ps 110:1–4; and 1 Chr 15:11–15.

7. But see Barzilay, "The Law of the King in the *Temple Scroll*."

8. See Sarah J. Pearce, *The Words of Moses: Studies in the Reception of Deuteronomy in the Second Temple Period* (Tübingen: Mohr Siebeck, 2013), 275–288.

9. 11Q19 57:12–13.

10. Tellingly, the king must also consult with the high priest wearing the *Urim* and *Thummim* regarding matters of warfare. 11Q19 58:18–21.

11. 11Q19 56:1 (judge, an incomplete citation based on Deut 17:9); 11Q19 56:9–10 (priest and judge, based on Deut 17:12); 61:8–9 (priests, Levites, judges, elaborating on Deut 19:17). See Yadin, *The Temple Scroll*, 350. Notice how 61:8–9 enumerates a threefold representation that arguably corresponds to the three duodecimal branches that comprise the LK's council of thirty-six. This may imply that a body with a threefold representation has autonomous judicial standing in Qumran, which the king presides alongside in certain situations.

12. See Aharon Shemesh, *Halakhah in the Making: The Development of Jewish Law from Qumran to the Rabbis* (Los Angeles: University of California Press, 2009), 53–54; and Gershon Brin, "Studies in Biblical Law: From the Hebrew Bible to the Dead

Sea Scrolls," Supplement, *Journal for the Study of the Old Testament* 176 (1994): 128–162.

Note that the use of brackets and parentheses in citations throughout this chapter follow the conventions of Qumran literature, which differ from the stylistic format used in other chapters: In Qumran literature, bracketed clauses contain scholarly reconstructions of fragmentary texts and parenthetical clauses contain explanatory interpolations. In the other chapters, by contrast, bracketed clauses contain explanatory interpolations and parenthetical clauses record source references.

13. See note 182.

14. Conversely, the TS can be better evaluated in light of other materials. See this chapter's conclusion.

15. They also debate about when during the Hasmonean dynasty TS was written. See the references in note 2 and in Steven D. Fraade, *Legal Fictions: Studies of Law and Narrative in the Discursive World of Ancient Jewish Sectarians and Sages* (Leiden: Brill, 2011), 291nn16–17.

16. 1QpHab 8.8–13. See Lawrence H. Schiffman and James C. VanderKam, eds., *Encyclopedia of the Dead Sea Scrolls*, 2 vols. (New York: Oxford University Press, 2000), 1:331.

17. 1QpHab 8:9 states that the wicked priest "was called loyal (*nikra al shem ha-emet*) at the start of his office," which may suggest that his priestly role is not per se illegitimate, but becomes delegitimized over time.

18. See, e.g., *Encyc. DSS*, 2:688–693; and Joseph L. Angel, *Otherworldly and Eschatological Priesthood in the Dead Sea Scrolls* (Leiden: Brill, 2010).

19. See Joseph Blenkinsopp, *David Remembered: Kingship and National Identity in Ancient Israel* (Grand Rapids, Mich.: Eerdmans, 2013), 167–168.

20. On whether the TS should be considered a sectarian text, contrast Israel Knohl, "The Bible Reworked at Qumran: The Temple Scroll and 4Q Reworked Pentateuch" [Hebrew], in *The Qumran Scrolls and Their World*, vol. 1, ed. Menahem Kister (Jerusalem: Yad Ben-Zvi Press, 2009), 162–164, with Schiffman, *The Courtyards of the House of the Lord*, 149–162.

21. This raises an additional complexity: Some texts focus on the present, whereas others formulate a utopian or eschatological vision. Texts may also diverge on whether they are grounded in Scripture or sectarian teachings. One should be mindful of these differences, even though drawing sharp distinctions based upon them is difficult. See also Steven D. Fraade, "Review: Aryeh Amihay, *Theory and Practice in Essene Law*," *Dead Sea Discoveries* 25, no. 2 (2018): 285–287.

22. Aspects of these issues have been explored by Aharon Shemesh, Joseph Baumgarten, and Lawrence Schiffman, among others. An exhaustive study of judicial authority at Qumran is still a desideratum.

23. I deliberately refer to Qumran writings in general; however, most of my evidence comes from what is often deemed "pre-sectarian and sectarian material." Throughout this

chapter, I aim to offer a survey of this eclectic corpus, and at the same time to not of-fend most (not all!) viewpoints of its nature. I hope thereby to sidestep the most con-tentious issues in scholarship relating to the community living at Qumran; their precise dates, predecessors, and successors; and the profile of their library, including which works they authored, revered, or collected. For an overview, see John J. Collins, *The Dead Sea Scrolls: A Biography* (Princeton, N.J.: Princeton University Press, 2012); and Kister, *The Qumran Scrolls and Their World,* 1:3–108. This chapter's conclusion pre-sents a thesis that necessarily relies on certain assumptions about the nature and dating of this material, delineated below.

24. Unlike Chapter 2, where I was able to explore Philo's jurisprudence by mostly focusing on one extended excursus structured around Deut 17, in this and subsequent chapters the analysis must necessarily move beyond Deuteronomy and examine numerous pas-sages related to the themes of legal authority and its relationship to royal power, or priestly or other extra-royal figures or bodies.

25. On possible external influences, see note 182.

26. See the references in Martin G. Abegg Jr., *The Dead Sea Scroll Concordance,* vol. 1, pt. 1 (Leiden: Brill, 2003), 451–453.

27. Amos 5:26–27 can be rendered: "You have lifted up the shrine [*sikut*] of your king, the pedestal of your idols, the star of your god which you made for yourselves. Therefore I will exile you beyond Damascus, says the Lord of Hosts." See Paul D. Mandel, *The Origins of Midrash: From Teaching to Text* (Leiden: Brill, 2017), 114. CD is interpreting these verses homiletically. This section is known as the *Amos-Numbers Midrash* (CD A 7:13b–8:1a), and is not found in CD B. See also John J. Collins, *The Scepter and the Star: The Messiahs of the Dead Sea Scrolls and Other Ancient Literature* (New York: Doubleday, 1995), 80–81.

28. The term *sikut* (shrine) is being vocalized by the scroll as *sukkat* (booth).

29. Note that the Amos 9:11 intertext explicitly refers to King David. This verse forms the basis of a pro-monarchic passage analyzed below, 4Q174:12–13.

30. CD 8:8ff, by contrast, clearly recognizes that gentile kings exercise sovereign power.

31. See George J. Brooke, "Exegesis at Qumran: 4QFlorilegium in Its Jewish Context," Supplement, *Journal for the Study of the Old Testament* 29 (1985): 302–309.

32. See 4Q246, 4Q252 and 4Q521, discussed briefly below.

33. CD 7:18–20.

34. Tellingly, even these passages do not depict the king filling a consequential con-temporary role in the community. See Jacob Licht, *The Rule Scroll* (Jerusalem: Mosad Bialik, 1965), 188–189.

35. Relative to Aramaic Levi, a contemporary work that transfers all sovereignty to the priestly class, the royalism of these Qumran texts is still noteworthy. See David C. Flatto, *Between Royal Absolutism and an Independent Judiciary: The Evolution of Separa-tion of Powers in Biblical, Second Temple and Rabbinic Texts* (Cambridge, Mass.: Har-vard University Press, 2010), 137–140.

36. See the earlier lines 4Q398 Frags. 11–13:1–5. See also 4Q470.

37. Some scholars argue that the addressee of 4QMMT has a kind of royal status, while others disagree or see this as a rhetorical construct. See the summary of earlier scholarship in Fraade, *Legal Fictions,* 79; and Aryeh Amihay, *Theory and Practice in Essene Law* (New York: Oxford University Press, 2017), 32–36. In terms of the substance of this passage, it notably presents kings as fallible. See also the discussion of sin in the LK (11Q57:10–11) above and CD 5:1–6 below.

38. Scholars sharply debate the identity and nature of this ruler. See, e.g., Arstein Justnes, *The Time of Salvation* (Frankfurt: Peter Lang, 2009), 137–162.

39. This passage is the controversial "Pierced Messiah" text, which has, of course, been subject to different interpretations. Note that in 4Q285 fragment 5:5 a priest is also mentioned. See note 57.

40. This passage is opaque. For a pro-monarchic reading, see David Goodblatt, "The Title Nasi and the Ideological Background of the Second Revolt" [Hebrew], in *The Bar Kokhba Revolt: A New Approach,* ed. Aharon Oppenheimer et al. (Jerusalem: Yad Ben Zvi, 1984), 118.

41. Scholars debate whether this scroll is genuinely positive in its praise (the majority position), or, in fact, negative, as captured in this article's title: Emmanuelle Main, "For King Jonathan or Against? The Use of Bible in 4Q448," in *Biblical Perspectives: Early Use and Interpretation of the Bible in Light of the Dead Sea Scrolls,* ed. M. E. Stone and E. G. Chazon (Leiden: Brill, 1998), 113–135. 4Q448's orientation toward monarchy should also be evaluated alongside my conjecture below about the shifting attitudes toward monarchy at Qumran over time.

42. The "Prince of the Congregation" is mentioned explicitly in Frag. 2–6:15. The *Kittim* are referenced several times in Frags. 8–10:1–10. *Kittim* is often a code word for the Romans. See Shani Tzoref, *The Pesher Nahum Scroll from Qumran: An Exegetical Study of 4Q169* (Leiden: Brill, 2004), 101–104.

43. Frags. 8–10:11–25.

44. The underlying verses are from 2 Sam 7; Ps 2, 89; Amos 9; and Exod 15.

45. 4Q174 Frag. 1:1–3.

46. Nevertheless, 4Q174 Frag. 1:18–19 construes Psalms 2:2's messiah as the elect ones of Israel. It also refers to the Sons of Zadok (17), the Temple of Men (6), and possibly the House of Judah (Frag. 4:7).

47. 4Q174 Frag. 1:7–13. See the comments of Milgrom in *The Dead Sea Scrolls: Hebrew, Aramaic, and Greek Texts with English Translations,* ed. James H. Charlesworth, vol. 6b (Mohr Siebeck: Tubingen, 2002), 248–249.

48. According to a common theory, 1QS is designated for the pre-messianic community, whereas these appendices anticipate a subsequent eschatological phase. See Joseph L. Angel, "Victory in Defeat: The Image of the Priesthood in the Dead Sea Scrolls" (PhD diss., New York University, 2008), 156.

49. 1QSa 2:11–22. See Collins, *The Dead Sea Scrolls,* 108–110.

50. See Bilhah Nitzan, *Qumran Prayer and Religious Poetry,* trans. Jonathan Chipman (Leiden: Brill, 1994), 155–167.

51. See Geza G. Xeravits, *King, Priest, Prophet: Positive Eschatological Protagonists of the Qumran Library* (Leiden: Brill, 2001), 32.

52. 1QSb 5:20–23.

53. The reconstructed word *ve-lishpot* and other clauses from Isaiah 11 that appear in this blessing seem to have juridical connotations. But 1QSb reorders the verses here, and conflates them with verses from Micah 4, 5; and also describes the priestly role in the previous blessings as juridical in nature (see below). Therefore, the terms here may be more focused on leadership.

54. 1QSb 5:23–28.

55. For an alternate reconstruction, see Yadin, *The Temple Scroll,* 1:352.

56. The last line arguably mandates that the royal messiah be clothed in priestly garments. See Alex Jassen, "Rereading 4QPesher Isaiah A (4Q161) Forty Years after DJD 5," in *The Mermaid and the Partridge: Essays from the Copenhagen Conference on Revising Texts from Cave Four* (Leiden: Brill Academic, 2011), 57–90.

57. A parallel revision of neighboring verses in Isaiah is evident in the "Pierced Messiah" text (4Q285, 11Q14), where the scroll seamlessly interpolates the figure of the priest or high priest.

58. 4Q174 Frag. 1:10–11. The interjection stands out as the continuation reverts back to the king: "'I will raise up the hut of David which has fallen,' This (refers to) the hut of David which has fall[en, w]hich he will raise up to save Israel" (4Q174 Frag. 1:12–13). But see note 46.

59. See Fraade, *Legal Fictions,* 57–58.

60. 1QSb 3:22–25.

61. Alt. translation, "to assess all his judgments."

62. See Angel, "Victory in Defeat," 166.

63. See Carol A. Newsom, "The Sage in the Literature of Qumran: The Function of the *Maskil,*" in *The Sage in Israel and the Ancient Near East,* ed. John G. Gammie et al. (Winona Lake, Ind.: Eisenbrauns, 1990).

64. See Nitzan, *Qumran Prayer and Religious Poetry,* 145–172.

65. See also 11QMelch (11Q13); and 4Q369.

66. 1QSa 2:12. Note that the term "the priest" in this line is reconstructed.

67. See also 4Q427:7, 1QHa25:34–27:3, and 4Q471b4Q431, which arguably are related texts (often labeled Recension A, while 4Q491:11 I is called Recension B).

68. 4Q491:11 I:5.

69. 4Q491:11 I:5. See also Dan 7:9.

70. "Never have I been instructed, yet there is no teaching [that compares to my teaching] . . . Who can challenge me and so compare with my judgment?" (4Q491:11 I:9–10).

71. See Joseph L. Angel, "The Liturgical-Eschatological Priest of the Self-Glorification Hymn," *Revue de Qumran* 96 (2010): 588–592.

72. See Angel, "The Liturgical-Eschatological Priest of the Self-Glorification Hymn," 585–605.

73. See Collins, *The Scepter and the Star,* 120. Several clauses are ambiguous about whether the subject is God or the messiah (the former is more likely). See Lawrence H. Schiffman, *Reclaiming the Dead Sea Scrolls: The History of Judaism, the Background of Christianity, the Lost Library of Qumran* (Philadelphia: Jewish Publication Society, 1994), 348–350. See also 4Q521:3 III:1.

74. The following titles appear: *shalit, mehokek, mashiakh,* and *tsemakh,* as well as the terms *memshal* and *malkhut.*

75. The text thereby subtly limits the promise of a royal leader to such periods.

76. Other scrolls referring to the Davidic dynasty include 4Q252, 1QSb, 4Q161, 4Q174 (discussed above); 4Q504, 4Q285; as well as the Davidic hymns. See also 11Q Psalms (11Q5). See Joseph Blenkinsopp, *David Remembered: Kingship and National Identity in Ancient Israel* (Grand Rapids, Mich.: Eerdmans, 2013), 161–181.

77. The term used is *shalit;* the masoretic text reads *shevet.*

78. The masoretic text reads *regalav.* See James L. Kugel, *Traditions of the Bible* (Cambridge, Mass.: Harvard University Press, 2009), 492–493.

79. See Moshe J. Bernstein, "The Blessing of Judah in 4Q252," in *Studies in the Hebrew Bible, Qumran, and the Septuagint Presented to Eugene Ulrich,* ed. Peter W. Flint et al. (Leiden: Brill, 2006), 250–260.

80. See Daniel R. Schwartz, "The Messianic Departure from Judah (4QPatriarchal Blessings)," *Theologische Zeitschrift* 37 (1981): 257–266.

81. CD 5:1–6. See Jacqueline C. R. de Roo, "David's Deeds in the Dead Sea Scrolls," *Dead Sea Discoveries* 6, no. 1 (1999): 44–65. But see Ben Zion Wacholder, "David's Eschatological Psalter 11Q Psalms," *Hebrew Union College Annual* 59 (1988): 23–72.

82. See Adiel Schremer, "Qumran Polemic on Marital Law: CD 4:20–5:11 and Its Social Background," in *The Damascus Document: A Centennial of Discovery* (Leiden: Brill, 2000), 147–160.

83. See Craig A. Evans, "David in the Dead Sea Scrolls," in *The Scrolls and the Scriptures: Qumran Fifty Years After,* ed. S.E. Porter et al. (Sheffield, UK: Sheffield Academic Press, 1997), 186.

84. For rabbinic comparisons, see Flatto, *Between Royal Absolutism and an Independent Judiciary,* 389–391.

85. See Chapter 2 for an analysis of Philo's use of the parallel term "archon."

86. Alexander Rofe, "Qumran Paraphrases, the Greek Deuteronomy and the Late History of the Biblical Nasi" [Hebrew], *Textus* 14 (1988): 163–174 (in this vein, the use of *Nasi* in CD 5:1–4 is also noteworthy, as David's behavior is criticized). Christine Hayes, however, has suggested that the term *Nasi* offers a rarefied way to refer to an idyllic king.

87. Collins, *The Scepter and the Star,* 74–77.

88. Xeravits argues that the emphasis is on a second (not necessarily Davidic) royal figure. *King, Priest, Prophet,* 205–213.

89. See esp. 4Q175 (*Testimonia*).

90. The literature on this issue is vast. See Michael A. Knibb, "Apocalypticism and Messianism," in *The Oxford Handbook of the Dead Sea Scrolls,* ed. Timothy H. Lim et al. (New York: Oxford University Press, 2010), 417–432.

91. The entry on "Kingship" in *Encyc. DSS,* 1:468–469, which primarily focuses on the LK, is too narrow in scope.

92. *Encyc. DSS* 1:455–456. While much of the judicial process in Jewish antiquity was no doubt ad hoc, Qumran records very regimented schemes. The sources of the juridical models at Qumran are far from certain. See note 182.

93. See Amihay, *Theory and Practice.*

94. Scholars have labored arduously to clarify these matters, with varying degrees of success.

95. See *Encyc. DSS* 1:455–460.

96. The next section draws on primary references cited by Aharon Shemesh, *Halakhah in the Making;* Charlotte Hempel, *The Laws of the Damascus Document: Sources, Tradition and Redaction* (Leiden: Brill, 1998); Moshe Weinfeld, *Organizational Patterns and the Penal Code of the Qumran Sect: A Comparison with Guilds and Religious Associations of the Hellenistic-Roman Period* (Fribourg: Vandenhoeck und Ruprecht, 1986); Lawrence H. Schiffman, *Sectarian Law in the Dead Sea Scrolls: Courts, Testimony, and the Penal Code* (Chico, Calif.: Scholars Press, 1983); Joseph M. Baumgarten, *Studies in Qumran Law* (Leiden: Brill, 1977), among other works. All of these works make helpful contributions to understanding aspects of judicial authority at Qumran, but none provides an exhaustive study.

97. See Charlotte Hempel, "Community Structures in the Dead Sea Scrolls," in *The Dead Sea Scrolls after Fifty Years,* vol. 2, ed. Peter W. Flint and James C. VanderKam (Leiden: Brill, 1998–1999), 79–84.

98. Some of the original positions in Qumran adopt a biblical term or title (e.g., *Maskil*).

99. CD 20.24 previously referred to the judgment of the holy council. See Mandel, *The Origins of Midrash,* 140n172.

100. The title *Moreh Hatsedeq* is often translated as "Teacher of Righteousness," but it has been translated in various ways. See James H. Charlesworth, *The Pesharim and Qumran History: Chaos or Consensus?* (Grand Rapids, Mich.: Eerdmans, 2002), 28–30.

101. See Loren T. Stuckenbruck, "The Teacher of Righteousness Remembered: From Fragmentary Sources to Collective Memory in the Dead Sea Scrolls," in *Memory in the Bible and Antiquity* (Tübingen: Mohr Siebeck, 2007), 75–95.

102. The Teacher of Righteousness was a historical leader of the sect, as described in CD. Various texts anticipate that a similar figure will lead the sect at the end of days. A

minority scholarly view contends that this is the perpetual title of a communal official. See Gabriele Boccaccini, "The Groningen Hypothesis Revisited," in *Enoch and Qumran Origins: New Light on a Forgotten Connection,* ed. Gabriele Boccaccini (Grand Rapids, Mich.: Eerdmans, 2005), 249–316.

103. See Loren T. Stuckenbruck, "The Legacy of the Teacher of Righteousness in the Dead Sea Scrolls," in *New Perspectives on Old Texts: Proceedings of the Tenth International Symposium of the Orion Center for the Study of the Dead Sea Scrolls and Associated Literature, 9–11 January, 2005,* ed. Esther G. Chazon et al. (Leiden: Brill, 2010), 27.

104. See Fraade, *Legal Fictions,* 57–58.

105. It is unclear whether the Interpreter of the Torah has a fixed role, or a role that is only assumed in the process of religious instruction.

106. This suggestive term can be translated alternatively as a legislator. In this context it clearly has a juridical connotation, designating a legal authority. The term pervades these lines, appearing three more times in different forms in the next line (9). See Fraade, *Legal Fictions,* 55–56.

107. See CD 6:10–11. See also Fraade, *Legal Fictions,* 52–58.

108. Mandel also relies on 1QS 6:6–8 and 8:11–12. According to Mandel, the former passage evidently is not referring to a fixed position. See Mandel, *The Origins of Midrash,* 118–119.

109. Mandel, *The Origins of Midrash,* 125. Mandel's primary argument, that "midrash" in Qumran means hierarchical instruction, is less relevant for this chapter.

110. See Amihay, *Theory and Practice,* 145–146 (with citations).

111. See 1QS 6:11–20 (*Mebaqqer* runs the community meetings); CD 13: 7–21 (*Mebaqqer* examines new members, and approves commercial transactions); 15:6–17 (*Mebaqqer* examines new members, teaches members, and suspends wayward members). See Fraade, *Legal Fictions,* 197n13.

112. Shlomo Naeh and Aharon Shemesh argue that this passage has Deuteronomic roots. "Deuteronomy 19:15–19 in the Damascus Document and Early Midrash," *Dead Sea Discoveries* 20 (2013): 179–199.

113. See also CD 15:8–17.

114. See also CD 13:22.

115. See Amihay, *Theory and Practice,* 145–149. He proceeds to argue that the *Maskil*'s role in 1QS is eschatological.

116. See also 4QSb, 4QSd.

117. The passage also enumerates the ideal attributes of the *Maskil* (9:21a–26), including constantly being alert to the precepts of God (9:24). See Mandel, *The Origins of Midrash,* 103.

118. See Menachem Kister, "Commentary to 4Q298," *Jewish Quarterly Review* 85, nos. 1–2 (1994): 237–238.

119. See also CD 12:19–20, 20:27–31.

120. See Shem Miller, *Dead Sea Media: Orality, Textuality, and Memory in the Scrolls from the Judean Desert* (Boston: Brill, 2019), 70–73.

121. The continuation states that if there is no proficient priest, a proficient Levite should preside.

122. Moreover, presumably the figures singled out in the vertical arrangements are selected in part for their embodiment, and representation, of sectarian ideals.

123. The leading figure may serve on a council, or operate alongside a council and / or the community. See the various texts cited below.

124. Recall that in the LK the king operates alongside a council of thirty-six.

125. A threefold division may be echoed in 1QM 2:1–3. A threefold division also exists in the structure of the Temple courtyard in the TS.

126. This structure bears a resemblance to the later rabbinic schemes of "institutional justice." See Chapter 6.

127. See *Encyc. DSS* 1:456.

128. See Joseph M. Baumgarten, "The Duodecimal Courts of Qumran, Revelation and the Sanhedrin," *Journal of Biblical Literature* 95, no. 1 (1976): 59–78.

129. See Lawrence H. Schiffman, *The Halakhah at Qumran* (Leiden: Brill, 1975), 76.

130. See Baumgarten, "The Duodecimal Courts," 59–64.

131. The passage is from 1QS. There are significant variants in parallels from the fourth cave. See Philip S. Alexander and Geza Vermes, *Qumran Cave 4.XIX: Serekh ha-Yahad and Two Related Texts: DJD*, vol. 26 (Oxford: Clarendon, 1998), 139–144. Scholars debate whether the council is an elite gathering from within the sectarian community (*yahad*), or more directly aligned with the entire community. See Mandel, *The Origins of Midrash*, 95n24, 139, and below.

132. Note that the phrase "community council" is also used for the community as a whole. See, e.g., 1QS 3:2; 5:7–9.

133. See also 1QS 8:11–12. 4Q265 Frag. 7 ii:7–9 also refers to a council of fifteen.

134. Alternatively, the council actually constitutes the holy house of Israel and the sacred chambers of Aaron.

135. 1QS 8:24–25 further states that one who is expelled from the community cannot participate in judging or in offering counsel. In all, the scroll advances a vision of a community that will live according to norms, and whose distinct manner of living is most manifest in the council. The council embodies justice, testifies, punishes, instructs (revealed) laws, and expels rebels. Merely describing its role as adjudication does not fully capture its all-encompassing juridical character.

136. Scholars debate the precise relationship of this passage to the 1QS8 passage about the fifteen-member council, along with the relationship of 1QS to CD. See John J. Collins, "Beyond the Qumran Community: Social Organization in the Dead Sea Scrolls," *Dead Sea Discoveries* 16, no. 3 (2009): 357–365.

137. Its precise makeup depends on different recensions. See Alison Schofield, "Rereading S: A New Model of Textual Development in Light of the Cave 4 Serekh Copies," *Dead Sea Discoveries* 15 (2008): 96–120. There is an ongoing debate about whether the 4QS manuscripts are earlier or later than 1QS. See Devorah Dimant, "The Composite Character of the Qumran Sectarian Literature as an Indication of Its Date and Provenance," *Revue de Qumran* 22 (2006): 615–630.

138. Mandel argues that this refers to the same council of ten referred to previously. Others disagree and say this refers to any gathering of ten communal members. See Mandel, *The Origins of Midrash*, 118.

139. See Charlotte Hempel, "Interpretive Authority in the Community Rule Tradition," *Dead Sea Discoveries* 10, no. 1 (2003): 62.

140. See also 1QS 8:20ff.

141. The shifting back and forth described below is especially noticeable in the juxtaposition of these lines about the nightly instruction of the Many with the previous lines about the daily and nightly instruction of the council of ten (according to Mandel).

142. The Many inquire of the council, but evidently also offer input to the council. So the Many is not just subject to the legal authority of the council, but also participates in legal instruction.

143. These terms do not appear in 1QS 1–4. See Sarianna Metso, "In Search of the *Sitz im Leben* of the Community Rule," in *The Provo International Conference on the Dead Sea Scrolls: Technological Innovations, New Texts, and Reformulated Issues,* ed. Donald W. Parry and Eugene Ulrich (Leiden: Brill, 1999), 311. Also, at one stage of the redaction the term "Many" is replaced by a reference to the sons of Zadok and the men of the community. See Metso, "In Search of the *Sitz im Leben* of the Community Rule," 311–312, 312n14.

144. See Mandel, *The Origins of Midrash*, 140, for his summary.

145. The interpretation of 1QS 5–7 may also influence how one interprets 1QS8. See note 136.

146. See notes 131 and 132.

147. On "Levites," see Fraade, *Legal Fictions*, 200–201nn23–24.

148. See Charlotte Hempel, "Do the Scrolls Suggest Rivalry between the Sons of Aaron and the Sons of Zadok, and if so Was It Mutual?," *Revue de Qumran* 24, no. 1 (2009): 135–153.

149. To express control over the law, the text uses the suggestive phrase *yimsholu be-mishpat*, which captures the significant political power that can be associated with judicial authority.

150. See, e.g., the following passages (several referenced in this chapter): 1QS 2:19–20; 5:21–22; 6:3–9, 18–19; 8:1; 1QSa 2:17–21; CD 4:6–9; 10:4–6; 13:2–4; 14:3–8; 4Q159 Frags. 2–4, lines 3–4; and 4Q266 9.i.13. See also Schiffman, *The Halakhah at Qumran*, 75–76.

151. An *Interpreter of the Torah* and *Maskil* may also operate along with the council and the community. See, e.g., 1QS 6, 8–9. More basically, the fact that there are multiple leadership figures (*Maskil, Mebaqqer,* etc.) also diffuses authority from a single person. The biblical model of the high priest is arguably absent in these texts.

152. The fact that in several arrangements there is more than one priest is also noteworthy.

153. See Geza Vermes, "Fragments of the Community Rule from Qumran Cave 4," *Journal of Jewish Studies* 42 (1991): 255.

154. This seems compounded by the continuation of 1QS 6:8–10, which distinguishes the priestly sector as the primary division in the Many but attributes no additional authority to it.

155. See also 1QSa 1:25–2:3. 1QSa also conflates legal administration, priestly and Levitical service, and military command, partially echoing the Bible (see, e.g., Num 8:23–26). Various constituent groups with diverse functions merge in the eschatological community.

156. These include studying the laws and committing to fulfill the precepts (1QSa 1:6–8, 11).

157. For additional analysis, see David C. Flatto, "Constructing Justice: The Selective Use of Scripture in Formulating Early Jewish Accounts of the Courts," *Harvard Theological Review* 111, no. 4 (2018): 494–498.

158. See, e.g., Magen Broshi, "Daily Life at Qumran" [Hebrew], in Kister, *The Qumran Scrolls and Their World,* 27. Perhaps 1QSa intends to divide between the practical authority of members of the community, and the substantive authority of priestly teachings and traditions.

159. There are other echoes of simultaneous vertical and horizontal dynamics operating within Qumran jurisprudence, such as the individual figures who operate alongside the council and community, and a council that operates alongside the Many. Even in the royalist TS and the LK, the king shares jurisdiction with the council of thirty-six.

160. Recall that priests, judges, and Levites also have independent legal authority elsewhere in the TS. See note 11.

161. The king's judicial role in the LK may be more limited than it appears, given that the council, or analogous personnel, appear to operate autonomously elsewhere. See 11Q19 61, 4Q164, 1QM 2:1–3, CD 10:4–10. When the king presides over legal matters, he may be joining the primary judicial officials. Such an arrangement has loose analogs in rabbinic and Western jurisprudence. See Flatto, *Between Royal Absolutism and an Independent Judiciary,* 109. Either way, it is undeniable that the LK incorporates the king into the judicial process, while other texts assign judicial authority to nonroyal personnel.

162. Note that the Temple Scroll's scheme is utopian, but not necessarily messianic. See Schiffman, *The Courtyards of the House of the Lord,* 502–504.

163. The stature of the TS stands out from the perspective of its reputation and its conceptual significance. In terms of its prevalence in manuscripts, see Devorah Dimant, *History, Ideology and Bible Interpretation in the Dead Sea Scrolls* (Tübingen: Mohr Siebeck, 2014), 51.

164. Given the intensive debates surrounding the dating, authorship, and redactional history of various Qumran writings, this conclusion will necessarily be speculative, but I have attempted to rely on assumptions supported by numerous scholars. In speaking of a diachronic development, I refer to several foundational texts that arguably intersect.

165. See the references in Elisha Qimron, *The Temple Scroll: A Critical Edition with Extensive Reconstructions* (Beer Sheva: Ben-Gurion University of the Negev Press, 1996), 119–121.

166. See, e.g., Hanan Eshel, "4QMMT and the History of the Hasmonean Period," in *Reading 4QMMT: New Perspectives on Qumran Law and History,* ed. John Kampen and Moshe J. Bernstein (Atlanta: Scholars Press, 1996), 64–65. Contrast Israel Knohl, "The Date of 4QMMT," in *Fifty Years of Dead Sea Scrolls Research: Studies in Memory of Jacob Licht,* ed. Gershon Brin et al. (Jerusalem: Yad Ben Zvi, 2001), 166–170.

167. See, e.g., *Encyc. DSS* 2:932.

168. See Schiffman, *The Courtyards of the House of the Lord,* 123–148.

169. This formulation is based on *Encyc. DSS* 1:560.

170. See *Encyc. DSS* 1:560.

171. See Hanan Eshel, *The Dead Sea Scrolls and the Hasmonean State* (Grand Rapids, Mich.: Eerdmans, 2008).

172. See Eshel, *The Dead Sea Scrolls and the Hasmonean State,* 22–27, 131.

173. This text may reflect a later sectarian reconstruction of the earlier period. For its dating, see *Encyc. DSS* 2:649.

174. See, e.g., George J. Brooke, *Qumran Cave 4,* XVII: *Parabiblical Texts,* part 3, *Discoveries of the Judean Desert,* in vol. 22 (Oxford: Clarendon Press, 1996), 205.

175. See the references in David M. Goodblatt, *The Monarchic Principle: Studies in Jewish Self-Government in Antiquity* (Tübingen: Mohr [Siebeck], 1994), 74n53.

176. At the outset of this chapter, I remarked that Qumran writings respond to Hasmonean rule mostly by formulating an alternate vision of the ideal priesthood. Nevertheless, in early strata there was also a secondary focus on kingship, even as there may have been a growing distrust in monarchy as an institution.

177. My hypothetical reconstruction may have implications for dating other Qumran material, especially 4Q246, cited above. See Flatto, *Between Royal Absolutism and an Independent Judiciary,* 132n126.

178. The leading Hasmoneans were essentially monarchic figures from early on, even though they officially adopted the royal title only later. See Kenneth Atkinson, *A History of the Hasmonean State: Josephus and Beyond* (London: Bloomsbury, 2016), 32.

179. This is because the king also serves as a spiritual exemplar. See Eyal Regev, "The Temple Impurity and Qumran's 'Foreign Affairs' in the Early Hasmonean Period" [Hebrew], *Zion* 64 (1998): 141–145.

180. See 1QpHab 8:9 (see note 17).

181. See Seth Schwartz, *Imperialism and Jewish Society, 200 B.C.E. to 640 C.E.* (Princeton, N.J.: Princeton University Press, 2001), 33–52.

182. Weinfeld attributes these judicial arrangements to Greco-Roman influences, whereas Schiffman asserts that they are internally derived (see note 96). The biblical, Second Temple, and rabbinic sources he cites are of questionable relevance. It is more likely that these are novel judicial arrangements that acquired a sacred status in Qumran due to the doctrine of perpetual revelation. On the latter, see Aharon Shemesh and Cana Werman, "Hidden Things and Their Revelation," *Revue de Qumran* 18 (1998): 409–427.

183. The dissemination of legal responsibility is a far cry from democracy (notwithstanding the term's invocation by various scholars), but instead arises from the expectation that the entire community will live according to the true norms revealed to the sect. At the same time, the sweeping role of law makes alternate configurations of power in the sectarian community possible. With the marginalization of monarchy, sectarian society relies upon sacral law, priests, and communal bonds as sources of authority and order. The collective commitment at Qumran to law helps to reify the vital role of law in structuring the community (see Chapter 8).

4. Josephus on Kingship, Theocracy, and Law

1. Brent D. Shaw, "Josephus: Roman Power and Responses to It," *Athenaeum* 83 (1995): 357–390.

2. But Josephus's "constitutionalism" can influence his description of Roman history in certain respects. See below.

3. Throughout this book I use the terms "Jews," "Jewish," and "Judaism" because they have popular currency. Nevertheless, "Judean" and related terms are often more precise and should be understood as the intended meaning where appropriate. See John J. Collins, *The Invention of Judaism* (California: University of California Press, 2017), 1–20.

4. For an abbreviated version of this chapter's argument, which also explores certain related issues in legal and intellectual history not addressed herein, see David C. Flatto, "Theocracy and the Rule of Law: A Novel Josephan Doctrine and Its Modern Misconceptions," *Dine Israel* 28 (2011): 5–30.

5. The descriptions of judicial administration during or prior to his lifetime reveal a complex web of personal and institutional dynamics. See, e.g., *Ant.* 20.200–203 (the high priest could convene a judicial council, but required imperial sanction, and was subject to the king's supervision); and *Ant.* 20.216–218 (the people request that the king initiate a legal action). Another significant depiction of legal authority in Josephus's writings are his

accounts of the trial of Herod, which are descriptive in nature but also shed light on his political theory. See David C. Flatto, "Justice Retold: The Seminal Narrations of the Trial of the Judean King," *Journal of Law and Religion* 30 (2015): 1.

6. See Sarah J. Pearce, *The Words of Moses: Studies in the Reception of Deuteronomy in the Second Temple Period* (Tübingen: Mohr Siebeck, 2013), 120–141, 306–326.

7. Although I shift between the terms legal-political "philosophy," "theory," and "theology" throughout this chapter, the latter seems most apt for *Apion*, which especially emphasizes the sacral dimension of law and politics.

8. See 2 Chron 19:1 and 34:13, and Neh 8:11.

9. The same number of judges are mentioned in *Ant.* 4.287, where Josephus restates another biblical norm (see Exod 22:7); and in *J.W.* 2.570–571, where Josephus describes the Galilean tribunals he established to adjudicate lesser disputes. So this is the standard basic tribunal, for Josephus, in theory and evidently in practice, too. See also *Ant.* 11.192.

10. These paragraphs also draw on Exod 22:27.

11. Sarah Pearce has argued that the Septuagint already makes a couple of subtle but consequential choices in its translation of Deuteronomy 17:8–13. See Pearce, *The Words of Moses*, 263–274.

12. Seth Schwartz has persuasively argued that the larger trend in Josephus's mature writings, relative to his earlier *Jewish War*, is to criticize various individual high priests (especially in *Ant.* 20), but this does not preclude his having high regard for the office in general. See Seth Schwartz, *Josephus and Judaean Politics* (Leiden: E. J. Brill, 1990), 58–109.

13. Wayne Meeks goes a step further and argues that for Josephus the prophet was a regular administrative office. See Meeks, *The Prophet-King: Moses Traditions and the Johannine Christology* (Leiden: Brill, 1967), 142.

14. *Gerousia* is a notoriously difficult term to define in Josephus. Scholars since Mantel understand this to refer to a judicial body such as the Sanhedrin. But Goodblatt insists that this was an ad hoc gathering of elders, not a permanent judicial body. See David M. Goodblatt, *The Monarchic Principle: Studies in Jewish Self-Government in Antiquity* (Tübingen: Mohr [Siebeck], 1994), 103–130. See also Seth Schwartz's review of this book in *Journal of Jewish Studies* 47 (1996): 167–169. The leading role of this council appears at various points throughout Josephus's writings, especially in *Antiquities*—see, e.g., 4.255–256, 324–325; 5.15, 43, 55.

15. *Ant.* 4.186. See also *Ant.* 4.165, 4.311, and 9.4. See Pearce, *The Words of Moses*, 120–141. While I agree with linking *Ant.* 4.218 with *Ant.* 4.186, I would argue that their relationship operates in the opposite direction, with *Ant.* 4.186 foreshadowing the scheme of *Ant.* 4.218.

16. See also Jer. 18:18.

17. Josephus deliberately prefaces the judiciary section in *Ant.* 4.209–211 with a separate norm (Deut 31:10–13, 6:7–9) that accents the centrality of law, and follows it in

4.219–223 with other legal procedures (Deut 17:6, 19:15–19) that are administered by similar officials to those referenced in 4.214–218.

18. By inserting this claim here, Josephus is appealing for an aristocracy over a monarchy.

19. See, e.g., *Ant.* 6.262–267, where Josephus elaborates on certain vices of kingship, analyzed by Jan Willem van Henten, "Good and Bad Rulers in Josephus," lecture delivered at the XIth Congress of the European Association for Jewish Studies, Krakow, Poland, July 2018. For secondary references related to Josephus's antimonarchism, see Flatto, "Theocracy and the Rule of Law," 10n13.

Several recent works have challenged the antimonarchic characterization of Josephus. See Nadav Sharon, *Judea under Roman Domination* (Atlanta: SBL, 2017), 79–81; Jacob Feeley "Josephus as Political Philosopher: His Concept of Kingship" (PhD diss., University of Pennsylvania, 2017); and Jacob S. Abolafia, "A Reappraisal of *Contra Apionem* 2.145 as an Original Contribution to Political Thought," *Scripta Classica Israelica* 32 (2013): 153–172. These revisionary accounts are, at the very least, correct in complicating the picture. As I argue below (and in an earlier article that predates these studies), Josephus's political ideology advances a constitutional arrangement structured around the rule of law, and is less focused on targeting monarchy per se.

20. Julius Wellhausen, *Prolegomena to the History of Ancient Israel* (Gloucester, Mass.: Peter Smith, 1973), 247–256, 411–425.

21. For a helpful overview of the classical "constitutional" forms, see Christopher Rowe, "Aristotelian Constitutions," in *The Cambridge History of Greek and Roman Political Thought,* ed. Christopher Rowe and Malcolm Schofield (New York: Cambridge University Press, 2000), 366–389.

22. See the secondary references in note 19.

23. See, e.g., *Ant.* 11.111 and 20.238–251. Indeed, Josephus clearly acknowledges that certain kings were positive figures. Nevertheless, his broader constitutional vision, grounded in the rule of law, limits or marginalizes monarchy; and his ultimate political vision articulates a stronger version of separation-of-powers jurisprudence, which challenges the rule of men altogether.

24. Deut 17:14 can be read as stating that Israel's choice of a king is optional. In addition, Josephus's preference for an "aristocracy" over a monarchy is likely inspired by 1 Sam 8:7, which contrasts God's sovereignty with kingship.

25. Josephus interpolates the elders here. See also *Ant.* 4.218.

26. All three injunctions also mitigate the king's power, a complementary goal that further preserves the lawful order.

27. As I discuss in other chapters, other early exegetes also reorder these bans.

28. The addition of the *gerousia* suggests that, in addition to his exegesis, Josephus aims to present a consistent constitutional scheme. See also Robert P. Gallant, "Josephus' Exposition of Biblical Law: An Internal Analysis" (PhD diss., Yale University, 1988), 194–202.

29. *Ant.* 4:225 skips to Deut 19:14, and may serve as a kind of peroration for the previous sections. Warren Harvey interestingly suggests that Josephus (as explained in this chapter) is influenced by Aristotle's view that "one who asks the law to rule asks god or *nous* to rule, while one who asks a human being to rule asks the animal to rule" (*Politics* III:16). Even so, it is crucial to recognize how Josephus adapts this teaching. Aristotle clearly recognizes monarchy as a legitimate constitutional form. But Josephus understands that the rule of law negates or limits monarchy. Moreover, in *Apion,* Josephus argues that rule by god's laws negates the legitimacy of all classical forms of government that rely upon men. Veneration of rule of law existed in the classical world, but it did not translate into the radical constitutional template of the rule of law alone implicit in Josephus's theocracy. See also note 104.

30. Scholars have debated to what extent Josephus's biblical adaptations are deliberate, and, if they are, what inspired these modifications. Some assume that Josephus inherited various exegetical motifs, perhaps unwittingly; many contend that his changes derive from aesthetic, historic, and apologetic considerations. See Flatto, "Theocracy and the Rule of Law," 9n10. See also *Ant.* 1.17, 4.196–197, 10.218. My argument herein claims that at least in certain instances, Josephus reworked biblical materials in order to propound a certain political-theological ideology. On the somewhat related question of Josephus's conception of, and attitude toward, ancestral laws, see Flatto, "Theocracy and the Rule of Law," 9n11.

31. The whole issue of constitutional forms is paramount in Josephus's restatement of Samuel. See, e.g., *Ant.* 6.35–36. 81, 84–85, 88–94.

32. Samuel's role in *Ant.* 6 exemplifies Moses's remarks in *Ant.* 4.184–187 that future leaders of the people will offer the best advice about governance.

33. As a prophet, Samuel serves as a leading legal authority. See *Ant.* 4.218, discussed above.

34. See Christopher T. Begg, *Judean Antiquities 5–7* (Leiden: Brill, 2005), 104n115.

35. *Ant.* 14.41 records a reverse dynamic that reinforces these same themes. For Josephus, Jewish history is viewed through the prism of political history. See *Ant.* 1.5–20. Josephus deliberately underscores parallel political constructs at different phases in order to gain insight about different modes of administration, and to single out an optimal constitutional form.

36. Martin Buber, *Kingship of God* (New York: Harper and Row, 1967). See, e.g., Judg 8:22–23.

37. See, e.g., *The Jewish Study Bible,* ed. Adele Berlin et al. (Oxford: Oxford University Press, 2004), 509.

38. See Fred Skolnik, ed., *Encyclopedia Judaica,* 2nd ed., vol. 11 (Detroit: Macmillan, 2007), 565.

39. A widespread scholarly hypothesis is that Judg 19–21 contain a polemical attack on the house of Saul, and champion the Davidic dynasty instead. See, e.g., Yairah Amit, "The Book of Judges: Dating and Meaning," in *Homeland and Exile: Biblical and Ancient Near*

Eastern Studies in Honour of Bustenay Oded, ed. Gershon Galil et al. (Leiden: Brill, 2009), 297–322.

40. The translation in this paragraph comes from Louis H. Feldman, "Josephus' Portrayal (Antiquities 5.136–174) of the Benjaminite Affair of the Concubine and Its Repercussions (Judges 19–21)," *Jewish Quarterly Review* 90 (2000): 263.

41. In addition, the turbulence is due to various vices of the Israelites, including pleasure seeking, greediness, and indolence. See *Ant.* 5.132–134.

42. See Josephus's interpretation of Deut 13, Judg 17–18, and Num 25, all discussed below. In *Ant.* 4.214–224 he skips over the laws of idolatry recorded in Deut 16–17, although he deals with some of this material elsewhere.

43. The scholarly consensus is that the final chapters of the book of Judges are a discrete biblical source. See, e.g., Amit, "The Book of Judges," 307. See also *Seder Olam* 12, *Eliyahu Rabbah* 11:57.

44. See Feldman, "Josephus' Portrayal," 266.

45. See Pearce, *The Words of Moses,* 313.

46. This is in accord with the law recorded in Deut 20:10–11 (involving warfare with the Canaanites), as elaborated upon by Josephus in *Ant.* 4.296.

47. The inimical spread of anarchy and the undermining of lawful order are also markers of decline in other periods described below.

48. See *Ant.* 5.100–114 (a restatement of Josh 22), where Josephus describes an administration comprised of Joshua (the prophet), Eleazar the high priest, and the *gerousia*. Thus, the continuation of *Ant.* 4, followed by *Ant.* 5, extends the themes of the Deuteronomic constitution, as restated by Josephus.

49. See also Josephus's related description of the tyrannical behavior of John of Gischala, in *J.W.* 4.208, 6.98, 129, as noted by Begg, *Judean Antiquities 5–7,* 57n626.

50. Various of the themes emphasized in Moses's speech, including the notion of "piety," resonate with themes emphasized in *Apion.* See, e.g., *Ag. Ap.* 2.146, 170, 291–293.

51. *Ant.* 4.186 now takes on additional significance: "Listen to them (Eleazar et al.) without annoyance, knowing that all who know well how to be ruled also will know how to rule, once they have come to a position of authority." Because law is the mode of ruling, those who submit to laws (i.e., know how to be ruled) will know how to administer laws (i.e., know how to rule). This also resolves Zimri's complaint. See note 52.

52. Nodet argues that *Ant.* 4.186 is the paragraph where Josephus articulates Moses's response to Zimri's charge in *Ant.* 4.145–149 (cited in *Flavius Josephus: Judean Antiquities 1–4,* trans. Louis H. Feldman [Boston: Brill Academic, 2004], 394n552).

53. Even an aristocratic regime can fail if it is not committed to the rule of law. See Josephus's comments in *Ant.* 5.135, analyzed above.

54. I explored aspects of Josephus's treatment of idolatry and covenant in a lecture, "Legal and Political Motifs in *Antiquities* 3–4," presented at the conference "Josephus between the Bible and the Mishnah," Neve Ilan, Israel, April 10, 2019.

55. See, e.g., *Ant.* 5.185; 6.84–85; 11.111; 12.138–142; 13.166–169, 300–301; 14.41, 91; 20.229–235. See also *J.W.* 4.319, 358.

56. See, e.g., *Ant.* 4.14–20, 189; 7.194–196; and 20.160–188.

57. For additional examples, see Flatto, "Theocracy and the Rule of Law," 14.

58. For an illuminating example of Josephus's political ideology informing his record of an earlier postbiblical event, see Isaiah M. Gafni, "Josephus and I Maccabees," in *Josephus, the Bible, and History*, ed. Louis H. Feldman and Gohei Hata (Detroit: Wayne State University Press, 1989), 116–131.

59. Josephus also describes his own outstanding legal erudition and role (*Life* 9).

60. For an analysis of parallels between *J.W.* and *Life*, see Shaye J. Cohen, *Josephus in Galilee and Rome: His Vita and Development as a Historian* (Leiden: Brill, 1979).

61. Later in *J.W.*, Josephus blames those connected with the Fourth Philosophy for the revolt against the Romans. See note 67.

62. See *Ant.* 18.1–25.

63. See *Ant.* 18.9. The sharp criticisms leveled against the founders and followers are recorded in *Ant.* 18.6–10. In the continuation of *Ant.* 18.6–10, 23–25, however, Josephus's remarks contain both a critical and a positive dimension, as explained herein. Scholars have largely amplified Josephus's negative assessment of the Fourth Philosophy. But Seth Schwartz, *Josephus and Judean Politics*, 188, already notes some ambivalence in the *Ant.* 18 account.

64. *Ant.* 18.23.

65. This link ironically undermines to a certain degree the charge that the Fourth Philosophy abandoned ancestral traditions. But see note 66.

66. It seems that for Josephus, the error of those who established the Fourth Philosophy was not only related to their message (as I describe in the continuation of the paragraph), but their very establishment of a new school, which itself may constitute an "innovation and reform in ancestral traditions." Now that Josephus characterizes them as presenting a competing philosophy, not just as a marginal offshoot, he also negatively assesses the effrontery involved in their staking out a novel position.

67. Josephus concludes this segment by blaming the uprising on Florus, the Roman procurator (*Ant.* 18.25, 20.252–258), which differs considerably from *J.W.* 7.252–255, where he holds the rebelling Jews (including those connected with the Fourth Philosophy) as primarily culpable for the revolt against Rome. By shifting the blame to Florus, Josephus further vindicates the Fourth Philosophy in *Antiquities*. See also Cohen, *Josephus in Galilee*, 152–160.

68. Thus, in his later works Josephus identifies a fourth approach in the sects / schools and the constitutional structures, which to a certain extent overlap. Yet he argues that theocracy promotes liberty through law, whereas the anarchic Fourth Philosophy operates on the brink of lawlessness. On *libertas* in Josephus, see Daniel R. Schwartz, "Rome and the Jews: Josephus on 'Freedom' and 'Autonomy,'" in *Representations of Empire:*

Rome and the Mediterranean World, ed. Alan K. Bowman et al. (Oxford: Oxford University Press, 2002), 65–81.

69. There is widespread scholarly consensus that this material originates from one or more external sources that Josephus relied upon, although the identity of the author(s) remains uncertain. See Klaus Scherberich, "Josephus und seine Quellen im 19. Buch der 'Antiquitates Iudaicae' (ant. Iud. 19, 1–273)," *Klio* 83, no. 1 (2001): 134–151. Even so, Josephus's decision to include this material in *Antiquities,* and in some cases undoubtedly to rework it, must be evaluated.

70. Compare, for example, *Ant.* 20.157, where Josephus states that he will limit his discussion about Nero because he intends to stay focused on his theme, the history of the Jews.

71. See Louis H. Feldman, *Studies in Hellenistic Judaism* (Leiden: Brill, 1996), 164–176.

72. See, e.g., Cohen, *Josephus in Galilee,* 59.

73. Cohen and others describe Josephus's writings as occasionally "sloppy." See, e.g., Cohen, *Josephus in Galilee,* 110.

74. Aspects of the Caligula episode echo tensions in contemporary political affairs under Domitian (see Feldman, *Studies in Hellenistic Judaism,* 172) and resonate with Josephus's broader political philosophy, especially as it developed in his later writings. For a loosely parallel thesis, see Brent D. Shaw, "Tyrants, Bandits and Kings: Personal Power in Josephus," *Journal of Jewish Studies* 44 (1993): 176–204. Most germane to my analysis are the introductory comments in Feldman, *Flavius Josephus,* xxvii–xxix.

75. See *J.W.* 2.204–205. Josephus's use of this term to describe the restoration of the Republic is noteworthy.

76. This initiative is the only event from this period in Roman history referred to in *J.W.* that does not relate directly to the Jews.

77. Arnaldo Momigliano, *Claudius: The Emperor and His Achievement,* trans. W. Hogarth (Cambridge, Mass.: Heffer, 1961), 20.

78. See Gavin Townsend, "Literature and Society," in *The Cambridge Ancient History,* vol. 10, ed. Alan K. Bowman et al. (Cambridge: Cambridge University Press, 1996), 913.

79. Dio's *Roman History,* bk. LX; Suet. *Div. Claud.* 10:3ff.; *Div. Calig.* 60. See also Flatto, "Theocracy and the Rule of Law," 18n29.

80. See T. E. J. Wiedemann, "Tiberius to Nero," in Bowman et al., *The Cambridge Ancient History,* 10:230n38.

81. Chaim Wirszubski, who considered this episode to be significant, understands it to signify the perils of challenging the Principate. See Wirszubski, *Libertas as a Political Idea at Rome during the Late Republic and Early Principate* (Cambridge: Cambridge University Press, 1950), 126–127. This is certainly not Josephus's understanding of its legacy, as I explain below.

82. K. R. Bradley, *Lives of the Caesars: Suetonius,* Loeb Classical Library, vol. 31, trans. J. C. Rolfe (Cambridge, Mass.: Harvard University Press, 1998), 21.

83. For references, see Flatto, "Theocracy and the Rule of Law," 18nn29–30.

84. The primary purpose of Josephus's description, which is much more elaborate than Suetonious's, was not to inspire Romans to change their administration (Josephus favorably depicts the imperial rise of Claudius, and Agrippa's role in facilitating his ascent, even though Josephus likely prefers a republican government). Rather, Josephus's "political act" is meant to underscore the limitations of the various constitutional forms of Roman politics. They rely on powerful men, and might deteriorate into tyrannical rule, rather than on durable and just laws. According to Josephus, the rule of law can be vouchsafed only by the kind of aristocracy he refers to in *Ant.* 4—or better, a theocracy, as he discovers in the mature philosophy of *Apion.* So Josephus differs from Suetonius who preferred a Republic, and Tacitus who was indifferent to constitutional forms.

85. Notice that freedom here is manifest by living according to one's own laws. See also Chapter 8, note 110. Gafni, "Josephus and I Maccabees," 123, similarly explains that freedom according to Josephus means being able to live according to the ancestral laws (based on *Ant.* 12.303). However, it is actually stronger than that, as freedom is manifest through laws and lawfulness. Josephus's description of the reaction to the Consul's assignment of the watchword *"Libertas"* after the senatorial debate reverberates loudly during his lifetime. See David C. Flatto, *Between Royal Absolutism and an Independent Judiciary: The Evolution of Separation of Powers in Biblical, Second Temple and Rabbinic Texts* (Cambridge, Mass.: Harvard University Press, 2010), 181–182.

86. Sentius traces the origins of tyranny back to Julius Caesar, who violated "law and order, setting himself above justice in order to achieve his own private gratifications." Subsequent emperors repeated this ruinous conduct, culminating in the egregious corruptions of Caligula. All of these indictments, of course, resonate for Josephus. But ultimately Josephus is not truly pro-Republic, but pro the rule of law and skeptical about the rule of men.

87. Still, Josephus mocks Sentius's excessive rhetorical flourish. *Ant.* 19.185.

88. The importance of safeguarding the law and the threat posed by tyrannical leaders echo themes stressed in the accounts of Moses and Phineas (*Ant.* 4.145–155, 178–186); the law of the king (*Ant.* 4.222–224); and Samuel (*Ant.* 6.36, 86–94). Rejecting the legal order for personal gratification stands at the root of the sin of Judges (*Ant.* 5.132). Exalting political rule over uniform justice represents the fundamental error of the Greeks, as opposed to the Jews (*Apion* 2; see below).

89. One semantic note is in order: Throughout his later works, Josephus repeatedly invokes the term "constitution," albeit in different senses. Sometimes he speaks of the constitution of the Jews as the form of government of a particular administration during a given historical period. At other times he speaks of the constitution of the Jews as the laws to which they adhere. Ultimately these two concepts are interrelated for Josephus, since the laws of the Jews form the foundation of their optimal form of government.

90. See Flatto, "Theocracy and the Rule of Law," 10n13.

91. See David C. Flatto, "Constructing Justice: The Selective Use of Scripture in Formulating Early Jewish Accounts of the Courts," *Harvard Theological Review* 111, no. 4 (2018): 501nn59–64.

92. Note the Deuteronomic influence on the latter set of laws. See Flatto, "Constructing Justice," 501n64.

93. Josephus thus transposes a normative system into a political structure. This transfiguration is the heart of Josephus's political-theological project. In his final work, *Apion*, it receives its ultimate articulation.

94. Martin Goodman, *Rome and Jerusalem: The Clash of Ancient Civilizations* (London: Allen Lane, 2007), 209.

95. See Flatto, "Theocracy and the Rule of Law," 20n34.

96. See especially *Ag. Ap.* 2.193, which projects the Temple as a central and unifying religious institution, notwithstanding its recent destruction or the intense sectarianism that divided the Jews when it was standing. But see note 97.

97. Scholars debate about whether to view this material as a discrete unit or as part of a broader apology, and whether it was authored by Josephus or by others, or whether Josephus here reworked earlier material. See Flatto, "Theocracy and the Rule of Law," 21n35. Even if Josephus depended in part on earlier sources, he carefully selected or even adapted this material. Indeed, an important implication of my analysis below is that the political theology recorded in *Apion* reflects a mature and sweeping formulation of ideas that play a profound role already in *Antiquities*. These ideas also have an important apologetic dimension that especially resonates post–70 CE. See also Mira Balberg, *Blood for Thought: The Reinvention of Sacrifice in Early Rabbinic Literature* (Oakland: University of California Press, 2017), 223–224.

98. Whereas *Antiquities* enumerates the high priest, prophet, and *gerousia* as leading judges, *Apion* only designates the priests, headed by the high priest, for this role. This revised account is also based on Deut 17. See Flatto, "Constructing Justice," 502–504. Josephus here adds that those who disobey the priests will be penalized, an allusion to Deut 17:12. This is consistent with *Apion*'s penal emphasis. See Flavius Josephus: *Against Apion*, trans. and commentary John M. G. Barclay (Leiden: Brill Academic, 2007), 368.

99. Josephus hails the choice of the priests because they are persuasive and moderate (qualities that are characteristic of the Pharisees, according to *Ant.* 18.12–15, 20.199–200). Moreover, Josephus essentially views the priests as God's proxies—they lead the worship of God (*Ag. Ap.* 2.185), and a violation of priestly rulings constitutes a sacrilegious act toward God (*Ag. Ap.* 2.194). Josephus thereby elevates the sacral nature of law and underscores its proximity to God. See also Barclay, *Against Apion*, 273–274, n732.

100. *Ag. Ap.* 2.164–165.

101. In one paragraph, Josephus focuses on certain virtuous traits (*Ag. Ap.* 2.170). But these are also cultivated by obedience to law (see, e.g., *Ag. Ap.* 2.146; see also *Ant.* 1.23). The

broader context of the argument in *Apion* makes the centrality of law even more plain (see note 102).

102. See, e.g., *Ag. Ap.* 2. 159–163, 172–174, 182–185, 190–217, 291–295, and the passages analyzed in the continuation below. Evidently, what drives the evolution in Josephus's political thought is not just the distinctiveness of God's rule, but also the primacy of laws, coupled with the extinction of conventional institutions of governance in contemporary Jewish life. For all these reasons, Josephus coins a new term—"theocracy"—to characterize the optimal form of the Jewish polity, the rule of God through laws (a kind of "nomocracy"). See also Daniel Boyarin, "An Isogloss in First-Century Palestinian Jewry: Josephus and Mark on the Purpose of the Law," in *The Faces of Torah: Studies in the Texts and Contexts of Ancient Judaism in Honor of Steven Fraade*, ed. C. Hayes et al. (Göttingen: Vandenhoeck und Ruprecht), 63–80.

103. Moses the legislator likewise exceeds Lycurgus, Solon, and Zaleukos in his antiquity. See *Ag. Ap.* 2.154.

104. Josephus criticizes the Spartans, who are often praised for their legal commitment but, "when changes of fortune came to affect them, they completely forg[e]t almost all the laws!" (*Ag. Ap.* 2.227). By contrast, Jews are willing to suffer onto death to uphold their norms. See *Ag. Ap.* 2.228, 232–235, 273–275. According to Josephus, only the Jews, with their distinctive constitutional form of theocracy, are truly committed to the rule of law—in two significant senses. First, only the Jews are truly dedicated to their superior laws. Second, a true dedication to laws means a complete rejection of the rule of men. It is this second point that distinguishes the dedication of the Jews, not only from the Spartan commitment (since Xenophon, for example, praises the Spartan preservation of monarchy) but also from all other classical accounts that extol the rule of law, while still promoting the rule of men.

105. This insight is meant as an important addition and corrective to recent scholarly works that describe *Apion* as an attempt by Josephus to frame Judaism in terms that are appealing to Roman civilization. See Flatto, "Theocracy and the Rule of Law," 22n38.

106. See Shaw, "Josephus."

107. Josephus approached political issues from a unique vantage point that combined Greco-Roman and Jewish perspectives on the themes of power and governance. During the latter decades of the first century CE, however, both of these viewpoints were colored by a political landscape filled with turmoil and confusion. See Flatto, "Theocracy and the Rule of Law," 24n40.

108. Of course, this would become a charge that circulated widely following Augustine's "Doctrine of Jewish Witness."

109. Josephus operates with the conventional barometer in *Ag. Ap.* 2.134 and highlights the past political success of the Jews, but this could have hardly been satisfactory in the present, and accordingly he modifies his argument. See Flatto, "Theocracy and the Rule of Law," 24n42. Indeed, when Josephus refers to the string of military defeats suffered

by the Jews in *Ag. Ap.* 2.272, he readily acknowledges these losses, seeing them as almost inevitable (see also 2.228–231, 276–277). Elsewhere Josephus insists that he was right to surrender to Rome, and that the Jews should never have revolted against Rome at this time (*J.W.* 2.345–404; *Life* 17–19). Sovereignty and autonomy are subject to the vicissitudes of history. Yet this mindset does not lead Josephus to capitulate to the formidable theologico-political challenges he confronts. Instead, he offers a profound response to these piercing questions in the form of his political philosophy. In addition, Josephus may have aspired to steer his Jewish audience in the direction of their ancestral laws, and away from other political ambitions.

110. *Ant.* 20.224–234.

111. Of course, their predicaments also differed considerably. For instance, the scale of political sovereignty of Christians for nearly a century prior to 410 CE was entirely different from that exercised by Jews prior to 70 CE.

112. *Apion* seeks to introduce this optimal template to the entire civilized world. Sounding a triumphant note near the end (2.284), Josephus asserts that just as God permeates the whole universe, so too law, as ideally realized in the Jewish theocratic polity, has influenced all of humanity.

113. See the Introduction regarding the different iterations of separation of powers.

114. Several recent scholarly works analyze the substantive law of the pre-rabbinic era. This chapter contributes to this discourse from another angle, by helping to illuminate a distinctive legal ideology from this period. See Flatto, "Theocracy and the Rule of Law," 26n47.

5. Kingship and Law in Tannaitic Literature

1. The Talmud is the foundational work of the next phase of rabbinic literature. For general background, see Herman Strack and Gunter Stemberger, *Introduction to the Talmud and Midrash* (Minneapolis: Fortress Press, 1992).

2. The ambivalence in rabbinic literature reflects a mixed legacy in the biblical and historical record. Medieval rabbinic commentators continued to debate the king's status. See generally Gerald Blidstein, *Political Principles in Maimonidean Thought* [Hebrew], 2nd ed. (Ramat Gan: Bar-Ilan University, 2001).

3. The primary (halakhic) rabbinic sources on monarchy are *m. Sanh.* 2; *t. Sanh.* 4; *Sifre Deut.* 156–162; *Midrash Tannaim Deut.* 17; *y. Sanh.* 2; *b. Sanh.* 2.

4. See *Sifre Deut.* 156; *t. Sanh.* 4:5.

5. This chapter primarily focuses on the Mishnah and Tosefta's conception of kingship, since these sources engage most directly with the relationship of the king to the judicial and legal system, as well as the priesthood. Additional rabbinic sources will be introduced selectively. An exhaustive review of rabbinic sources is beyond the scope of this book.

6. The manuscript variants have minor significance for this chapter's analysis. When a significant variant occurs, I will refer to it in the notes.

7. The content of these passages has been treated with varying degrees of comprehensiveness elsewhere (see citations below), but some of their nuances require elaboration. In addition, their rich rhetoric has not been adequately noticed or analyzed. Further, these analyses have not read the Mishnah and Tosefta synoptically or paid sufficient attention to the distinctive contributions of the Mishnah.

8. Below, I attempt to steer a middle course between two extremes that often characterize synoptic studies of the Mishnah and Tosefta by critically examining particular passages and at the same time culling information relating to larger themes.

9. In advancing an argument about the Mishnah's orientation, I have been informed by several considerations: a close analysis of the most consequential Mishnaic passages regarding the monarchy serves as my foundation; these passages are carefully crafted, and their rhetoric is suggestive of a broader orientation of the redactor(s); there are repeated contrasts with analogous material in the Tosefta; and there is remarkable consistency among all such Mishnaic passages, unlike the equivocal treatment in various other rabbinic texts. Still, I do not deny that certain similar themes can be detected outside of the Mishnah, and at times I refer to such parallels.

10. Scholars consider this material to be early, but on questionable grounds. See Efraim Elimelech Urbach, *The Sages: Their Concepts and Beliefs*, trans. Israel Abrahams (Jerusalem: Magnes, 1979), 441; and Jacob N. Epstein, *Introduction to Tannaitic Literature* [Hebrew] (Jerusalem: Magnes, 1957), 55, 417–419. They have also been influenced by the Bavli's interpretation, discussed below.

11. See also *m. B. Bat.* 6:7. Efraim Elimelech Urbach already notes the Mishnah's sweeping formulation in *The World of the Sages: Collected Studies* [Hebrew] (Jerusalem: Hebrew University, 1988), 44. See also *Sifre Deut.* 161.

12. See note 53. I hope to expand upon this topic in another context.

13. Fraade further expands on the way the Mishnah softens, and carefully reorders, the biblical prohibitions of Deuteronomy 17:15–19. Steven D. Fraade, *Legal Fictions: Studies of Law and Narrative in the Discursive World of Ancient Jewish Sectarians and Sages* (Leiden: Brill, 2011), 299–307.

14. *Halitsa* is a severance ritual that releases a widow from her levirate bond with her brother-in-law (the brother of her deceased husband). See Deut 25:5–10.

15. This structure has a slight echo in the trial of Jesus. See, e.g., Mark 15:1–20, where the high priest is involved in trying Jesus, the alleged "King of the Jews." Although there is an abundance of literature on the trial, this parallel and other aspects of its jurisprudential scheme deserve additional consideration.

16. On the broad jurisdiction of the Sanhedrin, see Chapter 6.

17. The phrase "standard halakhah" is a bit misleading, given the distinctive rules applicable to the high priest. But the important point is that the Mishnah emphasizes that a form of these laws applies to the high priest, not the king.

18. The opinion of R. Judah (b. Ilai) recorded in the Mishnah diverges from the primary position of the Mishnah, thus the Mishnah is not univocal. See also the discussion of *m. Sanh.* 2:4 below; and Fraade, *Legal Fictions,* 299–307. Overall, however, the primary, anonymous teachings of the Mishnah advance a uniform and coherent approach. The Mishnah notably focuses on levirate marriage and mourning, which are categories that have relevance to the high priest, but strikingly offers more exemptions for the king.

19. Moreover, the Mishnah generally depicts an all-encompassing normative system. The king's standing outside of this system in various respects is therefore certainly noteworthy. Interestingly, *Sifre Deut.* 161 frames some of the Mishnah's teaching in a manner that underscores the normative commitments of the king and others.

20. Possible weak sources for the king's withdrawal from the funeral procession would be Deut 17:15 (see *m. Sanh.* 2:5, which expands upon this verse) or verse 17:18 (see Midrash Tannaim ad loc., which uses this as a source for certain royal regulations), but these are never cited. The exact description of the high priest's participation in the funeral procession varies slightly in the Kaufman, Cambridge, and Parma manuscripts.

21. The Tosefta and Bavli suggest that an alternative reading of Lev 21:11–12 informs the regulated protocol which the high priest must follow when attending a funeral procession. Still, there is obvious biblical pressure barring a high priest from a funeral, which easily could have justified an opposite ruling.

22. See *y. Sanh.* 2:2, 2:4, and R. Yonatan of Lunel ad loc., which interpret the Mishnah in this vein (but see Nahmanides (Mo'ed Qat.), and Maimonides (Hilkhot Avel 7:7), who claim that the king is obligated to mourn). A similar phenomenon happens with the issue of levirate marriages. There is a strong scriptural case to exempt a high priest from (at least aspects of) this process, based on Lev. 21:13–14, while there is no scriptural source for a king's exemption. Yet the Mishnah fully exempts the king but not the high priest.

23. The use of a loan word (based on *praetorium*) also suggests that a positive conception of a royal palace is a foreign one. In the Bible, the primary source detailing the dimensions of a royal palace (1 Kgs 7:7) is largely a critique of royal extravagance.

24. In the Mishnah, the Temple is the situs of the high priest, not the king. The latter is far from obvious, given that kings built the Temples. Certain rabbinic sources mentioned below clearly link the king to the Temple (*t. Sanh.* 4:3; *m. Shebu.* 2:2; *m. Sotah* 7:8; *m. Yoma* 3:10, 7:5; *m. Yebam.* 6:4; and *m. Bik.* 3:4). See also Mordechai Sabato, "The Appointment of the King and the Building of the Temple: A New Analysis" [Hebrew], *Tarbiz* 76, nos. 3–4 (2007): 353–384.

25. To be sure, this mandate cannot be taken literally. Indeed, *m. Sanh.* 2:4 describes various instances where the king moves around outside of the palace. But in a sense, this only underscores the symbolic significance of the Mishnah's spatial imagery.

26. The Mishnah's king does not intermingle with the people. He does not judge, testify for or against, mourn with, nor marry them. He stands apart, and is held in awe by them. Thus, they are forbidden to observe his intimate conduct (see *m. Sanh.* 2:5). By

contrast, the Mishnah's high priest does engage in the normative and social order, and is more connected to the people. He judges, testifies, mourns, marries, etc. Likewise, he resides in the Temple, where people ascend to worship, and where he helps disseminate Torah instructions to them. The Mishnah maintains this account of the high priest, notwithstanding his elevated purity regulations, which would seem to distance him from the people.

27. These should be compared to the parallel, but at times subtly different, teachings of the Sifre, Sifre Zuta, and Midrash Tannaim on Deut. 17:14–20.

28. See Yair Lorberbaum, *The Disempowered King* [Hebrew] (Ramat Gan: Bar-Ilan University, 2009), 65–75.

29. See note 13; Blidstein, *Political Principles in Maimonidean Thought*, 183–189.

30. According to the Mishnah, the king has a singular stature in terms of his autonomy and the respect he commands, but he remains on par with the high priest in terms of his overall standing as a leader.

31. J. N. Epstein sees *m. Sanh.* 2:4 as an echo of the Bavli. This is dubious, but undoubtedly this source is problematic. Fraade, *Legal Fictions*, 303n51, proposes a distinction between a king's joining the judiciary and presiding over his own court (*m. Sanh.* 2:4's "yoshev badin" may connote sitting in royal judgment, whereas *t. Sanh.* 4:4's "be-bet din" may connote a standard court). I am inclined to interpret *m. Sanh.* 2:4 (a kind of midrash halakhah on Deut 17:18–19) as being in conflict with 2:2.

32. That is, the Mishnah presents a symmetric opposition between the king and high priest, but according to the Bavli, Davidic kings and high priests are similar in terms of their judicial role.

33. See *m. Sanh.* 2:2–4.

34. *Deut. Rab. Shoftim* 8. Bernard Septimus brought the midrash and the sources in note 35 to my attention, and highlighted the drastic change in tone in the continuation of the midrash (which raises the question of whether the king not being judged is idyllic or realistic).

35. Certain medieval commentators also interpret the Mishnah according to its plain sense. See R. Yonatan of Lunel on the Mishnah; and arguably the Arukh (*erekh melekh*).

36. See *y. Sanh.* 2:3; *Sifre Zuta Deut.* 21:2; *Midrash Tannaim Deut.* 17:14.

37. This reading is also supported by *m. Hor.* 2:6, which no doubt refers to all kings, not just non-Davidic ones; but see *t. Hor.* 2:2. See below.

38. Others have concluded that the king is superior. See Tosafot, *b. Sanh.* 18a ("ve-ha"). See also *b. Sotah* 42a; and Fraade, *Legal Fictions*, 299–307.

39. The reciprocity suggests that the point is to create distance between the institutions, which will enable the cultivation of two distinct spheres of practice.

40. See Chapter 6.

41. Exceptions abound in all directions. See, e.g., *t. Sanh.* 4:1–3, 5, 7–8.

42. See Num 35:28 and *m. Mak.* 2:6–7.

43. *T. Sanh.* 3:4 is traditionally understood as referring to appointing the king and high priest (see Maimonides *Hilkhot Klei Hamikdash* 4:14, *Hilkhot Sanh.* 5:1), but Yair Lorberbaum has argued that it refers to judging these officials in a court of seventy-one judges. See *Disempowered King,* 116. Aside from the novelty of this latter reading, it would also lead to a discrepancy with *t. Sanh.* 4:1–2's claim that the king and high priest are treated as ordinary people, which implies that they are judged by a smaller tribunal in the same manner that "ordinary people" are judged. See also *y. Sanh.* 2:1 and *b. Sanh.* 18b.

44. The Mishnah here appears to be later than the Tosefta parallels. See David C. Flatto, *Between Royal Absolutism and an Independent Judiciary: The Evolution of Separation of Powers in Biblical, Second Temple and Rabbinic Texts* (Cambridge, Mass.: Harvard University Press, 2010), 221n40, 222n44.

45. *B. Sanh.* 18b harmonizes this pronouncement with the Mishnah, but this is not the simple sense of the Tosefta. See also *t. Sanh.* 4:6, which implies that the "king's bench" operates autonomously. See Flatto, *Between Royal Absolutism and an Independent Judiciary,* 221n41.

46. On this reading, this source sounds like the king is presiding alone. Likewise, *m. Sanh.* 2:4 has a similar connotation. Other sources may imply that he is presiding on a tribunal.

47. *T. Sanh.* 4:4 declares that only Davidic kings can sit in the Temple court. This source is less clear about why they sit, especially given that standing in the Temple is mandatory for priests (see *m. Zev* 2:1). It seems likely that the kings sit for a purpose (*pace y. Sotah* 7:7), and this gives rise to an alternate, if novel, understanding of this passage. In tannaitic terminology, sitting is synonymous with judging—e.g., the king "sits in judgment" (*yoshev bedin*) in *m. Sanh.* 2:4. Therefore, it is possible that this Tosefta is alluding to a Davidic king sitting in the Temple as the supreme arbiter, which would cohere with certain biblical and rabbinic traditions where the Temple is the locus of supreme justice (e.g., Deut 17:8–10, *m. Sanh.* 11:2). Parenthetically, this source differentiates between Davidic and non-Davidic kings. If this passage is privileging the former as judges, it may serve as a precursor for the Babylonian "revision" of *m. Sanh.* 2:1 that distinguishes between Davidic and non-Davidic kings. See also note 111.

48. According to the Erfurt manuscript, their levirate marriage regulations are identical. In contrast, the Vienna manuscript records that a high priest's widow, as opposed to a king's widow, can be wed in a levirate marriage. Both manuscripts recognize differences in their mourning laws. See *t. Sanh.* 4:1–2.

49. The precise meaning of this rule is unclear. See also *t. Sanh.* 4:2, which seems to differ.

50. My hypothetical reconstruction of the redaction history of these texts is the most plausible one, in my estimation, but it is not crucial for my broader thesis. See notes 44 and 82.

51. Perhaps the Mishnah expands on the rationale of the Tosefta ruling, as explained in *y. Sanh.* 2:1, that the king is barred from the Sanhedrin "due to suspicion." See Chapter 6.

52. See note 43.

53. The former is recorded in *m. Mak.* 2:7; the latter is recorded in *m. Shebu.* 2:2 (which presents the king as leading a procession to increase the size of the Temple courtyard, unlike *m. Sanh.* 1:5, which describes the Sanhedrin as heading this procession, arguably to avoid conflating the role of the king and the Sanhedrin). *M. Sanh.* 2:4, concerning the waging of a voluntary war, is the only mishnaic passage that presents the king and the Sanhedrin as having overlapping responsibilities, although the king seems to initiate the decision (but see *m. Sanh.* 1:5). Moreover, *m. Sanh.* 2:3–4 allows the king to build a cavalry and raise money for his garrison (notwithstanding the biblical strictures cited in Deut 17:16–17), implying that waging war is his prerogative. Further, *m. Sanh.* 2:4 continues to broadcast the overall autonomy of the monarch. Once again, the rhetoric of the Mishnah is particularly noteworthy. Finally, the Mishnah does not mention the high priest and *Urim* and *Thummim* as a prerequisite for waging a war. Perhaps *m. Yoma* 7:5 reflects a deliberate relocation and adaptation of this idea in order to maintain a dichotomy between the king and the high priest. Compare to *Sifre Num.* 139, and the parallel Sifre Zuta.

54. The Tosefta sources are likely earlier. Wendy Amselem points out its division is more intuitive: The high priest's rituals require him to change, bathe, and cut his hair; whereas the king has a cavalry, crown, scepter, throne, and royal implements. In addition, the *t. Sanh.* 4:1 list essentially protects the high priest from shame, which is conceptually different from the *t. Sanh.* 4:2 list, which demands heightened respect for the king. Further, traces of two distinct lists are found in Midrash Tannaim, even as they both apply to the king. The first list is recorded on verse 17:14 (and seen as deriving from the king's awe), the other on verse 17:18 (and seen as deriving from the exalted status of the king's throne). Finally, the Kaufman, Cambridge, and Parma manuscripts of *m. Sanh.* 2:5 record three different variants of the *t. Sanh.* 4:1 list as applied to the king (all different from the Bavli's Mishnah), which likely reflects that the application to the king is secondary (in the Tosefta this list is stable, whereas the 4:2 list of the king's items has variants in the Erfurt and Vienna manuscript).

    A plausible reconstruction is that initially there were two distinct lists, as recorded in the Tosefta; then both were applied discretely to the king, recorded in separate passages in Midrash Tannaim; finally, they were concatenated into one list, recorded in *Sifre Deut.* 17:14 (perhaps influenced by the mention of the king being in a bathhouse in *t. Sanh.* 4:8, which is absent from the parallel *m. Sanh.* 2:4) and *m. Sanh.* 2:5. The latter caps the carefully redacted *m. Sanh.* 2, and is likewise anchored in an exegesis of *Deut.* 17:14 (demanding awe, or, perhaps more accurately when set in this new light, heightened respect, for the king). This reconstructed process would further support the hypothesis that the Mishnah is a later adaptation of the Tosefta's raw material, which aims to elevate the stature of the king.

55. But see *Sifre Deut.* 161, which has a different emphasis. See also *t. Sanh.* 4:5, which may operate with a nexus that functions in an opposite direction (i.e., an opinion in the Tosefta restricts the king's powers, and the king is also subjugated to the jurisdiction of the court).

56. The Mishnah's dual arrangement establishes distinct, parallel spheres of leadership (beneath the supreme role of the judiciary). Accordingly, these passages never introduce any mechanism of "checks and balances" between the royal and priestly "branches."

57. See Josephus, *Ant.* 4.574–577; and Philo, *Hypoth.* (in Eusebius, *Praep. Ev.* 7:13), who follow the plain sense of Scripture. The Mishnah's identification may be partially based on the king's duty to transcribe the Torah (reinterpreted in Josephus, and a priestly duty in TS). See Fraade, *Legal Fictions,* 305–306. Also, Josephus's position is perhaps informed by his broader ambivalence toward monarchy. See Chapter 4.

58. While the deliberateness of the juxtaposition in *m. Sotah* 7:2 seems clear, it is possible that the elaborations of *m. Sotah* 7:7–8 reflect a subsequent phase. So the initial juxtaposition lays the seeds for the "cross-pollination" of the next phase. In all, according to Mishnah Sotah the roles of the king and high priest are similar, while in Mishnah Sanhedrin their responsibilities are clearly different, even as their standing remains parallel. The Horayot passages are discussed below.

59. The straightforward reading of the Mishnah is that the king even says the seventh blessing, "on behalf of the priests."

60. Priests have the principal role of blessing the people. See Num 6:22–27. Moreover, this duty is recorded in the proximate passage, *m. Sotah* 7:6. Consistently, *m. Sotah* 7:7 labels the high priest's ritual as the "benediction of the high priest" rather than the "portion read by the high priest." Still, the king also has a role of blessing the people. See 1 Kgs 8:14. Likewise, reading the Torah is a monarchic role because *Hakhel* is assigned to the king in rabbinic tradition. Consistently, *m. Sotah* 7:8 labels this ritual as the "portion read by the king," rather than the "benediction of the king." Still, the high priest also has a role of reading the Torah, according to rabbinic tradition. See also *m. Yoma* 7:1.

61. See, e.g., Lorberbaum, *Disempowered King,* 120–123, and Fraade, *Legal Fictions,* 305–306, and the references they cite.

62. The particular comparison here is noteworthy, as the king's role at *Hakhel* is equated with the high priest's function on Yom Kippur, the pinnacle of the Jewish calendar. At the same time, the importance of assigning the king a leading role in the Temple in conjunction with the unique Temple celebrations of Sukkot is also significant (the Mishnah manuscripts all state that the *Hakhel* ceremony transpires at the climax of the last day of Sukkot). So here the king and the cult are linked, unlike in *m. Sanh.* 2 or *m. Hor.* 1–3.

63. See also note 47.

64. It is unclear whether the Tosefta assigns a distinct reading to the high priest altogether. By citing the model of Ezra, the Tosefta may not be operating with the sharp dichotomy of the Mishnah. But see *t. Yoma* 4:18.

65. See *t. Sanh.* 4:7. Other texts depict Nehemiah as a monarchic figure, alongside Ezra the Priest. See David M. Goodblatt, *The Monarchic Principle: Studies in Jewish Self-Government in Antiquity* (Tübingen: Mohr [Siebeck], 1994), 59.

66. R. Judah's position should be contrasted with the Mishnah's emphasis on the king's prerogative to even sit in the Temple courtyard.

67. This priestly ensemble only appears in the Tosefta (in the context of Ezra's recital), where the ceremony combines priestly and monarchic rites.

68. See also *Sifre Deut.* 157. On Agrippa's identity, see, e.g., Dalya Trifon, "Keta MiMishna Ke'edut Lema'amado shel Hamelech Agrippas Hasheni," *Cathedra* 53 (1989): 27–48.

69. See also *Midrash Tannaim Deut.* 17:15.

70. The Mishnah also adduces supporting evidence about proper ritual practice from the King Agrippa episode, which further accents the king's positive leadership role in the *Hakhel* ceremony. Other scholars have drawn speculative inferences from the varying reactions to Agrippa's reading recorded in the Mishnah and Tosefta. See Trifon, "Keta," 35.

71. See also *t. Bikk.* 2:10.

72. This chapter uncovers the Mishnah's selective use of history. Elsewhere, the Mishnah provides sparse information about actual kings, almost all positive. It refers to towering figures (e.g., David), and even marginal ones (e.g., Munbaz), but states almost nothing about wicked or corrupt kings. Even when the Mishnah refers to a king with an uneven record (e.g., Agrippa), it transforms his legacy into an illustrious one. The programmatic history of the Mishnah idealizes and spiritualizes the role of the king. In contrast, the Tosefta and other rabbinic writings present a more checkered history. See Flatto, *Between Royal Absolutism and an Independent Judiciary*, 258–261.

73. While the Mishnah's framing of monarchy is positive, its depiction of the king's role is carefully constructed (Lorberbaum's characterization of the mishnaic monarch as a middling figure is thus insufficient). I hope to elaborate on this in another forum.

74. See Avraham Walfish, "Individual and Communal Sin: Tractate Horayot, Chapter 1" [Hebrew], *Netuim* 6 (2000): 9–36; Zvi Aryeh Shteinfeld, *Tractate Horayot: Studies in the Mishna and Talmud* [Hebrew] (Ramat Gan: Bar Ilan Press, 2016), 9–45.

75. On the high court in the Mishnaic exegesis of Lev 4, and the reordering of the pericopes, see Chapter 6.

76. See Chapter 7.

77. The differences between the king and the others include the nature of the sin (an action versus a ruling), the specific sacrifices required (but see the Cambridge manuscript on *m. Hor.* 3:1), and the rules governing the obligation to bring those sacrifices. Mishnah Horayot has conflicting signals about the exact standing of the king. See Flatto, *Between Royal Absolutism and an Independent Judiciary*, 232n71.

78. An accidental transgression cannot be prosecuted. Still, *Horayot* confirms the king's accountability. Apparently the king is expected to acknowledge his own error. See also *Midrash Tannaim Deut.* 17:14. By contrast, the high priest is punished in court (for an intentional violation). See *m. Sanh.* 1:5, 2:1, *t. Sanh.* 4:1, *y. Sanh.* 2:1.

79. The only difference mentioned in *m. Hor.* 3:1–2 is that a king who vacates his position loses his title, in contrast with the high priest. Arguably, kingship necessitates actual sovereign powers. Nevertheless, the standing of the king while he reigns is the focus of the above discussion.

80. See the parallel *Sifra* (*Hova*) 5:6.

81. The line's precise semantics are a little ambiguous. See Hameiri, *Bet Habehira LeHorayot,* 276. I assume that it at least partially relates to the king's sovereign immunity (*m. Sanh.* 2:2, *m. Hor.* 2:6), which would then corroborate interpreting the king's immunity as an essential principle (unlike the Bavli), as argued above. See Blidstein, *Political Principles in Maimonidean Thought,* 37–39.

82. Still, it is sufficient for this chapter's thesis to note that the teachings of the Mishnah and the Tosefta differ in these various contexts—the Tosefta has a more variegated view of the king's role and status, while the Mishnah appears to be more consistently pro-monarchic. This observation stands whether the mishnaic passages examined are earlier, later, or independent of the Tosefta.

83. At the same time, the nexus between the Sanhedrin and the high priest that emerges in Mishnah Horayot is less apparent in the Tosefta. See *t. Hor.* 1:2, 8, 10; 2:4. In terms of the king and the court, *t. Hor.* 1:10 seems to require the king to offer testimony. This passage needs further study, and should be compared with *m. Hor.* 2:5, 7, and *t. Sanh.* 4.

84. This Tosefta passage undermines the singular stature of the *Nasi* (evidently, the special sacrifice is due to each king's actual political clout). But see Maimonides, *Hilkhot Shegagot* 15:9.

85. The Tosefta interestingly discusses these distinct kingdoms explicitly, unlike the Mishnah. Perhaps, the Mishnah wants to project an ideal of a unified kingdom, along-side its depiction of a national and tribal courts.

86. Even as the Mishnah also refers to non-Davidic kings (e.g., Agrippa), it nevertheless envisions a single sovereign commanding all royal powers. In contrast, the Tosefta recognizes the diminished sovereignty of two simultaneous kings. See also *b. Hor.* 11b.

87. *T. Hor.* 2:8–9 (these passages notably refer to the king as *melekh* rather than *Nasi*). See also Trifon, "Keta," 35.

88. The Tosefta's claim about kingship is striking in light of Davidic lineage presumably being a prerequisite for ideal kingship, as emphasized in *m. Abot* 4:13.

89. *T. Hor.* 2:8–10 appears to contain earlier, less-edited material than *m. Hor.* 3:8.

90. See also Shteinfeld, *Tractate Horayot,* 75–104.

91. R. Shimon is a third-generation tanna, which makes this source pertinent, even if it is recorded in *Abot,* which may have been composed later. Still, as a discrete

teaching it is less probative than the anonymous, rhetorically rich, mishnaic units analyzed above. See Flatto, *Between Royal Absolutism and an Independent Judiciary*, 236–237.

92. Strikingly, the Mishnah records only positive royal actions, despite ample negative history. The Tosefta registers some of the latter. See, e.g., *t. Pesah.* 4:18, which criticizes King Munbaz. See note 72.

93. *Tosafot Yoma* 12b adduces this as a normative precedent to establish that a king may appoint the high priest. See also *t. Sanh.* 3:4; and *t. Yom.* 1:4. Some of these sources link the king to the high priest and the Temple. See note 24.

94. *M. Pesah.* 4:9, which describes the sages passing judgment on (and partially criticizing) the actions of King Hezekiah, was not originally part of the Mishnah, as Maimonides states in his Mishnah commentary.

95. See Flatto, *Between Royal Absolutism and an Independent Judiciary*, 237–239.

96. An important interpretive question is whether these mishnaic passages are truly pro-monarchic, or do they subtly camouflage the king's marginalization? The above analysis suggests that the Mishnah takes its pro-monarchic vision seriously (even as the monarch is secondary to the Sanhedrin). Moreover, given that these passages were redacted when there had been no king for more than a century, it is difficult to imagine the Mishnah's use of such subtle techniques to marginalize kingship. The Mishnah's only possible contemporary target would be the Patriarchate, but it was only burgeoning at this stage and its early leaders were rabbinic figures (who probably were instrumental in redacting the Mishnah).

97. The Mishnah's pro-monarchic orientation may have contributed to the stature of the Patriarchate, as it burgeoned over the next century. Minimally, the Mishnah provides a conceptual foundation for the notion of political autonomy that may have been instrumental for the Patriarchate's subsequent growth. As the Patriarchate evolves into more mature, less rabbinic phases, this notion of political autonomy may become more consequential, even as the later Patriarchate would subsequently be subject to rabbinic criticisms as well. See also Emanuel Friedheim, "Politique et rabbinisme en Palestine romaine: Opposition, approbation et réalités historiques," *Theologische Zeitschrift* 59, no. 2 (2003): 97–112; Goodblatt, *The Monarchic Principle*, chap. 5; and Chapter 7.

98. Moreover, by depicting the king as an established leader (*m. Sanh.* 2, *m. Hor.* 2–3 and *m. Abot* 4:13), commanding vital administrative powers (*m. Sanh.* 2, *m. Shebu.* 2:2, and *m. Yebam.* 6:4), conducting religious rituals (*m. Sotah* 7:8, *m. Bikk* 3:4), and warranting special treatment (*m. Sanh.* 2, *m. Hor.* 2–3, and *m. Yoma* 7:5, 8:1), the Mishnah projects him as a significant figure in its worldview. The prestige of the king is further elevated by the Mishnah's deliberate presentation of monarchic laws alongside the high priest. The noticeable dearth of rabbinic sources devoted to kingship emerges within the

mishnaic scheme not as a reflection of inferiority but as a function of the monarchy's flexible, autonomous nature. This dearth somewhat parallels the limited Pentateuchal record. Still, in the Pentateuch this dearth likely reflects a devaluation of kingship, whereas in the Mishnah's recasting of monarchic laws it has a positive cast. Further, the Pentateuch only imposes limits on the king, while the Mishnah enumerates positive powers.

99. See David Flatto, "The Historical Origins of Judicial Independence and Their Modern Resonances," *Yale Law Journal Pocket* 117 Part 8 (2007), http://yalelawjournal.org/forum /the-historical-origins-of-judicial-independence-and-their-modern-resonance; Flatto, "The King and I: The Separation of Powers in Early Hebraic Political Theory," *Yale Journal of Law and the Humanities* 20, no. 1 (2008), https://digitalcommons.law.yale .edu/yjlh/vol20/iss1/3.

100. See Erwin Chemerinsky, "Against Sovereign Immunity," *Stanford Law Review* 53 (2001): 1201.

101. See *m. Sanh.* 1:6.

102. The Bavli limits immunity to non-Davidic kings. Yet even though the Bavli differs from the Mishnah's plain sense, it also does not embrace the general rationale for sovereign immunity. For the Bavli, non-Davidic kings have immunity but do not judge, whereas Davidic kings judge but do not have immunity. Evidently, the critical issue for the Talmud is whether the king is integrated into, or separated from, the legal process. Other rabbinic sources concur with Mishnah Sanhedrin's doctrine of sovereign immunity. See notes 34 and 36. For further analysis, see David C. Flatto, "Justice Retold: The Seminal Narrations of the Trial of the Judean King," *Journal of Law and Religion* 30, no. 1 (2015): 3–35.

103. See *y. Ros. Has.* 1:2; and *Lev. Rab.* 35:3. The Greek adage relates to the idea of unwritten law (see Chapter 2). It should be noted, however, that the Mishnah presumably concurs with the bottom line of this rabbinic passage. Notwithstanding the Mishnah's emphasis on how normative law does not apply to the king, this no doubt has its limits (as affirmed by his need to atone in Horayot). Numerous written laws do apply to the king; but he cannot be judged in court.

104. This is also the ruling of *Horayot.* Tracing this anomalous proposition to its Deuteronomic roots invites a follow-up question: Why does the Deuteronomic model prevail over the widely held assumption of royal justice? See Chapter 8.

105. Robert Cover, "Folktales of Justice: Tales of Jurisdiction," *Capital University Law Review* 14 (1985): 183.

106. See, e.g., Nicholas, *An Introduction to Roman Law*, 18.

107. See, e.g., Christopher Rowe and Malcolm Schofield, eds., *The Cambridge History of Greek and Roman Political Thought* (New York: Cambridge University Press, 2000), 366–389, 464–476.

108. But see the enigmatic *Midrash Tannaim Deut.* 17:14, which imputes to the gentiles a scheme wherein the king may neither judge nor be judged.

109. *Y. Sanh.* 2:3 and Josephus (see Flatto, "Justice Retold," 30) seem to affirm only the doctrine of sovereign immunity. In contrast, the plain sense of Deut 17 is that the king is subject to the rule of law and does not participate in the judiciary.

110. The Mishnah's overall implication is that the king has, beyond specific royal powers, a distinct, albeit ill-defined, political role. See note 144. See also Gerald J. Blidstein, "Review of Yair Lorberbaum's 'Disempowered King,'" *Mehkerei Mishpat* 25, no. 3 (2010): 921–928.

111. The more variegated Tosefta influenced the Bavli in this context, which inevitably led to its revision and adaptation of the Mishnah's teachings. While the Bavli's narrowing of the Mishnah's principle to non-Davidic kings is not directly derivative of the Tosefta, it may be influenced by the latter. First, the Tosefta links the king to the legal order (see *t. Sanh.* 2:15, 4:2). Second, the Tosefta distinguishes Davidic kings in terms of their legal stature (see *t. Sanh.* 4:4). See also note 47.

112. The printed text states Rabbi Joseph, but manuscripts attribute this teaching to R. Pappa.

113. For a fuller analysis, see Flatto, "Justice Retold," 13–20.

114. 1 Kgs 11:29–39.

115. See Jon D. Levenson, *Sinai and Zion: An Entry into the Jewish Bible* (Minneapolis: Winston Press, 1985), 156–157.

116. See *Midrash Tannaim Deut.* 17:14, which already introduces a division (albeit among Davidic kings) between righteous kings who behave properly (e.g., David), and others who fail to do so (e.g., Solomon).

117. Other accounts of this epic trial diverge substantially from the Bavli's rendition. See Flatto, "Justice Retold," 20–33.

118. By associating the mishnaic rule with the infamous King Jannaeus, who is strongly censured elsewhere (e.g., *b. Qidd.* 66a), the passage further signals the inferiority of this alternate arrangement.

119. This is the common understanding, in light of Rabbi Pappa's teaching. But see Flatto, "Justice Retold," 15n51.

120. An earlier Talmudic gloss explains: "And if they are not subject to judgment, how can they judge others? For . . . Resh Lakish expounded: 'Examine yourself and only then examine others!'" See Flatto, "Justice Retold," 15n51.

121. See Cover, "Folktales of Justice," 183–190.

122. Cover, "Folktales of Justice," 190.

123. See Flatto, "Justice Retold," 17n59.

124. I have challenged aspects of Cover's analysis of the redacted Bavli, but concur that its kernel accents the theme of judging the king, and that the larger Bavli sugya promotes the ideal model. See Flatto, "Justice Retold," 16–20.

125. Later interpreters include traditional commentators, as well as scholars such as Urbach, Epstein, and Albeck. See Flatto, *Between Royal Absolutism and an Independent Judiciary*, 249n132.

126. The reciprocal nature of the king's relationship to the judiciary distinguishes the Bavli from the absolutist form of royal justice. In addition, the idea of Davidic king judging may mean as a member of the established judiciary. The Bavli's jurisprudence, thus, is more about incorporating the ruler into the legal sphere of the Sanhedrin and courts. At the same time, my analysis above primarily focuses on the king's capacity to judge, which seems to be a central pivot in the opening of the Bavli.

127. At times the Yerushalmi leaves its objections to the Mishnah unresolved. See Zacharias Frankel, *Mevo ha-Yerushalmi* (Breslau: Shletter, 1870), 29.

128. Further, the king cannot judge as a member of the Sanhedrin. See *t. Sanh.* 2:15.

129. The recording of disparate voices in *m. Sanh.* 2 seems to be the result of juxtaposing two conflicting sources rather than a careful editorial decision.

130. The manuscripts of *m. Sanh.* 2:4 have slight variants. On the conflict between 2:2 and 2:4, see note 31.

131. The precise rationale behind *t. Sanh.* 2:15 is not obvious. Although this scheme refrains from asserting a total separation of powers, it does curb the judicial role of the king in a significant manner. Certainly, restricting the king from participating in the highest tribunal is unusual in ancient jurisprudence. On the Talmudic explanations, see Chapter 6.

132. The rhetoric of this teaching is broad, even though the context is specific. *Y. Sanh.* 1:2 and *b. Sanh.* 14b use this verse to derive more general principles about the judiciary.

133. See *Sifre Zuta Deut.* 21:2; *y. Sotah* 9:1; *y. Sanh.* 1:2; *b. Sotah* 45a; and *b. Sanh.* 14b. These sources record different versions of the first part of the lemma, which identifies "your elders" as the high court, Sanhedrin, or court of seventy (the relationship among these terms is difficult to decipher, but matters little for present purposes). The second part, which refers to the king and high priest, may envision them functioning as independent judicial officials, who preside here alongside the judiciary. By contrast, the Mishnah integrates the high priest into the judiciary.

134. See Menachem Kahane, *Sifre Zuta Devarim* [Hebrew] (Jerusalem: Magnes Press, 2002), 294.

135. See, e.g., *Sifre Deut.* 9, 346. See, more generally, the classic study of Ignaz Ziegler, *Die Königsgleichnisse im Midrasch* (Breslau, 1903). A related motif is the rabbinic conception of Rosh Hashana as the day of God's kingship and judgment.

136. *Mekh.* Rabbi Ishmael *Yitro, Parsha* 2 (Horovitz ed., 196, line 10–11).

137. The previous paragraph in the Mekhilta specifically describes Moses as judging.

138. See *b. Sanh.* 13b, 16b; and Chapter 6.

139. See David C. Flatto, "It's Good to Be the King: The Monarch's Role in the Mishna's Political and Legal System," *Hebraic Political Studies* 2–3 (2007): 255–283.

140. See Hayim Lapin, *Rabbis as Romans: The Rabbinic Movement in Palestine, 100–400 CE* (Oxford: Oxford University Press, 2012).

141. "Engaging Rabbinic Literature: Four Texts," in *Why Study Talmud in the Twenty-First Century: The Relevance of the Ancient Jewish Text to Our World*, ed. Paul Socken (Lanham, Md.: Lexington Press, 2009), 213–215.

142. Josephus's response to Roman power differed substantially. See Chapter 4.

143. The Mishnah does not elaborate on the political sphere, beyond the notion that it should be separated from the legal sphere. Indeed, the Mishnah's approach to separation of powers is to make a very general statement about the distinct responsibilities of the king and the judiciary. Overall the primary mishnaic contributions to this discourse are, first, in its bold proclamation of this stark division, and second, in its original conception of an independent judiciary (see Chapter 6).

6. Juridical Models in Tannaitic Literature

1. The formulations in this paragraph reflect my assumption that rabbinic juridical writings are often programmatic in nature. See David C. Flatto, "Constructing Justice: The Selective Use of Scripture in Formulating Early Jewish Accounts of the Courts," *Harvard Theological Review* 111, no. 4 (2018): 489–493. The Pentateuchal juridical schemes share this quality to a certain degree.

2. I refer to the ideal system. See below.

3. For further background on the rabbinic court system, see the references in David C. Flatto, *Between Royal Absolutism and an Independent Judiciary: The Evolution of Separation of Powers in Biblical, Second Temple and Rabbinic Texts* (Cambridge, Mass.: Harvard University Press, 2010), 274n4. Although these works are helpful, they interpret the rabbinic material in a manner that is too positivistic and monolithic.

4. *M. Sotah* 9:11 already states that the Sanhedrin was canceled. See also *y. Sanh.* 1:1 about the suspension of capital and civil courts. For more on the historicity of the rabbinic courts, see Flatto, "Constructing Justice," 489nn6–7.

5. Max Weber famously distinguished among traditional, charismatic, and legal-rational forms of authority and related this to legal systems. Weber, "The Three Types of Legitimate Rule," trans. Hans Gerth, *Berkeley Publications in Society and Institutions* 4 (1958): 1–11. On critiques of Weber, see Aryeh Amihay, *Theory and Practice in Essene Law* (New York: Oxford University Press, 2017), 144.

6. Thus, a juridical scheme built around individual, charismatic sages was a reality; a centralized and empowered Sanhedrin was not. But the reality of rabbinic society may have inspired a vision of an expansive and autonomous legal regime. See this chapter's conclusion.

7. It is best to analyze these templates separately, even though they may overlap to a certain degree.

8. H. P. Chajes, "Les juges juifs en Palestine de l'an 70 a' l'an 500," translated in *Shenaton Hamishpat Haivri* 20 (1997): 429–443.

9. See, e.g., *m. B. Qam.* 8:6; *m. B. Mesi'a* 5:3, 8:8; *m. B. Bat.* 9:7, 10:8; *m. Ned.* 9:5; *m. Ketub.* 13:1; *m. Pe-ah* 2:6. See also Shaye J. D. Cohen, "The Rabbi in Second-Century Jewish Society," in *The Cambridge History of Judaism*, vol. 3: *The Early Roman Period*, ed. William Horbury et al. (Cambridge: Cambridge University Press, 1999), 961–971, 980–987.

10. Some noticed and criticized Chajes's argument. See Gedaliah Alon, *Jews and Judaism in the Classical World: Studies in Jewish History in the Times of the Second Temple and Talmud* (Jerusalem: Magnes Press, 1977), 382–386.

11. See Haim Shapira, "The Court in Yavneh: Status, Authority and Functions," in *Studies in Mishpat Ivri and Halakha: Judges and Judging* [Hebrew], ed. Ya'akov Habba and Amihai Radziner (Ramat-Gan: Bar-Ilan University, 2007), 318–319; and Seth Schwartz, "Historiography on the Jews in the 'Talmudic Period' (70–640 CE)," in *The Oxford Handbook of Jewish Studies*, ed. Martin Goodman (Oxford: Oxford University Press, 2002), 86.

12. See Seth Schwartz, *Imperialism and Jewish Society, 200 B.C.E. to 640 C.E.* (Princeton, N.J.: Princeton University Press, 2001), 105–110.

13. Presumably, the individual sages offered rulings on an ad hoc basis. See Flatto, *Between Royal Absolutism and an Independent Judiciary*, 280n18. For more on the templates of "informal justice" and "local justice" in rabbinic literature, see ibid., 330–344.

14. The Mishnah's continuation describes a ruling of R. Tarfon. See also *t. Yebam.* 4:7. At the same time, the notion of an (authorized) expert approved by the court may be a way of aligning an individual with an institutional template. See Chapter 7.

15. This "*baraita*" has no other attestations in tannaitic literature.

16. See also *b. Sanh.* 3a, 5b; *b. Git.* 32b–33a; *b. Yebam.* 25b; and *b. Ketub.* 22a.

17. The Tosefta also states that civil disputes require three or five judges.

18. See below. See also *b. Sanh.* 3a; *b. B. Qam.* 74b–75a; and the possible inference from the end of *m. Ros. Has.* 4:4 (but see 3:1).

19. An exhaustive analysis of all relevant rabbinic sources is beyond the scope of this chapter.

20. The term "instructions" connotes a broad range of subjects, not just the enumerated priestly rituals. This is also its meaning in tractate Horayot. For an alternate reading, see Aharon Shemesh and Cana Werman, *Revealing the Hidden: Exegesis and Halakha in the Qumran Scrolls* [Hebrew] (Jerusalem: Bialik Press, 2011), 84–86.

21. See the analysis in Chapter 5.

22. See also *m. Hor.* 2:3–4.

23. It is not clear from this passage whether the high priest rules for himself or for others. This may depend on varying recensions recorded in the Kaufman, Cambridge, and Parma manuscripts. The parallel Tosefta clearly refers to the high priest ruling for others. See *t. Hor.* 1:2, 8. See also Zvi Aryeh Shteinfeld, *Tractate Horayot: Studies in the Mishna and Talmud* [Hebrew] (Ramat Gan: Bar Ilan Press, 2016), 135–156.

24. See Daniel Tropper, "Bet Din Shel Kohanim," *Jewish Quarterly Review* 6, no. 33 (1973): 204–221. Regarding Courts of Levites, see *Sifre Num.* 122.

25. But see *t. Ketub.* 1:2; Tropper, "Bet Din Shel Kohanim," 211.

26. See Tropper, "Bet Din Shel Kohanim," 206–207; and Shlomo Zevin, ed., *Encyclopedia Talmudit,* vol. 3 (Jerusalem: Bohak, 1951), 181. Several of these sources will be analyzed below.

27. For secondary references and analysis, see Flatto, *Between Royal Absolutism and an Independent Judiciary,* 284nn33–37.

28. These alternate models have received little scholarly attention, as they have been overshadowed by the institutional justice passages.

29. For a more subtle displacement of royal justice, see the novel interpretation of Prov 29:4 in *b. Sanh.* 7b and *b. Ketub.* 105a; and see *b. Git.* 62a.

30. Resh Laqish's homily before the Patriarch cited in the continuation of the Yerushalmi may touch on a related motif.

31. This is likewise the sense of the previous verse, Exod 23:1.

32. See *Mekh.* R. Ishmael, *Kaspa, Parsha* 20; and *t. Sanh.* 3:7–8. See also Efraim E. Urbach, *Mehkarim be-Madae ha-Yahadut,* vol. 2 (Jerusalem: Magnes Press, 1998), 503–509.

33. The Talmud, however, focuses on the opening clause of this verse ("*lo taaneh al rib*"), and interprets the term "*rib* [legal dispute]" as "*rab* [a master who exercises legal authority]."

34. The Mishnah's aim may be to formalize the voting procedures in different kinds of matters. If, alternatively, there is a genuine concern about protecting the integrity of each judge's viewpoint, it is not clear why this should not also be a concern in civil or ritual matters. See also *b. Sanh.* 36a.

35. A third view follows: "Rav said, 'Do not speak, even after a hundred.'" The Leiden manuscript concludes with a dangling extraneous clause "the words of R. Pinhas."

36. This becomes apparent from the continuation of the Yerushalmi, which identifies a different verse (1 Sam 25:13) as a source that teaches that capital cases must commence from the side. See also *b. Sanh.* 36a, and *b. Git.* 59a; and Avraham Weiss, *Seder Ha-Diyun* [Hebrew] (New York: Yeshiva University Press, 1957), 176–177.

37. This may be a vestige of the models of individual justice or royal justice. See also Chapter 7.

38. Rashi ad loc. explains that one is not allowed to contradict the judicial master; therefore, if the king reaches a verdict (and serves as master judge), nobody else would be able to demur.

39. While focusing on the master's role in dispensing justice, this passage highlights the ultimate incompatibility of power and justice.

40. While medieval commentators wonder why the king cannot just be required to opine last (see *b. Sanh.* 36a), the Bavli implies that the king's powerful voice must be completely sequestered from the court. The Bavli's exegesis somewhat parallels its nearby

account of the Jannaeus trial (*b. Sanh.* 19a-b). Both passages reflect a determination to keep power separated from justice.

41. In the Yerushalmi's idiom, the king is expelled from the Sanhedrin because he is suspicious; in the Bavli's, the king is expelled because he is big, i.e., powerful. (The continuation of the Yerushalmi may have an opposite connotation: the king cannot participate on a tribunal that is too small in size and, therefore, beneath his dignity.)

42. See, e.g., *b. Sanh.* 2b.

43. See also *b. Sanh.* 33a for additional interpretations of this mishnaic source.

44. See *m. Sanh.* 3:2.

45. These will be discussed below. Other sources include *t. Sotah* 11:14; *Midrash Tannaim Deut.* 17:8; *b. B. Qam.* 61a; *b. Yoma* 80a; *b. Mak.* 23b.

46. Paul Mandel has recently offered a penetrating reconstruction of the world of the sages, which highly valued the authority of individual figures. See *The Origins of Midrash: From Teaching to Text* (Leiden: Brill, 2017). But as I argue in a forthcoming piece, rabbinic discourse deliberately represents this world as embodying an institutional ideal.

47. See Gedalyahu Alon, "*Elen deMitmanin be-Kesef,*" in *Mehkarim be-Toldot Yisrael: Bi-Yeme Bayit Sheni uvi-Tekufat ha-Mishnah veha-Talmud,* 2 vols. (Tel Aviv: Hakibutz ha-Meuhad, 1967–1970), 2:47n131.

48. To be sure, *m. Abot* 4:8 uses the language of persuasion, rather than prohibition, in polemicizing against single judges. But see the citation of this source in Yerushalmi Sanhedrin below.

49. Abot Rabbi Nathan B, 34, attributes this teaching to Rabbi Eliezer (son of Rabbi Eliezer Haqafar).

50. See *Mekh.* Rabbi Ishmael, *Beshalach, Parsha* 6, and parallels.

51. The Yerushalmi may frame the breaching of *m. Abot* 4:8 as a violation of the Torah. Evidently, accepting a single judge is valid from the litigant's perspective, but problematic from the judge's vantage point.

52. See also 1 Kgs 22:19–22; Isa 6:1–8; and *Gen. Rab., Parsha* 8.

53. These lines record a dispute about whether God seals the decree of judgment alone or when accompanied by the divine court.

54. This section also includes an instance where a judge thinly bypasses the restriction on judging alone by having a subordinate present.

55. Elsewhere, rabbinic discourse reflects both poles: portraying God as a sole judge or consulting with a celestial tribunal, and conceiving of Moses as a sole (royal) judge, as a chief judge on a court, or as embodying the Sanhedrin.

56. According to *m. Sanh.* 1, the lower, civil (monetary) courts are composed of three judges, rather than one (but see note 57). The intermediate court is composed of twenty-three judges. The supreme tribunal is composed of seventy / seventy-one judges. Note the greater the court's stature, the larger its size; with the largest panel of judges atop the judicial pyramid, instead of a single figure such as Moses. So the scheme of *m. Sanh.* 1 is

actually an inverted pyramid. Nevertheless, the validity of individual judges may continue to be upheld in restricted circumstances.

57. The degree to which a panel is envisioned to supplant individual justice may depend on whether it is designed to be level (see Chapter 7), or merely technically satisfy a proscription on judging alone by adding token judges (see *b. Sanh.* 2b–3a, and note 54 above).

58. See, e.g., *m. Pesah.* 5:8.

59. See also *m. Ohal.* 17:5. See Zacharias Frankel, *Darkhei ha-Mishnah* (Tel Aviv: Sinai, 1959 offset of Leipzig: H. Hunger, 1867), 62.

60. Notably, individual rabbis make the assessment.

61. See *m. Ed.* 8:3; and *m. Seqal.* 1:3–4.

62. The Mishnah strikingly inverts the order of Lev 4, which lists the anointed priest's sin offering before that of the people (the rabbis interpret the latter as referring to the sin offering of the court and the people). Moreover, *y. Hor.* 2:1–2 and *b. Hor.* 7a–b constrict the scope of the priest's role, and thereby further subordinate his juridical position to that of the court.

63. See also *y. Sanh.* 2:1, which discusses the size of the tribunal that judges the high priest, and may imply that the high priest joins a tribunal of the same size when he judges.

64. *M. Sanh.* 1:5 reflects a much more sweeping subordination of the high priest to the Sanhedrin. See below. See also Tosafot *b. Sanh.* 18a, *Ve-ha.*

65. See also the tribunal of ten judges—including one priest—in *m. Sanh.* 1:2, discussed below.

66. The Sifre refers to the Yavneh court, which functions as a kind of Sanhedrin. See notes 11 and 92. See also Midrash Tannaim ad loc.

67. Alon claims that the court of seventy-one (Sanhedrin) was a composite of three lower courts (of twenty-three), plus two court leaders. See Gedaliah Alon, *The Jews in Their Land in the Talmudic Age, 70–640 C.E.*, trans. and ed. Gershon Levi (Cambridge, Mass.: Harvard University Press, 1989), 176–252.

68. According to *m. Sanh.* 1:1, 4, and 4:1, civil courts correspond to courts of three, and capital courts to courts of twenty-three.

69. Although the contexts differ in these synoptic passages (focusing on the makeup of the supreme court, the editing of the King's Torah, and the lineage qualifications for a judge on a capital court), I do not think that this bears upon the overall analysis. All four texts share similarities, but each promotes a distinct scheme (with the possible exception of the Yerushalmi). See also *Sifre Zuta Deut.* 19:17; and Menahem Kahane, *Sifre Zuta Devarim* [Hebrew] (Jerusalem: Magnes Press, 2002), 287.

70. The red heifer: Num 19:3–7; broken-necked heifer: Deut 21:5; woman suspected of adultery: Num 5:15–31; leprosy of men: Lev 13:1–46; and leprosy of houses: Lev 14:33–57. Among these, only the ritual of the broken-necked heifer includes other officials. See Deut 21:2–4, 6–8.

71. The red heifer: *t. Sanh.* 3:4; broken-necked heifer: *m. Sanh.* 1:1, *t. Sanh.* 3:4 and *Sifre Deut.* 152; woman suspected of adultery: *m. Sotah* 1:3–4 and *Sifre Deut.* 152; and leprosy plagues: *Sifre Deut.* 152. See also *Sifre Zuta Deut.* 17:8.

72. See *m. Meg.* 4:3. The decimal tribunal's reference in a parallel list, its inclusion of a priest, and its unusual size are all indications that it constitutes a distinct juridical arrangement deriving from an external source. Likewise, courts of five / seven for intercalation (*m. Sanh.* 1:2) may reflect a distinct juridical scheme. See also *y. Sanh.* 2:1.

73. See *m. Kelim* 1:8.

74. See *t. Menah.* 7:5.

75. I am not commenting on the historical veracity of this or other rabbinic passages, but arguing that, regardless of their historicity or date, they have a conceptual and rhetorical function (even in the period of their redaction).

76. In practice, there was likely (sectarian and / or ongoing) tension between sages and priests surrounding Temple regulations, which may be reflected in certain rabbinic sources. See, e.g., *m. Seqal.* 1:3–4. Descriptive sources about Rabbi Yohanan b. Zaqqai's legislation relating to Temple matters are not addressed here, but may assume additional significance in light of the phenomenon described above.

77. See, e.g., *m. Menah.* 10:3 (depicting the court's role in the *Omer* offering); *m. Sukkah* 4:4 (the court's role and enactment relating to the lulav and the Temple precincts); *m. Seqal.* 1:1, 3–4 (the court's collection of a half *shekel* for the Temple); *m. Parah* 3:1, 7–11 (especially 7–8) (the court's supervision of the high priest preparing for the red heifer ritual; see also *t. Parah* 3:8); and *m. Bik.* 3:7 (rabbinic legislation pertaining to the first-fruits ritual). See also Joshua Efron, *Studies on the Hasmonean Period* (Leiden: Brill, 1987), 298n43.

78. For a parallel phenomenon where the rabbinic court takes charge of a priestly ritual, see *m. Sotah* 1:3–4.

79. Undoubtedly, an underlying factor here and elsewhere is the legacy of sectarianism and past tensions between Sadducees and Pharisees over the control and conduct of the Temple and priesthood, and presumably ongoing tensions between priests and rabbis. But the result is a restructuring of authority, which is also driven by other factors.

80. Presumably this refers to elders from the leading institutional court, the Sanhedrin.

81. The "rabbinization" of priestly rituals is an extensive phenomenon. For example, rabbinic discourse not only elevates the court's responsibility for the Sotah ritual, but also transforms it into a more legalistic (i.e., rabbinic) one. Moreover, rabbinic sources depicts the sages as being the ultimate arbiters of cultic laws. See, e.g., *t. Pesah.* 4:11 and parallels.

82. Parallels include: *Sifre Deut.* 152; *t. Hag.* 2:9; *t. Sanh.* 7:1; *y. Sanh.* 1:4 (19c); and *b. Sanh.* 88b. See also Michael Ben-Ari, "The Chamber of Hewn Stone and the Sanhedrin on the Temple Mount" [Hebrew], *New Studies on Jerusalem* 10 (1995): 110.

83. Parenthetically, this source involves an individual sage transmitting an ancestral tradition (located in a central venue).

84. Ben-Ari ("Chamber of Hewn Stone," 95–118) argues that the Chamber of Hewn Stone was most likely a priestly chamber, and that the rabbinic location of the Sanhedrin there is an ideal-literary construct based on exegesis of Deut 17. I would add that it is also part of a dominant juridical vision that is advanced in rabbinic literature.

85. By this formulation, Ben-Ari means to distinguish it from a judicial chamber, but also from other chambers that were more directly involved in Temple services.

86. The actual development of this tradition may be more complicated, and requires further study. See, e.g., *m. Pe'ah* 2:6; *m. Ed.* 7:4; *m. Miqw.* 5:5; and note 87. Of course, there is a biblical backdrop as well. See, e.g., Deut 17:8–9; 1 Kgs 8:31–32; Isa 2:1–4.

87. See also the references in Efron, *Studies in the Hasmonean Period,* 297n37. Note that the chamber of the high priest (*Palhedrin*) is adjacent to the Chamber of Hewn Stone, which supports Ben-Ari's thesis. Conversely, in rabbinic tradition their proximity may offer another indication of how the high priest is absorbed into the judiciary.

88. The passage's placement at the tractate's conclusion further punctuates this point. See also *t. Sanh.* 7:1 (and parallels).

89. See also Josephus's *Ag. Ap.* 1.32–37, cited in Ben-Ari, "Chamber of Hewn Stone," 97. The Sanhedrin "judging" the priesthood (perhaps in a different sense) also surfaces in *m. Sanh.* 1:5. See below.

90. Institutional justice does not necessarily efface the other models. Thus, a residual role of individual judges and priests continues to be accented in certain depictions.

91. The influence of both of these terms or typologies is manifest in *m. Sanh.* 1. On these terms, see Michael Walzer, *In God's Shadow: Politics in the Hebrew Bible* (New Haven, CT: Yale University Press, 2012), 185–198.

92. Some of these rabbinic circles evolved into "courts," especially Yavneh. See, e.g., *Sifre Deut.* 153. See Steven D. Fraade, *From Tradition to Commentary: Torah and Its Interpretation in Midrash Sifre to Deuteronomy* (Albany: State University of New York Press, 1991), 83–87, 238n63. But see Shaye Cohen, "Patriarchs and Scholarchs," *Proceedings of the American Academy for Jewish Research* 48 (1981): 57–85.

93. The borrowed terminology signals that the concept of a Sanhedrin is not entirely indigenous, although it is not simply derivative from foreign constructs either. On "Sanhedrin," see Daniel Sperber, *A Dictionary of Greek and Latin Legal Terms in Rabbinic Literature* (Ramat-Gan: Bar-Ilan University Press, 1984), 123–126.

94. This term has no biblical roots. It etymology deserves further study.

95. Deut 17 underpins rabbinic accounts of administering justice, and influences rabbinic jurisprudence, including its notions of separation, centralization, and hierarchy. Nevertheless, perhaps the most salient feature of rabbinic jurisprudence that is evident in the rabbinic interpretation of Deut 17—its institutional scheme—has no scriptural basis. This act of eisegesis vividly captures the importance of this rabbinic motif.

96. See Fraade, *From Tradition to Commentary,* 238n63.

97. See also *Sifre Deut.* 152; and Flatto, "Constructing Justice," 509–511.

98. See Kahane, *Sifre Zuta Devarim*, 254–255. The supreme judicial institution has various names recorded in rabbinic sources. See Alon, *The Jews in Their Land*, 187. Alon rebuts Buchler's theory that these names reflect distinct institutions. See also Ishay Rosen-Zvi, "The Protocol of the Court at Yavne? A New Reading of Tosefta Sanhedrin 7" [Hebrew], *Tarbiz* 78 (2009): 30n160.

99. There is a structural parallel between the hierarchical arrangement of the Mosaic judiciary and the vertical scheme of *m. Sanh.* 1. Further, the brief reference to "officers of ten" in 1:6, which is elaborated upon in the Talmudim, suggests that this scriptural source is (loosely) linked to the Mishnah. See Flatto, "Constructing Justice," 512–513. Nevertheless, this link is not developed in the Mekhilta. The only allusion to the Sanhedrin is *Mekh.* Rabbi Ishmael 18:18's reference to the seventy elders. Even when Exod 18 / Deut 1 is adduced by the Mishnah, it may be more as a way of affirming (rather than generating) a rabbinic tradition.

100. The Kaufman manuscript transcribes *kedei*, instead of *keneged*, which led Ephraim E. Urbach to a novel interpretation: 23 judges are selected out of 230 eligible judges. Still, the institutional emphasis remains intact (the 23 selected judges join a tribunal). See Urbach, *The Halakhah: Its Sources and Development* (Jerusalem: Yad la-Talmud, 1986), 61–62. Urbach's thesis has been rejected by others. See David Henshke, "The Number of Judges in Ancient Israel," *Jewish Law Annual* 17 (2007): 33n27; and Kahane, *Sifre Zuta Devarim*, 235n7.

101. The Talmudim are fully aware of the verses' plain sense. See the *baraita* (*y. Sanh.* 1:4; *b. Sanh.* 17a) which tallies the number of individual judges in the Mosaic judiciary.

102. See *b. Sanh.* 13b, 16b (and Rashi "*de-uke sanhedraot*"). Moses's role is also viewed institutionally in a different sense, i.e., in the calculation of seventy / seventy-one judges. See *m. Sanh.* 1:6; *t. Sanh.* 3:5.

103. See also *Sifre Num.* 11. Some attempt to harmonize these disparate sources. See, e.g., Chanoch Albeck, *Shisha Sidre Mishnah*, 6 vols. (Jerusalem: Bialik; Tel-Aviv: Devir, 1952–1959), 4:163–165. Others offer alternate perspectives. See, e.g., Rosen-Zvi, "The 'Protocol,'" 30n160.

104. The distinction between capital and monetary matters is manifest throughout *m. Sanh.* 1, 3–5. On these courts, see Urbach, *The Halakhah*, 61–62, who also notes the Sifre Numbers tradition of a court of thirty. See also *Sifre Zuta Deut.* 16:18, cited by Henshke, "The Number of Judges," 44–51.

105. The judiciary's preeminence is also manifest in its expansive jurisdiction, which swells well beyond judicial affairs. See Flatto, *Between Royal Absolutism and an Independent Judiciary*, 317n132.

106. See *Sifre Deuteronomy*, ed. Louis Finkelstein (New York: Jewish Theological Seminary, 2001), 97n6, which notes the alternate sequence of the tiers in *b. Sanh.* 16b.

107. *Sifre Deut.* 144 also discusses the role of the officers, who are never mentioned in the Mishnah.

108. While the Sifre here interprets Deut 16, the notion of centralization is also emphasized in Deut 17, which likely also informs this midrashic scheme.

109. This structure would be loosely parallel to the Mosaic judiciary, which is also hierarchical.
See also *Midrash Tannaim Deut.* 17:18, which seems to envision the high court in Jeru-
salem as having a supervisory role over other courts, comparing it to the superior role of
Moses's court (note how Moses here is joined by a tribunal). Traces of the Sifre's juridical
design surface elsewhere, sometimes in conjunction with other traditions. See, e.g., *m.
Sanh.* 1:5–6; *b. Sanh.* 16b (linking the Mishnah and Sifre); *m. Mak.* 1:10; and *t. Sanh.* 3:5.

110. This overall scheme is a striking example of institutionalization, as Lev 4:13–21 refers
to the sin of the congregation.

111. In the very least, Horayot does not mention the juridical function. Likewise, *m. Sanh.*
11:2 and *t. Sanh.* 7:1 describe an institution that issues instructions and resolves halakhic inquiries or debates, not one that adjudicates. On the interrelationships among
adjudication, instruction, and teaching, see Rosen-Zvi, "The 'Protocol.'"

112. See generally Jon D. Levenson, *Sinai and Zion: An Entry into the Jewish Bible* (San Francisco: Harper & Row, 1987), 15–88.

113. See Flatto, "Constructing Justice," 510. The Isaiah verse is linked to legal jurisdiction in
other passages. See *y. Sanh.* 1 (19a); *y. Ned.* 6 (40a); and *b. Ber.* 63b. For somewhat different, but related, elaborations on this verse, see Abot Rabbi Nathan, B 48; *b. B. Bat.*
21a; *Pesiq. Rab.* 40; and other parallels.

114. Arguably, Horayot's court represents the people, even as it instructs them. See Flatto,
Between Royal Absolutism and an Independent Judiciary, 341n204.

115. Scholars have argued that *m. Sanh.* 11:2 is an edited abridgment of *t. Sanh.* 7:1. There
are also other rabbinic parallels. See Flatto, "Constructing Justice," 513n122.

116. Later, this passage refers to seventy-one members.

117. The *baraita* (*b. Sanh.* 88b) states that the Temple-area courts were of twenty-three,
which makes more intuitive sense, but this may well be a revised source. The *baraita*
also locates these two courts at the opening of the Temple Mount and courtyard. This
latter variant is also found in *m. Sanh.* 11:2; *Sifre Deut.* 152; *Gen. Rab. Parshah* 70. See
also Avraham Weiss, "On the Question of the Nature of the Court of Seventy-One,"
in *Jubilee Volume in Honor of Louis Ginzberg on the Occasion of His Seventieth Birthday*
[Hebrew] (New York: American Academy for Jewish Research, 1945), 207–209.

118. See Saul Lieberman, *Tosefta Ki-Feshuta Hagiga,* vol. 5 (Jerusalem: Jewish Theological
Seminary, 1992), 1298.

119. This passage states that the questioner and the most distinguished court member would
ascend to the higher courts, whereas Midrash Tannaim states only that the judge who
did not know the law would ascend. See also Kahane, *Sifre Zuta Devarim,* 254–255.

120. The final lines may be an interpolation. See Rosen-Zvi, "The 'Protocol,'" 25–29. The
Tosefta proceeds to discuss the traits that qualify a person to judge, and the way lower

courts serve as "feeders" for the upper ones—further indicators of "institutionalization." For variants, see Lieberman, *Tosefta Ki-Feshuta Hagiga*, 1298–1299.

121. The Tosefta addresses resolving halakhic inquiries in general, in contrast with the Mishnah's narrower focus on the prohibition of the "rebellious elder," i.e., a dissenting local judge who continues issuing a ruling that contravenes the ruling of the Temple tribunals.

There are subtle differences in the interpretation of Deut 17:8–13 among various sources: Midrash Tannaim attributes the process's initiation to a judge who is uncertain about the law; the Mishnah and Sifre depict a lower-court debate concerning a *derasha* and *limud;* and the Tosefta describes a questioner who wants to know the halakhah, with the lower court solely reporting traditions (but see *b. Sanh.* 88b and *Sifre Zuta Deut.* 16:18). The Mishnah's context is the rebellious elder, which is also alluded to in Midrash Tannaim. See also the different contexts of *b. Sanh.* 88b and *y. Sanh.* 1:6; Rosen-Zvi, "The 'Protocol,'" 25–29.

122. The Tosefta further accents sacred motifs by describing the courts as clustered on the Temple Mount, and synchronizing the high court's hours of operation with the daily schedule of sacrifices.

123. See also *t. Seqal.* 3:27.

124. The Mishnah has a broader emphasis on the court teaching Torah, while the Tosefta focuses on issuing legal pronouncements. See also *Sifre Zuta Deut.,* 16:18; Kahane, *Sifre Zuta Devarim,* 236–237.

125. Lieberman contends that the Sanhedrin would issue instructions then. *Tosefta Ki-Feshuta Hagiga,* 1299.

126. See Chapter 7.

127. See note 105.

128. Deuteronomy's centralization of the cult influences its centralization of justice. See Moshe Weinfeld, *Deuteronomy and the Deuteronomic School* (Oxford: Clarendon Press, 1972), 233–236. In rabbinic literature, the latter becomes a dominant motif.

129. Seth Schwartz, *The Ancient Jews from Alexander to Muhammad* (Cambridge: Cambridge University Press, 2014), 118n18.

130. See Schwartz, *The Ancient Jews from Alexander to Muhammad,* 118n18. See also Fraade, *From Tradition to Commentary,* 86–87.

131. Schwartz, *The Ancient Jews from Alexander to Muhammad,* 118n18. The preference for institutional justice over priestly justice also reflects the historic and ongoing tension between sages and priests.

132. See *b. Ros. Has.* 25b, commenting on *m. Ros. Has.* 2:10 and elaborating on *t. Ros. Has.* 1:17 (and then citing *Sifre Deut.* 153). Both the Mishnah and Tosefta also stress aspects of institutional justice.

133. See Chapter 7.

134. See Chapter 9. On the broader phenomenon of law as a social and cultural force, see, e.g., Lawrence Rosen, *Law as Culture: An Invitation* (Princeton, N.J.: Princeton University Press, 2006), 14–67; and Paul Kahn, *The Cultural Study of Law: Reconstructing Legal Scholarship* (Chicago: University of Chicago Press, 2000).

135. A similar point may obtain from the shift from individual, royal, or priestly justice to institutional justice. Individual justice tends to be more ad hoc, royal justice often derives from the ruler's whim, and priestly justice may rely on cultic inspiration. In contrast, institutional justice advances laws that are set, rational, and general.

136. Consistent with this characterization, the Mishnah stations the king and high priest beneath the Sanhedrin. See Chapter 5.

7. The *Nasi* and the Judiciary in Rabbinic Literature

1. Chapters 5–6 have already documented dissenting views. But this chapter explores changes that transpire within the institutional scheme.

2. The programmatic scheme is transformed in various ways, undoubtedly in part due to an encounter with real power dynamics.

3. Robert W. Gordon ("Foreword: The Arrival of Critical Historicism," *Stanford Law Review* 49]1996–1997]: 1029) makes this claim about law and power, in general. Regarding the rabbinic partition between law and power, I have argued in Chapters 5–6 that this is largely an imaginative construct that is historically contingent.

4. Alternatively, these structural changes can be viewed as a breakdown in the institutional scheme under the corroding pressure of power dynamics within and outside of the court.

5. See note 11.

6. See, e.g., *y. Shab.* 16:15; *y. Ta'an.* 4:68; *y. Kelim* 9:32b; *b. Sanh.* 38a; *b. Sanh.* 98b; *b. Ketub.* 103b. See also Aharon Oppenheimer, *Rabbi Judah the Prince* [Hebrew] (Jerusalem: Merkaz Zalman Shazar, 2007), 35–40.

7. If anything, the *Nasi* is inferior in stature to a king; still, his legal authority is more expansive.

8. Scholars debate the precise role of the yeshiva, but it seems to clearly include legal responsibilities. See Haim Shapira, "The Court in Yavneh: Status, Authority and Functions," in *Studies in Mishpat Ivri and Halakha: Judges and Judging* [Hebrew], ed. Ya'akov Habba and Amihai Radziner (Ramat-Gan: Bar-Ilan University, 2007), 329–330; and Paul D. Mandel, *The Origins of Midrash: From Teaching to Text* (Leiden: Brill, 2017), 172–173.

9. For the Tosefa (*t. hag.* 2:9 = *t. Sanh.* 7:1), the ongoing debate between the *zugot* may also be indicative of a certain erosion of the institutional scheme. Maybe its root cause is not the lack of dedication of the students to their masters (ibid.), but the infiltration of power into the institution.

10. See, e.g., *t. Hag.* 2:4; *t. Sanh.* 7:8; *m. Sem.* 9:2; *b. Mo'ed Qat.* 22b. See also *y. Pesah.* 6:1; *y. Ber.* 4:1.

11. See the references in Hayim Lapin, *Rabbis as Romans: The Rabbinic Movement in Palestine, 100–400 CE* (Oxford: Oxford University Press, 2012), 20–24, 52–55; and David C. Flatto, *Between Royal Absolutism and an Independent Judiciary: The Evolution of Separation of Powers in Biblical, Second Temple and Rabbinic Texts* (Cambridge, Mass.: Harvard University Press, 2010), 349n6.

12. When Sacha Stern attempts to date the term *Nasi* as Patriarch, he writes, "The title nasi is attributed to Hillel the Elder . . . but this is in the significantly different sense of 'head of the Sanhedrin' or of some other, specific assembly." Stern, "Rabbi and the Origins of the Patriarchate," *Journal of Jewish Studies* 54, no. 2 (2003): 196–197. See also his equivocation about whether "*Nasi*" in certain pre-70 sources means "head of the Sanhedrin specifically (as opposed to some other assembly)." Ibid., 197n11.

13. Shmuel Safrai, review of *Mehqarim Betoldot Ha-Sanhedrin*, *Kiryat Sefer* 39 (1964): 69–75.

14. Chanoch Albeck was already sensitive to the complexities of the term *Nasi* and its evolution over time. Albeck, "The Sanhedrin and Its President (*Nesiah*)" [Hebrew], *Zion* 8 (1943): 165–178. See also the early scholarship surveyed in Hugo Mantel, *Mehqarim Betoldot Ha-Sanhedrin* (Tel Aviv: Devir, 1969), 50–53.

15. See Martin Jacobs, *Die Institution des Judischen Patriarchen: Eine Quellen-und Traditionskritische Studie zur Geschichte der Juden in der Spantantike* (Tübingen: Mohr Siebeck, 1995), 27–98 (esp., 60), 353–368; and Mantel, *Mehqarim,* 3–63.

16. See the relevant discussions in Chapters 2–3.

17. See *Theological Dictionary of the Old Testament* (Grand Rapids, Mich.: Eerdmans, 1999), 10:44–53. The term *Nasi* appears 126 times. Most of these citations have a political, not a juridical, connotation; but see Num 27:2, 31:13; Josh 17:4, and *Theological Dictionary,* 10:49.

18. See, e.g., the sources cited in Martin G. Abegg Jr. et al., eds., *The Dead Sea Scrolls Concordance,* vol. 1, pt. 2 (Leiden: Brill, 2003), 522.

19. See Alexander Rofe, "Qumran Paraphrases, the Greek Deuteronomy and the Late History of the Biblical Nasi" [Hebrew], *Textus* 14 (1988): 163–174.

20. See note 11.

21. See the analysis in Chapter 5.

22. For example, *Targum* translates *Nasi* as *rav,* Septuagint as *archon,* and Vulgate as *princeps.*

23. The parallel passages in *Sifra Hova, Parsha* 5, and *t. Hor.* 2:2 also confirm the royal connotation of *Nasi.*

24. This seems plain for the rest of Mishnah and Tosefta Horayot, and *Sifra Hova.* See also *t. B. Qam.* 7:5; *t. Sheb.* 1:6; *t. Zebah.* 10:2; *t. Parah* 1:5; *Sifre Num.* 112; *Sifre Zuta Num.* 15.

25. See also *t. Shab.* 8:9. But see *Sem.* 8:6, which contrasts kings and *Nesiim*.

26. *B. Hor.* 11b.

27. Scholarship has extensively analyzed which rabbis were labeled *Nesiim* by rabbinic sources (certain references clearly project back from a later period), including Hillel (Second Temple period), Rabbi Yohanan b. Zakkai and Rabban Gamaliel II (Yavneh), Rabbi Simeon b. Gamaliel II (Usha), and Rabbi Judah the Patriarch I (the Galilee). See note 11.

28. Some of these sources expound biblical verses that explicitly relate to tribal leaders. See, e.g., *Sifre Num.* 47, 52.

29. This is the way Albeck and Ginzberg understood this passage. See Mantel, *Mehqarim*, 55n266. Stern, following Mantel and Jacobs, suggests that the implication of *m. Ned.* 5:5 is that each city had its own *Nasi,* a landowning aristocrat who acted as a kind of magistrate. Stern believes that when rabbinic literature referred to this position, they immediately rabbinized it (during Judah the Patriarch's lifetime). Stern, "Rabbi," 213–214.

30. One line may suggest otherwise. It distinguishes between a judge / *Nasi* and a *bor* (attested to in all manuscript variants), not a *hedyot.* Arguably, this contrast implies that a *Nasi* is a learned sage.

31. If "*Nasi*" has a distinct juridical meaning, it is as chieftain of the judiciary (perhaps drawing on certain biblical citations; see note 17). Still, considering the consistent political connotation of this title, and the absence of a definitive role of chief judge, this seems less likely.

32. The main indications of a hierarchy are discussed below, including court seating protocols. The arguable indicators of a chief judge position are also discussed below. In addition, see the viewpoint of the sages in *m. Sanh.* 1:6 about Moses being distinct from the seventy elders (but this may just be a way of calculating an odd number for majority rule, see *t. Sanh.* 3:9); an ambiguous line in *Sifre Deut.* 144 about *ehad al gabei kulam* (although the context makes it sound like it is referring to a supreme tribunal rather than an individual). See also Flatto, *Between Royal Absolutism and an Independent Judiciary,* 400–401.

33. See, e.g., *Sifre Deut.* 144; *m. Hor.* 1:1–5; *m. Sanh.* 11:2.

34. See, e.g., *m. Sanh.* 1:1–6; *t. Sanh.* 7:1.

35. The biblical elders only serve as loose precursor for institutional justice. See Chapter 6.

36. The context is R. Dosa b. Hyrkanus cautioning R. Joshua not to defy the binding ruling of the Yavneh court (led by Rabban Gamliel). Underscoring this point, R. Dosa cites the following homily.

37. Likewise, R. Dosa focuses upon, not the towering authority of R. Gamliel, but instead the binding authority of a tribunal of three.

38. *M. Ros. Has.* 2:9 suggests an equivalence among courts of all sizes, in contrast with sources that envision a hierarchy among the tiers of courts, such as *m. Sanh.* 1:1–6;

m. Sanh. 11:2; and perhaps *Sifre Deut.* 144. See also the principle of *gadol be-hokhma u-ve-minyan* (*m. Ed.* 1:5). Note, incidentally, the striking fact that this principle grades the collective body, rather than the (much easier to gauge) status of individuals (which one can conjecture was perhaps the original meaning of this principle; see *m. Abot* 5:7). I hope to explore this principle and its relationship to the themes analyzed herein in a separate study.

39. To be sure, limited hierarchies in the court can conform with these aims, assuming they are just conferring respect on more-senior judges, and / or intending to safeguard each judge's voice. See notes 49, 54, 59, and 86. But hierarchies can reflect or enable the domination of a leading figure, or subset of figures.

40. See *t. Sanh.* 7:1; *t. Hag.* 2:9; *Mekh.* Rabbi Ishmael 18:21; *Sifre Deut.* 13; *Midrash Tannaim Deut.* 1:15, 16:18.

41. See, e.g., *T. Sanh.* 7:1, which identifies the same set of characteristics for all judges, even as it recognizes different tiers of tribunals and implies that there is a method for promoting judges from one tier to the next.

42. *B. Sanh.* 17a.

43. Of course, I am not claiming that these standards were ever implemented, let alone achieved. Some of them are clearly idealized. Nevertheless, the ideal is to appoint similar judges. Contrast this with the modern desideratum of judicial diversity. See, e.g., Richard A. Posner, *The Federal Courts: Challenge and Reform* (Cambridge, Mass.: Harvard University Press, 2009), 16ff.

44. Numerous rabbinic sources endorse majority rule. See Flatto, *Between Royal Absolutism and an Independent Judiciary,* 403n164.

45. See *m. Sanh.* 5:5.

46. See also *m. Sanh.* 5:4, which states that when a student has a meritorious argument on behalf of a defendant, he is installed among the judges.

47. See *m. Sanh.* 3:7.

48. The latter is the connotation of the Mishnah's citation of Lev 19:16.

49. See also *y. Sanh.* 3:7; *b. Sanh.* 30a. Notably, *m. Sanh.* 3:7 affirms the role of a chief judge, even as it merges his opinion into the court (i.e., he may be the dissenter who has to announce the majority position as the court's holding). This reflects the subtlety of certain sources, and demonstrates that the position of a chief judge can coexist with the majority rule principle, and does not necessarily destabilize the overall egalitarian nature of institutional justice.

50. There is a certain tension between the themes of this paragraph and the prior one, even though they are not mutually exclusive. Arguably, each judge's voice matters for the collective viewpoint, but the impact of any one voice in isolation is minimal.

51. So justice does not depend on a leading figure, or a given subset of influential judges.

52. See *m. Sanh.* 11:2 (see Chapter 6).

53. See *m. Sanh.* 4:3.

54. Note that even in a hierarchical arrangement, the integrity of each judge's vote may be protected by following a prescribed voting order. See note 39.

55. The various protocols and procedures listed in the above paragraphs may coexist, or may be in some tension with one another. See, e.g., note 50. They do not necessarily follow from one another, and there is little reason to think that they were formulated in concert. Still, they all are consistent with a broader jurisprudential orientation, as emphasized below.

56. Alt. senior. It is unclear what the metric is for determining seniority: age, merit, teaching position, reputation, etc. (one source quoted below about the *Ab Bet Din* even refers to a bequeathal of this title). It would appear that some of these metrics are more consonant with an aspiration for a level court (for instance, age, which is an objective metric).

57. See also the alternate position (on noncapital matters) recorded in the Yerushalmi ad loc. (cited in Chapter 6).

58. See *t. Sanh.* 8:2. While these Tosefta sources recognize a gradation among the various tribunals and the rows of students, there is no set hierarchy within each tribunal or row. Evidently all members of a given tribunal or row are on par. See also *t. Sanh.* 7:1.

59. Indeed, the egalitarian construct of institutional justice described above is easiest to envision with a level court. But see note 39. A hierarchical judiciary, in turn, can be understood as a variant of institutional justice; a vestige of a royal or individual template; or a reflection of a mounting hierarchy that arises due to a political intervention. See below.

60. See the references cited in note 32. See also Gerald Blidstein, "On the Character of the *Nesiut* in the Halakhic Teachings of Maimonides," *Shenaton Hamishpat Haivri* 20 (1997): 38–43.

61. But see note 32.

62. *M. Sanh.* 3:7, 4:2; *Sifra Kedoshim, Parsha* 2:4; *t. Sanh.* 7:7.

63. *M. Ros. Has.* 2:7; *m. Ros. Has.* 4:4.

64. *M. Hor.* 1:4; *Sifre Deut.* 152.

65. *Lev. Rab., Parsha* 2, *Siman* 3. Interestingly, tannaitic sources do not describe R. Eleazar b. Azariah as head of the yeshiva, but as joining the yeshiva. See *m. Zebah.* 1:3; *m. Yad.* 3:5; *t. Ed.* 3:1. See also Catherine Heszer, *The Social Structure of the Rabbinic Movement in Roman Palestine* (Tübingen: Mohr Siebeck, 1997), 198–199.

66. *Sifre Deut.* 144. See note 32.

67. See the analysis of this term below. Other relevant terms may include: *zaqen* (*m. Ta'an.* 2:1; *t. Seqal.* 3:27; *t. Sanh.* 8:1); and *parnas* (*Sifre Deut.* 162; *b. Hor.* 13b).

68. Arguably, as powerful judges exercised more influence on increasingly hierarchical courts, they assumed leadership roles, and these labels reflect their rise in prominence.

69. See Mantel, *Mehqarim*, 50–51 (citing Jelski's hypothesis); and Adolf Buchler, *Ha-Sanhedrin* [Hebrew] (Jerusalem: Mosad ha-Rav Ḳuḳ, 1974), 152–156.

70. See also *b. B. Qam.* 74b; Chanoch Albeck, "Semikhah ve-Minuy Bet Din" [Hebrew], *Zion* 8 (1943): 91.

71. See the parallel *Derekh Eretz, Perek Haminin,* 25.

72. See the Mishnah of the Bavli. The manuscripts, by contrast, refer to the *Bet Din.* See Buchler, *Ha-Sanhedrin,* 152. Perhaps the early phase reflected in the manuscripts focuses on the entire institution, while the latter phase reflected in the Bavli focuses on a chief judge, an *Ab Bet Din.* Arguably, over time the court becomes more hierarchical.

73. Buchler argues that such sources reflect a later phase, when the Patriarch was already weakened. *Ha-Sanhedrin,* 154–156. This seems implausible in light of contemporary scholarship's dating of the ascension of the Patriarchate to a later phase.

74. Yalkut Devarim 18: 815 (the Yalkut is a later collection, but may contain some earlier materials). See Buchler, *Ha-Sanhedrin,* 156.

75. If the *Nasi* is a legal official, it would arguably be sufficient for him to officiate alone. Likewise, one would expect him to lead the admonition recital (instead this is assigned to the *zaqen*). But see *m. Ta'an.* 1:5–7, which describes a distinctive role for the court in fast-day rites. This may imply that these officials are all members of the court.

76. See *Sifra Kedoshim* 10:7; *b. Sanh.* 66a. See also Mantel, *Mehqarim,* 52–53; and Blidstein, "On the Character," 44n52.

77. See also *Sifre Zuta Num.* 35:22, which refers to *Nasi, dayan,* and *dayan be-Bet Din Hagadol.*

78. The Oxford, Munich, and Vatican manuscripts refer to Ahaz. The printed Horvitz edition refers to Ahav. The Geniza fragments and first edition omit this line altogether.

79. See the parallel accounts in *y. Pesah.* 6:1; *b. Pesah.* 66a.

80. See *b. Mo'ed Qat.* 22b; see also *y. Mo'ed Qat.* 3:7; *Sem.* 9:2.

81. This source (and parallels) bestows greater honor upon the *Nasi* than upon the *Ab Bet Din* and *hakham.*

82. See, e.g., *t. Sanh.* 7:8; *b. Hor.* 13b; *b. Mo'ed Qat.* 17a.

83. Distinguishing between the Mishnah and other tannaitic sources raises the question of the respective dating of these materials. In the synoptic case discussed shortly, the Mishnah seems to preserve an earlier strata. But a concluding gloss may be later, in any event. See note 84.

84. See Gedalyahu Alon, "The Patriarchate of Rabbi Johanan ben Zakkai," in *Studies in Jewish History in the Times of the Second Temple, the Mishna and the Talmud* (Tel Aviv: Hakibbutz Hameuchad, 1967), 254n4. Daniel Boyarin argues that this line is "an artifact of the latest editing of the Mishna." Boyarin, *Border Lines: The Partition of Judaeo-Christianity* (Philadelphia: University of Pennsylvania Press, 2004), 81.

85. See David M. Goodblatt, *The Monarchic Principle: Studies in Jewish Self-Government in Antiquity* (Tübingen: Mohr [Siebeck], 1994), 185–186.

86. The relationship between *m. Sanh.* 4:2, 4 (the seating and voting order) and 4:3 (seating configuration) requires further study. They may be inconsistent, but—certainly as redacted—they can be harmonized. See note 90.

87. This reconstruction seems likely, as the Mishnah is straightforward, and the Tosefta's additional clause seems to undermine the parity achieved by the Mishnah's seating arrangement.

88. The Yerushalmi's emendation relocates and adapts the explanatory clause ("so that they all might see . . .") to better integrate the *Nasi* interpolation, and thereby transforms the purpose of the seating arrangement, the role of the *Nasi*, and the distribution of authority within the judiciary.

      The change in the purpose of the "half of a round threshing-floor (*hatsi goren*)" seating configuration reflected in these sources is partially enabled by its dual function. In *m. Mid.* 2:5, the Levites are described as standing in this configuration during Temple service, where they presumably act in concert (but see *m. Seqal.* 5:1 and *m. Tamid.* 7:2–4 on their hierarchy). In contrast, *Exod Rab., Parsha* 5 represents the king presiding before his court, and God before the future assembly of elders, seated in this configuration. Arguably, *M. Sanh.* 4:3 invokes the egalitarian model reflected in *Middot*, while *y. Sanh.* 1:6 invokes the hierarchical model reflected in *Exod Rab.*

89. Maimonides *Hil. Sanhedrin* 1:3's account of the seating configuration represents a fourth iteration. See also Blidstein, "On the Character," 26n4.

90. *M. Sanh.* 4:2, 4, which depicts a set arrangement for the judges and disciples, may reflect a different rabbinic viewpoint, but not necessarily; perhaps these passages only relate to the order in which the judges vote and are promoted.

91. Alongside the synoptic textual evidence, my chronological reconstruction is based upon the dearth of references to the *Nasi* as chief judge in the Mishnah.

92. Historical developments likely spur this programmatic reconfiguration. See below.

93. See *t. Sanh.* 8:1, which cites this tradition in the name of R. Elazar b. Zadok. See also Haim Shapira, "The Study Hall in the Late Second Temple Era and Mishnaic Period: Institutional and Philosophical Perspectives" [Hebrew] (PhD diss., Hebrew University, 2002), 184–192.

94. Even during this phase, the *Nasi* does not command extra voting power.

95. It is difficult to know whether in the Yerushalmi the *Nasi* serves as the focal point in his capacity as a ruler, or whether the term has already morphed into the title of the chief judge and rabbinic head.

96. See Seth Schwartz, "Big-Men or Chiefs: Against an Institutional View of the Palestinian Patriarchate," in *Jewish Religious Leadership: Image and Reality*, ed. J. Wertheimer, vol. 1 (New York: Jewish Theological Seminary Press, 2004), 155–173.

97. Over time, this political office may have evolved into the Patriarchate. While the cumulative power of "big men" may have influenced the formation of the *Nesiut* (Patriarchate), as Schwartz argues, I am inclined to think there was also a prior rabbinic con-

ception (influenced by pre-rabbinic conceptions) of a leadership office. What probably was projected back was the identification of specific figures such as Hillel, etc., as *Nesiim*. What seems less clear is whether the title *Nasi* attached to these figures as a result of their clout or due to their position as leading sages, since by then the term had already become associated with the head of the rabbinic academy and court (see Stern, "Rabbi," 197n12).

98. In theory, one can view these alternate accounts diachronically or synchronically. I am inclined to the former option, given the later appearance of the term *Nasi*, which seems to signal a change.

99. It is, of course, hard to pinpoint the dating of this line. See note 84. In any case, the Yerushalmi may operate with a legal semantic of *Nasi*. See note 95.

An interesting parallel transformation is the change in the late antique Greek nomenclature for *Nasi* from "Ethnarch" to the more commonly used "Patriarch."

Returning to the final transformation of the *Nasi*, it remains difficult to decipher: Was the *Nasi* initially a political figure in fact, whose position then becomes rabbinized? Or was this office merely envisioned as a political one, but in reality it was rabbinic? Or was the *Nasi* originally a prominent rabbi who then amassed political clout (an approach advanced in certain historiographical accounts, but not supported by this source)? See note 97. As Christine Hayes points out, to the extent that this source reflects a process of rabbinization of the *Nasi*, it should be considered alongside a broader rabbinic "program" of "rabbinizing" positions of authority.

100. See *m. Hag.* 2:2; *t. Hag.* 2:8; *y. Pesah.* 6:1; *y. Ber.* 4:1 (*y. Ta'an.* 4:1); and *Deut Rab., Parsha* 2, *Siman* 19. The other sources that depict the *Nasi* before or above the *Ab Bet Din* (e.g., *m. Ta'an.* 2:1; *t. Sanh.* 7:8; *y. Mo'ed Qat.* 3:7; *b. Mo'ed Qat.* 22b–23a, 26a) may be conceiving of an autonomous political figure, alongside the rabbinic judiciary or academy.

101. See the analysis of *Semahot* 9:19; *b. Mo'ed Qat.* 26a; *t. Sanh.* 7:8; *b. Hor.* 13b; *b. Mo'ed Qat.* 17a; and other references in Flatto, *Between Royal Absolutism and an Independent Judiciary*, 364n57.

102. This last shift was perhaps enabled by the fact that the early Patriarchate operated within rabbinic circles, and also played an important juridical role. At the same time, rabbinic literature even depicts an increasingly non-rabbinic Patriarchate as rabbinic in origin in order to maintain the social role of the rabbinic class. See Seth Schwartz, *The Ancient Jews from Alexander to Muhammad* (Cambridge: Cambridge University Press, 2014), 119.

103. The analogous process, however, may have transpired at a later time period. See below.

104. Historically, rulers have used this capacity to influence the court's jurisprudence. With the modern ascent of independent judiciaries, there have been increasing attempts to curb this effect. Nevertheless: "The power to make judicial appointments is the most important check on judicial policy." Kermit L. Hall et al., eds., *The Oxford Companion to American Law* (Oxford: Oxford University Press, 2002), 442.

105. It is likely that during the early rabbinic period there was no formal appointment process, and that this only developed over time. Still, certain schematic sources examined below speak in more formal terms.

106. See, e.g., the references in Heszer, *The Social Structure of the Rabbinic Movement*, 79–110, 185–213.

107. *Sifre Deut* 13, for example, implies that judicial authority often emanates from a de facto accrual of popular support. From a normative perspective, however, it likely requires a formal appointment, as seen from the Sifre's continuation.

108. It is worth noting that recent scholarship has challenged the assumption that *semikhah* and *minuy* refer to the appointment of judges. See Shapira, "The Court in Yavneh," 328–333. Yet even this revisionist position acknowledges that these terms connote an authorization for other legal functions (e.g., voting on rabbinic legislation). Moreover, scholarly skepticism pertains only to tannaitic literature's earlier strata. All agree that in layers following the Bar Kochba generation an appointee had judicial responsibilities. Finally, the earlier scholarly consensus operated with the plausible assumption that the purpose of any conferral of a rabbinic license at least also included judicial powers. See Albeck, "Semikhah ve-Minuy Bet Din," 85–93; and Shalom Albeck, *Bate ha-Din bi-Yeme ha-Talmud* (Ramat Gan: Bar-Ilan University Press, 1980), 109–122.

109. See also *m. Sanh.* 1:1; *y. Sanh.* 1:3; *b. Sanh.* 13b–14a. According to *t. Sanh.* 7:1, high-court judges are selected from among the lower-court judges, while according to *m. Sanh.* 4:4, they are selected from among the rows of students that accompany the high court. The Tosefta also refers to such rows (see *t. Sanh.* 8:2, albeit with a less regimented hierarchy; see above), but never states they serve as a supply pool for the high court.

110. Noah Aminoah argues that initially the exemption of an expert was limited to rulings regarding firstborn animals, and later it was expanded to other domains. Aminoah, "Mumhim be-Masoret ha-Halakha," *Dine Yisrael* 8 (1977): 141–168; and Shapira, "The Court in Yavneh," 330–331. The exemption's expansion might also reflect the increasing formalization of the appointment process over the course of the rabbinic period.

111. The court presumably attests to the judge's proficiency. See also *m. Bek.* 4:5, which has a similar connotation.

112. See *Sifre Zuta Num.* 27:19 and *b. Sanh.* 4b–5a, which imply that this designation derives (also) from the people.

113. The depiction of this council or academy is presumably an idealized account of an actual convocation of leading sages. See also Shapira, "The Court in Yavneh," 328–330.

114. See also *t. Ed.* 3:1.

115. See *m. Zeb.* 1:3; *m. Yad.* 3:5, 4:2. See also *Sifre Deut.* 16; *y. Ber.* 4:1.

116. Presumably, *Nasi* here refers to the Patriarch, given that he exercises appointment power according to other sources. Alternatively, it refers generically to a political leader.

117. This seems to be the connotation of the phrase "seats the elders." See Albeck, "Semikhah ve-Minuy Bet Din"; Alon, *"Eleh de-Mitnamnin be-Kesef,"* in *Mehkarim be-Toldot*

Yisrael, vol. 2 (Tel Aviv: Hakibutz Hameuchad, 1958), 15–57. But see Shapira, "The Court in Yavneh," 318–319, 328n111. A legal connotation also emerges from the pericope's reference to the seventy elders of Num 11 (who arguably had legal authority). See also *Sifre Num.* 92.

118. It is plausible that the one "who is appointed to authorize judges" is a political underling (an appointee?) of the Patriarch. See also Alon, "*Eleh de-Mitnamnin be-Kesef,*" 29n58.

119. See Alon, "*Eleh de-Mitnamnin be-Kesef.*" See also Schwartz, *The Ancient Jews,* 120–121; and Lapin, *Rabbis as Romans,* 86–87.

120. On *minuy,* see Lapin, *Rabbis as Romans,* 82–87, and the references on 229n94.

121. Elsewhere, "*minuy*" is used in descriptive accounts, where someone is appointed as a *zaqen, hacham, parnas,* or without a referent, and recent scholarship has questioned whether historically these roles or titles included judicial responsibilities. See note 108. In any event, "*minuy*" clearly has a juridical connotation in this Yerushalmi. See Shapira, "The Court in Yavneh," 329–330.

122. See also Louis Ginzberg, *Commentary on the Palestinian Talmud,* vol. 3 [Hebrew] (New York: Jewish Theological Seminary, 1941), 178; and Albeck, "Semikhah ve-Minuy Bet Din," 85–86.

123. Lapin, *Rabbis as Romans,* 85–86.

124. *Maimonides Hilkhot Sanhedrin* 4:5 records *Ab Bet Din* instead of *Bet Din.* See also Alon, "*Eleh de-Mitnamnin be-Kesef,*" 33n77.

125. Sages evidently continued to exercise certain appointment power even later on. See *t. Ta'an* 1:7; *y. Hag.* 1:7; *y. Ned.* 11:10.

126. There are also, no doubt, social reasons for this framing. See note 102.

127. This phase is of dubious historicity. In contrast, the first two phases likely have a historical basis, even if the normative structure attributed to them is superimposed.

128. See Flatto, *Between Royal Absolutism and an Independent Judiciary,* 378–383.

129. Recasting is a way of responding to the Patriarch's intervention in legal affairs.

130. Interestingly, the topics of these two sections—hierarchy and appointment—intersect in a segment of this Yerushalmi passage (i.e., R. Simeon's jealousy of R. Meir); and also in *y. Ros. Has.* 2:6 (i.e., "to proclaim an intercalation we go by the *minuy*").

131. See also Steven D. Fraade, *Legal Fictions: Studies in Law and Narrative in the Discursive Worlds of Ancient Jewish Sectarians and Sages* (Leiden: Brill, 2011), 323–344.

132. Recall the Talmudic texts that override the separation in other respects, analyzed in Chapter 5.

133. See also *y. Ros. Has.* 1:3; *b. Ros. Has.* 16a; *b. Abod. Zar.* 2b; *Num. Rab., Parsha* 13.

134. It also discusses reinstating the high priest after he is punished.

135. Although this episode appears in Yerushalmi Sanhedrin, its original context is Horayot. Responding to *m. Hor.* 3:1, which discusses the laws of a high priest and *Nasi* (= king) who sin (accidentally), *y. Hor.* 3:1 relays Resh Laqish's teaching regarding a contemporary *Nasi* (= Patriarch) who sins (deliberately).

136. When *y. Hor.* 3:1 is read against the background of Mishnah Horayot it is also problematic. Although the Mishnah declares the *Nasi* blameworthy, and obligates a sacrificial atonement for his accidental sin, he still remains immune from judgment in court (see *m. Hor.* 2:6).

137. While the former option seems less likely, recall that *y. Sanh.* 2:2 countermands the Mishnah and states that a king can serve as a judge (see Chapter 5), which raises the possibility of a symmetric ruling that a king is judged (even though the Yerushalmi states that a king is not judged in a human court, perhaps Resh Laqish teaches otherwise). See also the Sifre Zuta and Tanhuma about judging the king analyzed in David C. Flatto, "Justice Retold: The Seminal Narrations of the Trial of the Judean King," *Journal of Law and Religion* 30, no. 1 (2015): 20–24.

138. The concern of shielding powerful men from legal accountability is no doubt heightened when they have arrogated to themselves legal powers.

139. Of course, enforcing this revised rule is untenable, as is seen in the continuation of the Resh Laqish narrative.

140. See the parallel account in *Gen. Rab., Parsha* 80.

141. *Gen. Rab.* reads, "the members of the house of the Patriarch" instead of "the king."

142. The above passage differentiates between priestly and royal prerogatives. See also *y. Hor.* 3:4, which states that priests may not serve as kings. Both passages, which resonate with passages surveyed in Chapter 5 (including *m. Sanh.* 2:1–2), may reflect a critique of the Hasmonean dynasty, which combined these roles.

143. See 2 Chron 31:4.

144. See note 141.

145. See note 148.

146. The homily exhibits poetic justice: because the king violated the boundaries of the priests, he will no longer be buffered from legal judgment.

147. In later rabbinic literature, the king's subordination to the law is at times more far-reaching. See, e.g., *b. B. Qam.* 60b, describing King David's inquiry into the halakhic parameters of his royal prerogative to act above the law(!).

148. Even though the transgressions of the priests and House of Israel do not have a valid excuse, their sins are considered to be an outgrowth of sovereign rule gone astray. A corrupt ruler is thus the ultimate cause of society's transgressions.

149. While these passages focus on particular leaders, they may suggest that rulers in general tend to become powerful and corrupt, akin to 1 Samuel 8:11–21; or in the famous words of Lord Acton, "Power tends to corrupt, and absolute power corrupts absolutely." *Essays on Freedom and Power*, ed. Gertrude Himmelfarb (Boston: Beacon Press, 1948), 364.

150. Two other Yerushalmi passages in this same chapter relate to this final turn. See *y. Sanh.* 2:6 on the deposal of King Solomon due to his violation of the law (Torah), and, from a different vantage point, the royal aura of the legal master, R. Hizqiyyah. See also *b. Gittin* 62a; *b. Ketub.* 105b; *b. Sanh.* 7b; Flatto, *Between Royal Absolutism and an Independent Judiciary*, 392–395.

151. A different kind of response to an intractable conflict is recorded in the Bavli's rendition of the Jannaeus trial: erecting a strong partition between law and politics, not as an ideal form of separation (i.e., the mishnaic scheme), but as an exigent act of self-preservation. See Chapter 5; and Flatto, "Justice Retold," 13–20.

8. Formative Factors

1. Philo, too, expounds upon Deut 17, but still depicts the ruler's principal role in administering justice.

2. See Julius Wellhausen, *Prolegomena to the History of Ancient Israel* (Gloucester, Mass.: Peter Smith, 1973), chapter 11; Tacitus, *Hist.* 5.1–13.

3. See, e.g., Jon D. Levenson, *Sinai and Zion* (San Francisco: Harper & Row, 1987), 42–45. But see David P. Wright, *Inventing God's Law: How the Covenant Code of the Bible Used and Revised the Laws of Hammurabi* (Oxford: Oxford University Press, 2009), 3–28.

4. Most scholars situate Deuteronomy, including Deut 16–17, within a monarchic framework. See the commentary of Bernard M. Levinson in Adele Berlin and Marc Zvi Brettler, eds., *The Jewish Study Bible,* 2nd ed. (New York: Oxford University Press, 2014), 357.

5. I refer to ideas about law and legal authority in works that are not analyzed in this book, such as 1 *Macc.,* 2 *Macc.,* and *Aristeas.*

6. Recent scholarship has challenged the conventional account of post-destruction Judaism as powerless, and highlighted various forms of Jewish power that materialized throughout the centuries of Diaspora life. See David Biale, *Power and Powerlessness in Jewish History* (New York: Schocken Books, 1986); and Ruth R. Wisse, *Jews and Power* (New York: Nextbook, 2007).

7. See the nuanced discussion of early Christian attitudes towards law and commandments in Jon D. Levenson, *Inheriting Abraham* (Princeton, N.J.: Princeton University Press, 2012), 149–163.

8. A substantial growth of canon law happened only in a later period of empowerment.

9. This undoubtedly is a result of the fact that Christians were not just responding to disempowerment but also informed by the Pauline rejection of aspects of the legalism of carnal Israel.

10. See, e.g., Robert M. Cover, "The Supreme Court, 1982 Term—Foreword: Nomos and Narrative," *Harvard Law Review* 97 (1983): 4; and Michael Walzer, "Introduction: The Jewish Political Tradition," in *The Jewish Political Tradition,* vol. 1, *Authority,* ed. Michael Walzer et al. (New Haven, Conn.: Yale University Press, 2000), xxi–xxxi.

11. Bailyn borrows this concept from the art critic Kenneth Clark. Bernard Bailyn, *To Begin the World Anew: The Genius and Ambiguities of the American Founders* (New York: Knopf, 2003), 6–8.

12. To be clear, I am not claiming that the impetus for the formulation of early Jewish jurisprudence was purely ideational. Presumably there were also pragmatic or strategic

reasons for it and its rhetoric, some of which I have gestured at in the chapters above. But whatever the impetus, the political conditions helped nurture, or at least enable, the formulation of certain striking jurisprudential ideas.

13. Another (related) challenge was the limited ability to enforce the law throughout most of Jewish history over the last two millennia. The Deuteronomic jurisprudence of postbiblical writings helped to elevate the role of law, which likely contributed to its self-enforcement at various times and places (even if their discourses imagined enforcing the law).

14. See the sociohistorical analyses interspersed throughout the chapters of this book.

15. See *b. B. Qam.* 2b; *b. Hag.* 10b; and *b. Nidd. 23a.*

16. See Ephraim E. Urbach, "Law and Prophecy," in *The World of the Sages: Collected Studies* [Hebrew] (Jerusalem: Magnes Press, 1988), 21–50.

17. See Assaf Rosen-Zvi, "'Even Though There Is No Proof to the Matter, There Is an Indication of the Matter': The Meaning, Character and Significance of the Phrase in the Tannaitic Literature" [Hebrew], *Tarbiz* 78, no. 3 (2009): 323.

18. See also *y. Meg.* 1:7; *b. Ned.* 22b.

19. See, e.g., *b. Shab.* 13b.

20. See, e.g., *m. Meg.* 3:1; *t. Meg.* 3:20; *Sifra Behukotai* 13:7; *y. Meg.* 1:5, 7; *b. Tem.* 16a. See also A. Rosen-Zvi, "Even Though There Is No Proof to the Matter,'" 343–344.

21. See, e.g., John J. Collins, *The Invention of Judaism* (Oakland: University of California Press, 2017), 21–61; Gary N. Knoppers and Bernard M. Levinson, eds., *The Pentateuch as Torah: New Models for Understanding Its Promulgation and Acceptance* (Winona Lake, Ind.: Eisenbrauns, 2007).

22. For "*Torat Moshe,*" see Josh 8:31–32; 1 Kgs 2:3; 2 Kgs 14:6, 23:25; Mal. 3:22; Dan 9:11, 13; Ezra 3:2, 7:6; Neh 8:1; 2 Chron 23:18, 30:16. For "*Sefer Moshe,*" see 2 Kgs 14:6; Ezra 6:18; Neh 13:1; 2 Chron 25:4, 35:12.

23. See, e.g., Sara Japhet, "'Law' and 'The Law' in Ezra and Nehemia," in *From the Rivers of Babylon to the Highlands of Judah: Collected Studies on the Restoration Period* (Winona Lake, Ind.: Eisenbrauns, 2006), 137–151.

24. The Samaritans attributed the entire Pentateuch to Moses. See N. Sarna and S. Sperling, "Bible: The Canon, Text, and Edition," in *Encyclopedia Judaica,* ed. F. Skolnik et al., 2nd ed. (New York: Macmillan Reference, 2007), 578.

25. Scholars now speak of a canonical process. The literature is voluminous. See, e.g., John Barton, *A History of the Bible: The Story of the World's Most Influential Book* (New York: Viking, 2019), 215–238; Timothy H. Lim, *The Formation of the Jewish Canon* (New Haven, Conn.: Yale University Press, 2013).

26. See Benjamin D. Sommers, "Psalms 1 and the Canonical Shaping of Jewish Scripture," in *Jewish Bible Theology: Perspectives and Case Studies,* ed. Isaac Kalimi (Winona Lake, Ind.: Eisenbrauns, 2012), 208–210.

27. See, e.g., Tessa Rajak, *Translation and Survival: The Greek Bible of the Ancient Jewish Diaspora* (Oxford: Oxford University Press, 2009), 20–23. See also Alex P. Jassen, *Scrip-*

ture and Law in the Dead Sea Scrolls (New York: Cambridge University Press, 2014), 53–54.

28. See Jassen, *Scripture and Law in the Dead Sea Scrolls*, 7–11.

29. See, e.g., Shani Tzoref, "Qumran Pesharim and the Pentateuch: Explicit Citation, Overt Typologies, and Implicit Interpretive Traditions," *Dead Sea Discoveries* 16, no. 2 (2009): 190–220.

30. See Michael Segal, "Biblical Interpretation—Yes and No," in *What Is Bible?*, ed. K. Finsterbusch and A. Lange (Leuven: Peeters, 2012), 67–80.

31. See Timothy H. Lim, "Authoritative Scriptures and the Dead Sea Scrolls," in *The Oxford Handbook of the Dead Sea Scrolls*, ed. Timothy H. Lin and John J. Collins (Oxford: Oxford University Press, 2010), 307–314; and Jassen, *Scripture and Law in the Dead Sea Scrolls*, 46–55.

32. Gershon Brin records thirteen such references. Brin, *Studies in the Prophetic Literature* (Jerusalem: Mosad Bialik, 2006), 381–398.

33. See Shani Tzoref, "The Use of Scripture in the Community Rule," in *A Companion to Biblical Interpretation in Early Judaism*, ed. Matthias Henze (Grand Rapids, Mich.: Eerdmans, 2012), 203–234.

34. See Alex P. Jassen, "The Presentation of the Ancient Prophets as Lawgivers at Qumran," *Journal of Biblical Literature* 127 (2008): 307–337.

35. See also Pesher Hosea (4Q166) 2:3–5, 4Q390 Frag. 2I:5, and (the broader implication of) 4Q375:1–8.

36. See Jassen, *Scripture and the Law in the Dead Sea Scrolls*, 334–335.

37. This is in consonance with the conclusion of Jassen's study.

38. See Jassen, *Scripture and the Law in the Dead Sea Scrolls*, 247–252.

39. This requirement also serves as an anchor for, and a limit on, the judges' rulings.

40. This does not deny that exegesis of extra-Pentateuchal Scripture may also be a source of law. But see the non-Scriptural account of legal authority in Paul D. Mandel, *The Origins of Midrash: From Teaching to Text* (Leiden: Brill, 2017), 87–88, 123–125.

41. See, e.g., Tzoref, "The Use of Scripture in the Community Rule," 230.

42. See James C. Vanderkam, "Authoritative Literature in the Dead Sea Scrolls," *Dead Sea Discoveries* 5 (1998): 382. In the Temple Scroll, Deuteronomy's role is further intensified, as it is reworded as direct revelation. See also Hindy Najman, *Seconding Sinai: The Development of Mosaic Discourse in Second Temple Judaism* (Boston: Brill, 2003), 41–69.

43. An additional function of prophetic texts in Qumran is to serve as a foundation for predicting the present and future of the sect.

44. See 1QpHab 2:1–10, 7:2–5. See also Michael Fishbane, "Use, Authority and Interpretation of Mikra at Qumran," in *Mikra: Reading and Interpretation of the Hebrew Bible in Ancient Judaism and Early Christianity*, ed. Martin Jan Mulder (Philadelphia: Fortress, 1988), 361–362.

45. See Aharon Shemesh, "Halakhah between the Scrolls and Rabbinic Literature," in Lin and Collins, *The Oxford Handbook of the Dead Sea Scrolls*, 600–605. But see note 40.

46. See, e.g., his extraordinary praise of the Mosaic laws in *Ant.* 3.223, *Ag. Ap.* 2.145–186, and numerous other *Apion* 2 passages cited in Chapter 4.

47. See *Ant.* 3.224–286, 4.196–301; *Ag. Ap.* 2.190–218.

48. Josephus refers to twenty-two biblical books. See *Ag. Ap.* 1.37–41.

49. Similarly, Josephus relied on postbiblical sources for the subsequent events that he covers in *Antiquities* 11–20, and he derives lessons from these materials as well.

50. See Louis H. Feldman, *Josephus's Interpretation of the Bible* (Berkeley: University of California Press, 1998), 37–46.

51. See, e.g., *Moses* 2.12–14. See also Najman, *Seconding Sinai*, 70–106.

52. This generalization does not extend to his short philosophical treatises.

53. See Naomi G. Cohen, *Philo's Scriptures: Citations from the Prophets and Writings; Evidence for a Haftarah Cycle in Second Temple Judaism* (Boston: Brill, 2007), 25–54.

54. See *Decalogue* 154.

55. For references and analysis, see Cohen, *Philo's Scriptures*, 1–54.

56. See Cohen, *Philo's Scriptures*, 175–198; and David T. Runia, "Philo's Reading of the Psalms," *Studia Philonica Annual* 13 (2001): 102–121.

57. See Urbach, "Law and Prophecy," 22n16.

58. See the analysis of the concept of a living law in Chapter 2.

59. Christine Hayes, *What's Divine about Divine Law? Early Perspectives* (Princeton, N.J.: Princeton University Press, 2015), 114 (citing Adele Reinhartz).

60. See Najman, *Seconding Sinai*, 70–106.

61. This also explains why Philo bases his version of royal justice analyzed in Chapter 2 on Exod 18 and Deut 17, notwithstanding the exegetical challenges this raises, rather than on more obvious non-Pentateuchal sources.

62. See David C. Flatto, "Constructing Justice: The Selective Use of Scripture in Formulating Early Jewish Accounts of the Courts," *Harvard Theological Review* 111, no. 4 (2018): 504–508.

63. Another example of the plurality of interpretive options is the diverse rabbinic attitudes toward monarchy, reflected in their commentary on Deut 17.

64. This function became more central over time. Aspects of this historical process are surveyed in Collins, *The Invention of Judaism.*

65. Marc Z. Brettler, "Torah," in Berlin and Brettler, *The Jewish Study Bible,* 1–2.

66. See Jassen, *Scripture and the Law in the Dead Sea Scrolls,* 52n39.

67. Consider, for example, the foil of New Testament literature, which derives numerous teachings from a cross section of Hebrew Bible verses. See, e.g., G. K. Beale and D. A. Carson, eds., *Commentary on the New Testament Use of the Old Testament* (Ada, Mich.: Baker Academic, 2007).

68. James L. Kugel, "Some Unanticipated Consequences of the Sinai Revelation: A Religion of Laws," in *The Significance of Sinai: Traditions about Sinai and Divine Revelation*

in Judaism and Christianity, ed. George J. Brooke, Hindy Najman, and Loren T. Stuckenbruck (Leiden: Brill, 2008), 7–8.

69. Accordingly, when Kugel describes Josephus's motivations in writing *Antiquities,* he omits Josephus's emphasis on the value of obeying the law.

70. The three models are outlined in Moshe Halbertal, "God's Kingship," in Walzer et al., *The Jewish Political Tradition,* 1:128–132, and evaluated in Yair Lorberbaum, *Disempowered King: Monarchy in Classical Jewish Literature* (New York: Continuum, 2011), 1–36. But see Doron Mendels, *Why Did Paul Go West? Jewish Historical Narrative and Thought* (London: Bloomsbury, 2013), 145n5.

71. See the Introduction, note 20.

72. See Halbertal, "God's Kingship," 128–132.

73. See Marc Z. Brettler, *God Is King: Understanding an Israelite Metaphor* (Sheffield, UK: Sheffield Academic Press, 1989), 44–45, 76–78, 109–116.

74. This formulation (i.e., suggesting that a vacuum triggers a crisis, which is then resolved) is only used for expository purposes and is not meant literally; rather, it is intended to highlight that a reduction in the scope of royal power makes room for other leadership figures.

75. See note 72; see also Moshe Halbertal and Avishai Margalit, *Idolatry,* trans. Naomi Goldblum (Cambridge, Mass: Harvard University Press, 1992), 214–235.

76. See 1 Sam. 8:11–17, 20.

77. To be sure, Halbertal is more focused on Samuel and the overall typologies of kingship, than on Deut 17 (and its afterlife).

78. See the Introduction.

79. Classifying legal authority as sacral may be even more essential for works authored in a post-Temple and post-prophetic age, as law becomes the primary vehicle of revelation and religious life. See below.

80. I thank Moshe Halbertal for this suggestion. The Sinaitic Covenant, where God the Suzerain instructs all of Israel in the laws, can certainly be conceptualized in this manner. See the Introduction. This line of thinking is also implicit in Chapter 4. At the same time, the category of royal justice obviously has different resonances when applied to God versus a terrestrial ruler. Of course, this book's focus is on the (latter and other forms of) human administration of justice. See also note 106.

81. The (divine) sovereign can also enforce the law by way of (divine) punishment (in contrast with the models of postbiblical jurisprudence that cannot be enforced in practice).

82. Likewise, royal justice mirrors a royalist theology (although one could easily imagine a more secular account of monarchy also espousing royal justice solely on political grounds).

83. See Martin Buber, *Kingship of God* (New York: Harper & Row, 1967), 61–62. See also David C. Flatto, "Theocracy and the Rule of Law: A Novel Josephan Doctrine and Its Modern Misconceptions," *Dine Israel* 28 (2011): 5–30. Further, traditions that trumpet

the kingship of God do not necessarily preclude human kingship (e.g., 1 Samuel 8), and ample biblical sources invest legal authority in the hands of the latter (see the Introduction).

84. The foil of certain Christian theological writings again comes to mind, where the kingdom of God demands absolute faith and devotion, but not legal obeisance.

   Another indication of the possible incongruity between the juridical and monarchic templates is the fact that the weaker and stronger jurisprudence are anomalous in the Bible, whereas the two monarchic responses to a royalist theology are mainstream ideas.

85. See Chapter 4.

86. See, e.g., Haim Shapira, "'For the Judgment Is God's': On the Metaphysics of Judging" [Hebrew], *Bar-Ilan Law Review* 26 (2010): 51–89.

87. Rabbinic literature at times portrays the halakhah as an autonomous realm; and mastering and fulfilling its dictates as the exclusive mode of serving God (at least following the Temple's destruction). See, e.g., *b. Ber.* 8a.

88. A robust system of Jewish law structures late antique rabbinic society. I explored certain social-legal implications of this phenomenon in a lecture titled "Who Is Wicked? Adapting Witness Disqualification Standards," presented at the Columbia University Conference in Honor of David Weiss Halivni, May 2005.

89. Indeed, all three of these initial factors point in the direction of a fourth factor—disempowerment is addressed in part by further cultivating a distinctive legal ideology; the special canonical status of Deuteronomy (and the Pentateuch) is largely due to the primacy of its norms; and God's kingship is especially manifest through the rule of law.

90. See Steven D. Fraade, *Legal Fictions: Studies of Law and Narrative in the Discursive Worlds of Ancient Jewish Sectarians and Sages* (Leiden; Boston: Brill, 2011), 209. Like the Sinaitic Covenant, Deuteronomy also arguably takes the form of a treaty. See note 97. On the relationship of Deuteronomy to Exodus's Sinaitic Covenant, see, e.g., Bernard M. Levinson, *Deuteronomy and the Hermeneutics of Legal Innovation* (New York: Oxford University Press, 1997), 98–118; and the studies of Jeffrey Stackert, Marc Brettler, and John Van Seters, among others.

91. Several related studies are collected in John T. Strong and Steven S. Tuell, eds., *Constituting the Community: Studies on the Polity of Ancient Israel in Honor of S. Dean McBride, Jr.* (Winona Lake, Ind.: Eisenbrauns, 2005).

92. See other examples in Fraade, *Legal Fictions*, 213–225.

93. Whereas Deut 5 has clear signs of dependency on Exodus's Sinaitic account, primary covenantal motifs also surface elsewhere in Deuteronomy, in particular Deut 17, as explained below. Only after highlighting these elements within the Sinai Covenant, and then turning to their recurrence in Deuteronomy and beyond, can the full thrust of Deuteronomy 17 and its postbiblical afterlife be appreciated. The repeated convergence

of these elements in subsequent writings suggests that these are constitutive elements of an essential early Jewish conception of law and legal authority.

94. See Levenson, *Sinai and Zion*, 42–50.

95. Often these Sinaitic innovations are highlighted for the surprising ways the Bible deploys royal metaphors, and transforms absolutist motifs. While the Bible in numerous places portrays God as the supreme king, it also depicts mankind or Israel in royal terms. A similar construct may inform how the Bible structures the administration of justice: God the Suzerain issues laws; the Vassal Israelites exercise legal authority as royal emissaries; and so on.

Beyond the deployment of royal motifs, though, Sinai represents law as the crucial medium in Israel's relationship with God. More, it espouses a distinct conception of law (marginalizing the influence of powerful figures, etc.). While the Exodus covenant signals that justice must be administered autonomously, it is Deuteronomy (especially Deut 17) that allocates jurisdiction in such a manner. Early Jewish jurisprudential writings, in turn, advance striking permutations of the Deuteronomic scheme in order to uphold the ideal of the primacy of law, which is only enabled when justice is unbound from the shackles of power.

96. See James L. Kugel, *How to Read the Bible: A Guide to Scripture Then and Now* (New York: Free Press, 2007), 240–243.

97. See Weinfeld's discussion about the genre of Deuteronomy—whether it is a code of law or a treaty. Moshe Weinfeld, *Deuteronomy and the Deuteronomic School* (Oxford: Clarendon Press, 1972), 146–157. Either way, law is at the fore.

98. Another way of classifying these chapters is that they are composed of a middle section of Deut 12–26:15, followed by a depositing of the law, and blessings and curses in Deut 27–28. See also Weinfeld, *Deuteronomy and the Deuteronomic School*, 66.

99. See, e.g., Deut 4:6–9, 6:6–9, 10:12–13, 11:18–20, 30:20.

100. See Deut 16:18–20, 17:8–13. Nevertheless, Kugel emphasizes the limits of law beyond the town centers. See Kugel, *How to Read the Bible*, 309–310.

101. This formulation draws on Kugel, "Some Unanticipated Consequences," 11. See also James L. Kugel, *The Great Shift: Encountering God in Biblical Times* (Boston: Houghton Mifflin Harcourt, 2017), 181–186.

102. See Weinfeld, *Deuteronomy and the Deuteronomic School*, 233–235. (Weinfeld refers to this as a "secularization" of the law, but this is a relative matter, and does not preclude my comments in the text near note 79). See also Levinson, *Deuteronomy and Hermeneutics*, 127–129 (Levinson openly emphasizes the sacral nature of Deuteronomy's jurisprudence).

103. Moshe Greenberg highlights the dispersion of political power in the Bible: "In the divinely ordained polity provided for Israel, power is dispersed among the members of society." Alluding to Deut 17, he comments, "No central government is recognized in the laws, except for an isolated paragraph in Deuteronomy that treats the monarchy,

the purpose of this paragraph is to curb the king's appetite for power and prestige." Moshe Greenberg, *Studies in the Bible and Jewish Thought* (Philadelphia: Jewish Publication Society, 1995), 54. In addition, one should also stress how Deut 17's "separation of powers" is emblematic of the Torah's dispersion of *legal* power.

104. See the Introduction.

105. See Simeon Chavel, "The Legal Literature of the Hebrew Bible," in *Literature of the Hebrew Bible: Introductions and Studies* [Hebrew] (Jerusalem: Ben-Zvi Press, 2011), 228–232.

106. See the Introduction, notes 50, 88, and 91.

107. See Fraade, *Legal Fictions,* 212. In particular, Deut 17 offers an "interpretive foundation" for the articulations of postbiblical jurisprudence examined throughout this book.

108. Moshe Halbertal, "The Origins of the Halakhah and the Emergence of the Halakhah" [Hebrew], *Dine Israel* 29 (2013): 1–23.

109. Shapira, "'For the Judgment Is God's,'" 64–77. See also Hayes, *What's Divine about Divine Law?*, 6–8, 168, and, more generally, 166–370.

110. These templates also enhance a wider pursuit of liberty (*herut*). See Shlomo Pines, "On the History of the Term Freedom" [Hebrew], *Iyyun* 33 (1984): 247–265; and Chapter 4.

9. Ancient and Modern Jurisprudence

1. The early Jewish analogs have largely gone unnoticed. Accordingly, modern scholarship conventionally associates concepts such as the separation of powers and an independent judiciary with the American founding fathers, who in turn were inspired by Enlightenment philosophy and political theory. Even studies with a broader historical perspective have identified the origins of these theories in Greco-Roman works. For discussions of the classical origins of these notions, see, e.g., Carl J. Richard, *The Founders and the Classics: Greece, Rome and the American Enlightenment* (Cambridge, Mass.: Harvard University Press, 1995); David A. Richards, *Foundations of American Constitutionalism* (New York: Oxford University Press, 2001); Gilbert Chinard, "Polybius and the American Constitution," in *The American Enlightenment*, ed. Frank Shuffelton (Rochester, N.Y.: University of Rochester Press, 1993), 217–237.

Despite the importance of the classical political tradition as a source for early democratic principles, its relevance for the notion of an independent judiciary is rather limited. Thus, the kernel of the separation of powers doctrine derives from the notion of a mixed constitution advanced by Polybius and later Cicero. Nevertheless, for Polybius and Cicero, the branches that they sought to separate are (to use modern taxonomy) the executive and legislative. Under Polybius's model, judicial responsibility belonged to the consuls and assemblies, and was not allocated separately to an independent body. See David Flatto, "The Historical Origins of Judicial Independence and Their Modern Resonances," *Yale Law Journal Pocket* 117 Part 8 (2007), http://

yalelawjournal.org/forum/the-historical-origins-of-judicial-independence-and-their -modern-resonance; and this book's Introduction.

2. Advancing a genealogical claim would require a careful reconstruction of the sources that informed influential early modern political theorists and practitioners to determine the role, if any, of "Hebraic" materials. Several important studies in the burgeoning field of political Hebraism have presented persuasive arguments about the "Hebraic" roots of other Western political tropes and ideals. See, e.g., Eran Shalev, "'A Perfect Republic': The Mosaic Constitution in Revolutionary New England, 1775–1788," *New England Quarterly* 82 (2009): 235–263; Eric Nelson, *The Hebrew Republic: Jewish Sources and the Transformation of European Political Thought* (Cambridge, Mass.: Harvard University Press, 2010); and Nathan R. Perl-Rosenthal, "The 'Divine Right of Republics': Hebraic Republicanism and the Debate over Kingless Government in Revolutionary America," *William and Mary Quarterly*, ser. 3, 66 (2009): 535–564. In any event, exploring early Jewish conceptions may contribute to a deeper understanding of contemporary issues in modern constitutional theory and discourse. See David Flatto, "The King and I: The Separation of Powers in Early Hebraic Political Theory," *Yale Journal of Law and Humanities* 20, no. 1 (2008), https://digitalcommons.law.yale.edu/yjlh/vol20/iss1/3.

Other scholarly works have discerned constitutional themes in biblical writings. See, e.g., Joshua Berman, *Created Equal: How the Bible Broke with Ancient Political Thought* (New York: Oxford University Press, 2008); and Bernard M. Levinson, "The First Constitution: Rethinking the Origins of Rule of Law and Separation of Powers in Light of Deuteronomy," in *Cardozo Law Review* 27 (2006): 1853–1888.

3. There are other differences, too, such as checks and balances and the notion of judicial review.

4. For one highly influential account of this period, see Jonathan Israel, *A Revolution of the Mind: Radical Enlightenment and the Intellectual Origins of Modern Democracy* (Princeton, N.J.: Princeton University Press, 2011). Israel's work has also engendered much argument and criticism, and alternative reconstructions. See the references cited in Israel, "Rousseau, Diderot, and the 'Radical Enlightenment': A Reply to Helena Rosenblatt and Joanna Stalnaker," *Journal of the History of Ideas* 77, no. 4 (2016): 649–677.

5. See John Locke, *Two Treatises on Government* (London: Printed for R. Butler, 1821), secs. 143–159; and Montesquieu, *The Spirit of Laws*, in *The Great Legal Philosophers*, ed. Clarence Morris (Philadelphia: University of Pennsylvania Press, 1971), 161–184.

6. Jeremy Waldron, "Separation of Powers in Thought and Practice," *Boston College Law Review* 54 (2013): 433–468.

7. Madison's authorship of *Federalist* 47 is certain, and 51 is widely assumed.

8. Bruce Ackerman, "The New Separation of Powers," *Harvard Law Review* 113 (2000): 633–729.

9. See M. C. Vile's classic study, *Constitutionalism and the Separation of Powers* (Oxford: Clarendon Press, 1967). See also William B. Gwyn, *The Meaning of Separation of Powers*

(New Orleans: Tulane University, 1965); and Jeremy Waldron, "The Rule of Law," in *The Stanford Encyclopedia of Philosophy,* ed. Edward N. Zalta, fall 2016 ed., online at plato.stanford.edu.

10. Athens was a precursor for these ideas, but Jerusalem certainly was not. See, e.g., Arlene W. Saxonhouse, *Athenian Democracy: Modern Mythmakers and Ancient Theorists* (Notre Dame, Ind.: University of Notre Dame Press, 1996); and Moses I. Finley, *Democracy Ancient and Modern* (New Brunswick, N.J.: Rutgers University Press, 1985).

11. See Robert M. Cover, "Obligation: A Jewish Jurisprudence of the Social Order," in *Law, Politics, and Morality in Judaism,* ed. Michael Walzer (Princeton, N.J.: Princeton University Press, 2006), 3–11.

12. Scholarship has advanced various theories. See, e.g., Scott D. Gerber, *A Distinct Judicial Power: The Origins of an Independent Judiciary, 1606–1787* (New York: Oxford University Press, 2001); and Philip Hamburger, *Law and Judicial Duty* (Cambridge, Mass.: Harvard University Press, 2008).

13. See, e.g., Faith Thompson, *A Short History of Parliament, 1295–1642* (St. Paul. Minn.: North Central, 1953); and Robert R. Palmer, "The British Parliament between King and People," in *The Age of the Democratic Revolution: A Political History of Europe and America, 1760–1800* (Princeton, N.J.: Princeton University Press, 2014).

14. See Laurence Claus, "Montesquieu's Mistakes and the True Meaning of Separation," *Oxford Journal of Legal Studies* 25 (2005): 419–451.

15. For a nuanced account of Marbury and the Marshall Court's legacy, see, among many works, William E. Nelson, *Marbury v. Madison: The Origins and Legacy of Judicial Review* (Lawrence: University Press of Kansas, 2000).

16. See, e.g., Ari Afilalo, Dennis Patterson, and Kai Purnhagen, "Statecraft, the Market State and the Development of European Legal Culture," in *Towards a European Legal Culture,* ed. Geneviève Helleringer and Kai Purnhagen (Portland, Ore.: C. H. Beck / Hart / Nomos, 2013), 277–302.

17. See, e.g., Larry Kramer, "Popular Constitutionalism, circa 2004," *California Law Review* 92 (2004): 959–1011; and Valerio Fabbrizi, "The Debate on Constitutional Courts and Their Authority between Legal and Political Constitutionalism," *Philosophica Critica* 2, no. 2 (2016): 47–70.

18. See, e.g., the studies in K. D. Ward and C. Castillo, eds., *Judiciary and American Democracy: Alexander Bickel, the Countermajoritarian Difficulty, and Contemporary Constitutional Theory* (Albany: State University of New York Press, 2005).

19. Alexander Bickel, *The Least Dangerous Branch: The Supreme Court at the Bar of Politics* (Indianapolis: Bobbs-Merrill, 1962).

20. John Hart Ely, *Democracy and Distrust: A Theory of Judicial Review* (Cambridge, Mass.: Harvard University Press, 1980); Bruce Ackerman, *We the People: Foundations,* vol. 1 (Cambridge, Mass.: Harvard University Press, 1991); Bickel, *The Least Dangerous Branch;* Larry Kramer, "Popular Constitutionalism"; Mark Tushnet, *The New Constitutional*

Order (Princeton, N.J.: Princeton University Press, 2003); and Jeremy Waldron, "The Core of the Case against Judicial Review," *Yale Law Journal* 115 (2006): 1346–1406.

21. See, e.g., *Law Under a Democratic Constitution: Essays in Honour of Jeffrey Goldsworthy*, ed. Lisa Burton Crawford et al. (Oxford: Hart, 2019); Alon Harel, "Rights-Based Judicial Review: A Democratic Justification," *Law and Philosophy* 22 (2003): 247–276; and Annabelle Lever, "Democracy and Judicial Review: Are They Really Incompatible?," *Perspectives on Politics* 7 (2009): 805–822.

22. See, e.g., the surprising candor expressed in the title of one leading scholar's defense of the judiciary and judicial review: Richard H. Fallon Jr., "The Core of an Uneasy Case for Judicial Review," *Harvard Law Review* 121 (2008): 1693. The author's uneasiness does not match the long-standing constitutional fixity of the doctrine.

23. See, e.g., Mirjan R. Damaška's provocative and critical formulation about the centrality of law and judges in American society: "There is, accordingly, an ever-present risk inherent in the American propensity, registered already by Tocqueville, to convert all social issues, including those of high politics, into legal ones, and to entrust their resolution to the judges." Damaška, "Reflections on American Constitutionalism," *American Journal of Comparative Law* 38 (1990): 443. Of course, this phenomenon can be described in more neutral or positive language; and can be arguably extended, albeit perhaps in more moderate terms, to Western society at large.

24. See generally J. H. Baker, *An Introduction to English Legal History*, 3rd ed. (London: Butterworths, 1990); and John H. Langbein et al., *History of the Common Law: The Development of Anglo-American Legal Institutions* (New York: Aspen, 2009).

25. See Prohibitions del Roy, 12 Co. Reports 63 (1658).

26. *Marbury v. Madison*, 5 U.S. 137 (1803).

27. In *Marbury*, Chief Justice Marshall essentially declared the principle of judicial review, even as he refused to order Secretary of State Madison to deliver the commission to Marbury, due to a lack of jurisdiction. Accordingly, some commentators describe Marshall's ruling as a shrewd political move. For more background, see Michael W. McConnell, "The Story of Marbury v. Madison: Making Defeat Look Like Victory," in *Constitutional Law Stories*, ed. Michael C. Dorf (New York: Foundation, 2004), 13–32.

28. Paul W. Kahn, *The Reign of Law: Marbury v. Madison and the Construction of America* (New Haven, Conn.: Yale University Press, 1997), 16.

29. See Kahn, *The Reign of Law*, 27–34, 69–74.

30. See Kahn, *The Reign of Law*, 27–34, 69–74.

31. See generally Ronald Dworkin, *Justice for Hedgehogs* (Cambridge, Mass.: Belknap Press of Harvard University Press, 2011); and *Justice in Robes* (Cambridge, Mass.: Belknap Press of Harvard University Press, 2006).

32. See generally Harold J. Berman, *Faith and Order: The Reconciliation of Law and Religion* (Atlanta: Scholars Press, 1993); and Berman, *Law and Revolution: The Formation of the Western Legal Tradition* (Cambridge, Mass.: Harvard University Press, 1983).

33. See generally Frederick F. Schauer, *Thinking Like a Lawyer: A New Introduction to Legal Reasoning* (Cambridge, Mass.: Harvard University Press, 2009).

34. See Philippe Nonet and Philip Selznick, *Law and Society in Transition: Toward Responsive Law* (New York: Octagon Books, 1978).

35. A sociological perspective on the question of legal authority may also reveal that there are competing and overlapping sources of authority operating at once. See the classic study of Hendrik Hartog, "Pigs and Positivism," *Wisconsin Law Review* 4 (1985): 899.

36. The drive to maintain the integrity of law is at least what is evinced within the discourse of these texts. What lies beneath this drive may be another matter. See the Introduction.

37. See, e.g., Berman, *Faith and Order;* Austin Sarat et al., *Law and the Sacred* (Stanford, Calif.: Stanford University Press, 2007); Sanford Levinson, *Constitutional Faith* (Princeton, N.J.: Princeton University Press, 2011); and Jaroslav Pelikan, *Interpreting the Bible and the Constitution* (New Haven, Conn.: Yale University Press, 2004).

38. Berman, *Faith and Order,* 1–22.

39. For related arguments, see Mark Lilla, *The Stillborn God: Religion, Politics, and the Modern West* (New York: Knopf, 2007); and Ronald Dworkin, *Religion without God* (Cambridge, Mass.: Harvard University Press, 2013).

40. Identifying resemblances of the second and third iterations of separation of powers in contemporary jurisprudence is a way of revealing jurisprudential dimensions that are less recognizable and little noticed.

41. See Kahn, *The Reign of Law,* 105–106. Even though US constitutional decisions are usually signed by individual justices, rather than being announced as *per curiam* verdicts, it is the opinion of the institution of the Supreme Court, as reflected in the majority's holding, which carries legal weight. Accordingly, from *Marbury* onward the ideal is to produce a single authoritative "opinion of the court."

42. In rabbinic literature this latter emphasis may intersect with other jurisprudential themes, including the development of the majority rule principle.

43. This phrase is already cited by John Adams, "'Novanglus Papers,' no. 7," in *The Works of John Adams, Second President of the United States,* vol. 4, ed. Charles Francis Adams (Boston: Little, Brown, and Co., 1850–1856), 106.

44. The stronger version of early Jewish jurisprudence would thus counter the claim of critical legal scholars that law is inherently political by stating this is only an apt characterization of law that operates alongside political actors, but when a fully autonomous legal system governs society, then law transcends the problem (and limits) of the political.

45. In popular discourse, this term is often used to censure forms of fundamentalist religious leadership that undermine lawful values. Even those who apply this label in a more neutral manner frequently associate it with an absence of formal rules. Returning to the origins of this term, however, reveals a very different, almost opposite, notion.

See David C. Flatto, "Theocracy and the Rule of Law: A Novel Josephan Doctrine and Its Modern Misconceptions," *Dine Israel* 28 (2011): 5–30.

46. To be sure, there are different models of separation of powers that exist in modern Western jurisprudence, but all depend on a political sphere composed of ruling men and women.

47. To be sure, this is more of an aspiration or a conception of the legal-political imagination, than a reality. Obviously a judiciary must operate with human actors. Yet the stronger (and internal) thesis of Jewish jurisprudence seeks to eliminate the most powerful political personalities, and to disseminate legal authority broadly to a collective body that can faithfully apply the rule of law. The more this ideal can be realized, the more people will be led by norms rather than the whims of powerful actors. See Kahn, *The Reign of Law,* 21–23, 44–45; and Waldron, "The Rule of Law." Of course, given that human actors are necessary for mediating the legal process, it is always possible that the rule of law will break down, and legal authority will be usurped by powerful individuals. See Chapter 7, which describes this latter phenomenon in the context of rabbinic literature.

48. One could have conceived of the US Constitution as an exclusively political instrument which constituted a federal government, but Marshall in *Marbury* and *McCulloch* helped shape its conception as a fundamental, legal document. In a lecture entitled "Covenants and Constitutions," presented at the conference on "People of the Book: Judaism and Constitutional Law" at DePaul University School of Law, April 2014, I argued that the latter reading is essentially correct, and that the entire design of the US Constitution is to achieve "rule *by* law."

49. For a helpful analysis of the debate between Schmitt and Kelsen, see Sandrine Baume, "On Political Theology: A Controversy between Hans Kelsen and Carl Schmitt," *History of European Ideas* 35 (2009): 369–381. Other leading German legal and political theorists of the Weimar period included Gerhard Anschutz, Richard Thoma, Henrich Triepel, Erich Kaufmann, Hermann Heller, and Rudolf Smend. For more background, see Arthur J. Jacobson and Bernhard Schlink, eds., *Weimar: A Jurisprudence of Crisis* (Berkeley: University of California Press, 2000).

50. Carl Schmitt, *The Concept of the Political,* trans. George Schwab (Chicago: University of Chicago Press, 1996).

51. For more on Schmitt, see Ellen Kennedy, *Constitutional Failure: Carl Schmitt in Weimar* (Durham, N.C.: Duke University Press, 2004); Heinrich Meier, *The Lesson of Carl Schmitt: Four Chapters on the Distinction between Political Theology and Political Philosophy* (Chicago: University of Chicago Press, 1998); and Paul Kahn, *Political Theology: Four New Chapters on the Concept of Sovereignty* (New York: Columbia University Press, 2011).

52. See, e.g., David Dyzenhaus, *Legality and Legitimacy: Carl Schmitt, Hans Kelsen, and Hermann Heller in Weimar* (Oxford: Oxford University Press, 1997), 102–160; and Lars

Vinx, *Hans Kelsen's Pure Theory of Law: Legality and Legitimacy* (Oxford: Oxford University Press, 2007).

53. Kelsen articulated his thesis most fully in his *Pure Theory of Law*. For more on Kelsen, including his relationship to Kant and Positivism (especially H. L. A. Hart), see Dyzenhaus, *Legality and Legitimacy;* Iain Stewart, "The Critical Legal Science of Hans Kelsen," *Journal of Legal Studies* 17 (1990): 273; Stanley L. Paulson, "Four Phases in Hans Kelsen's Legal Theory? Reflections on a Periodization," *Oxford Journal of Legal Studies* 181 (1998): 153; and Richard Tur and William Twining, eds., *Essays on Kelsen* (Oxford: Oxford University Press, 1986).

54. This formulation comes from Kelsen's essay, "Rechtsstaat und Staatsrecht," *Österreichische Rundschau* 36 (1913) (cited in Vinx, *Hans Kelsen's Pure Theory*, 1).

55. In Vinx's words, "the utopia of legality is a system in which people are subject, as far as this is possible, only to the objective rule of laws, and not to the rule of men." Vinx, *Hans Kelsen's Pure Theory*, 25.

56. But see the critical evaluation of Kelsen's thought in Petra Gumplova, *Law, Sovereignty and Democracy* (Baden-Baden: Nomos, 2011).

Conclusion

1. I refer broadly to any medieval work that builds upon the foundation of the early Jewish (especially rabbinic) jurisprudence analyzed throughout this book. See David C. Flatto, *Between Royal Absolutism and an Independent Judiciary: The Evolution of Separation of Powers in Biblical, Second Temple and Rabbinic Texts* (Cambridge, Mass.: Harvard University Press, 2010), 13n27.

2. See the characterization in Robert M. Cover, "Obligation: A Jewish Jurisprudence of the Social Order," in *Law, Politics, and Morality in Judaism*, ed. Michael Walzer (Princeton, N.J.: Princeton University Press, 2006), 65. See also Suzanne Last Stone, "Religion and State: Models of Separation from within Jewish Law," *International Journal of Constitutional Law* 6 (2008): 631–661.

3. R. Nissim b. Reuben Gerondi, *Derashot* [Hebrew], ed. Leon A. Feldman (Jerusalem: Institute Shalem, 1973).

4. See the references in Flatto, *Between Royal Absolutism and an Independent Judiciary*, 13n27, and those cited below.

5. See Gerondi, *Derashot*, 192 ("The matter of judgment, in its greater part and in its principal part, is given over the Sanhedrin, and in its lesser part to the king.") See also the striking formulation in the next homily, *Derashot*, 211. Both of these lines are analyzed by Harvey (see note 6).

6. The formulation is inspired by Warren Zev Harvey, who contrasts the court's pursuit of deontological ethics (the "judicial branch"), with the king's preservation of welfare through utilitarian politics (the "executive branch"). See, e.g., Harvey, "Liberal Demo-

cratic Themes in Nissim of Girona," in *Studies in Medieval Jewish History and Literature, III,* ed. Isadore Twersky and Jay M. Harris (Cambridge, Mass.: Harvard University Press, 2000), 201–206.

7. While earlier rabbinic sources (e.g., *b. Sanh.* 19a) incorporate the king into the judicial system (see Chapter 5), they do not treat him as an autonomous legal authority.

8. Contrast Gerondi with Abravenel, who agrees with Gerondi's division into two tracks of justice, but argues that the Sanhedrin is in charge of both. See the citation of Abravenel in Gerondi, *Derashot,* 190n11 (Gerondi himself, in *Derashot,* 192, concurs that this happens when there is no king). Abravenel's approach is truer to the spirit of early Jewish jurisprudence, although Abravenel is primarily motivated by his own antimonarchic polemic.

9. See, e.g., Aaron Kirschenhaum, "The Role of Punishment in Jewish Criminal Law: A Chapter in Rabbinic Penological Thought," *Jewish Law Annual* 9 (1991): 123–143. For a summary of scholarship on how to interpret Gerondi's eleventh homily, see Itzhak Brand, "Religious Recognition of Autonomous Secular Law: The 'Sitz im Leben' of R. Nissim of Girona's Homily (No. 11)," *Harvard Theological Review* 105, no. 2 (2012): 163–188.

10. See Menachem Lorberbaum, *Politics and the Limits of Law: Secularizing the Political in Medieval Jewish Thought* (Stanford, Calif.: Stanford University Press, 2001), 129–133.

11. See Lorberbaum, *Politics and the Limits of Law,* 124–159.

12. See Harvey, "Liberal Democratic Themes," 211n17, for a trenchant critique of certain interpretations of Gerondi. But this does not preclude recognizing—to use a more moderate formulation—Gerondi's division between the adjudication of the courts and the legal determinations of the political body. In general, Harvey focuses more on the first motif in Gerondi's homily (the Sanhedrin, and its distance from utilitarian concerns), and Lorberbaum focuses more on the second (the king and the political sphere). See also Julie E. Cooper, "Review of *Politics and the Limits of Law,*" *Political Theory* 31, no. 4 (2003): 604–607. In any event, Lorberbaum is convincing in situating Gerondi within a medieval discourse, positing that the king signifies the political sphere more generally, and noticing a larger trend among other medieval thinkers.

13. Note the significant difference between Gerondi's scheme and the mishnaic scheme (Chapter 5). The Mishnah separates the king and the court. In contrast, according to Gerondi both the king and the Sanhedrin exercise legal authority.

14. In medieval Jewish communities, the legal system is the most influential social force. Notice how Gerondi applies *m. Abot* 3:2 (about kingship) to the judiciary at the opening of this homily (*Derashot,* 189). When Gerondi's homily, in turn, identifies the distinct standing of the political body, its authority is only meaningful within medieval Jewish society if it has a role in reaching legal determinations.

15. See Steven Nadler, *Spinoza: A Life* (Cambridge: Cambridge University Press, 1999), 7–15.

16. See, e.g., the political theory of Jean Bodin, cited in Anne Oravetz Albert, "'A Civil Death': Sovereignty and the Jewish Republic in an Early Modern Treatment of Genesis 49:10," in *Jewish Culture in Early Modern Europe: Essays in Honor of David B. Ruderman*, ed. Richard I. Cohen et al. (Jerusalem: Hebrew Union College Press, 2014), 69.

17. See Albert, "'A Civil Death,'" 69.

18. See Albert, "'A Civil Death,'" 63–74.

19. See Albert, "'A Civil Death,'" 64, citing Isaac Orobio de Castro, *Prevenciones divinas contra la vana idolatria de las gentes* (hs. ros 631), 74: "The doctors of the law . . . have so much authority over the people, conceded by God himself in the law . . . that it is not lawful for anyone to repudiate their decrees. . . . These same doctors . . . are absolute judges of the people throughout the world."

20. If there is a link between Orobio and Josephus's jurisprudence, it is likely through the writings of (Protestant) early modern political thinkers on Jewish republicanism. See Albert, "'A Civil Death,'" 68. But some of them misunderstood his thought. See below.

21. I am referring to Orobio's theme that commanding legal authority constitutes sovereignty. Albert also tries to identify a precedent for Orobio's emphasis on the Jews having the supreme legal authority to take the life of a subject that he finds in the Jewish power of excommunication (*herem*), which he interprets as a civil death.

22. Eric Nelson, *The Hebrew Republic: Jewish Sources and the Transformation of European Political Thought* (Cambridge, Mass.: Harvard University Press, 2010), 23–56.

23. Nelson, *The Hebrew Republic*, 88–137. See also David C. Flatto, "Theocracy and the Rule of Law: A Novel Josephan Doctrine and Its Modern Misconceptions," *Dine Israel* 28, no. 5 (2011): 27–30.

24. Accordingly, the imprimatur of the civic authority is necessary to authorize religious laws. See Nelson, *The Hebrew Republic*, 90–91.

25. Nelson notes that the early modernist reading of Josephus, which understands legal authority as belonging to the civic authority rather than the priests, may not be the simple reading. Nelson, *The Hebrew Republic*, 179n13. This formulation is too equivocal. Josephus understands legal authority to be the sacral responsibility of priests, and deems sacred laws to be the essence of the polity. This is especially true in *Apion*, where the notion of a theocracy is introduced. See Chapter 4.

26. It is doubly ironic. One irony is that a particular religious tradition fueled an expansive doctrine of religious toleration. A second is that a doctrine that underscores the primacy of law as the foundation of civic life came to be understood as espousing the centrality of civic governance in administering all normative matters.

27. See Nelson, *The Hebrew Republic*, 91.

28. See the discussion regarding the constitutional judiciary and Kelsen's theory in Chapter 9.

Acknowledgments

While this book has been in formation for a long period, its final touches were made in an unusually fraught time and place: Spring 2020, New York City. As the world was in the throes of battling a terrifying virus and protesting for the most basic human rights, many faced acute anxieties and stresses, myself included. A surprising anchor for me during this surreal season was an all-too-familiar manuscript, reminiscent of happier times in the past when its earlier iterations were formulated, and containing within its pages reflections upon sublime and noble ideals of justice that will no doubt prevail again in the future. Its words, arguments, and revisions retain marks of the indelible influence of my mentors and colleagues. And the spirit that animates it is vitalized by values and pursuits I share with family and friends: a burning quest to fathom historically elusive concepts, a love of Torah, and an urge to exchange ideas with others.

Upon completion of my manuscript, I have the privilege to express my abundant gratitude to many mentors, colleagues, friends, and family. A few must be singled out for specific words of appreciation.

Extraordinary efforts on behalf of this project were extended by Noah Feldman and Elisheva Carlebach. World renowned for their academic achievements, I was privy to witness generous facets of their personalities that are perhaps less public, but equally exceptional. Producing this book would not have been possible without their assistance. For this I am deeply grateful.

Several other scholars have not flinched whenever I turned to them for critical feedback, sage advice, or timely assistance: Shaye Cohen, Steven Fraade, Moshe Halbertal, and Christine Hayes. I am blessed to have benefited from their mentorship in my academic career.

Over the years, various scholars have guided me along at various phases and taken keen interest in my scholarship. A special thanks to Suzanne Last Stone, Joseph Weiler, Yuval Shany, Zev Harvey, Celia Fassberg, Tom Baker, Phil McConaughay, Hari Osofsky, Jon Levenson, James Kugel, and Yair Lorberbaum. Numerous colleagues at Penn State Law, Penn Law, NYU Law, the Hebrew University, and other Israeli institutions have enlarged my academic worldview. I have especially benefited from ongoing conversations with Benny Porat, Judah Galinsky, and Avi Helfand. I am also indebted to several scholars who have reviewed or discussed various sections of this book, including Shani Tzoref, Seth Schwartz, Moshe Benovitz, Aharon Shemesh z'l, Hanan Eshel z'l, Gerald Blidstein, and Paul Kahn.

A few close friends have read sections of the manuscript and offered invaluable suggestions that greatly enhanced its quality: Alex Sztuden, Tal Kastner, Gilaad Deutsch, Ari Blech, and Julie Cooper. Others, including David Becker, Josh Hain, David Yudin, and Evyatar Marienberg, have been by my side throughout the highs and lows of this project (among other "projects"). True to the teaching in tractate *Avot* (2:9, certain recensions), they have all helped steer me onto the straight path.

This book benefited from the guidance of Harvard University Press's superb editorial team, led by Sharmila Sen and Heather Hughes. I also wish to thank John Donohue of Westchester Publishing Services for his excellent work in preparing the manuscript for publication, and Marc Sherman for compiling the indexes. The Lubin Fund has generously given financial support for the final phases of this work.

My love for the field of rabbinics traces back to the exceptional teachers who trained me in Talmudic studies. In particular, I have boundless gratitude to Rabbi Michael Rosensweig for opening the portals of advanced Torah study for me. He is a singular exemplar of brilliance and piety, and I cherish the many years I have studied with him.

Lastly, I wish to thank my precious family members and loved ones who form our tightly knit circle. My sister, Professor Sharon Flatto, has always been the person I looked up to most, even to the point of following her into a career in Jewish studies. Her passion, intensity, and integrity as a scholar continually inspire me, and her affection and guidance touch my core. I could not have asked for a more wonderful and loving older sister. I walk in her footsteps, always, with the utmost pride. Her beautiful family is an extension of my own: my immensely learned and charismatic brother-in-law, Rabbi Ysoscher Katz, and my amazing nephews Avi and Gabi.

Over the past several years, I have been especially fortunate to share most of my days with Yael Kristen Zatarski. She has graciously assumed the challenging task of escorting me along this path with her love, vast intelligence, psychological depth, and fortitude. To the extent I have succeeded, it is largely due to her. I eagerly look forward to our future chapters together.

This work is dedicated to the beloved memory of my late mother, Dr. Zehava Flatto z'l, and in honor of my father, Dr. Leopold Flatto. My mother had an inimitable and infectious way of living fully: with great curiosity, wisdom, adventure, courage, and joy, and the utmost pride in, and dedication to, her family. As much as her presence was pulsating, her absence is palpable. Yet she bequeathed a unique "*Torat ha-Em*" to me that I strive to live by and will always treasure. My father is a brilliant and humble scholar. From an early age, I have memories of him sitting with a pencil and paper fixated on a math problem and scribbling down notes, or leaning over a Talmud captivated by its inner logic. And astoundingly this image remains constant nearly a Jubilee later. He has never retired, since the pursuit of knowledge is his lifeblood. My parents together demonstrated to me that education is of utmost priority; that the pursuit of knowledge is a lifelong quest; that our aspirations demand great effort and sacrifice; and that there is a distinct kind of exuberance in life's journey.

Unlike later rabbinic law that prescribes a blessing of gratitude for certain discrete occasions, the biblical thanksgiving offering is open ended. And in some sense, so it needs to be. I close by paraphrasing the traditional blessing of gratitude to the One who bestows bounty upon us— in myriad forms, and in the most unpredictable of circumstances. May God continue to bestow bounty and kindness upon us all, *Selah*.

Index of Names and Terms

Index Locorum

Writings of Philo

Writings of Josephus